A ZRH LU SAE BRU NDB ATR-42-300 A31A
J GYE UPN VV SAK VHHH ZCL SAL AC
GPS B777 SAQ OS SA MM FRU SAS P
AS VN 544 SAW KLAX 1 SAY C3
DF DI DN DR DT LH3117 DX STOL TW
EH BBJ EI CY EK EL DH8-300 AGNIS EN
FD FE FG LX FH FI MACH FK RWY F
B FS FT FV FW FY SAR FX FZ GA IKEC
REX SJO GG GL KL1046 PEK ORY CA1108
AC IATA GU GV HA MLA HB SIN CA134
0377 HC DH4 HD OAX HE SLOT L10 TU
T HL HR HS OSE NBO HT HU K LA BKH
P LE LF KGL COK LG LH CGN JED LI L
M LR LS CCU LT LV YYR LW LX CAG L
MG TP MH MK C9 B735 HAJ DH8-100 LIS
ZRH MW JED SYD ISB MY LX024 WAV
AM MCO OK BKO UTC NL MCT LAE KIX
19 CUN OB LG9302 OE OI OJ AA664 MS
OR MAS OT PA A300-600 PG HKG PH F
TRC ZIH RJ BCN RK RO RP SA SB ZNZ
L SM SO LHR DXB SP GOT SU FNA SY
B TD DXB TF TG ORD TI TJ KWI NRT T
AVRO RJ100 TR IGH MX757 TT TU TV DK
JI UK AVRO RJ100 UL UM UN KU171 UO U
VC VD VE VG VH FOR VI VL SFO VM
WB LHE WI WM AA WP MD-82 DHC30
A LOS SAN LAS DEL DUR FNA GLA DCA
I SEL JFK SOF TPE DOH GMT SYZ . LBA
40 DEN YYZ COK B777 LG6574 BA DL107
Z MAG HIR RAB MUC KE IR GA FM W
TC MNM S4 500 ATP SN3618 MSY AT LO
011 ONT IDO QLI A340 YJR KU171 DEL BK
ZFA ASQ GLO CA1858 PEK KHI TYO LX

THE COMPLETE BOOK OF

FLIGHT

FACTS, FIGURES AND THE STORY OF
AIRPORTS, AIRLINES AND AIRCRAFT

LUDWIG KÖNEMANN (EDITOR)
ANDREAS FECKER

THE COMPLETE BOOK OF
FLIGHT

FACTS, FIGURES AND THE STORY OF
AIRPORTS, AIRLINES AND AIRCRAFT

PaRragon

Bath·New York·Singapore·Hong Kong·Cologne·Delhi·Melbourne

CONTENTS

LIGHT

AIRLINER

PORTS OF THE WORLD

INES OF

S

ETAILS

READY FOR TAKE-OFF?

This book is dedicated to all those who are interested in, fascinated by, or mad about flying – to those who follow in-flight maps mile for mile, devour every flying-related article they can lay their hands on, track the development of new aircraft or keep an eye out for airline mergers. It is aimed at travellers who are not content merely to fly from one point on the earth to another, but who are intrigued by the complexities of air travel and want to know more about flying than just their departure time and gate number.

Problem-free flying is not just an enormous technical and engineering achievement – it requires planning, investment, logistics and co-operation between different institutions. It depends on people: pilots who are passionate about their work, motivated flight attendants, conscientious technicians and decisive crisis managers in the aviation nerve centres. All these people make a visible or invisible contribution to making our flight what we want it to be: an enjoyable experience.

- According to the International Air Transport Association (IATA), there are three billion air passengers per year – or eight million per day. This is the equivalent of the entire population of New York City taking off on a daily basis.
- There are some 460,000 people in the air at any given time. At 400 passengers per Boeing 747-400, this equates to 1,150 packed jumbos, consuming around 14,000 tonnes of kerosene per hour.
- Commercial flights clock up some 4.5 trillion passenger km/2.8 trillion passenger miles per year, corresponding to 100 million times around the Equator or approximately 12 million trips from the earth to the moon.
- Some 16,000 aircraft are flown by around 200,000 pilots.
- Every 30 minutes, a plane takes off in London bound for New York. Each year, some two million people travel this route – the world's busiest – in both directions.
- According to the CIA, there are around 44,000 airports in the world.

THE
STORY
OF
FLIGHT

LEARNING FROM THE BIRDS

Daedalus and Icarus. The first disaster in the history of flying took place in Greek mythology.

1505 Leonardo da Vinci – architect, painter, sculptor, musician, mechanical engineer, natural philosopher and inventor – studies the anatomy of birds and designs machines propelled by human muscle-power that imitate the way they fly.

1720 Swiss mathematician Daniel Bernoulli discovers that flowing air creates low pressure.

1783 The Montgolfier brothers construct the world's first hot-air balloon, known as the *Montgolfière*.

1783 Jacques Charles builds the world's first hydrogen balloon, known as the *Charlière*.

1783 Jean-François Pilâtre de Rozier makes the first balloon flight over Paris.

1785 Jean-Pierre Blanchard makes the first balloon crossing of the English Channel.

1785 Jacques Charles takes the first hydrogen-only balloon to a height of nearly 3,000 m/ 10,000 ft.

1810 Albrecht Berblinger, the 'Tailor of Ulm', constructs a flying machine that crashes on its maiden flight due to unfavourable fall winds.

1810 After 21 years of study, Thomas Walker publishes his *Treatise upon the Art of Flying*.

1848 John Stringfellow from Attercliffe near Sheffield, England, experiments with an aircraft powered by a steam engine and contrarotating propellers.

1857 Frenchman Félix du Temple de la Croix patents a flying machine with two wings constructed of curved wooden or metal spars covered with silk. These wings are fixed to either side of a carriage carrying the engine. An airscrew designed to pull the craft forward is positioned at the front of the machine. A horizontal rudder regulates the angle of flight, while a vertical rudder steers the plane to the right or left. However, the machine proves too heavy to fly.

1867 Retired Russian artillery officer Nikolai Teleshov applies for a patent for an 'improved lighter-than-air system' that would be described today as a jet-powered aircraft with delta wings. The craft has a solid wing that slopes backwards at an angle of 45 degrees with a straight rear edge and a cylindrical fuselage that has a conical nose. It is powered by a jet engine. Because Teleshov was 100 years ahead of his time he was refused a patent in Russia and had to go to France. Sadly, the plane was never built and exists only on paper.

1871 Francis Wenham builds the world's first wind tunnel in order to measure lift. He makes the astonishing discovery that shallow angles of incidence between 5 degrees and 15 degrees generate greater lift than more oblique angles. He also ascertains that long, narrow surfaces (like those of modern gliders) generate more lift than stub wings with the same surface area.

1879 Frenchman Victor Tatin builds a model aeroplane with a fuselage that serves as a reservoir for

Jacques Charles in his hydrogen-filled airship, 1783.

Albrecht Berblinger, the 'Tailor of Ulm', was a colourful character. The young master tailor had an unusually strong interest in mechanics, for which he was mocked. In 1810, he fell out with his guild when he designed a flying machine. Despite all the obstacles, he succeeded in building his glider and waited for the right opportunity to show it off. This came when King Frederick of Württemberg visited the town. Berblinger erected a scaffold on the Adlerbastei ('Eagle's Bastion'), a high wall on the banks of the River Danube, but at the last moment his courage deserted him. Under the pretext that there was something wrong with his machine, he postponed the flight. The next day he ascended the scaffold again and looked down at the assembled crowd. By this time the king had departed. It is not known whether he jumped or was pushed, but in any case he and his flying machine crashed into the Danube after travelling no more than a few feet.

Berblinger immediately became the laughing stock of the town. Reduced to poverty, he died at the age of 58 and was buried in an unmarked pauper's grave.

In 1986, his flight was simulated and it was discovered that he might have succeeded had he chosen a different launch venue. Prevailing fall winds at the spot he chose meant that his attempt was doomed from the outset.

Da Vinci, Airscrew (detail), 1487–90.

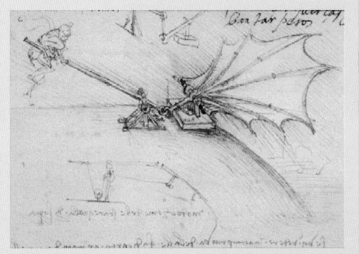

Da Vinci, Stress-testing of a wing (detail), 1487–90.

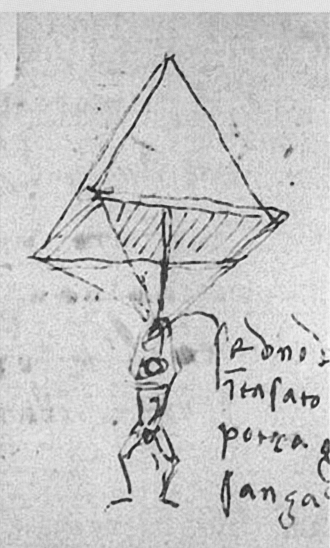

Da Vinci, Parachute (detail), 1485–87.

compressed air. When a tap is opened, air streams out, driving two tractor propellers. The model has a wingspan of 190 cm/75 inches and flies in a circle around the peg to which it is tethered.

1884   An Englishman by the name of Horatio Phillips patents eight wing-like lift surfaces of differing widths and profiles. He uses a wind tunnel to determine the speed of airstream needed to generate the required lift for each different lift surface, discovering that wings with a curved surface generate more lift than flat wings. In 1893,

he builds a model aeroplane weighing 158 kg/348 lb that flies a 180-m/590-ft circuit

At the 1889 Universal Exhibition in Paris, Commander **Charles Renard** of the French aviation authority exhibits a steerable balloon, as well as another flying machine he developed 16 years earlier: a steerable paraglider that anticipated the future of flying. This craft consists of an oval, hollow body on runners connected to a framework of ten superimposed wings with a rear rudder.

Renard is convinced that his glider could be launched either from a balloon or (equipped with an engine) from the ground. Despite having observed that birds have curved wings, he gives his machine flat wings in imitation of butterflies, insects in general and paper kites.

around a central post to which it is tethered. This model is equipped with a small engine

that drives a propeller at 400 rpm. It flies in a circle at 64 km/h /40 mph at an altitude of just over 1 m/3 ft. The wings comprise 50 curved sections superimposed in an arrangement resembling a venetian blind, with a gap of just 5 cm/2 inches between each section.

1889   Otto Lilienthal publishes his observations on the flight of storks in his book *Birdflight as the Basis of Aviation* and attempts to solve the problem of what was then called 'manflight'. Between 1891 and 1896 he attempts 2,000 flights from

Learning from the Birds

Otto Lilienthal.

a hill using ever-improving designs of a glider. He succeeds in flying up to 500 m/1,640 ft but suffers a fatal crash on 9 August 1896.

1890   Frenchman Clément Ader develops a heavier-than-air flying machine. The first model is steam-powered and resembles a bat. The craft is ready in 1890 but the drive unit proves unsuitable. The war ministry later withdraws Ader's research funding and the project is terminated.

1894   Australian inventor Lawrence Hargrave binds four box kites together, installs a simple seat, and flies a distance of just over 5 m/16 ft.

1895   Like Lilienthal, Percy Pilcher experiments with gliders, using a hill at Cardross, outside Glasgow, as his launch venue. He models his craft on the various creatures he has observed in flight. One glider resembles a bat, another a beetle and another a gull. He then turns his attention to a fourth design, a hawk, which he is planning to equip with an engine. While giving a

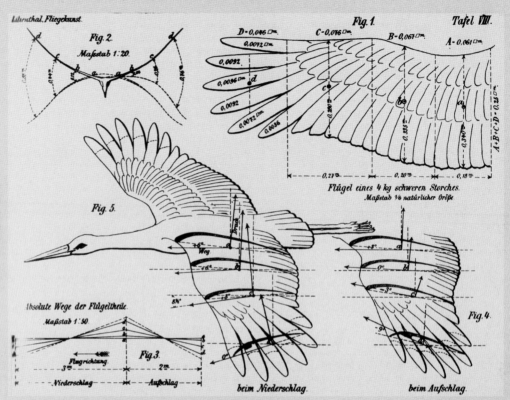

Study by Lilienthal entitled Our Mentors in Flight, *1889.*

public demonstration, a wire snaps causing the tail of his glider to collapse. Pilcher crashes in front of the crowd. He dies from his injuries two days later.

1896   Octave Chanute, a Frenchman who emigrated to the United States, collates data and expertise on flying machines from all over the world. He reconstructs these machines and also develops his own models. The Wright brothers make use of his collection *Progress in Flying Machines* (1894).

1908   On 4 July an article appears in *Scientific American* entitled 'The Winning Flight of the "June Bug" Aeroplane for the Scientific American Trophy'. This piece describes in great detail the work of the young

Octave Chanute's glider being tested in 1896.

Glenn Curtiss, who has teamed up with Alexander Graham Bell (the future inventor of the telephone) to develop aeroplanes that are widely regarded as superior to those of the Wright brothers (*see p15*). The Curtiss works later develop into the first mass producer of aircraft.

1910 **7 January** – flying an Antoinette VII, Englishman Hubert Latham becomes the first to reach a height of 1,000 m/3,280 ft.
10 March – Frenchman Emil Aubrun, flying a Blériot aircraft, makes the world's first night flight in Buenos Aires.
18 May – start of the first International Aviation Conference in Paris. Air traffic between sovereign states is the main issue on the agenda.

1911 **18 February** – Henri Pecquet, in a Humer-Sommer, makes the first airmail flight in Allahabad, India, with sacks of post containing 6,000 letters and postcards. His flight ends five miles away at Naini Junction, where the post is transferred to a train. This flight also marks the inauguration of a regular airmail service.
12 April – Frenchman Pierre Prier, carrying passengers, pilots the first non-stop flight from London to Paris. The Blériot takes 3 hours and 45 minutes to complete the journey.

1912 **19 September** – Delag Zeppelin LZ13, the *Hansa*, begins the first regular passenger service (between Hamburg, Copenhagen and Malmö), making Delag, a forerunner of Lufthansa, the world's first airline.

1914 **1 January** – the St. Petersburg-Tampa Airboat

Otto Lilienthal flying his glider from the hill that came to be known as the Fliegerberg ('hill of flight').

Line in Florida inaugurates a regular passenger service, becoming the first airline in the United States. The Benoist Flying Boat that makes the 32-km/20-mile journey from St. Petersburg to Tampa over Tampa Bay is piloted by Anthony Jannus. Abe C. Pheil, the mayor of

St. Petersburg, buys the first ticket at auction for 400 dollars. The regular fare is five dollars.

1919 **5 February** – In Germany, Deutsche Luft Reederei (DLR) begins the first scheduled passenger service between Berlin

and Weimar. The service uses former warplanes manufactured by AEG (*Allgemeine Elektrizitäts-Gesellschaft*) and DFW (*Deutsche Flugzeug-Werke*).
3 March – William Boeing and Edward Hubbard launch an airmail service between Seattle and Victoria in British Columbia.
25 June – the world's first all-metal passenger craft, the Junkers F13, is unveiled; 322 are built in quick succession.
21 July – Anthony Fokker opens an aircraft factory in his own name at Schiphol, near Amsterdam.
28 August – founding of the International Air Traffic Association (IATA) at The Hague.
7 October – *Koninklijke Luchtvaart Maatschappij voor Nederland an Kolojien* (KLM for short) is founded in the Netherlands.
13 October – the League of Nations concludes the Paris Convention, by which international air traffic is regulated. Among other things, this treaty stipulates that radio call signs are to consist of five letters.

French flying pioneer Louis Blériot is given an enthusiastic reception in England in 1909 after winning the 1,000-pound prize for the first crossing of the English Channel. He made the journey in a monoplane of his own design.

THE DAWNING OF THE PASSENGER AGE

The first commercial airline to carry passengers in **aeroplanes** as opposed to airships was the **St. Petersbug-Tampa Airboat Line**, whose service, using a Benoist Flying Boat, was inaugurated in 1914. The first few tickets were auctioned and **Abe C. Pheil**, the former mayor of St. Petersburg, Florida, secured the first with a bid of 400 dollars. The launch was watched by a crowd of 3,000 onlookers. The plane flew at a height of around 10 m/ 33 ft above Tampa Bay and covered the 32 km/ 20 miles in 23 minutes. During the short journey the engine consumed ten gallons of fuel and one gallon of oil.

This was the start of a regular service with tickets costing five dollars. The airline flew two trips a day, six days a week for over four months, but the service was eventually suspended

Abe C. Pheil.

due to a lack of long-term profitability.

In 1995, a descendant of Mr Pheil honoured the ten billionth passenger to be carried by an American airline.

Today, air passengers number some 3 billion per year, a figure that could double by 2025.

In 2007 another auction was held, offering tickets for the inaugural flight of a **Singapore Airlines** Airbus A380 flying from Singapore to Sydney. Julian Hayward, a 39-year-old Briton, was the highest bidder. He paid 100,380 US dollars for two suites equipped, among other things, with a double bed and a flat-screen television set.

Landing in Tampa.

INCIDENTALLY...

The **millionth** passenger in the United States was celebrated in 1937.

The **ten billionth** made the world's newspapers on 13 June 1995.

The **hundred billionth** is expected in 2031 and the **one trillionth** in 2124 – that

is, if there is any kerosene left by then.

The world's shortest flight Scottish carrier Loganair offers the shortest scheduled flight in the world. Flight LOG 313 from Westray to Papa Westray in the Orkney Islands is only 1.5 km/1 mile long and

is scheduled to take just two minutes (departs Westray 9.51 am, arrives 9.53 am). With a favourable wind, the journey time can be as little as 56 seconds, but thanks to frequent storms in this part of the world it is not unusual for it to take up to 12 minutes.

THE FIRST FLIGHT

On 23 March 1903, the **brothers Wilbur and Orville Wright** applied for the patent for an aircraft based on their Number III glider.

On 14 December 1903, Wilbur Wright attempted an initial flight in the *Flyer*. He was unsuccessful and the aircraft was damaged. The breakthrough came in Kitty Hawk, North Carolina three days later, on **17 December 1903**, when **Orville Wright** achieved the first official flight in history, piloting the *Flyer* over a distance of 36.5 m/120 ft. The flight lasted 12 seconds. Since it had been announced in advance and took place before witnesses, it is regarded as the first manned, sustained and controlled flight in a heavier-than-air craft. That same day the brothers made three more flights, the longest of which lasted for almost a minute.

The Wright brothers made hundreds of flights and refined their technology. In September 1904, Wilbur made his first successful circular flight and a month later achieved a distance of 4.43 km/2.75 miles during the first flight of more than five minutes' duration. Now their patent could be marketed. The first customer was the US government. The Wright brothers ended their series of test flights. The history of powered flight had begun.

The **first aircraft passenger** was Charles W. Furnas, a mechanic who assisted the Wright brothers with the construction of their aeroplanes. He was taken up by Wilbur Wright on a number of flights (the first on 14 May 1908) by way of thanks for his work. Most importantly, these flights demonstrated to the US Army that passengers could be carried by aircraft. Furnas suddenly lost interest in flying after a plane, piloted by Orville on a separate occasion, broke up in mid-air and crashed, resulting in the death of the passenger.

Probably the most famous picture in the history of aviation: Orville Wright during the first powered flight at 10.35 am on 17 December 1903 in Kitty Hawk, North Carolina. The undulating flight lasted 12 seconds and covered a distance of 36.5 m/120 ft. The biplane took off under its own power along a wooden rail. The engine weighed 90 kg/198 lb and the two propellers were chain-driven. The wingspan was 13.2 m/43 ft and the wing surface area 47 sq m/506 sq ft. To put the flight into perspective, in terms of distance, it could have started and finished inside the fuselage of a Boeing 747.

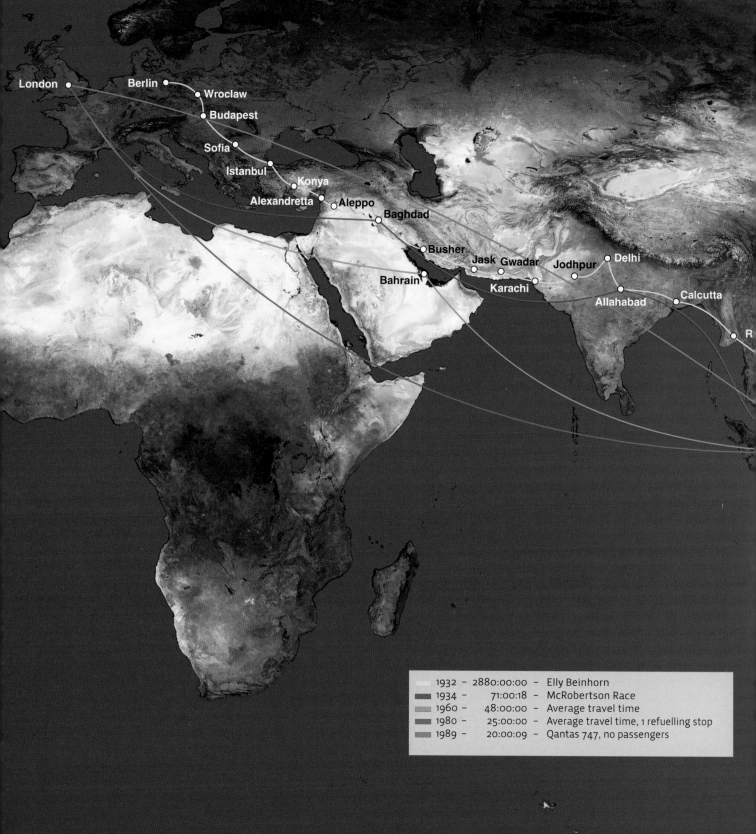

THE LONG WAY TO NON-STOP

London
Berlin
Wroclaw
Budapest
Sofia
Istanbul
Konya
Alexandretta
Aleppo
Baghdad
Busher
Jask
Gwadar
Jodhpur
Delhi
Bahrain
Karachi
Allahabad
Calcutta
R

	1932	2880:00:00	Elly Beinhorn
	1934	71:00:18	McRobertson Race
	1960	48:00:00	Average travel time
	1980	25:00:00	Average travel time, 1 refuelling stop
	1989	20:00:09	Qantas 747, no passengers

gapore

Jakarta
Surabaya
Bima
Kupang
Darwin
Newcastle-Waters
Cloncurry
Longreach
Charleville
Brisbane
Sydney
Melbourne

Aviation pioneer **Elly Beinhorn**, born 30 May 1907 in Hanover, Germany, set a number of long-distance records in the 1930s.

In 1931, she was working on an aerial photography assignment in Africa. On her journey back to Germany, she suffered a ruptured fuel line in her engine and had to make an emergency landing in a swampy region of the Niger between Bamako and Timbuktu in what is now Mali. She received a friendly reception from the warlike Songhai tribe and eventually found someone who could speak French and could take her to Timbuktu. Upon her arrival there, exhausted and feverish after four days of walking, she discovered to her astonishment that the whole of Germany was in agitation over her disappearance. After spending a few days recovering, she hired some helpers and returned to the scene of her crash-landing in order to recover the aeroplane's engine and instruments. In the meantime, the news of Elly Beinhorn's rescue had spread throughout the world and an aeroplane was sent from Germany to Africa to pick her up. The heroic pilot travelled by train and ship to Casablanca, where she met the plane. After her triumphant arrival in Berlin she observed with a shake of her head: 'My emergency landing has made more headlines than the greatest aviation triumph.'

On 4 December 1931 she set off again, bound this time for Australia. She flew her single-engined Klemm from Berlin via Wroclaw, Budapest, Sofia, Istanbul, Konya, Alexandretta, Aleppo, Baghdad, Bushehr, Jask, Gwadar, Karachi, Jodhpur, Delhi, Allahabad, Calcutta, Rangoon, Bangkok, Alor Star, Singapore, Jakarta, Surabaya, Bima, Kupang, Darwin, Newcastle Waters, Cloncurry, Longreach, Charleville and Brisbane to Sydney, where she arrived on 2 April 1932.

As the Pacific Ocean could not yet be crossed by plane, the 24-year-old pilot dismantled her Klemm, packed it into crates and loaded it onto a freighter bound for Panama. She then flew along the coast to Chile, crossed the Andes and continued to Buenos Aires. From there she returned by ship to Bremerhaven, Germany. Elly Beinhorn had demonstrated that with the exception of the major oceans, the world could be circumnavigated by a small aeroplane with a single 80 hp engine.

After many more flights – to Africa, North America and Central America – she eventually settled in Freiburg, Germany, where she wrote books and radio plays. Elly Beinhorn died on 28 November 2007 at the age of 100.

Flying Becomes Socially Acceptable: the 1920s and 1930s

The 12-engine Dornier Do-X , 1929.

1920 12 December – maiden flight of the Blériot-Spad 33 airliner.

1921 5 June – first attempt to pressurize an aircraft cabin (in an Airco USD-9A).

Transcontinental & Western Air started its coast-to-coast service in 1930.

1922 7 April – first aerial collision of two airliners: in northern France a French Farman Goliath belonging to Grands Express strays into the path of a de Havilland DH-18 operated by Daimler Airways. There are seven fatalities.
9 June – first scheduled night flight from Paris to London.

1923 22 August – maiden flight of the Witteman-Lewis XNBL-1. This long-range bomber becomes the world's largest plane to date.

1924 1 July – inauguration in the United States of the first regular transcontinental airmail service.
28 September – first circumnavigation of the earth. The Douglas World Cruisers *Chicago* and *New Orleans* take off and land in Seattle. Flying time: 371 hours and 11 minutes with 57 stops.
  Also... founding of Huff Daland Dusters in Macon, Georgia. The world's first aerial crop-dusting company later becomes better known as Delta Air Lines.

1925 12 March – maiden flight of the Fokker F.VIIa.
13 April – Henry Ford sets up the United States' first aerial freight service, operating between Detroit and Chicago.

1926 6 January – Deutsche Aero Lloyd and Junkers Luftverkehr merge to form Deutsche Luft Hansa. Flights commence on 6 April.
6 April – founding of Varney

A passenger boarding a Luft Hansa Fokker-Grulich F.III in 1926.

Speed Lines, the future Continental Airlines.
11 June – maiden flight of the Ford 4AT Trimotor.
24 July – two Luft Hansa Junkers G24s fly from Berlin to Beijing and arrive back on 26 September.
  Also... unveiling of the Junkers G31.

1927 15 January – founding of the Boeing Air Transport Company in order to carry airmail between San Francisco and Chicago.
14 March – founding of Pan American World Airways (known as 'Pan Am') to carry airmail between Key West,

Florida and Havana, Cuba.
20–21 May – flying solo in the *Spirit of St. Louis*, Charles Lindbergh makes the first non-stop flight between New York and Paris. He covers the 5,800 km/3,600 miles in 33 hours and 39 minutes.
4–6 June – Charles A. Levine becomes the first passenger on a transatlantic flight. Clarence D. Chamberlain pilots *Columbia*, a Wright-Bellanca WB-2, from New York to Eisleben, Germany – a distance of 6,294 km/3, 911 miles.
14–15 October – Dieudonné Costes and Joseph Le Brix make the first non-stop flight

across the South Atlantic in a Bréguet 19 GR, taking off in Saint-Louis du Sénégal and landing in Puerto Natal, Brazil.

Cover of a book about passenger air travel in Germany (1925).

1928 **12–13 April** – first transatlantic flight from east to west: Hermann Köhl, Freiherr von Hünefeld and James Fitzmaurice fly a Junkers W33 from Dublin, Ireland, to Greenly Island off the coast of Labrador, Canada.

31 May–8 June – Charles Kingford Smith and his crew are the first to cross the Pacific. Their Fokker F.VIIb-3m, the *Southern Cross*, takes 83 hours to fly from Oakland, California, via Honolulu and Fiji to Brisbane, Australia.

17 June – Amelia Earhart of the United States becomes the first woman to fly across the Atlantic.

18 September – airship LZ127, the *Graf Zeppelin*, enters service.

11 October – the LZ127 *Graf Zeppelin* crosses the Atlantic from Friedrichshafen, Germany, to Lakehurst, New Jersey in 71 hours.

Also... in 1926 and 1927 there are 24 airline crashes. In 1929 the figure is 51, the highest to date. It is the equivalent of one accident per million miles flown. The same rate today would amount to 7,000 crashes per year. However, the current accident rate for air travel lies at only one accident per two billion air miles.

1929 **1 January** – founding of LOT (Polish Airlines) in Poland.

30 March – Imperial Airways, one of the forerunners of British Overseas Airways Corporation (BOAC), inaugurates a scheduled service between London and India.

25 July – maiden flight of the Dornier Do-X.

4–16 August – the first international passenger flight competition, a 3,692-mile/5,942-km rally through the heart of Europe, starting and finishing in Paris. It is won by a German crew led by Fritz Morzik. The BFW M.23 achieves a top speed of 140 km/h /87 mph.

8–29 August – Hugo Eckener achieves the first circumnavigation of the earth by airship in the LX127 *Graf Zeppelin*. Starting from, and returning to, Lakehurst, New Jersey, with stops in Germany, Japan and Los Angeles, the 35,200-km/21,900-mile trip takes a total of 21 days, 5 hours and 31 minutes.

The weighing of passengers in 1926. Could this procedure make a comeback?

24 September – Lieutenant James H. Doolittle achieves the first 'blind' flight: taking off, flying and landing the plane by instrument alone. The cockpit windows are blacked out for the experiment.

21 October – the Dornier Do-X sets a world record by taking off with a crew of ten, 150 paying passengers and nine stowaways.

The Ford Trimotor. Unlike Ford's 'Tin Lizzy', 17 million of which were produced, only 199 'Tin Geese' were built.

THE 1920S AND 1930S

A Luft Hansa Junkers G38 in 1931.

1930   25 January – founding of American Airways.
15 May – Ellen Church becomes the world's first stewardess. The former nurse from Iowa welcomes 11 astonished passengers on board a three-engined United Airlines Boeing 80A in Oakland, California. From now on, United Airlines employs air hostesses at a salary of 125 dollars per month to serve their passengers fruit cocktail, roast chicken, and tea or coffee.
18 May – the airship LZ127 *Graf Zeppelin* crosses the South Atlantic.
25 October – Transcontinental & Western Air (TWA) starts its coast-to-coast service.
  Also … Deutsche Luft Hansa becomes the fastest-growing airline in Europe, with the most extensive network of routes.

1931   29 August – the airship *Graf Zeppelin* launches its Germany–Brazil service.
3–5 October – flying a Bellanca Skyrocket, Clyde Pangborn and Hugh Herndon make the first non-stop flight from Japan to the United States.
1 October – Air France becomes the first European airline to employ stewardesses.

1932   19–24 May – the Dornier Do-X flying boat flies from New York to Friedrichshafen, Germany.
20–21 May – Amelia Earhart becomes the first woman to fly solo across the Atlantic, piloting her Lockheed Vega from Harbor Grace in Newfoundland to Londonderry, Northern Ireland.
21 July – A Dornier Do J 'Wal' ('whale') flown by Wolfgang von Gronau takes off from

the German island of Sylt on a three-week trip around the world during which it will cover 60,000 km/37,300 miles.

1933   30 March – the Boeing 247 is the first airliner equipped with a retractable undercarriage.
7 June – the *Monsun*, a Dornier Do J 'Wal' flying boat, crosses the South Atlantic with a stopover on the steamer *Westfalen* and lands in the sea off Natal, Brazil.
1 July – roll-out of the Douglas DC-1.

1934   30 January – a new altitude record is set by the Soviet stratospheric balloon *Osoaviakhim*, which attains a height of 22,000 m/72,200 ft. During the descent, the pressure cabin becomes coated with ice and grows so heavy that it eventually

breaks away from the balloon and crashes to the ground. The crew perish.

1935   A new flight endurance record is set. Brothers Fred and Al Key, known as the Flying Keys, borrow a Curtiss Robin in Meridian, Mississippi. They eventually land on 1 July after staying up for 27 days, having flown over 84,000 km/52,200 miles using 22,700 litres/5,000 gallons of fuel. This record of 635 hours and 34 minutes has never been broken. For their feat the brothers developed an in-flight refuelling system that was later adopted by the US Army Air Corps.

1935   The American aviation pioneers Will Rogers and Wiley Post suffer a fatal accident during take-off at Point Barrow, Alaska.

1935   Douglas unveils the Douglas Sleeper Transport (DST). Based on the DC-2, it is equipped with 14 berths (or 28 seats in the day version) and like the DC-3, Dakota or C-47 is later to become one of the most famous transport planes in aviation history.

1936   Hans Joachim Pabst von Ohain and Max Hahn are engaged by Ernst Heinkel to start work on the development of a jet engine.

1936   Frenchman Georges Détré breaks the aircraft altitude record, achieving a height of 14,843 m/48,697 ft in a Potez 50.

1937   A new world altitude record for an aircraft is set by Italian Lieutenant Colonel Mario Pezzi in a Caproni 161. The new height to beat is 15,655 m/51,361 ft.

Handley Page H.P. 42 of Imperial Airways.

1937 The American aviation pioneer Amelia Earhart and her partner Captain Fred Noonan disappear over the Pacific during an attempted circumnavigation of the globe in a Lockheed Electra 10E.

1938 Deutsche Luft Hansa introduces the Focke-Wulf FW 200 on its Berlin–London route.

1938 Howard Hughes, the American billionaire and later the richest man in the world, lands in New York after circling the globe in a Lockheed 14, covering 24,700 km/15,350 miles in 3 days, 19 hours and 17 minutes.

1938 A Focke-Wulf FW 200 flies non-stop from Berlin to New York.

1938 Lieutenant Colonel Mario Pezzi breaks his own world altitude record, taking his supercharged Caproni Ca161bis to a height of 17,083 m/56,047 ft (Flight Level 560) above Montecelio Airfield. No piston-engined aircraft has ever broken this record.

1938 Focke-Wulf FW 200 'Brandenburg' D-ACON flies from Berlin to Tokyo. With three refuelling stops, the journey takes 46 hours and 15 minutes.

1938 First flight of a passenger aircraft with a pressurized cabin. The Boeing 307 Stratoliner is the forerunner of the B-17 Flying Fortress bomber.

1939 The first Boeing 314 in the Pan Am fleet is named *Yankee Clipper* by Mrs Roosevelt, wife of the US president.

1939 A new world speed record of 746 km/h /463 mph is set by a Heinkel He 100 V8.

1939 This record is then broken by Captain Fritz Wendel, who achieves 755 km/h /469 mph in a Messerschmitt Me 209 V1. Wendel's record – for a piston-engined aircraft – is to stand for 30 years.

1939 First flight of a rocket-powered Heinkel He 176 in Peenemünde, Germany.

1939 A Deutsche Luft Hansa Focke-Wulf FW 200 flies from Berlin to Bangkok, inaugurating a regular service between the two cities.

1939 European air travel is brought to a standstill by World War II.

1939 Luft Hansa and Aeroflot launch a regular service between capitals Berlin and Moscow.

Airline service 1930s-style in a Focke-Wulf FW 200 'Condor'.

TOWARDS THE JET ERA: FROM THE 1940S TO THE 1950S

1941 Japan attacks the US Navy in Pearl Harbor, Hawaii. Six Japanese aircraft carriers transport 400 aircraft to the battle zone. Five American battleships and ten other vessels are destroyed, with a further three battleships badly damaged. In the evening, Tokyo declares war against the United States and Great Britain.

1943 Ernst Jachmann catches a good thermal in his single-seat glider and manages to stay airborne for 55 hours and 51 minutes.

1944 The Convention on International Civil Aviation (also known as the Chicago Convention) is signed in Chicago.

1945 Founding of the International Air Transport Association (IATA) in Havana, Cuba.

1946 Colonel William H. Council sets a new US transcontinental speed record. Flying in a Lockheed P80 Shooting Star from Long Beach in Los Angeles to La Guardia, New York, Council completes the journey (which a few years earlier still took days) in just 4 hours, 13 minutes and 26 seconds. This is also the longest non-stop flight by a jet.

1946 A Pan Am Constellation lands at Heathrow, inaugurating the first scheduled airline service between New York and London.

1946 The US military declares knots and nautical miles to be the official standards for aviation speed and distance measurement.

1946 A Lockheed P2V Neptune sets a new non-stop distance record, travelling 18,081 km/11,235 miles from Perth, Australia, to Columbus, Ohio.

1946 A Boeing B-29 makes the first non-stop flight from Hawaii to Egypt over the North Pole – a distance of 17,498 km/10,873 miles.

1947 The International Civil Aviation Organization is formed in Montreal, Canada. The ICAO is an agency of the United Nations.

1947 Pan Am launches a west–east service from New York to San Francisco; the route circles the globe, connecting all the world's major cities.

1947 Fully automatic flight of a C-54 Skymaster from Stephenville, Newfoundland, to England.

1947 Captain Charles 'Chuck' Yeager breaks the sound barrier in a rocket-powered Bell X-1 in level flight. He attains a speed of 1,127 km/h /700 mph (Mach 1.06) at a height of 12,800 m/41,995 ft.

1948 Orville Wright dies at 76 years of age.

1948 1 April – train services between Berlin and West Germany are suspended by the Soviets.
18–19 April – all roads between Berlin and West Germany are blocked by the Soviets.

A transport plane landing at Tempelhof Airport during the Berlin Airlift of 1948.

24 June – rail traffic between Berlin and West Germany through the Soviet occupation zone is suspended until further notice for 'technical reasons'.
26 June – start of the Berlin Airlift. American, British and French transport planes fly to West Berlin from eight airports and air bases in West Germany, landing at intervals of one or two minutes.

23 July – the US Air Force (USAF) and the Military Air Transport Command make preparations to extend the airlift in order to ensure the continued supply of food and fuel to the city.
21 August – C-54 Skymasters are used in the airlift.
14 September – the Royal Australian Air Force takes part in the airlift.
16 October – the South African Air Force contributes personnel to the airlift.

The jet age began in 1947 with test planes such as the Bell X-1.

A *Boeing B-29, 1946.*

1951 1 August – founding of Japan Airlines.
21 August – improvements made on Cocos Island in the Indian Ocean, allowing Qantas Empire Airways to operate a passenger service from Perth, Australia, to Johannesburg via Cocos Island and Mauritius.

1952 29 July – first non-stop flight by a jet (a North American RB-45) over the Pacific from Alaska to Japan.
5–6 December – a Scandinavian Airlines System (SAS) DC-6 flies non-stop over the North Pole from Los Angeles to Copenhagen.

1953 6 January – founding of LUFTAG (*Aktiengesellschaft für Luftverkehrsbedarf*) which later becomes Lufthansa.
15 May – Central British Columbia Airways changes its name to Pacific Western Airlines.

3 November – the Royal New Zealand Air Force also sends crews to Berlin.

1948 A USAF Consolidated B-36 flies 15,128 km/9,400 miles from Fort Worth, Texas, to Hawaii and back without air-to-air refuelling.

1949 First non-stop circumnavigation of the globe by Captain James Gallagher of the US Air Force. His B-50, the *Lucky Lady II*, is refuelled in flight four times. The trip covers 37,742 km/23,452 miles in 94 hours and 1 minute.

1949 16 April – peak day during the Berlin Airlift: 13,000 tonnes of freight are delivered to Berlin in 1,398 flights within a space of 24 hours.

1949 Americans Bill Barris and Dick Riedel pilot the *Sunkist Lady*, their slow-flying Aeronca Sedan, from Fullerton, California, to Miami and back without landing, spending a total of 1,008

hours and 1 minute in the air. This is the equivalent of six weeks. Their record-breaking flight requires an immense logistical effort. While the pilots take turns sleeping, a crew of three accompany the plane in a second Aeronca, the *Lady's Maid*. This second plane lands at airfields along the route where the auxiliary crew fill 11-litre/2.5-gallon canisters with fuel and race along the runway in a jeep below the low-flying *Sunkist Lady* while the fuel and provisions are loaded into the plane. In Miami, the *Sunkist Lady* is forced to circle for 14 days due to bad weather before continuing her journey to California. This labour-intensive record stands for just six months.

1949 12 May – the Soviet Union ends its blockade of West Berlin. The airlift continues in order to build up reserves.
30 September – the Berlin Airlift is called off. During the 15 months of its operation, 2.35 million tonnes of freight

are delivered to Berlin, including 1.44 million tonnes of coal and 490,000 tonnes of food. Among the other supplies, 160,000 tonnes of building materials are also transported by air. A total of 277,804 flights are made, during which 41 Britons and 31 Americans lose their lives.

1950 17 May – Transcontinental & Western Air is renamed Trans World Airlines (TWA).

Offering passengers cigarettes was considered stylish and a normal part of in-flight service in the 1950s.

What goes around, comes around. Main picture: On board a Pan Am Boeing 377. Below: On board a Singapore Airlines A380. By contrast, some airlines today are seriously considering asking their passengers to stand during flights!

THE 1950S TO THE 1960S

1954 15 May – Qantas Empire Airlines takes over the Australia–Canada and Australia–United States routes from British Commonwealth Pacific Airlines.

6 August – in Germany, the first chapter in the rebuilding of civil aviation comes to a close when LUFTAG decides to change its name to Deutsche Lufthansa (without becoming the legal successor the Deutsche Luft Hansa that existed before the war). Three months later, the Allies issue a special permit for the introduction of aircraft and training. However, this does not include an automatic licence to operate.

1955 1 April – Lufthansa makes its first official post-war flight.

16 May – Lufthansa starts to fly to other European countries.

27 July – an EL AL airliner strays into Bulgarian airspace and is shot down by two MiG 15 fighters with the loss of all 58 people on board.

16 October – a prototype of the Boeing 707 (model 367-80) flies non-stop from Seattle to Washington, DC in 3 hours and 58 minutes.

1 November – a bomb on board a United Airlines DC-6 explodes over Colorado with the loss of all 44 passengers and crew. A man who wanted to claim his mother's life insurance had hidden a bomb in her suitcase prior to the flight.

1956 1 June – the Douglas DC-7 is brought into service by Pan Am.

15 September – Aeroflot adds the Tupolev Tu-104 turbojet to its fleet.

1957 18 January – three Boeing B-52 Stratofortress jets make the joint first non-stop round-the-world flight by a jet-powered aircraft, taking 45 hours and 19 minutes.

1958 14–20 January – Qantas launches a round-the-world service in a Lockheed Super Constellation. The *Southern Aurora* flies east from Sydney to London over the United States while the *Southern Zephyr* travels west over India and the Middle East.

An SAS DC-6 in 1965.

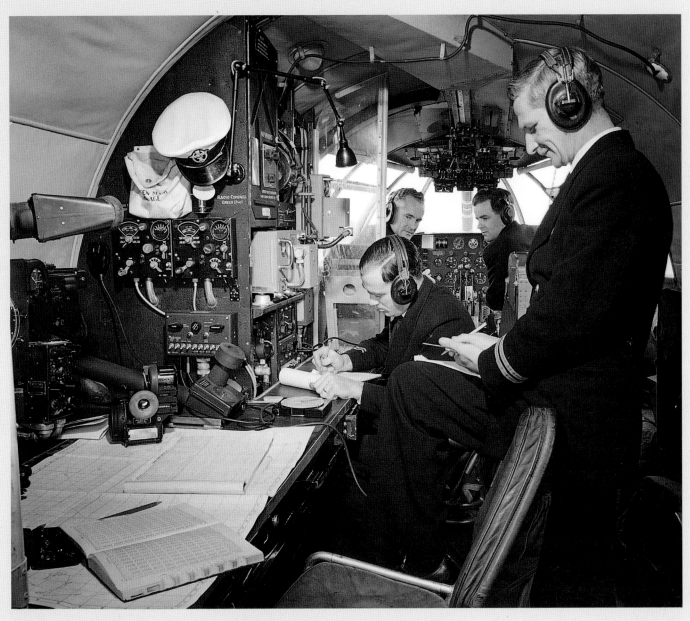

Until the 1970s, flight crews included navigators and radio operators as well as pilots.

1 April – economy class is introduced on the transatlantic route.

1959   18 September – the Douglas DC-8 enters service.

1960   9–28 July – the Belgian airline Sabena airlifts 25,711 Belgian nationals back to Europe after the Belgian Congo gains its independence.

1961   19 July – Trans World Airlines (TWA) shows films in

the first-class lounge of its long-haul flights.

1962   31 December – the last US airship is scrapped.

1963   19 July – Joe Walker flies to the edge of space, climbing to an altitude of 106 km/66 miles in an X-15A.

1965   15 November – a Boeing 707 of the Flying Tiger Line is the first aircraft to fly around the world via both poles.

1966   6 December – in Germany, the Luftwaffe grounds its 770 Starfighters after the number of crashes by interceptor aircraft of this type reaches 65.

1967   5 June – roll-out of the one-thousandth Boeing jet, a 707-120B destined for American Airlines.

1968   30 June – maiden flight of the Lockheed C-5A Galaxy.
31 December – maiden flight by the prototype of the

supersonic Tupolev Tu-144. Due to its resemblance to Concorde, which is currently under construction, it is nicknamed the 'Konkordski'.

1969   9 February – maiden flight of a Boeing 747.
2 March – the United Kingdom withdraws from the European Airbus programme. Germany and France develop the Airbus A300 together.

The Oil Crisis and the First Insolvencies: the 1970s and 1980s

A Scandinavian Airlines DC-7 in the 1970s.

1970 **21 January** – the Boeing 747 enters service.
6 September – Palestinian terrorists hijack a BOAC VC-10, a TWA Boeing 707 and a Swissair DC-8 and fly them to Dawson's Field in Jordan. A fourth aircraft, a Pan Am Boeing 747, is flown to Cairo.
12 September – the terrorists blow up all four aircraft after the release of most of the passengers.

1972 **30 May** – in the arrivals hall of Tel Aviv Airport, three Japanese Red Army terrorists fire their guns indiscriminately at passengers who have just disembarked from an Air France flight. There are 28 fatalities (including 16 pilgrims from Puerto Rico) and 69 people are injured.
29 October – a Lufthansa Boeing 727 is hijacked and diverted to Zagreb, Croatia, by Libyan terrorists seeking to obtain the release of prisoners.
29 December – discovery of the survivors of the Andes plane crash of 13 October 1972.

1973 **3 June** – the thirtieth Paris Air Show ends with the break-up and crash of the second Tupolev Tu-144 prototype.
29 November – roll-out of the one thousandth Boeing 727.
17 December – after police discover weapons in the luggage of a passenger at Rome Fiumicino Airport, four other terrorists open fire indiscriminately in the airport's packed lounge. They take hostages and manage to board a Pan Am plane. When the terrorists throw hand grenades into the aircraft, 29 people (including 14 American employees of an oil company) are killed. The assailants then seize a Lufthansa airliner and fly it to Kuwait, where they give themselves up to the authorities.

1974 **3 March** – a Turkish Airlines McDonnell Douglas DC-10 crashes north of Paris with the loss of all 346 people on board.
8 March – opening of Charles de Gaulle Airport in Paris.
23 May – the Airbus A300-B-2 enters service.

26 August – Charles Lindbergh dies of cancer at the age of 72.

1975 **4 April** – an American C-5 Galaxy carrying 311 orphans crashes 12 minutes after taking off from Saigon in Vietnam. Of the 311 children, only 161 survive.

1976 **4 March** – first non-stop flight of a Japan Airlines jumbo jet from Tokyo to New York. The Boeing 747 travels the 10,000 km/6,200 miles in 11 hours and 30 minutes.
24 March – a passenger plane world distance record of 16,500 km/10,253 miles is set by a Boeing 747SP.
22 December – first fully automatic landing by an Airbus A300 airliner.

1977 **27 March** – the worst aviation accident in history occurs when two Boeing 747s collide in fog on the runway of Santa Cruz Airport on Tenerife with the loss of 579 lives.
21 May – Concorde memorial flight from New York to Paris marks the fiftieth anniversary of Charles Lindbergh's transatlantic flight. While Lindbergh took 33 hours and 29 minutes, Concorde needs just 3 hours and 44 minutes to travel the same route.
13 June – Freddie Laker launches Skytrain, the first low-cost carrier.

1978 **1 January** – an Air India Boeing 747 crashes into the sea off the Indian coast with the loss of all 213 people on board.
20 April – a Korean Airlines Boeing 707 strays into Soviet airspace and is forced to make an emergency landing after being attacked by Soviet fighters.
21 May – after four years of protest, Narita International Airport, Tokyo's second major airport, opens with certain restrictions that are still in force today.
24 October – deregulation of aviation in the United States.

1979 **25 May** – a McDonnell Douglas DC-10 loses an engine after take-off and crashes. All DC-10s are grounded until 13 July.
29 November – an Air New Zealand DC-10 takes off in

Voyager as it returns after circumnavigating the globe in 1986.

The Antonov 124, unveiled in 1985, was the world's largest aircraft for several years.

Auckland for a sight-seeing trip over the Antarctic and crashes into a mountainside. All 257 people on board are killed.

1980   1–8 August – the air show at Oshkosh, Wisconsin, sets a new record with 250,000 spectators and 6,000 aircraft.

1981   6 August – US president Ronald Reagan fires 10,000 striking air traffic controllers and bars them from their profession for life.

1982   16 February – roll-out of the first A310.

1983   1 September – a Russian fighter shoots down a Korean Airlines Boeing 747 with the loss of 269 lives off the coast of Sakhalin Island in the North Pacific.
9 December – roll-out of the thousandth Boeing 737.

1984   23 July – an Air Canada Boeing 767, dubbed the 'Gimli Glider', runs out of fuel halfway between Montreal and Edmonton. A mistake had been made refuelling the plane because of a

recent switch from gallons to litres. However, the captain is a gliding enthusiast and succeeds in dramatically glide-landing the plane at a disused military airbase at Gimli near Winnipeg.

1985   29 May – unveiling of the world's largest aircraft, the Antonov An-124, at the Paris Air Show (Le Bourget).
23 June – an Air India jumbo jet is blown up by a suitcase bomb south of Ireland, resulting in 329 fatalities.

1986   17 August – Boeing celebrates the roll-out of its five thousandth airliner.

1986   14–23 December – A new distance record is set for a non-stop flight without refuelling. The Rutan Model 76 Voyager ends its flight around the world after 9 days, 3 minutes and 44 seconds, having travelled a distance of 40,812 km/ 25,359 miles.

1987   23 November – of the 128 new airlines created after deregulation in the United States, only 37 are still in business.

1988   28 March – roll-out of the Airbus A320.
3 July – an Iranian Air Airbus A300 is accidentally shot down by the American cruiser USS *Vincennes* with the loss of all 286 on board.
21 December – the Pan Am Boeing 747 *Maid of the Seas* is blown up over Lockerbie in Scotland. The 16-strong crew, 243 passengers and 11 people on the ground are killed. The attack is attributed to Libyan terrorists.

1989   Maiden flight of the Northrop B-2. Costing 516 million dollars per plane, this is the most expensive aircraft in the history of aviation.

1989   18 August – the Qantas Boeing 747-400 *Spirit of Australia* flies non-stop from London to Sydney in 19 hours and 10 minutes.

1989   Russian aircraft designer Alexander Yakovlev dies at the age of 84.

Enormous progress in both military and civil aviation was made during the 1970s and 1980s. While DC-7s were still in use, modern, elegant designs were coming to the fore, such as this Northrop B-2 Stealth Bomber.

From 1 Cent to 100,000 Dollars Per Seat: the 1990s and 2000s

1990 11 January – roll-out of the three-engined McDonnell Douglas MD-11.

1991 1 September – Boeing ends production of the 707 after 37 years. Pan Am experiences financial difficulties and is wound up after 73 years. Its remaining profitable assets are taken over by Delta Air Lines.

1993 16 August – Concorde flies round the world in 31 hours and 27 minutes (New York–Toulouse–Dubai–Bangkok–Guam–Honolulu–Acapulco–New York).

1996 16 March – the Dutch aircraft manufacturer Fokker folds after 77 years.
15 December – Boeing takes over McDonnell Douglas.

1997 8 September – roll-out of the Boeing 777-300. At 73 m/240 ft it is the world's longest aircraft to date.

1998 16 January – in the interests of safety, the Russian aviation authority shuts down over 200 small Russian airlines that have come into being since 1992. Of the 315 airlines that existed previously, only 53 remain.
17 October – US Airways places an order for 276 Airbus A319s. Never before has an airline ordered so many aircraft at once.

1999 22 December – a Korean Air Boeing 747 Cargo crashes after taking off from London Stansted.

2000 25 July – a Concorde crashes with the loss of 114 lives immediately after taking off from Charles de Gaulle Airport in Paris. The crash, the first in the aircraft's history, is caused by a piece of metal that had fallen onto the runway from another plane. The metal bursts one of the Concorde's tyres and pieces of rubber penetrate the fuel tank above. The fuel tank catches fire causing the aircraft to lose power and crash into a hotel near the airport.

2000 Singapore Airlines places an order worth 235 million dollars for ten Airbus A380s and signs an option for a further 15 aircraft of the same type.

2000 Qantas orders 12 Airbus A380s. Qantas has hitherto been one of Boeing's most loyal customers.

2001 11 September – Boeing 767s belonging to American Airlines and United Airlines are hijacked by al-Qaeda terrorists. Both aircraft, fully fuelled for domestic flights from Boston to Los Angeles, are flown on different trajectories into the World Trade Center in Manhattan. The buildings collapse with the loss of over 2,800 lives. An American Airlines Boeing 757 flying from Washington Dulles to Los Angeles is also hijacked and is crashed into the Pentagon. A second 757 is hijacked after taking off from Newark, New Jersey. The passengers overpower the terrorists and instead of being crashed into the Capitol or the White House, the plane crash-lands in an open field. Aviation security reacts immediately, closing down US airspace. The international airline industry is badly affected.
12 September – The financially stricken airline Ansett Australia is finished off by the events of 11 September and declares itself bankrupt.
2 October – Swissair declares itself bankrupt.
7 November – Sabena's 73-year history also ends in bankruptcy.

2002 United Airlines files for bankruptcy but continues to operate under certain conditions laid down in Chapter 11 of the US bankruptcy code.

2003 Concorde is definitively retired on 26 November, bringing an era to a close.

2004 A Singapore Airlines Airbus A340-500 flies the shortest route between Singapore and New York, a distance of 16,500 km/10,253

Following the terrorist attacks of 11 September 2001, the United States closed down its airspace. All planes either had to land immediately or exit American airspace and land in Canada. This picture shows the situation at Halifax, Nova Scotia.

At subsonic speeds, Concorde had a rather unstable wing profile. It compensated for this with powerful engines.

miles, non-stop. At over 18 hours, this is the longest non-stop passenger-carrying flight in the world. It leaves Singapore at 11 pm and arrives two days later at 6 am local time. The in-flight food and drink is carefully adapted to long-distance flying, with the three meals consisting of light fare.

Singapore Airlines was the first to place an order for the Airbus A380, the world's largest passenger aircraft.

THE GENEALOGY OF AN AIRLINE

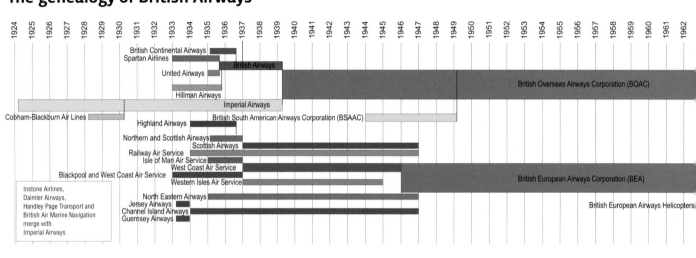

The genealogy of British Airways

Genealogy is a fascinating science. It involves the tracing of a living person's ancestry backwards through time, uncovering liaisons, unions, parents, grandparents and siblings along the way. Changes of name add to the difficulty of the task. The same problem is true of airlines, very few of which were founded more than 50 or 60 years ago under their current names. In contrast to Delta Air Lines, which has had 'Delta' in its name from a very early stage and played the role of 'son and heir' until its merger with Northwest (which has its own rich tradition), the history of US Airways is extremely convoluted. Founded in 1937 as All American Aviation, it later changed its name to Allegheny Airlines and gradually bought up various local competitors and other regional airlines until it was large enough to call itself USAir. This name, in turn, was changed to US Airways. By 2004, however, its finances had deteriorated to such an

extent that it was put up for sale. The ailing mega-carrier was bought by America West, an Arizona-based airline that had been in business for no more than 20 years. After the take-over, the company was subsumed into America West's operations and its headquarters transferred to Tempe, Arizona. Going against normal practice, however, America West changed its name to that of the company it had acquired, since 'US Airways' was an older and more established name that had become very well known.

Equally misleading were the names of two Fiji-based airlines. Initially there was Air Fiji, whose dominion was the entire Pacific region, and Air Pacific, whose small fleet merely plied backwards and forwards between the Fijian islands. Only after swapping names did the airline's titles match their route maps.

Subsidiaries founded in different parts of the world for political regions can also be confusing. KLM Asia, for

example, was founded in Taiwan in 1995 so that the parent company would not endanger its destinations in China. Its livery displayed neither the Dutch flag nor the royal crown. Another KLM subsidiary operated between 1928 and 1947 under the name KNILM (*Koninklijke Nederlansch-Indische Luchtvaart Maatschappij* or Royal Netherlands Indian Airways).

The history of nearly all the colonial powers is reflected in the history of their airlines. These companies set up subsidiaries in the colonies which were later often nationalized. Or else they conducted a proxy war against competitors, as in the case of the American PANAGRA, which challenged Lufthansa's dominance in South America.

Since civil aviation is subject, by its very nature, to turbulence, we can be certain that the airline industry will continue to be an arena for interesting pairings, mergers and take-overs. These often

begin with a codeshare agreement and then develop into an alliance before a full take-over is announced. Such was the case with Kingfisher and Deccan of India. The latter is now called Kingfisher Red and, as a low-cost carrier, it complements the services of its ambitious parent in the luxury sector. Genealogists of the future can rest assured that there will be plenty more fun to be had from tracing the ancestry of airlines.

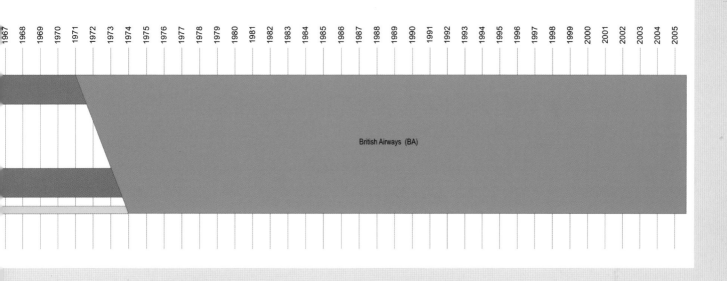

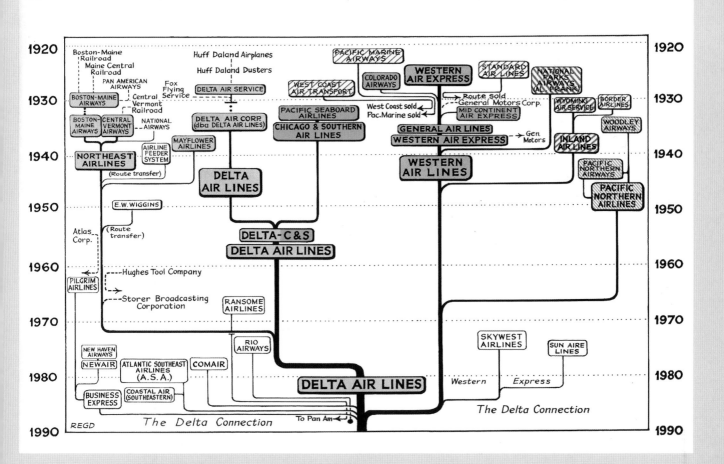

Following a merger with Northwest Airlines in 2008, Delta Air Lines is now the largest airline in the world, with almost 800 aircraft and numerous regional subsidiaries. Delta developed out of a small crop-spraying business called Huff Daland Dusters.

Chapter 11 – A Safe Haven for US Companies

Chapter 11 has provided countless American companies with protection from their creditors. Companies that file for insolvency under Chapter 11 no longer have to worry about their debts and can undertake restructuring. It was airlines that made Chapter 11 famous.

1979	New York Airways	1982	Aero Virgin Islands
1979	Aeroamerica		
1980	Florida Airlines	1982	Altair
1980	Indiana Airlines	1989	Partnair
1980	Air Bahia	2002	US Airways
1980	Tejas Airlines	2002	United Airlines
1981	Mountain West	2003	Air Canada
1981	LANICA	2004	Flash Airlines
1981	Coral Air	2004	US Airways re
1981	Pacific Coast	2004	Aloha Airlines
1981	Swift Air Line	2005	Northwest Airlines
1981	Golden Gate (Airline)	2005	Delta Air Lines
1982	Pinehurst Airlines	2007	Maxjet Airways
1982	Silver State Airlines	2008	Aloha Airlines
1982	Air Pennsylvania	2008	ATA Airlines
1982	Air South	2008	Skybus Airlines
1982	Cochise Airlines	2008	Frontier Airlines
1982	Braniff International	2008	Eos Airlines
1982	Astec Air East	2008	Sun Country Airlines
1982	Will's Air	2008	Primaris Airlines
1982	Aero Sun International		

Airline Deregulation

The world of commercial aviation changed forever when American president Jimmy Carter signed the Airline Deregulation Act on 24 October 1978.

Airlines could now select their own routes, based on profitability. From now on they could also set their own seat prices.

- The end of state protection forced airlines to adopt a form of management based on the principles of free enterprise.
- Seat prices were now determined by supply and demand.
- Price competition created a need to reduce costs.
- The pressure on costs led to industrial disputes with the unions.

Over 100 airlines went under, including big names such as Air Florida, Braniff, Capitol, Eastern, MarkAir, Pacific Southwest PSA, Republic Airlines, Texas International, Trans World Airlines (TWA) and Western Airlines.

The most important consequence of deregulation was that short-haul flights became more expensive and long-haul flights became cheaper.

Numerous airlines throughout the world were privatized around this time, with the result that unprofitable routes simply disappeared.

Genealogy of Airline Companies (Selection)

1909	*	DELAG
1916	*	NORTHWEST AIRWAYS
1916	*	AIRCRAFT TRANSPORT AND TRAVEL
1917	*	CHALK'S OCEAN AIRWAYS
1918	*	DET DANSKE LUFTFARTSELS-KAB
1918	*	SOCIÉTÉ DES LIGNES LATÉCOÈRE
1919	*	KLM
1919	*	SVENSKA LUFTTRAFIK
1919	*	LIGNES AÉRIENNES FARMAN
1919	*	GRANDS EXPRESS AÉRIENS
1919	*	COMPAGNIE DES MESSAGERIES AÉRIENNES
1919	*	DAIMLER AIRWAYS
1919	*	KLM
1919	*	SCADTA
1919	*	HANDLEY PAGE TRANSPORT
1919	*	INSTONE AIR LINE
1920	*	COMPAGNIE FRANCO-ROUMAINE DE NAVIGATION AÉRIENNE
1920	*	QANTAS
1921	*	MEXICANA
1921	*	WEST AUSTRALIAN AIRWAYS
1921	*	AEROMARINE WEST INDIES AIRWAYS
1921	*	HUFF DALAND DUSTERS
1921	†	AIRCRAFT TRANSPORT AND TRAVEL
1921	†	SVENSKA LUFTTRAFIK
1922	*	MALERT
1923	*	AIR UNION
1923	*	AEROFLOT
1923	*	SABENA
1923	*	CZECH AIRLINES
1923	*	FINNAIR
1923	*	AB AEROTRANSPORT
1923	*	TAJIK AIR
1923	†	GRANDS EXPRESS AÉRIENS
1923	†	COMPAGNIE DES MESSAGERIES AÉRIENNES
1924	*	BRITISH MARINE AIR NAVIGATION CO LTD
1924	*	IMPERIAL AIRWAYS
1924	*	DELTA AIR LINES
1924	∞	DAIMLER AIRWAYS → IMPERIAL AIRWAYS
1924	∞	HANDLEY PAGE TRANSPORT → IMPERIAL AIRWAYS
1924	∞	INSTONE AIR LINE → IMPERIAL AIRWAYS
1924	†	AEROMARINE WEST INDIES AIRWAYS
1924	†	BRITISH MARINE AIR NAVIGATION CO LTD
1925	*	WESTERN AIR EXPRESS
1925	*	CIDNA
1925	*	LLOYD AÉREO BOLIVIANO
1926	*	DEUTSCHE LUFT HANSA
1926	*	EASTERN AIRLINES
1926	*	DEUTSCHE LUFT HANSA AKTIENGESELLSCHAFT
1926	*	VARNEY AIRLINES
1926	*	NORTHWEST AIRLINES
1926	*	COLONIAL AIR TRANSPORT
1926	*	SERVIÇOS AÉREOS CRUZEIRO DO SUL
1927	*	PAN AM, PAN AMERICAN WORLD AIRWAYS INC
1928	*	BRANIFF
1928	∞	HUFF DALAND DUSTERS → DELTA AIR SERVICE
1929	*	PANAGRA, PAN AMERICAN GRACE AIRWAYS
1930	*	TWA, TRANS WORLD AIRLINES
1930	∞	WESTERN AIR EXPRESS; STANDARD AIRLINES + TRANSCONTINENTAL AIR TRANSPORT → TWA
1930	*	WESTERN CANADIAN AIRWAYS
1930	∞	WESTERN CANADIAN AIRWAYS → CANADIAN AIRWAYS
1930	∞	COLONIAL AIR TRANSPORT → AMERICAN AIRLINES
1931	*	SWISSAIR
1932	†	SOCIÉTÉ DES LIGNES LATÉCOÈRE
1933	*	NORTHEAST AIRLINES
1933	∞	LIGNES AÉRIENNES FARMAN → AIR FRANCE
1933	∞	COMPAGNIE FRANCO-ROUMAINE DE NAVIGATION AÉRIENNE → AIR FRANCE
1933	†	AIR UNION
1933	∞	CIDNA → AIR FRANCE
1933	*	NATIONAL AIRLINES
1934	∞	VARNEY AIRLINES → UNITED AIRLINES
1935	†	DELAG
1936	†	WEST AUSTRALIAN AIRWAYS
1937	*	MALAYSIAN AIRLINES SYSTEM (MAS)
1938	*	DERBY AIRWAYS
1939	*	BRITISH OVERSEAS AIRWAYS CORPORATION, BOAC
1939	∞	IMPERIAL AIRWAYS → BRITISH OVERSEAS AIRWAYS → BRITISH AIRWAYS
1940	*	AVIANCA
1940	∞	SCADTA → AVIANCA
1941	*	WESTERN AIR LINES
1941	∞	WESTERN AIR EXPRESS → WESTERN AIRLINES
1942	*	CANADIAN PACIFIC AIRLINES – CP AIR
1944	*	LOFTLEIDIR ICELANDIC AIRLINES
1944	†	MALERT
1945	*	FLYING TIGER LINE
1945	†	DEUTSCHE LUFT HANSA
1945	*	MOHAWK AIRLINES

1946	*	BRITISH EUROPEAN AIRWAYS, BEA
1946	*	BRITISH WORLD AIRWAYS
1946	*	CAPITOL AIRWAYS
1946	*	EAST AFRICAN AIRWAYS
1946	*	SOBELAIR
1946	†	DET DANSKE LUFTFARTSELSKAB
1947	*	AIR CEYLON
1948	*	AVIACO
1949	*	C A A C
1949	*	PACIFIC SOUTHWEST AIRLINES
1950	∞	AB AEROTRANSPORT → SAS
1952	*	NORTH CENTRAL AIRLINES
1953	*	ALLEGHENY AIRLINES
1953	*	BALAIR
1953	*	DAN-AIR SERVICES LTD
1953	*	WARDAIR
1953	∞	HUFF DALAND + CHICAGO & SOUTHERN AIR LINES → DELTA C&S
1954	*	DEUTSCHE LUFTHANSA
1954	*	AIR INTER
1954	*	INTERFLUG GESELLSCHAFT
1956	*	SOUTHEAST AIRLINES
1957	*	BAVARIA
1959	*	SPANTAX
1961	*	INEX ADRIA AIRWAYS
1961	*	VIASA
1962	*	STERLING AIRWAYS
1963	*	ALIA
1963	*	ALISARDA
1963	*	UTA – UNION DE TRANSPORTS AERIENS
1964	*	GERMANAIR
1964	†	DERBY AIRWAYS
1966	*	DAT DELTA AIR TRANSPORT
1966	*	LAKER AIRWAYS
1967	†	PANAGRA, PAN AMERICAN GRACE AIRWAYS
1967	†	CAPITOL AIRWAYS
1967	∞	WESTERN AIRLINES + PACIFIC NORTHERN AIRLINES
1968	∞	PACIFIC AIR LINES → AIR WEST
1969	*	TEXAS INTERNATIONAL AIRLINES
1970	*	BRITISH CALEDONIAN
1970	*	PANINTERNATIONAL
1970	∞	Air West → HUGHES AIR WEST
1971	†	PANINTERNATIONAL
1972	*	AIR LITTORAL
1972	†	NORTHEAST AIRLINES
1972	†	MOHAWK AIRLINES
1972	∞	NORTHEAST AIRLINES → DELTA
1973	†	LOFTLEIDIR ICELANDIC AIRLINES
1974	*	DLT (DEUTSCHE LUFTVERKEHRSGESELLSCHAFT)
1974	*	NFD – NÜRNBERGER FLUGDIENST

1974	∞	BRITISH OVERSEAS AIRWAYS CORPORATION, BOAC → BRITISH AIRWAYS
1974	∞	BRITISH EUROPEAN AIRWAYS, BEA → BRITISH AIRWAYS
1974	*	BRITISH AIRWAYS
1974	†	BAHAMAS WORLD AIRWAYS
1975	*	CROSSAIR
1977	†	EAST AFRICAN AIRWAYS
1978	*	AIR EUROPE
1978	*	DELTA AIR REGIONALFLUGVERKEHR
1978	†	OVERSEAS NATIONAL AIRWAYS
1979	*	AIR LANKA
1979	*	BRITISH EUROPEAN
1979	†	AIR CEYLON
1979	†	NORTH CENTRAL AIRLINES
1979	†	ALLEGHENY AIRLINES
1979	†	SOUTHEAST AIRLINES
1979	†	BAVARIA
1979	†	GERMANAIR
1979	∞	NORTH CENTRAL AIRLINES + SOUTHERN AIRWAYS → REPUBLIC AIRLINES
1980	†	NATIONAL AIRLINES
1980	∞	REPUBLIC + HUGHES AIR WEST
1981	*	AEROLLOYD
1981	*	CORSE AIR
1981	†	GREAT LAKES AIRLINES
1982	†	BRANIFF
1982	†	TEXAS INTERNATIONAL AIRLINES
1984	†	CANADIAN PACIFIC AIRLINES – CP AIR
1984	†	C A A C
1985	†	LAKER AIRWAYS
1985	†	AIR FLORIDA
1986	*	INTEROT
1986	†	INEX ADRIA AIRWAYS
1986	†	ALIA
1986	∞	REPUBLIC → NORTHWEST AIRLINES
1986	†	WESTERN AIR EXPRESS
1987	*	AIR BOTNIA
1987	*	CANADIAN AIRLINES INTERNATIONAL
1987	*	EMERY WORLDWIDE
1987	†	MALAYSIAN AIRLINES SYSTEM (MAS)
1987	†	WESTERN AIR LINES
1987	†	BRITISH CALEDONIAN
1987	∞	WESTERN AIR LINES → DELTA
1988	*	LTU SÜD
1988	†	PACIFIC SOUTHWEST AIRLINES
1988	†	SPANTAX
1989	*	GERMAN WINGS
1989	†	WARDAIR
1990	†	GERMAN WINGS
1991	†	EASTERN AIRLINES
1991	†	PAN AM, PAN AMERICAN WORLD AIRWAYS INC

1991	†	ALISARDA
1991	∞	DELTA → PAN AM (Routes)
1992	*	SHOROUK AIR
1992	†	DAN-AIR SERVICES LTD
1992	†	UTA – UNION DE TRANSPORTS AERIENS
1992	†	DLT (DEUTSCHE LUFTVERKEHRSGESELLSCHAFT)
1993	∞	SERVIÇOS AÉREOS CRUZEIRO DO SUL → VARIG
1994	*	SABRE AIRWAYS
1994	†	INTERFLUG GESELLSCHAFT
1994	†	NFD – NÜRNBERGER FLUGDIENST
1994	†	RFG REGIONALFLUG
1995	†	AIR INTER
1995	†	INTEROT
1997	*	GO
1997	*	KLM UK
1997	*	VOLARE
1997	†	VIASA
1997	†	LTU SÜD
1998	†	AIR BOTNIA
1999	*	BUZZ
1999	*	JMC AIRLINES
1999	†	AVIACO
1999	†	AIR LANKA
1999	†	CANADIAN AIRLINES INTERNATIONAL
2000	†	SABRE AIRWAYS
2001	†	SABENA
2001	†	TWA, TRANS WORLD AIRLINES
2001	†	SWISSAIR
2002	∞	CROSSAIR → SWISS INTERNATIONAL
2002	†	DAT DELTA AIR TRANSPORT
2002	†	NATIONAL AIRLINES
2002	†	GO
2002	†	VG AIRLINES
2003	*	V-BIRD
2003	†	AEROLLOYD
2003	†	SHOROUK AIR
2003	†	BUZZ
2003	†	JMC AIRLINES
2004	†	SOBELAIR
2004	†	AIR LITTORAL
2007	∞	SWISS → LUFTHANSA
2007	†	CHALK'S OCEAN AIRWAYS
2007	†	LLOYD AÉREO BOLIVIANO
2008	∞	DELTA + NORTHWEST
2008	∞	ALITALIA → AIR FRANCE/KLM
2009	∞	AUA → LUFTHANSA
2009	∞	BMI → LUFTHANSA

Key to symbols used in the chart:
* founding
∞ merger
† closure
→ take-over

THE
COMMERCIAL
AIRLINER

JUNKERS JU-52, ('AUNTIE JU')

The Ju-52 was a further development of the Ju-52/1m, originally conceived as a single-engined aircraft for military use. It was designed to be used in regions with poor infrastructure as a robust transport plane and auxiliary bomber requiring minimum maintenance. However, pursuing the vision of Professor Hugo Junkers and at the request of Luft Hansa, it was eventually fitted with three engines and became the world's first mass-produced airliner. It was purchased by numerous airlines, and a total of 4,800 were produced, of which a number are still flying today. The Ju-52 was used by airlines in Argentina, Austria, Belgium, Bolivia, Brazil, Colombia, Germany, Great Britain, Italy, Norway, Peru, South Africa, the Soviet Union, Sweden, Uruguay and elsewhere. It was also used by Luft Hansa subsidiary Eurasia in China. Luft Hansa's in-flight brochure of the day stated: 'Travelling by air is a joyful, recuperative and time-saving experience. The fast airliners of today complete even the longest of journeys in a very short time.'

At that time, the airline still showed great consideration to smokers: 'Passengers who wish to smoke take precedence in the smoking compartment. In the spirit of in-flight camaraderie, we ask passengers in the smoking compartment to give up their seats, as and when necessary, to those wishing to smoke.'

The consequences of airsickness were also carefully regulated: 'Luft Hansa makes no charge for soiling as a result of airsickness. However, if the soiling is caused by dogs travelling in the cabin with their owners, the owner will be required to pay a cleaning fee of one Reichsmark. This fee will be passed on to the individual along with the responsibility of cleaning up the mess.'

JUNKERS JU-52

Length	18.5 m/60 ft 8 in
Wingspan	29.25 m/96 ft
Wing area	110.5 sq m/1189 sq ft
MTOW	10 500 kg/23 149 lb
Maximum speed	250 km/h /155 mph
Cruising speed	190 km/h /118 mph
Range	1200–1300 km/746–808 miles
Service ceiling	6300 m/20 669 ft
Crew	3
Passengers	15–17
Engines	3
Maiden flight	7 March 1932

Thanks to its low-maintenance design, the Ju-52 won a reputation for punctuality and reliability. It achieved great popularity and before long was in use all over the world.

Starting in 1929, Wulf-Diether Graf zu Castell-Rüdenhausen built up an extensive network of routes for Luft Hansa subsidiary Eurasia in China. It was not all easy going. After days of continuous rain, it was not unusual for the makeshift airstrips to become boggy. This picture shows him trying to pull an 8-ton Ju-52 out of the mire with the help of a team of ten water buffaloes.

To the astonishment of industry observers, United Airlines purchased 20 Caravelles in France.

CARAVELLE VI

Length	32 m/105 ft
Wingspan	34.4 m/112 ft 7 in
Wing area	146.7 sq m/1579 sq ft
MTOW	50 000 kg/110 231 lb
Maximum speed	825 km/h /513 mph
Cruising speed	785 km/h /488 mph
Range	2650 km/1647 miles
Service ceiling	11 000 m/36 086 ft
Crew	5–6
Passengers	64–99
Engines	2
Maiden flight	1955

Sud Aviation of France was an early precursor of EADS (European Aeronautic Defence and Space Company). In 1951, it began work on the development of an aircraft designed to meet a specification issued by the French civil aviation authority for a plane capable of carrying a load of 6–7 tonnes at a speed of 700 km/h /435 mph over a distance of 2,000 km/1,250 miles, thereby competing with the de Havilland Comet. Initially, the aircraft was to be powered by three rear-mounted French engines, but in the end the designers opted for the British Rolls-Royce Avon turbojet, two of which would deliver the same performance.

Instead of mounting these two engines under the wings, the rear-mounted design was retained, producing an aerodynamically 'clean' wing, unencumbered by engine pods. The first production models could accommodate between 60 and 90 passengers, while later variants could carry up to 139 people.

The Caravelle was a great success. In addition to French airlines Air France and Air Inter, which purchased a total of 92 between them, many other European and African airlines also operated the French-built aircraft. Even United Airlines of the United States ordered 20. A total of 283 aircraft were produced between 1953 and 1973.

One of the seven Caravelles belonging to Middle East Airlines. On 17 April 1964 this aircraft crashed into the sea during its approach to Dharan, Saudi Arabia. The cause was never identified.

The Lockheed Constellation, Super Constellation and Star Liner brought the turboprop era to a close. Thereafter, long-distance air travel would be dominated by the Boeing 707 and the DC-8.

LOCKHEED SUPER CONSTELLATION L-1049G

Length	35.42 m/116 ft 2 in	Range	8700 km/5406 miles
Wingspan	38.47 m/126 ft 2 in	Service	
Wing area	153.7 sq m/1654 sq ft	ceiling	7050 m/23130 ft
MTOW	62370 kg/137502 lb	Crew	5
Maximum		Passengers	62–109
speed	610 km/h /379 mph	Engines	4
Cruising		Maiden	
speed	570 km/h /354 mph	flight	13 October 1950

Lockheed L-1049G Super Constellation

In 1939, Trans World Airlines and Pan Am contracted Lockheed to produce a 40-seat long-distance aircraft driven by four piston engines. The resulting plane flew for the first time on 9 January 1943. However, during the war the military had first refusal of all aircraft produced. After the war, KLM, Air France, Air India and South African Airways joined Pan Am and TWA in purchasing the aircraft. Taking into account all its variants, a total of 856 Constellations were built.

In response to rapidly growing seat requirements during the post-war period, Lockheed extended the fuselage by 5.6 m/18 ft 4 in and upgraded the engines.

With close seating, this allowed the plane to carry up to 99 passengers. At 6,500 km/4,040 miles, however, the range was too small for non-stop transatlantic flights and so the operating airlines scheduled stopovers at Gander in Newfoundland or Shannon in Ireland.

It was not unusual for one of the four finely tuned engines to fail, so the 'Super Connie' came to be known as the 'world's finest trimotor'. Nevertheless, the plane was highly popular. TWA had 48 in its fleet, Eastern 46 and KLM 35. Air France, Qantas, Lufthansa, VARIG and all other airlines offering long-distance services also wanted to acquire it.

Altogether, 259 Super Connies left the factory. There are still a number around today, and aircraft enthusiasts seem to have developed an almost obsessive attachment to them.

The L-1049G was succeeded by the Lockheed Star Liner L-1649. However, only 44 of these were built – because the world was already gearing up for the jet age.

American airline ATA used the TriStar to carry sea cruise passengers to their embarkation point, as seen here in Ushuaia, Argentina.

LOCKHEED L-1011 TRISTAR

	L-1011-1	L-1011-200	L-1011-500
Length	54.2 m/177 ft 10 in	54.2 m/177 ft 10 in	50 m/164 ft
Wingspan	47.3 m/155 ft 2 in	47.3 m/155 ft 2 in	50.1 m/164 ft 4 in
Wing area	321.1 sq m/3456 sq ft	321.1 sq m/3456 sq ft	329 sq m/3541 sq ft
MTOW	195 000 kg/429 901 lb	209 000 kg/460 766 lb	225 000 kg/496 040 lb
Maximum speed	999 km/h /621 mph	999 km/h /621 mph	999 km/h /621 mph
Cruising speed	950 km/h /590 mph	950 km/h /590 mph	950 km/h /590 mph
Range	7419 km/4610 miles	7419 km/4610 miles	10 200 km/6338 miles
Service ceiling	10 670 m/35 007 ft	10 970 m/35 991 ft	12 496 m/40 997 ft
Crew	3	3	3
Passengers	253 (3-class)	263	234 (3-class)
Engines	3	3	3
Maiden flight	16 November 1970	12 August 1976	1 October 1978

LOCKHEED L-1011 TRISTAR

In 1966, American Airlines issued a specification for a short-to-medium-range aircraft for 350-plus passengers. Lockheed saw this as a gap in the market. Lockheed and Douglas submitted similar designs with three engines. As with the Boeing 727, Lockheed integrated the third engine into the tail. This soon proved to be a disadvantage, however, because in buying the aircraft the customers had already committed themselves to a manufacturer, in this case Rolls-Royce, and, as fate would have it, Rolls-Royce later experienced difficulties delivering the engine, delaying the entire project.

American Airlines therefore opted for the DC-10. Eastern Airlines and Trans World Airlines, on the other hand, each ordered around 50 Lockheed TriStars and Delta Air Lines ordered over 70. In the end, the L-1011 was launched almost simultaneously with the DC-10. However, only 250 TriStars were produced, and as the RB.211 engine gradually aged and became less economical, so the TriStar aged too. The DC-10, on the other hand, enjoyed considerable popularity, at least at the beginning, and later formed the basis for the MD-11.

THE BOEING STORY

In 1915 William E. Boeing learnt to fly and built his first aeroplane in a boathouse. He hired an experienced pilot for the test flight, but the pilot was late. Being impatient, William Boeing climbed into the cockpit himself and the pilot arrived at the boathouse, out of breath, just in time to see Boeing accelerating to the end of the lake and taking off for a 400 m/1,300-ft flight. With considerable foresight, Boeing paid for the construction of a wind tunnel at the University of Washington in Seattle so that the aviation faculty could train future engineers. In 1917, the young company had 28 employees – from pilots to welders. When America entered World War I, Boeing sold the US Navy 50 seaplanes. After the war, however, the market was saturated with aircraft and the company had to make furniture for a while just to stay in business. Eventually it managed to obtain a number of orders for mail planes and not long afterwards won a large order from United Airlines for 60 new Boeing 247s. It took a while for

Boeing's first home was an old boatyard. The 'Red Barn' is now a museum.

William Boeing to realize that this order actually benefited his competitors, since the contract gave United Airlines the monopoly on this model for two years, stipulating that it could not be supplied to other airlines until after the end of that period. Other airlines were therefore forced to look for alternatives from other manufacturers.

Boeing had just brought the 307 Statoliner into production when the country turned its attention to military aircraft: fighters, transport planes, and light and heavy bombers. Warplanes became the priority at both Boeing and Douglas. Naturally, aircraft design and construction benefited from the development effort, technical advances, competition and material constraints of building aircraft that were larger, faster, safer, capable of flying greater distances and required less maintenance.

After 1945, when people picked up their peace-time lives again, the industry began to build increasingly large and luxurious aircraft. Boeing scored a worldwide hit with the 707, selling 723 of the civil variant. In the 1970s, Boeing opened the door to a brave new world of aviation with the launch of the 747,

BOEING

	247D	307	314	377
Length	16.3 m/53 ft 6 in	22.6 m/74 ft 2 in	32.31 m/106 ft	33.63 m/110 ft 4 in
Wingspan	22.66 m/74 ft 4 in	32.6 m/106 ft 11 in	46.33 m/152 ft	43.05 m/141 ft 3 in
Wing area	77.6 sq m/	138 sq m/	266.34 sq m/	164.34 sq m/
	835 sq ft	1485 sq ft	2867 sq ft	1769 sq ft
MTOW	5950 kg/13 117 lb	19 050 kg/41 998 lb	37 422 kg/82 501 lb	66 000 kg/145 505 lb
Maximum speed	324 km/h /201 mph	396 km/h /246 mph	320 km/h /199 mph	695 km/h /432 mph
Cruising speed	304 km/h /189 mph	350 km/h /217 mph	296 km/h /184 mph	603 km/h /375 mph
Range	c. 1200 km/	3846 km/	5600 km/	8500 km/
	c. 746 miles	2390 miles	3480 miles	5282 miles
Service ceiling	3000 m/9843 ft	7985 m/26 197 ft	4085 m/13 402 ft	9800 m/32 152 ft
Crew/Passengers	3/10	5/33	3/74	4/55–100
Engines	2	4	4	4
Maiden flight	8 February 1933	31 December 1938	1938	8 July 1947

the largest and proudest airliner of all time.

In 1996, during a period of major consolidation in the American aviation industry, Boeing acquired McDonnell Douglas, thereby becoming the world's leading aviation and aerospace group. This is surely something that the citizens of Hohenlimburg, in Germany's Sauerland region, could never have imagined when Wilhelm Böing set out for the United States in 1868. Böing worked his way up and eventually made a fortune in timber and iron ore. When he died, he left his wife and three sons 1.5 million dollars. What his son William made of his inheritance is clear for all to see.

BOEING 247D
This was the first modern all-metal aircraft with retractable undercarriage, variable-pitch propellers, de-icing system and autopilot. It could fly from Los Angeles to New York in 20 hours with seven stopovers. Of the 75 which were built, 60 were operated by Boeing Air Transport, ten by United Airlines and five by Luft Hansa in Germany and China.

BOEING 307 STRATOLINER
This was Boeing's first passenger aircraft capable of flying at higher altitudes. Owing to its wide fuselage, Howard Hughes purchased one and fitted it out as a 'flying penthouse' with living room, bedroom, two bathrooms, kitchen and a bar. Only ten were ever built.

BOEING 314
Pan Am requested a four-engined flying boat from Boeing. The aircraft was nicknamed the 'Clipper', alluding to the great sailing ships of yore, and Boeing retained the name throughout the 314's entire existence. The flying boat could accommodate 74 passengers or 40 sleeping berths. It also offered spacious dressing rooms, a dining room that could be transformed into a lounge, and a wedding suite. Its catering was provided by chefs from the best hotels. In total 12 314s were built.

BOEING 377 STRATOCRUISER
Boeing's first passenger aircraft after World War II, the 377 possessed all the advanced technical features of the B-29 bomber, but was luxuriously fitted out and once again offered spacious dressing rooms. A spiral staircase led down to a 'cellar bar', and stewardesses prepared fresh meals for the passengers. Naturally, there was also an overnight version with 40 berths. In total 56 Stratocruisers were built.

BOEING 707

Sabena flew a total of 30 707s. Almost all belonged to the 320 series, with 141 seats (or 219 in the charter version). This aircraft could fly non-stop from Europe to destinations on the west coast of the United States or in Africa.

When Boeing was looking for a prototype for a new refuelling tanker after World War II, it settled on the 367-80 model, also known as the 'Dash 80', whose flying characteristics and range were suitable for a civil variant. In order to accommodate six seats in a row, the fuselage was widened by 10 cm/4 inches. Boeing offered to build customized versions for the different airlines: for example, a long-range version for Qantas and a high-altitude version for Braniff's South American routes.

This approach paid off and Boeing's first jet was a worldwide success, becoming the aircraft of choice for 600 different operators from Aer Lingus to Zambia Airways. TWA and Pan Am each had 130 of the aircraft in their fleets.

The 707 is remarkable for its longevity. Half a century after its introduction, it is still in use despite the fact that it is now anything but economical and can barely meet the current aircraft noise regulations of most European airports (sometimes having to pay high landing fee supplements). John Travolta is also the proud owner of a 707 (a 707-138B built in 1964).

A short-range variant (designated the 720) was also built. A total of 154 720s and 856 707s left the Boeing factory.

BOEING 707-320 (B)/(C)

Length	46.61 m/152 ft 11 in
Wingspan	43.4 m/142 ft 5 in
Wing area	273.7 sq m/2946 sq ft
MTOW	141700 kg/312395 lb
Maximum speed	950 km/h /590 mph
Cruising speed	885 km/h /550 mph
Range	8700 km/5406 miles
Service ceiling	12800 m/41995 ft
Crew	3–4
Passengers	219
Engines	4
Maiden flight	11 January 1959

*The Boeing 727 was Pan American Airlines'
workhorse. It was used both for shorthaul
flights and on transcontinental routes
of up to 5,000 km/3,100 miles.*

BOEING 727-200

Length	46.69 m/153 ft 2 in
Wingspan	32.92 m/108 ft
Wing area	157.93 sq m/1700 sq ft
MTOW	95 030 kg/209 505 lb
Maximum speed	980 km/h /609 mph
Cruising speed	965 km/h /600 mph
Range	4020 km/2498 miles
Service ceiling	12 192 m/40 000 ft
Crew	2
Passengers	145
Engines	3
Maiden flight	17 May 1964

Like the French Caravelle, Boeing experimented with a design for an airliner with rear-mounted engines. This reduced noise for the passengers; the uncluttered wings also promised lower aerodynamic drag, lower fuel consumption and higher speeds.

Other unusual features included the additional passenger door at the rear of the plane, and a built-in APU (auxiliary power unit) meant that the plane did not have to rely on a ground-based power supply and could start its own engines.

Initially sales were sluggish, so Boeing sent the 727 on a 120,000-km/75,000-mile world tour stopping in 26 different countries. In the end, the airlines were won over – not least by the plane's short take-off capability, 131-passenger capacity and APU.

The 727 was bought by 666 airlines (United Airlines alone operated 236 727s) and a total of 1,832 were produced. Over 400 are still in service and are particularly popular with freight airlines such as FedEx. Due to their power, they are also widely used in countries with short runways in Africa, South America and Asia. The plane can also be fitted with winglets in order to save fuel.

For many years more 727s were made than any other jet airliner.

BOEING 737

In the year 2000, the Boeing 737 became the first aircraft in the world to achieve an aggregate flying time of 100 million hours. This is the equivalent of one aeroplane circling the earth for 11,415 years.

BOEING 737

	737-100	737-900
Length	28.65 m/94 ft	42.11 m/138 ft 2 in
Wingspan	28.35 m/93 ft	34.3 m/112 ft 6 in
Wing area	91.1 sq m/980 sq ft	124.6 sq m/1341 sq
MTOW	49 940 kg/110 099 lb	79 016 kg/174 200 lb
Maximum speed	990 km/h /615 mph	990 km/h /615 mph
Cruising speed	917 km/h /570 mph	852 km/h /529 mph
Range	3440 km/2137 miles	3630–6660 km/
		2256–4138 miles
Service ceiling	11 000 m/36 089 ft	12 500 m/41 010 ft
Crew	3	2
Passengers	85–99	175–189
Engines	2	2
Maiden flight	9 April 1967	3 August 2000

By the early 1960s, Lufthansa was already an established Boeing customer. The German airline lacked a mid-range aircraft of the BAC 1-11 or DC-9 type and therefore asked Boeing to develop a small jet to its specifications. Delivery to Lufthansa of the first 30 737-100s commenced in 1965. In Germany the aircraft was known as the 'Bobby Boeing' whereas in the United States 'Baby Boeing' became the preferred nickname. The 737 went on to achieve unprecedented success throughout the world: by the end of 2009, over 6,000 aircraft had been produced in all the different variants. Southwest Airlines alone has 557 737s in its fleet with another 91 currently on order. Along with the Airbus A320, the Boeing 737 has been a hit with full-service providers and budget carriers alike. Thanks to the systematic development of its wings and materials, the aircraft is economical and boasts longer maintenance intervals than all of its predecessors. The 800 and 900 versions in particular stand out for their short turnaround times (the length of time between landing and take-off). This is due, among other things, to improved braking characteristics, a low undercarriage and simplified maintenance procedures. Furthermore, the capacity of the aircraft has also been continually improved.

The development of the 737 reached the end of its journey with the 900ER version. Under the designation 737RS ('Replacement Study'), Boeing is currently working on a derivative based on the 787. Although there are still 1,500 orders pending for the new generation 737, the 100–189-seat market segment is too important to allow the competition to gain the upper hand.

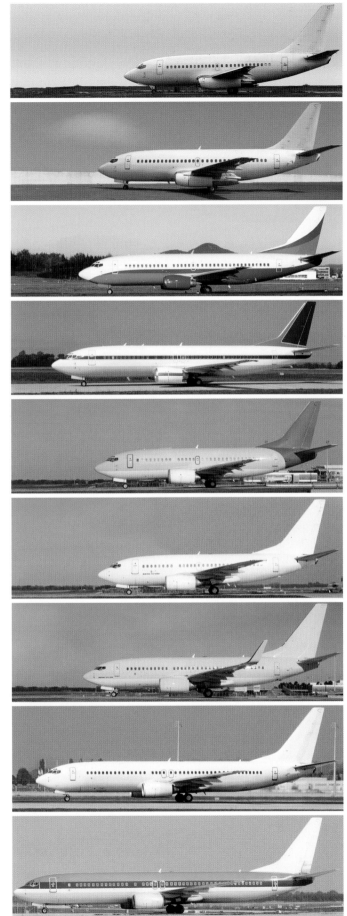

737-100 This model was the basis for one of the world's most successful aircraft. Lufthansa owned 22 of them, more than any other airline.

737-200 Over 1,100 of this version were produced. The 737-200 accommodates between 96 and 133 passengers and has a range of 4,200 km/2,610 miles.

737-300 More passengers, more economical, better performance. This model has between 123 and 149 seats and a range of 4,400 km/2,734 miles. Over 1,000 were built.

737-400 Quieter and with a longer range, the 737-400 can carry between 146 and 162 passengers over distances of more than 5,000 km/3,100 miles. Almost all of the 500 that were built are still in service.

737-500 This version departs from the trend for ever-increasing capacity, accommodating just 103–122 passengers. Its range, however, was increased to 5,200 km/3,231 miles. Just 289 were built.

737-600 In the 1990s, a series of 'Next-Generation' 737s were developed. Just 31 m/102 ft long, the 737-600 holds 110–122 passengers and has a range of 4,000–7,200 km/2,485–4,474 miles. Only 69 were built.

737-700 Over 1,000 of this version have been sold to date with another 476 in the pipeline. The 737-700 has 128-49 seats and is economical over distances of between 3,600 and 6,600 km/2,240–1,100 miles.

737-800 Production of the 737-800 has surpassed that of any other model. While 1,800 have left the factory, orders for a further 1,300 are pending. This version has the same range as the 737-700 but its stretched fuselage of 39 m/128 ft can hold 162–89 passengers.

737-900 This model is set to be the culmination of the 737 family. Its fuselage has been extended again and is 3 m/10 ft longer than the 737-800. It has a maximum capacity of between 175 and 189 passengers, while the ER version can hold up to 215.

BOEING 747

During the 1970s the Boeing 747 was so popular that none of the world's largest airlines could afford to be without it. The 747-400 is one of the most elegant aircraft ever built.

When the Boeing 747 was first unveiled, people rubbed their eyes in astonishment, barely able to believe that such a monster would be capable of flying. There was much amazed talk of four million individual parts, a landing gear comprising 18 wheels, a capacity of 366 passengers and a range of around 10,000 km/6,200 miles.

In 2009, the Boeing 747 – which is now bigger than ever – celebrated its fortieth birthday. A total of 1,419 jumbos have been produced and 3.5 billion people have flown in one. There are 820 currently in service while 182 have been mothballed awaiting the end of the aviation crisis. Some 126 are in breakers' yards, 230 have

already been scrapped and 12 are in museums. Another 49 have been destroyed in accidents, shot down or blown up by terrorists. Given the aggregate of 90 million flying hours and some 80 billion km/50 billion miles flown by 747s, these disasters represent a minute proportion of the total, although they are no less tragic for those affected.

Private individuals, freight carriers and air forces have also, for a wide variety of reasons, ordered jumbos. The Iranian air force owns 28 Boeing 747s and the USAF 29, one of which is still flying as Air Force One after 22 years of service. United Parcel Service has put 30 through its books over the years.

The largest single operator of jumbo jets, however, is Cathay Pacific Airways, which has acquired a total of 119, of which 74 are still active. Close on its heels are Japan Airlines with 118 aircraft and Saudi Arabian Airlines with 115.

Meanwhile, Boeing has already secured 681 orders for the 747's successor, the 787-8.

For many years the Boeing 747 formed the backbone of Lufthansa's long-haul fleet. Lufthansa has purchased 66 jumbos over the years, 30 of which are still in service. It was the first airline to order the 747-8.

Some 167 Boeing 747-100s were produced. The upper deck had just three round portholes on either side, as this area was designed to serve as a lounge.

The Boeing 747-200 offered an improved range. The row of windows on the upper deck was not extended until its first maintenance C-check.

The truncated version of the jumbo, the compact 747SP, had an exceptionally long range.

The Boeing 747-300 is similar to the 747-200 but with improved engines that consume 25 per cent less fuel. Its extended upper deck provides accommodation for 86 passengers.

BOEING 747

	747-100	747-200B	747-SP	747-300	747-400(ER)	747-8
Length	70.6 m /231 ft 8 in	70.6 m /231 ft 8 in	56.31 m /184 ft 9 in	70.6 m /231 ft 8 in	70.6 m /231 ft 8 in	76.4 m /250 ft 8 in
Wingspan	59.6 m /195 ft 6 in	59.6 m /195 ft 6 in	59.6 m /195 ft 6 in	59.6 m /195 ft 6 in	64.4 m /211 ft 3 in	68.5 m /224 ft 9 in
Wing area	511 sq m /5 500 sq ft	511 sq m /5500 sq ft	511 sq m /5500 sq ft	511 sq m /5500 sq ft	541.2 sq m /5825 sq ft	524.9 sq m /5650 sq ft
MTOW	333 400 kg/ 735 021 lb	374 850 kg/ 826 402 lb	317 515 kg/ 700 000 lb	374 850 kg/ 826 403 lb	368 000 kg/ 811 301 lb	439 985 kg/ 970 001 lb
Maximum speed	945 km/h /587 mph	945 km/h /587 mph	1044 km/h /649 mph	910 km/h /565 mph	988 km/h /614 mph	n/a
Cruising speed	895 km/h /556 mph	895 km/h /556 mph	999 km/h /621 mph	894 km/h /555 mph	913 km/h /567 mph	920 km/h /572 mph
Range	9800 km/ 6089 miles	12 700 km/ 7891 miles	15 400 km/ 9569 miles	12 400 km/ 7705 miles	14 205 km/ 8826 miles	14 815 km/ 9205 miles
Service ceiling	13 100 m /42 979 ft	13 100 m /42 979 ft	16 500 m /54 134 ft	13 100 m /42 979 ft	13 100 m /42 979 ft	13 100 m /42 979 ft
Crew/Passengers	3/366	3/366	3/316	3/412	2/416	2/467
Engines	4	4	4	4	4	4
Maiden flight	9 December 1969	11 October 1970	4 July 1975	5 October 1982	29 April 1988	8 February 2010

The upper-deck lounge of early 747s was a major draw. For many passengers it was what motivated them to pay the hefty surcharge for a premium ticket.

747 FACTS

- A 747-400 comprises six million individual parts, including three million rivets.
- A single aircraft contains 274 km/170 miles of cabling and 8 km/5 miles of hoses.
- The aluminium used in a single aircraft weighs 66 tonnes.
- The main landing gear has 16 wheels and the front landing gear just two.

- A single wing is 30 times as heavy as the first aeroplane built by Boeing.
- The engines measure 2.6 m/8 ft 6 inches in diameter.
- The cockpit of the first 747 contained 971 lights, switches and dials. Now the number is just 365.
- The typical take-off speed of a 747-400 is 290 km/h /180 mph and its typical landing speed is 260 km/h /162 mph.

- The Wright brothers' first flight could have taken off and landed within the fuselage of a 747.
- In total, the world's 747s have carried 3.5 billion passengers (equivalent to half the world's population) a total of 80 billion km/50 billion miles, roughly the same as 75,000 trips to the moon and back.
- Half the world's goods are carried by 747 freighters.

THE JOE SUTTER STORY

Joe Sutter was born in 1921. During World War II he served in the US Navy on a destroyer escort, and afterwards joined Boeing as an aircraft designer. Sutter hardly ever took a day off, but it was while spending a peaceful weekend in the mountains with his wife that he received the news: 'Joe, you're getting the 747.' This was shortly after Boeing lost out to Lockheed in the competition for the C-5 Galaxy transport plane, and Boeing was therefore extremely keen to take up a challenge laid down by Pan Am to build a large passenger aircraft. Designers of military aircraft have to follow a specifications catalogue that is over 1,000 pages long. The requirements for a passenger aircraft, on the other hand, run to something like 50 pages, and Sutter therefore had a relatively free hand. He was also assisted by a staff of 4,500 technicians and engineers.

Sutter was given just four years to develop, build and test the plane, despite the fact that there was not yet any factory big enough to build it in. In parallel to the development of the aircraft, therefore, work proceeded on the construction of the world's largest assembly plant.

Joe Sutter

In the early days, the airlines had major reservations about the plane, questioning whether it would actually fly, whether airports were big enough and whether their terminals could handle so many passengers at once. But there was no going back. Boeing had bet its very survival on the construction of the 747 and its assembly plant.

Joe Sutter wanted to give the world an aircraft that could be easily and safely flown in difficult situations as well as in perfect conditions. For this reason he equipped the plane with four hydraulic systems, four flight control systems, four engines and four sets of landing gears. His aim was to build a good, safe passenger aircraft that could also be sold as a large-capacity freighter.

Like many inventors, Joe Sutter was far ahead of his time.

An impressive example of the jumbo's carrying capability, with an interesting payload. NASA converted two Boeing 747-100s in order to transport the Space Shuttle from Edwards Air Force Base in California to Cape Canaveral in Florida.

BOEING 757

The Boeing 757 first flew in 1982. It was designed as a longer and more slender replacement for the three-engined 727, but shared its predecessor's short take-off characteristics. Its computerized cockpit is very similar to that of the Boeing 767, which was developed in parallel. This means that pilots can be easily switched between both aircraft.

The 757's performance was put to the test in 1991 under controlled conditions when it took off with only one engine at an altitude of 4,000 m/13,123 ft from Lhasa airport in Tibet, circled and landed again at the same airport.

The last aircraft in the series, number 1050, was delivered to Shanghai Airlines at the end of 2005. The 757 is one of just seven airliners in the history of civil aviation of which more than 1,000 have been produced.

The first Boeing 767 left the factory in 1981. Unlike the 757, the 767 is a widebody aircraft with two aisles. It was designed to fill the gap between the 727, 737 and 757 models on the one hand, and the 747 on the other. With a range of 12,000 km/7,500 miles, it was designed to be able to cross the North Atlantic comfortably.

The 767 can accommodate up to 375 passengers in a single-class configuration. The biggest operator of the 767 is Delta Air Lines, with over 100 aircraft. American Airlines and ANA of Japan also have large fleets of 767s. As of February 2010, 984 aircraft had been built.

The development of the Boeing 777 took just five years from initial design to maiden flight. This was the first aircraft to be designed exclusively on computer. As part of this process, Boeing invited representatives of eight airlines to Seattle and asked each one to complete a 23-page questionnaire concerning their expectations. The results were immediately integrated by means of CAD (computer-aided design).

This widebody aircraft with the largest engines in the world has become the backbone of numerous mega-carriers. For example, Singapore Airlines operates 75 of them, although the Boeing 777, capable of carrying 365 passengers, is still the smallest aircraft in its fleet. It was chosen for its excellent long-range capability.

There are currently over 700 of the type in circulation, with another 330 on order. It looks, therefore, as if this successful model is also set to break through the 1,000 barrier.

BOEING 767

BOEING 777

The 200LR version of the Boeing 777 can technically fly non-stop between any pair of cities in the world – 'technically' because no one has yet used the aircraft to fly passengers between London and Sydney.

BOEING

	757-200	757-300	767-200D	767-400ER	777-200	777-300ER
Length	47.32 m/155 ft 3 in	54.47 m/178 ft 8 in	48.5 m/159 ft 1 in	61.4 m/201 ft 5 in	63.7 m/209 ft	73.9 m/242 ft 5 in
Wingspan	38.05 m/124 ft 10 in	38.05 m/124 ft 10 in	47.6 m/156 ft 2 in	51.9 m/170 ft 3 in	60.9 m/199 ft 10 in	64.8 m/212 ft 7 in
Wing area	181.2 sq m/ 1950 sq ft	181.2 sq m/ 1950 sq ft	283.35 sq m/ 3050 sq ft	283.35 sq m/ 3050 sq ft	430 sq m/ 4628 sq ft	427.8 sq m/ 4605 sq ft
MTOW	115 665 kg/ 254 998 lb	122 470 kg/ 270 000lb	179 170 kg/ 395 002 lb	204 120 kg/ 450 007 lb	247 210 kg/ 545 005 lb	351 534 kg/ 775 000lb
Maximum speed	990 km/h /615 mph	990 km/h /615 mph	950 km/h /590 mph	950 km/h /590 mph	950 km/h /590 mph	950 km/h /590 mph
Cruising speed	950 km/h /590 mph	950 km/h /590 mph	851 km/h /529 mph	851 km/h /529 mph	890 km/h /553 mph	890 km/h /553 mph
Range	6276 km/ 3900 miles	6455 km/ 4011 miles	12 223 km/ 7595 miles	10 454 km/ 6496 miles	9649 km/ 5995 miles	14 594 km/ 9068 miles
Service ceiling	11 675 m/38 304 ft	11 005 m/36 106 ft	10 670 m/35 007 ft	13 137 m/43 100 ft	11 980 m/39 304 ft	10 270 m/33 694 ft
Crew/Passengers	2/200–231	2/243–280	2/255	2/375	2/305	2/365
Engines	2	2	2	2	2	2
Maiden flight	19 February 1982	10 March 1999	26 September 1981	26 September 1981	12 June 1994	24 February 2003

BOEING 787

Computer drawing of an Ethiopian Airways Boeing 787.

Even before its roll-out, the Boeing 787 had become the fastest-selling aircraft in history, with 857 orders secured. The plane was christened the 'Dreamliner', but it soon became a nightmare for the manufacturer, as supply difficulties and the non-availability of special rivets delayed completion.

The celebrated roll-out of the first prototype proved to be a little premature because the individual parts were joined together with construction rivets that subsequently had to be removed and replaced with aerospace fasteners. The first customer, ANA, was due to receive its first delivery in May 2008 but it turned out that the central wing box needed to be strengthened. More work was also needed on the software and improvements had to be made to the supply chain.

A significant amount of carbon fibre is used in the construction of the 787. This is designed to make the aircraft lighter and decrease its fuel consumption. With so many technical innovations, it is hardly surprising that delays have occurred. Had the competition with Airbus not become so overheated and emotionally charged, no one would have been particularly bothered by the hold-ups.

Given the way things are, however, the full order book for the new aircraft is proving problematic. Customers are expecting a 30-month delay and are demanding price discounts from Boeing, as well as aircraft to tide them over while they are waiting. And these aircraft could just as easily be supplied by another manufacturer...

BOEING 787

	787-3	787-9
Length	55.5 m/182 ft 1 in	63 m/206 ft 8 in
Wingspan	52 m/170 ft 7 in	60 m/196 ft 10 in
Wing area	n/a	n/a
MTOW	165 100 kg/363 983 lb	244 940 kg/540 000 lb
Maximum speed	c. 915 km/h /c. 569 mph	n/a
Cruising speed	n/a	n/a
Range	4650 km/2889 miles	15 750 km/9787 miles
Service ceiling	n/a	n/a
Crew	2	2
Passengers	210–330	250–290
Engines	2	2
Maiden flight (planned)	2010	2010

BOEING 787 ASSEMBLY

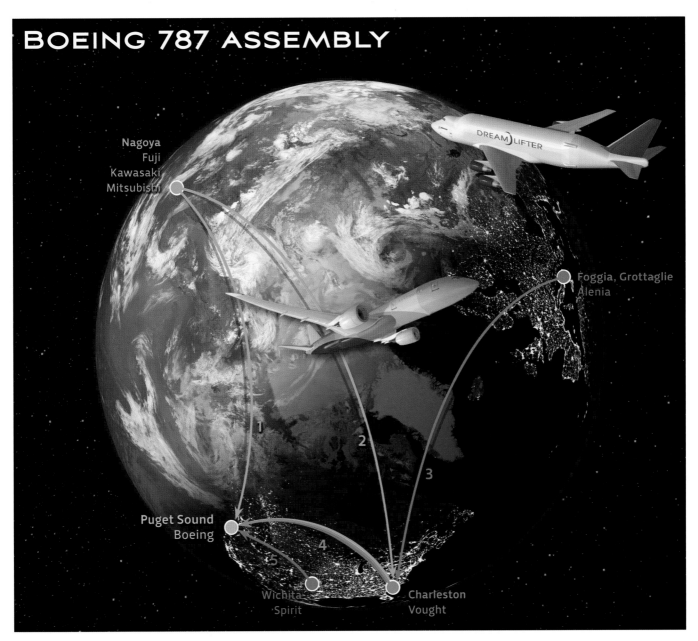

Nagoya
Fuji
Kawasaki
Mitsubishi

DREAM)LIFTER

Foggia, Grottaglie
Alenia

1

2

3

Puget Sound
Boeing

4

5

Wichita
Spirit

Charleston
Vought

It seems that Boeing has been unlucky in its outsourcing of component manufacture for the Dreamliner. It has therefore decided to fork out 580 million dollars for Vought Aircraft Industries' facility in South Carolina which makes the fuselage sections. Instead of assembling all the individual components in Boeing's own works, the assembly of large subsections has also been outsourced to external suppliers. These suppliers, however, are unable to cope because of difficulties getting hold of the individual parts. For a variety of reasons, changing the processes involved is no easy matter.

Weight is everything
If it turns out during the manufacturing process that rivets have to be brought in from a different supplier and each one weighs, for the sake of argument, 10 g/ ⅓ oz more than planned (roughly the weight of two sheets of paper), the

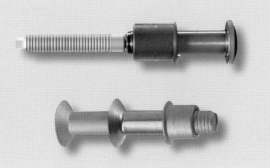

use of a million rivets will add up to excess weight of 10 tonnes! In an industry in which airlines remove from an aircraft anything that's not absolutely necessary, and even refrain from taking biscuits on board in order to save weight, this is a disaster.

THE MCDONNELL DOUGLAS STORY

Donald Wills Douglas founded the Davis-Douglas Company with a wealthy friend in a back room in 1920. The following year, Douglas circumnavigated the globe in three of his first planes in a journey that took five and a half months. This feat provided him with valuable experience that played an important part in the design of later aircraft. Initially, Douglas specialized in the manufacture of military planes, only later designing the DC-1 in response to TWA's request for a new airliner. This new aircraft seemed just as good as the Boeing 247 and TWA immediately placed an order for 20 of them. Although only 200 were produced (as with the DC-2), the aircraft was popular throughout the world and beat the Boeing

by two hours in the 1934 MacRobertson Air Race from England to Australia.

The DC-3 was developed out of the DC-2 in order to provide passengers with sleeping berths on longer flights. It went into production in 1939 and 15,592 (including 4,937 manufactured under licence) were eventually built. The DC-3 was followed by the DC-4, the DC-5, the DC-6 and the DC-7. Each new model was successful, but it was Boeing rather than the Davis-Douglas Company that wrote aviation history in 1954 with its 367-80, which was subsequently developed into the 707.

It was three years before Douglas unveiled the DC-8 and managed to make up some lost ground. Although 556 aircraft were ordered,

the DC-8 still lagged some way behind the Boeing 707 in terms of sales. The DC-9, on the other hand, was a highly successful medium-range jet and total production (including all of its later models) was 2,299. Despite this success, the company was by this time beset by financial difficulties.

James Smith McDonnell had founded the McDonnell Aircraft Corporation, a manufacturer of military planes only, in 1938. In 1967, McDonnell merged with Douglas to form the McDonnell Douglas Aircraft Corporation, which went on to produce some of the world's best passenger planes. The company launched the DC-10 (later renamed MD-10) as its

answer to the Boeing 747. A total of 446 were sold. The MD-10 was in turn developed into the MD-11, of which over 200 were produced.

In 1996, Boeing and McDonnell Douglas (MDD) surprised the industry by announcing a merger. Boeing effectively took over the ultimately loss-making aerospace group, allowing resources to be bundled and costs to be reduced. At that time, Boeing had a 60 per cent share of the airliner market, while Airbus had 35 per cent and MDD 5 per cent. However, McDonnell Douglas also had a successful military division, and at a single stroke, Boeing was able to take over all its engineers, aircraft designers, skilled workers and production centres.

DC-3, DC-4, DC-5, DC-7, DC-8, DC-10: United Airlines operated large fleets of all Douglas and McDonnell Douglas aircraft.

DOUGLAS DC-7

DOUGLAS DC-2

DOUGLAS

	DC-2	DC-3
Length	18.89 m/62 ft	19.66 m/64 ft 6 in
Wingspan	25.91 m/85 ft	29.98 m/98 ft 4 in
Wing area	87.23 sq m/939 sq ft	91.7 sq m/987 sq ft
MTOW	8419 kg/18 561 lb	13 190 kg/29 079 lb
Maximum speed	338 km/h /210 mph	368 km/h /229 mph
Cruising speed	306 km/h /190 mph	290 km/h /180 mph
Range	1750 km/1087 miles	2160 km /1342 miles
Service ceiling	6980 m/22 900 ft	7350 m/24 114 ft
Crew	2–3	4
Passengers	14	32
Engines	2	2
Maiden flighT	11 May 1934	17 December 1935

The DC-2 entered service in 1934 as an answer to the Boeing 247 and soon won a place in aviation history. In retrospect, it is significant above all as a precursor to the successful DC-3. In total 156 DC-2s were built.

The DC-3 was a logical development of the popular and highly promising DC-2. It was designed to have a longer range with sleeping berths and a galley. Nevertheless, three refuelling stops were necessary during a flight from the east to the west coast of the United States, which is why the journey still took 15 hours.

The sleeping berths took up a lot of space, so they were soon replaced by seats.

During World War II, the airlines had to surrender their DC-3s to the military. The Douglas Aircraft Company also worked flat out to produce a number of military variants. All in all, Douglas built a total of 10,655 DC-3s. Another 485 were produced under licence in Japan and a further 2,000 as the Lisunov Li-2 in Russia.

The DC-3 is still in service in the new millennium, not least in the Amazonian rainforest and extreme north of Canada, and seems fairly indestructible. It is loud, and rattles and clanks to such an extent that someone once described it as 'a collection of parts flying in loose formation'. Yet it is also reliable, rugged and easy to maintain.

DOUGLAS DC-3

Right: DC-2 (1934)

DC-3 (1935)

Caravelle (1955)

MD-87 (1987)

Boeing 747-400 (1995)

THE COCKPIT THROUGH THE AGES

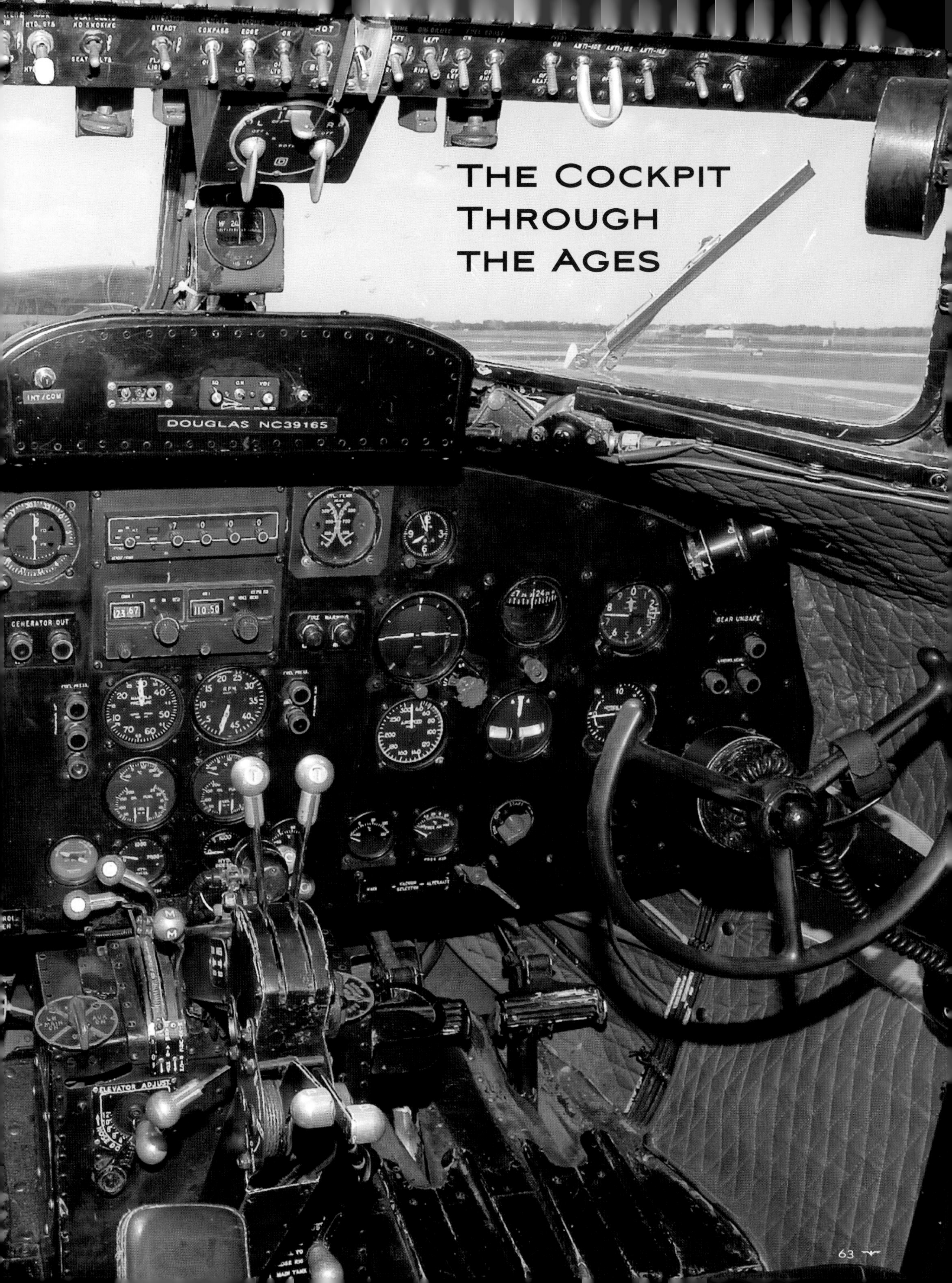
DOUGLAS NC39165
INT/COM
GENERATOR OUT
FIRE WARNING
GEAR UNSAFE
ELEVATOR ADJUST

DOUGLAS DC-4

The Douglas DC-4 Skymaster, whose military version was known as the C-54, was a hit. Total production was 1,241.

The DC-3 was so popular that when asked about a possible replacement, pilots used to say: 'The best replacement for a DC-3 is another DC-3!' Nevertheless, there was a need to carry more passengers over greater distances in a shorter time with fewer refuelling stops.

Douglas therefore developed a successor, the DC-4. The main advance in this model was to swap the tail wheel for a nose wheel. This allowed for a horizontal fuselage that also lent itself to easy stretching in later models. Furthermore, the aircraft had four engines, offering plenty of potential for the future. Some 1,241 DC-4s were built, of which 20 are still in daily use.

The DC-5 was not designed as a replacement for the DC-3 and DC-4; it was supposed to complement them. Demand, supply and product ranges were thrown into confusion by the war, however, with the result that only five of the civil version were built.

DOUGLAS DC-5

The DC-5 was conceived as a short-distance aircraft but failed to sell because of World War II. Despite considerable interest, only a dozen were built.

DOUGLAS DC-6

The DC-6 was designed to compete with the Lockheed Constellation, but it was not quite as successful.

Total production of the DC-7 was 338. American Airlines was the biggest customer with a fleet of 63. SAS also operated 18 of this popular aircraft.

The DC-6 was originally conceived as a military transport plane but its design was revised as the end of the war came into sight. After some initial difficulties with on-board fires and the need for a number of structural changes, the aircraft gradually won the approval of major airlines such as United, American, Pan Am, KLM, Sabena and SAS. In total 700 were produced, some of which are still in use.

The DC-7 was the last piston-engined aircraft built by Douglas. The performance yardstick at this time was New York to London non-stop. When an improved version made it possible to fly in the opposite direction without having to stop at Shannon or Gander, the DC-7C 'Seven Seas' became the queen of propeller airliners. It also opened up fast polar routes from Amsterdam via Anchorage in Alaska to Tokyo, and San Francisco to London. The jet age was dawning, however, and only 338 DC-7s were produced.

DOUGLAS DC-7

DOUGLAS

	DC-4	DC-5	DC-6	DC-7
Length	25.6 m/84 ft	18.96 m/62 ft 2 in	32.18 m/105 ft 7 in	37 m/121 ft 5 in
Wingspan	35.81 m/117 ft 6 in	23.77 m/78 ft	35.81 m/117 ft 6 in	42 m/137 ft 10 in
Wing area	135.63 sq m/1460 sq ft	76.55 sq m/824 sq ft	135.9 sq m/1463 sq ft	152 sq m/1636 sq ft
MTOW	33112 kg/72999 lb	9072 kg/20000 lb	48500 kg/106924 lb	65000 kg/143300 lb
Maximum speed	451 km/h /280 mph	325 km/h /202 mph	526 km/h /327 mph	720 km/h /447 mph
Cruising speed	365 km/h /227 mph	300 km/h /186 mph	507 km/h /315 mph	670 km/h /416 mph
Range	4023 km/ 2500 miles	2575 km/ 1600 miles	7590 km/ 4716 miles	9070 km/ 5636 miles
Service ceiling	6800 m/22310 ft	7225 m/23704 ft	7600 m/24934 ft	7600 m/24934 ft
Crew	5	6	3	4
Passengers	86	22	102	105
Engines	4	2	4	4
Maiden flight	7 June 1938	20 February 1939	15 February 1946	18 May 1953

DOUGLAS DC-8

DOUGLAS DC-8

	DC-8-32	DC-8-63CF
Length	45.87 m/150 ft 6 in	57.1 m/187 ft 4 in
Wingspan	43.41 m/142 ft 5 in	45.24 m/148 ft 5 in
Wing area	257.4 sq m/2771 sq ft	271.9 sq m/2927 sq ft
MTOW	140600 kg/309970 lb	161000 kg/354944 lb
Maximum speed	946 km/h /588 mph	959 km/h /596 mph
Cruising speed	459 km/h /285 mph	459 km/h /285 mph
Range	11260 km/6997 miles	9620 km/5978 miles
Service ceiling	10972 m/35997 ft	10972 m/35997 ft
Crew	3	3
Passengers	124	180
Engines	4	4
Maiden flight	10 May 1958	14 March 1966

Until the DC-7, Douglas had been the world's most successful manufacturer of passenger aircraft. This changed when Boeing brought out its 707. Douglas's answer was the DC-8, a four-engined jet that bore a strong physical resemblance to its rival. However, Boeing already had an unassailable lead in this market and won over the airlines with its 707.

DOUGLAS DC-9
McDONNELL DOUGLAS MD-81–MD-90

The DC-9, holding 90 to 100 passengers, was planned as a short-to-medium-range partner to the DC-8. Development work started as early as 1963 and the first flight took place in 1965. The merger with McDonnell occurred during the early days of delivery of this extremely successful aircraft. In order to compete with the Boeing 737, a number of variants were developed with stretched fuselage, additional seats and a longer range. At the beginning of the 1980s, McDonnell Douglas brought out the DC-9-88, which was subsequently developed into the MD-81, giving rise to a new family of models.

In Europe, meanwhile, Airbus was going from strength to strength, which damaged sales of the DC-9 and MD-81 to MD-87 models. With the MD-90, the company made a concerted effort to initiate a new programme. Due to technical difficulties with the rear-mounted engines, however, it proved difficult to widen and extend the fuselage. Following Boeing's 1996 take-over of McDonnell Douglas, the MD-90-50 project eventually evolved into the Boeing 717, which achieved no more than moderate

In the UK, the de Havilland Comet took up the challenge but experienced severe problems that led to a number of tragic crashes. Douglas had lost valuable time, but nevertheless succeeded in producing a well-designed aircraft. Some 556 were built, of which around 100 are still in service with cargo airlines.

DOUGLAS DC-9

	DC-9-10	DC-9-21	DC-9-30	DC-9-40	DC-9-50
Length	31.8 m/104 ft 4 in	31.8 m/104 ft 4 in	36.6 m/120 ft	38.3 m/125 ft 8 in	40.7 m/133 ft 6 in
Wingspan	27.3 m/89 ft 7 in	36.6 m/120 ft	36.6 m/120 ft	36.6 m/120 ft	36.6 m/120 ft
Wing area	86.8 sq m/934 sq ft	93 sq m/1,001 sq ft	93 sq m/1,001 sq ft	93 sq m/1,001 sq ft	93 sq m/1,001 sq ft
MTOW	41777 kg/92103 lb	44492 kg/98099 lb	49940 kg/110098 lb	51756 kg/114102 lb	54885 kg/121000 lb
Maximum speed	903 km/h /561 mph	910 km/h /565 mph	907 km/h /564 mph	917 km/h /570 mph	929 km/h /577 mph
Cruising speed	900 km/h /559 mph	900 km/h /559 mph	900 km/h /559 mph	900 km/h /559 mph	900 km/h /559 mph
Range	2340 km/1454 miles	3430 km/2131 miles	3030 km/1883 miles	3120 km/1939 miles	3030 km/1883 miles
Service ceiling	10058 m/32999 ft	10058 m/32999 ft	10058 m/32999 ft	10058 m/32999 ft	10058 m/32999 ft
Crew	2	2	2	2	2
Passengers	90	90	115	125	139
Engines	2	2	2	2	2
Maiden flight	25 February 1965	1 December 1968	30 January 1967	10 February 1968	20 August 1975

McDONNELL DOUGLAS MD-8X

	MD-81	MD-82/88	MD-83	MD-87	MD-90-30
Length	45.1 m/148 ft	45.1 m/148 ft	45.1 m/148 ft	39.7 m/130 ft 3 in	46.5 m/152 ft 7 in
Wingspan	32.8 m/107 ft 7 in	32.8 m/107 ft 7 in	32.8 m/107 ft 7 in	32.8 m/107 ft 7 in	32.87 m/107 ft 7 in
Wing area	92.97 sq m/1001 sq ft	92.97 sq m/1001 sq ft	92.97 sq m/1001 sq ft	92.97 sq m/1001 sq ft	112.3 sq m/1209 sq ft
MTOW	63503 kg/140000 lb	67812 kg/149500 lb	72575 kg/160000 lb	63503 kg/140000 lb	70760 kg/155999 lb
Maximum speed	811 km/h /504 mph	811 km/h /504 mph	811 km/h /504 mph	811 km/h /504 mph	811 km/h /504 mph
Cruising speed	810 km/h /503 mph	810 km/h /503 mph	810 km/h /503 mph	810 km/h /503 mph	810 km/h /503 mph
Range	2880 km/1789 miles	3790 km/2355 miles	4635 km/2880 miles	4395 km/2731 miles	3860 km/2398 miles
Service ceiling	11277 m/36998 ft	11277 m/36998 ft	11277 m/36998 ft	11277 m/36998 ft	11277 m/36998 ft
Crew	2	2	2	2	2
Passengers	172	172	172	139	172
Engines	2	2	2	2	2
Maiden flight	13 September 1980	5 August 1981	20 February 1985	1 November 1987	22 February 1993

success. The programme was terminated in 2006.

Nevertheless the DC-9 family remains one of the most successful jet airliner series in history. Around 2,288 aircraft were sold, 1,300 of which are still in service despite being less economical to operate than more modern aircraft.

McDonnell Douglas DC-10

N1818U is an aircraft of the inaugural DC-10-10 type. It was built in 1973 and is still in service with FedEx.

The first model produced after the merger between McDonnell and Douglas was the DC-10. The Boeing 747 was too big to land at every airport – due to insufficient length or load-bearing capacity of the runway, or lack of appropriate gates in the terminals – and MDD saw an opportunity for a large-capacity aircraft of somewhat smaller proportions.

Although the DC-10 was popular with pilots, it suffered from various design flaws that were only corrected after a number of major accidents. The loading hatch, for example, opened outwards and was therefore vulnerable to internal pressure. If it was not 100 per cent closed, the lock could fail, resulting in explosion-like decompression. Two aircraft lost their loading hatches in flight. One of

them, a Turkish Airlines DC-10, crashed near Paris in 1972 with the loss of 346 lives.

Another problem was that it was difficult to remove the engines from the external engine pods. Airline mechanics therefore devised a quicker procedure for engine maintenance which involved removing the entire pod. In 1979, this resulted in an American Airlines aircraft losing an engine during flight in an incident that claimed 271 lives.

In 1989, the rear engine of a DC-10 failed and a shard of metal ruptured all three hydraulic systems, which were located far too close together. The flight ended in an emergency landing at Sioux City Airport in Iowa with the loss of 111 of the 296 people on board.

Although the aircraft is now regarded as solid and reliable, its reputation has been permanently damaged by a total of 32 hull-loss accidents. As a result, a number of airlines parted

company with the aircraft prematurely and it is now operated mainly by cargo carriers. Of the 386 civil DC-10s produced, 138 are still flying.

MCDONNELL DOUGLAS DC-10

	DC-10-10	DC-10-40
Length	55.55 m/182 ft 3 in	55.04 m/180 ft 7 in
Wingspan	47.43 m/155 ft 7 in	50.39 m/165 ft 4 in
Wing area	329.8 sq m/3550 sq ft	338.8 sq m/3647 sq ft
MTOW	186 025 kg/410 115 lb	251 815 kg/555 157 lb
Maximum speed	960 km/h /597 mph	960 km/h /597 mph
Cruising speed	908 km/h /564 mph	908 km/h /564 mph
Range	10 220 km/6350 miles	11 190 km/6953 miles
Service ceiling	12 802 m/42 001 ft	12 802 m/42 001 ft
Crew	3	3
Passengers	265–380	265–380
Engines	3 turbofans	3 turbofans
Maiden flight	29 August 1970	28 February 1972

The DC-10 failed to sell in the hoped-for numbers and was therefore reworked. Its fuselage was lengthened, its range was increased and its cockpit was redesigned for a crew of two. However, despite orders from Alitalia, British Caledonian, Dragonair, FedEx, Finnair, Korean Air, SAS, Swissair, Thai Airways International and VARIG, the MD-11 was a 'flop'.

Competition from Airbus in the form of the A340 and Boeing with its 777 caused McDonnell Douglas problems. In addition, fuel consumption was higher than anticipated, and the poor reputation of the plane's predecessor did the rest.

Between 1990 and 2001, just 200 MD-11s were produced, 163 of them freighters.

The MD-11 is popular with FedEx, UPS and Lufthansa Cargo. The main customer for the passenger version is KLM.

McDONNELL DOUGLAS MD-11

	MD-11	MD-11CF	MD-11F	MD-11C	MD-11ER
Length	61.21 m/200 ft 10 in	61.23 m/200 ft 11 in	61.23 m/200 ft 11 in	61.23 m/200 ft 11 in	61.23 m/200 ft 11 in
Wingspan	51.66 m/169 ft 6 in	51.97 m/170 ft 6 in	51.97 m/170 ft 6 in	51.97 m/170 ft 6 in	51.97 m/170 ft 6 in
Wing area	333.9 sq m/3659 sq ft	333.9 sq m/3659 sq ft	333.9 sq m/3659 sq ft	333.9 sq m/3659 sq ft	333.9 sq m/3659 sq ft
MTOW	273314 kg/602554 lb	285990 kg/630500 lb	285990 kg/630500 lb	283700 kg/625451 lb	283700 kg/625451 lb
Maximum speed	945 km/h /587 mph	945 km/h /587 mph	945 km/h /587 mph	945 km/h /587 mph	945 km/h /587 mph
Cruising speed	876 km/h /544 mph	876 km/h /544 mph	876 km/h /544 mph	876 km/h /544 mph	876 km/h /544 mph
Range	13408 km/8331 miles	13408 km/8331 miles	13408 km/8331 miles	13408 km/8331 miles	13408 km/8331 miles
Service ceiling	9940 m/32612 ft	9940 m/32612 ft	9940 m/32612 ft	9940 m/32612 ft	9940 m/32612 ft
Crew	2	2	2	2	2
Passengers	410/323/293	410/323/293	26 pallets	410/214/181	410/323/293
Engines	3	3	3	3	3
Maiden flight	10 January 1990	1 April 1991	15 May 1986	21 August 1986	12 February 1994

CONVAIR

The Convair CV-240 was the first civil development of the military CV-110 aircraft. Its integrated steps made it independent of ground-based equipment. The CV-240 inaugurated a whole series of Convair passenger planes, ranging from a twin-engined aircraft with three-blade propellers to a four-engined jet.

Convair was the result of a merger between the American companies Consolidated Aircraft and Vultee Aircraft.

The Convair CV-240 was a success story whose general characteristics resembled those of the DC-3. It was powered by two engines with triple-bladed propellers. American Airlines had requested the aircraft as a replacement for the DC-3. In order to make it easier for passengers to board, however, it was to have a retractable nose wheel instead of a tail wheel.

Its successor, the CV-340, had an extended fuselage and larger wings, and all subsequent models were variants and developments of it.

The CV-990 Coronado was powered by four jet engines, but Boeing and Douglas had already launched competing models that proved to be better aircraft. The programme was terminated after the thirty-seventh CV-990 left the factory. The last CV-990, belonging to NASA, is on display at Mojave Airport in California.

In 1954, Convair joined the General Dynamics group, providing the latter with a foothold in the military market. It stopped making aircraft in 1965 in order to concentrate on the production of rockets and cruise missiles. In 1994 it was sold to Boeing and since 1996 has been fully integrated with the company.

CONVAIR

	CV-240	CV-340	CV-440-660	CV-990
Length	22.76 m/74 ft 8 in	24.13 m/79 ft 2 in	24.84 m/81ft 6 in	42.49 m/139 ft 4 in
Wingspan	29.97 m/98 ft 4 in	32.12 m/105 ft 5 in	32.12 m/105 ft 5 in	36.58 m/120 ft
Wing area	75.9 sq m/817 sq ft	85.5 sq m/920 sq ft	85.5 sq m/920 sq ft	209 sq m/2250 sq ft
MTOW	19 320 kg/42 593 lb	21 320 kg/47 003 lb	22 250 kg/49 052 lb	115 750 kg/255 185 lb
Maximum speed	500 km/h /311 mph	500 km/h /311 mph	500 km/h /311 mph	1030 km/h /640 mph
Cruising speed	450 km/h /280 mph	450 km/h /280 mph	450 km/h /280 mph	917 km/h /570 mph
Range	1930 km/1199 miles	935 km/580 miles	2800 km/1740 miles	6116 km/3800 miles
Service ceiling	4880 m/16 010 ft	4880 m/16 010 ft	7770 m/25 492 ft	12 495 m/40 994 ft
Crew	2–3	2–3	2	3
Passengers	40	52	52	90–149
Engines	2	2	2	4
Maiden flight	16 March 1947	5 October 1952	8 March 1956	24 January 1961

This CV-990A served with various airlines before ending life as a practice aircraft with the Denver fire brigade.

Production of the CV-990 Coronado totalled just 37 aircraft, which flew with eight different airlines including Alaska Airlines, American Airlines, Garuda Indonesian, SAS, Swissair and VARIG.

Finnair had a fleet of nine CV-440s. There are 75 aircraft of this type still active throughout the world.

THE AIRBUS STORY

France, Germany and the United Kingdom were among the first nations to develop successful aircraft industries in the twentieth century. However, the production of passenger aircraft was interrupted by the two world wars. Only in the 1950s did the Europeans start to build airliners once more. In the meantime, the American firms Boeing, Douglas and Lockheed had conquered the world market and largely carved it up between themselves. Compared to the Americans, European aircraft manufacturers such as Hawker Siddeley, VFW, Fokker, CASA, Sud Aviation and Dornier were of no more than marginal importance.

Eventually, in 1970, Airbus Industrie was founded, with considerable government involvement, as a multinational consortium of European aircraft manufacturers. Over time, the founding members from Germany were bought up by Daimler-Benz and brought under the umbrella of DASA, which, like the French company Aérospatiale, owned 37.9 per cent of Airbus equity. The remainder was owned by British Aerospace (20 per cent) and CASA of Spain (4.2 per cent). The development of the Airbus A300 was initially conceived as the consortium's sole project.

France built the cockpit, the flight controls and the lower section of the mid-fuselage, the United Kingdom built the wings and engines, and Germany built the cabin. The wing flaps came from the Netherlands and the tail from Spain. All these different parts were assembled in the French city of Toulouse. Before long, doubts surfaced in France and the United Kingdom about whether this 300-seat aircraft could succeed. As a result, the number of seats was reduced to 250 and the plane was redesignated the A300B. This failed to put a stop to disagreements between the participating nations, however, and threats were made to scupper the entire project. The British withdrew from the consortium, whereupon Germany increased its investment in the A300 to 50 per cent.

In the end, these difficulties proved to be mere teething troubles. While sales of the A300 had been sluggish, orders for its successor model, the A320, totalled 400 before the plane had even flown. The system of multi-nation production began to prove its worth and further models were developed. Before long, Airbus came to be regarded as a serious rival to Boeing.

In 1999, DaimlerChrysler Aerospace, Aérospatiale-Matra and CASA merged to form EADS as an umbrella organization for Airbus, Astrium, Defence & Security, Military Transport Aircraft and Eurocopter.

Whole families of economical and state-of-the-art aircraft followed, culminating most recently in the A380, the world's largest passenger plane.

The A380 project has not been without some tension, however. Boeing has complained to the World Trade Organization about illegal state subventions relating to aircraft development, while Airbus has in turn accused Boeing of receiving hidden subsidies for military projects. In 2005, the United States initiated legal proceedings against the European Union for illegal state assistance, whereupon the European Union launched a counteraction against the United States the very next day.

Ultimately at stake on both continents are 50,000 front-line jobs, plus hundreds of thousands more in the supply industry. At the end of the day, both companies are trying to meet the passengers'

Airbus and Boeing now use the production capacity of a number of different manufacturers. Individual sections are prefabricated and flown to the main works for final assembly. This means that even before its maiden flight, every aeroplane has already flown thousands of miles in the cargo bay of another aircraft.

AIRBUS A300

This A300B4 was on loan from Lufthansa.

AIRBUS A310

The A310 marked the beginning of a new era of Airbus widebodied aircraft.

desire for efficient and economical aircraft that will make air travel safer throughout the world.

As a result of the decline of the US dollar, Airbus has been hit financially: each ten cent fall in the value of the American currency costs Airbus one billion euros, since aircraft prices are currently quoted in dollars.

The A300 was the first aircraft produced by the Airbus consortium. It was the result of Europe's political determination to counter the American aircraft

manufacturers' dominance with a home-grown product. Inevitably, there were many bureaucratic hurdles to be overcome along the way.

Although the A300 is unrivalled in terms of fuel efficiency and very popular with pilots, the widebody jet was unable to make much of a mark in the United States. Eastern Airlines could only be persuaded to purchase the plane after being lent four aircraft for a year along with free maintenance and equipment. It was finally convinced and placed an order for 32.

Due to its relatively short range, the A300 proved inferior to the Boeing on transatlantic routes. As a large-capacity medium-haul aircraft, however, it is unbeatable – not least because its flight computer calculates the most efficient fuel consumption for any given speed.

More important, however, was the fact that the experiment succeeded. As a result, the A300 effectively served as a pilot project for a family of aircraft covering a whole range of distances and passenger loads.

By the time production was finally terminated on 12 July 2007, 561 A300s had been built.

The shorter, more modern A310 is a thoroughly reworked version of the A300. Its cockpit has been redesigned for a two-person crew, with the work of the flight engineer entrusted to a computer. Further weight savings were made thanks to the fly-by-wire system and the use – for the first time ever in an aircraft – of a composite tail unit.

Like the A300, the A310 was conceived as a medium-range jet and given a relatively modest range which was only extended with the A310-300. Not only was this version equipped with quieter engines, it was also given a fuel pumping system for adjusting the centre of gravity during take-off, cruising and landing, and an additional fuel tank in the tail unit that could be used as a trim tank.

Although only 255 A310s were sold, the plane was a total success, not least in providing a platform for many innovations that were to become standard on later Airbus types.

AIRBUS

	A300B2	A300B4	A300-600R	A310-200	A310-300
Length	53.62 m/175 ft 11 in	53.62 m/175 ft 11 in	54.08 m/177 ft 5 in	46.66 m/153 ft	46.66 m/153 ft
Wingspan	44.84 m/147 ft 1 in	44.84 m/147 ft 1 in	44.84 m/147 ft 1 in	43.9 m/144 ft	43.9 m/144 ft
Wing area	260 sq m/2799 sq ft	260 sq m/2799 sq ft	260 sq m/2799 sq ft	219 sq m/2357 sq ft	219 sq m/2357 sq ft
MTOW	142 000 kg/313 056 lb	165 000 kg/363 763 lb	165 000 kg/363 763 lb	157 000 kg/346 126 lb	157 000 kg/346 126 lb
Maximum speed	917 km/h /570 mph	917 km/h /570 mph	890 km/h /553 mph	897 km/h /557 mph	897 km/h /557 mph
Cruising speed	847 km/h /526 mph	847 km/h /526 mph	875 km/h /544 mph	840 km/h /522 mph	840 km/h /522 mph
Range	3430 km/2131 miles	5375 km/3340 miles	6968 km/4330 miles	6800 km/4225 miles	9580 km/5953 miles
Service ceiling	9500 m/31168 ft	9500 m/31168 ft	9500 m/31168 ft	12 500 m/41 010 ft	12 500 m/41 010 ft
Crew	3	3	3	2	2
Passengers	250	266	250	220	220
Engines	2	2	2	2	2
Maiden flight	28 October 1972	23 May 1975	5 July 1988	4 April 1982	25 March 1999

AIRBUS A318

The business model of Frontier Airlines, with its hub in Denver, Colorado, is based on economical medium-range aircraft.

The latest addition to the A320 family is also the smallest. Although conceived as a short-haul jet, the A318 has an ETOPS (Extended-range Twin-engine Operational Performance Standards) rating and can therefore be used on transatlantic routes. The 'Baby Bus' can carry 107 passengers, but has a weight disadvantage compared to the smallest Boeing 737, only coming into its own (due to the commonality benefit) when used as part of a fleet that includes larger Airbus models. Since its launch in 2007, 72 A318s have been produced with a further 11 on order.

The A320 family by size: a medium-range airliner for every market.

Most Airbus A318s are in service in America.

AIRBUS		
	A319-100	A318-100
Length	33.84 m/111 ft	31.45 m/103 ft 2 in
Wingspan	34.1 m/111 ft 10 in	34.1 m/111 ft 10 in
Wing area	122.6 sq m/1320 sq ft	122.6 sq m/1320 sq ft
MTOW	75 500 kg/166 449 lb	68 000 kg/149 914 lb
Maximum speed	900 km/h /559 mph	900 km/h /559 mph
Cruising speed	840 km/h /522 mph	840 km/h /522 mph
Range	6800 km/4225 miles	5950 km/3697 miles
Service ceiling	12 000 m/39 370 ft	12 000 m/39 370 ft
Crew	2	2
Passengers	124	107
Engines	2	2
Maiden flight	25 August 1995	15 January 2002

AIRBUS A319

Frontier won the hearts of its customers by decorating its planes with animal motifs.

At 4 m/13 ft shorter than the benchmark A320 model, the A319 holds 124 passengers in its usual seating configuration. There is also a business-class version, the A319LR (accommodating 48 passengers), equipped with supplementary fuel tanks. This enables Lufthansa to use it for business-class flights between Germany and the United States.

Frontier Airlines, based in Denver, Colorado, uses the A319 almost exclusively for its transcontinental network.

Production of the A319 totals 1,230 to date with a further 300 on order.

AIRBUS A320

The Classic: After the Boeing 737, the Airbus A320 is the world's best-selling medium-range aircraft.

After the success of its A300 and A310 widebody aircraft, Airbus set out to conquer the 100–200-seater market, entering into competition with the Boeing 737 and the MD-80. Between them, the American firms had the market more or less sewn up, achieving very high sales with their respective models.

In order to increase the attractiveness of the A320, a whole family of models was carefully planned from the outset. The decision was taken to offer the aircraft in a range of fuselage lengths in order to cover both the domestic and transcontinental markets for between 100 and 220 seats. This meant paying particular attention to the design of the wings. In addition, the jetliner had to be economical and offer a suitable fuselage cross-section for the expedient loading of freight.

The flight controls consist of five linked computers that monitor each other and ensure that the aircraft never exceeds it prescribed limits – even as a result of human error. The control surfaces are moved partly electronically and partly hydraulically by means of a sidestick.

Not surprisingly, Boeing was not exactly thrilled when a number of United States airlines placed orders for hundreds of A320s. Sales were helped by the price – five million dollars less than Boeing's competing model.

It seems reasonable to assume that Airbus precipitated the merger between McDonnell Douglas and Boeing and that the A320 ousted the MD-90 from the market.

Over 2,200 A320s have left the factory to date with another 1,800 on order.

AIRBUS A321

The largest aircraft in the A320 family has proved extremely popular and orders show no sign of drying up.

The A321, longer by 7 m/ 23 ft, needed new wing flaps to ensure rotational stability during take-off, otherwise the rear of the plane was liable to hit the ground as the nose lifted. The additional technology and heavier take-off weight also called for more powerful engines than the A320.

Accommodating a maximum of 220 passengers, the A321 covers the higher-capacity end of the A320 family.

Total production to date is 582 with another 196 on order.

With around 100 Airbus A320s, United Airlines is one of the largest operators of the type.

AIRBUS

	A320-200	A321-200
Length	37.57 m/123 ft 3 in	44.51 m/146 ft
Wingspan	34.1 m/111 ft 10 in	34.1 m/111 ft 10 in
Wing area	122.6 sq m/1320 sq ft	122.6 sq m/1320 sq ft
MTOW	77 000 kg/169 756 lb	93 500 kg/206 132 lb
Maximum speed	903 km/h /561 mph	900 km/h /559 mph
Cruising speed	840 km/h /522 mph	840 km/h /522 mph
Range	5700 km/3542 miles	5600 km/3480 miles
Service ceiling	12 000 m/39 370 ft	12 000 m/39 370 ft
Crew	2	2
Passengers	150	185
Engines	2	2
Maiden flight	22 February 1987	25 March 1993

AIRBUS A330

An A330 belonging to Northwest Airlines, which was taken over by Delta Air Lines in 2009.

flights had to be completed on just one engine.

Thanks to its outstanding long-distance characteristics and a further increase in its fuel efficiency, the A330 has proved extremely popular. Orders to date total 1,057: nearly three times as many as for the A340.

The A330 is due to be replaced by the A350 in 2012.

The A330 is a widebody jetliner for medium and long distances. It was conceived as a competitor to the DC-10 and Boeing 767 and developed in tandem with the A340. The fuselage of the A330 is based on the proportions of the A300 fuselage. The A330 and A340 share the same wing and tail unit design. The cockpit, meanwhile, is identical to the A320 flight deck, with the same fly-by-wire system.

In order to achieve ETOPS certification for Atlantic routes, numerous six-hour

AIRBUS A330

	A330-200	A330-200F	A330-300
Length	45 m/147 ft 8 in	58.37 m/191 ft 6 in	63.6 m/208 ft 8 in
Wingspan	60.3 m/197 ft 10 in	60.3 m/197 ft 10 in	60.3 m/197 ft 10 in
Wing area	361.6 sq m/3892 sq ft	361.6 sq m/3892 sq ft	361.6 sq m/3892 sq ft
MTOW	230 000 kg/507 063 lb	233 000 kg/513 677 lb	233 000 kg/513 677 lb
Maximum speed	913 km/h /567 mph	913 km/h /567 mph	913 km/h /567 mph
Cruising speed	871 km/h /541 mph	871 km/h /541 mph	871 km/h /541 mph
Range	c.12 500 km/c.7767 miles	c.7400 km/c.4598 miles	10 500km/c.6524 miles
Service ceiling	12 500 m/41 010 ft	12 500 m/41 010 ft	12 500 m/41 010 ft
Crew	2	2	2
Passengers	293	n/a	375
Engines	2	2	2
Maiden flight	13 August 1997	13 August 1997	2 November 1992

AIRBUS A340

The A340 is unmistakable. Along with the Boeing 747, these are currently the only aircraft of their size in the western world with four engines.

The A340 is a four-engined widebody jetliner for ultra-long distances. It was conceived for the market previously served by the DC-10 and Boeing 767.

During the design of the A340, Airbus adhered to the principle of commonality of its products. Many components are identical and therefore interchangeable. Apart from the additional throttle levers and control elements, the flight deck is identical to those of the A320 and A330 families as well as those of the A380 and planned A350, thereby facilitating the cross-rating of pilots.

Singapore Airlines currently holds the world record for the longest scheduled commercial flight. The 16,600-km/10,315-mile non-stop journey between Singapore and New York takes 18 hours. To make this possible, the airline has reduced the number of seats in the A340-500 to 181 in a two-class configuration and installed a bar in which passengers can stretch their legs.

AIRBUS A340

	A340-200	A340-300	A340-500	A340-600	A340-600HGW
Length	59.4 m/194 ft 11 in	63.6 m/208 ft 8 in	67.9 m/222 ft 9 in	75.3 m/247 ft	75.3 m/247 ft
Wingspan	60.3 m/197 ft 10 in	60.3 m/197 ft 10 in	60.3 m/197 ft 10 in	63.45 m/208 ft 2 in	63.45 m/208 ft 2 in
Wing area	361.6 sq m/3892 sq ft	361.6 sq m/3892 sq ft	439.3 sq m/4729 sq ft	439.3 sq m/4729 sq ft	439.3 sq m/4729 sq ft
MTOW	257 000 kg/566 588 lb	271 000 kg/597 453 lb	368 000 kg/811 301 lb	368 000 kg/811 301 lb	380 000 kg/837 756 lb
Maximum speed	940 km/h /584 mph	890 km/h /553 mph	920 km/h /572 mph	920 km/h /572 mph	920 km/h /572 mph
Cruising speed	880 km/h /547 mph	880 km/h /547 mph	905 km/h /562 mph	905 km/h /562 mph	905 km/h /562 mph
Range	14 800 km/9196 miles	13 350 km/8295 miles	16 050 km/9973 miles	13 900 km/8637 miles	14 600 km/9072 miles
Service ceiling	12 500 m/41 010 ft	12 500 m/41 010 ft	12 525 m/41 093 ft	12 525 m/41 093 ft	12 525 m/41 093 ft
Crew	2	2	2	2	2
Passengers	300	335	359	419	419
Engines	4	4	4	4	4
Maiden flight	1 April 1992	25 October 1991	11 February 2002	23 April 2001	18 November 2005

The A350 will be the first Airbus with both fuselage and wings made primarily of carbon fibre-reinforced plastic.

The A340-600 is currently the longest aircraft in the world. In making it this length, Airbus exploited the 80 m/262 ft maximum permitted length for aircraft handling at passenger terminals. The plane is fitted with external cameras to assist the pilots when taxiing because it is so long. The luggage and cargo bay is as big as that of a Boeing 747-400. Lufthansa opted to install the galley and washrooms on the lower deck of its A340-600s in order to create more space on the passenger deck. The trim tanks in the tail hold 4,800 kg/10,582 lb and 6,000 kg/13,228 lb of fuel for the A340-300 and A340-600 respectively.

Orders for the A340 total 378 to date.

The A350 is a European response to the Boeing 787. Airbus had regarded the 787 as Boeing's answer to its A330, and as late as 2004 was planning to win back market share from Boeing with a slightly improved and advanced variant of its highly successful earlier model. However, the airlines protested vehemently against this and valuable time was lost. Boeing took advantage of the delay to market its 787. In early 2006, Airbus unveiled an improved design that once more met with disdain, with the airlines announcing that they had decided in favour of the 787. At the 2006 Farnborough Air Show, however, Airbus finally presented a completely new design that met with the approval of the airlines. A year later, new details were released concerning the materials (relative Boeing 787 values in brackets): 52 per cent (50 per cent) CFRP (carbon fibre-reinforced plastic), 20 per cent (18 per cent) aluminium/lithium, 14 per cent (15 per cent) titanium, 7 per cent (10 per cent) steel and 7 per cent (7 per cent) diverse materials.

The cabin, wings, flight deck and engines will differ – in some ways substantially – from earlier Airbus models. The A350 is expected to make its maiden flight in 2012 and enter service in 2013. As of February 2010, 505 orders had been received, compared with Boeing's 876 orders for the 787.

AIRBUS A350

	A350-800	A350-900	A350-900R	A350-900F	A350-1000
Length	60.6 m/198 ft 10 in	66.9 m/219 ft 6 in	66.9 m/219 ft 6 in	66.9 m/219 ft 6 in	73.9 m/242 ft 5 in
Wingspan	64 m/210 ft	64 m/210 ft	64 m/210 ft	64 m/210 ft	64 m/210 ft
Wing area	443 sq m/4768 sq ft	443 sq m/4768 sq ft	443 sq m/4768 sq ft	443 sq m/4768 sq ft	443 sq m/4768 sq ft
MTOW	245 000 kg/540 132 lb	265 000 kg/584,224 lb	295 000 kg/650 364 lb	295 000 kg/650 364 lb	295 000 kg/650 364 lb
Maximum speed	945 km/h /587 mph	945 km/h /587 mph	945 km/h /587 mph	945 km/h /587 mph	945 km/h /587 mph
Cruising speed	903 km/h /561 mph	903 km/h /561 mph	903 km/h /561 mph	903 km/h /561 mph	903 km/h /561 mph
Range	15 400 km/9569 miles	15 000 km/9320 miles	17 600 km/10 936 miles	9250 km/5748 miles	14 800 km/9196 miles
Service ceiling	13 100 m/42 979 ft	13 100 m/42 979 ft	13 100 m/42 979 ft	13 100 m/42 979 ft	13 100 m/42 979 ft
Crew	2	2	2	2	2
Passengers	270	314	310	n/a	350
Engines	2	2	2	2	2
Maiden flight	n/a	2011	n/a	n/a	n/a

Airbus A380

The Long Journey from A3XX to A380

1970	Founding of Airbus.
1991	Initial exploratory talks with leading airlines about the requirements a possible super jumbo with the working designation A3XX would need to fulfil.
Jan 93	Boeing announces that it would be interested in producing a 'very large aircraft' in collaboration with Aérospatiale, Daimler-Benz Aerospace, Airbus, Construcciones Aeronauticas and British Aerospace.
Jun 93	Boeing starts to favour a smaller aircraft and the Airbus partners decide to go ahead with the super jumbo project.
1996	Founding of 'Airbus Large Aircraft Division'.
2000	Commercial launch of the A3XX, later to become the A380.
2001	The Airbus consortium becomes an integrated firm with four partners in France, Germany, Spain and the United Kingdom.
2002	Manufacture of components begins.
Feb 04	Rolls Royce delivers the first engines to Toulouse, France.
Apr 04	Start of preparations and structural changes at the world's major airports in order to enable them to handle the super jumbo.
May 04	Start of final assembly in Toulouse.
Dec 04	EADS (European Aeronautic Defence and Space Company) announces that the project will be 1.5 billion euros more expensive than planned.
Jan 05	Airbus and Boeing settle their dispute over alleged unfair competition and state subsidies.
27 Apr 05	Maiden flight in Toulouse. Test flights continue for the next 12 months.
Jun 05	Airbus announces a six-month delay.
Mar 06	In a successful test, 870 occupants evacuate the aircraft in 80 seconds with half the exits blocked.
Jul 06	Airbus announces a further six-month delay.
Oct 06	Airbus announces a further delay of one year. The programme is now 20 months behind schedule.
Oct 07	Singapore Airlines takes delivery of its first aircraft.

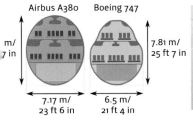

Airbus A380 | Boeing 747

m/
7 in

7.81 m/
25 ft 7 in

7.17 m/
23 ft 6 in

6.5 m/
21 ft 4 in

Comparison of the upper deck of the A380 and the Boeing 747.

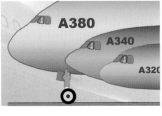

A380
A340
A320

Comparison of Airbus sizes at the same scale.

Flights on the A380 attract a surcharge, but are often fully booked.

The A380 is in a league of its own. Its size is breathtaking.

It would be possible to park 114 Volkswagen Golfs in the shade of the A380's wings.

AIRBUS A380

	A380-800	A380-900
Length	73 m/239 ft 6 in	79.4 m/260 ft 6 in
Wingspan	79.8 m/261 ft 8 in	79.8 m/261 ft 8 in
Wing area	846 sq m/9106 sq ft	846 sq m/9106 sq ft
MTOW	560 000 kg/1 234 589 lb	590 000 kg/1 300 727 lb
Maximum speed	955 km/h /593 mph	944 km/h /587 mph
Cruising speed	900 km/h /559 mph	900 km/h /559 mph
Range	15 200 km/9445 miles	14 200 km/8823 miles
Service ceiling	13 115 m/43 028 ft	13 115 m/43 028 ft
Crew	2	2
Passengers	555	c. 650
Engines	4	4
Maiden flight	27 April 2005	n/a

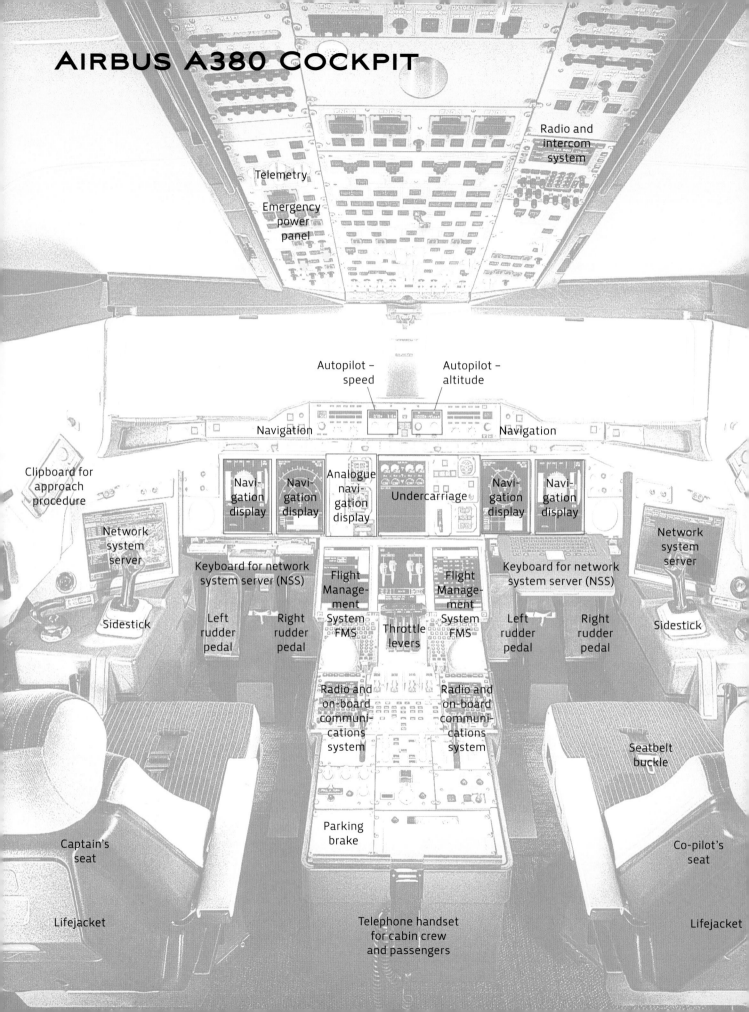

Airbus A380 Cockpit

Radio and intercom system

Telemetry

Emergency power panel

Autopilot – speed

Autopilot – altitude

Navigation

Navigation

Clipboard for approach procedure

Navigation display

Navigation display

Analogue navigation display

Undercarriage

Navigation display

Navigation display

Network system server

Network system server

Keyboard for network system server (NSS)

Flight Management System FMS

Flight Management System FMS

Keyboard for network system server (NSS)

Sidestick

Left rudder pedal

Right rudder pedal

Throttle levers

Left rudder pedal

Right rudder pedal

Sidestick

Radio and on-board communications system

Radio and on-board communications system

Seatbelt buckle

Captain's seat

Co-pilot's seat

Parking brake

Lifejacket

Telephone handset for cabin crew and passengers

Lifejacket

The Tupolev Story

Andrei Nikolayevich Tupolev was born in Pustomazovo, Russia, on 10 November 1888. His interest in aviation led him to enrol at the Moscow Technical School. In 1918, at the age of 30, he and his friend Nikolai Zhukovski founded the Central Aerohydrodynamic Institute (TsAGI) that would later develop into Russia's most important aviation research institute.

There he developed whole series of aircraft, including the world's first twin-engined, all-metal, cantilever bomber. This did not stop Stalin having him arrested on suspicion of treason, however, and in 1937 Tupolev was given a life sentence. While in prison he was required to continue designing aircraft. He was released in 1941, when Germany launched an attack on the Soviet Union. Stalin is even believed to have apologized to him in 1943. In addition to the development of bombers, Tupolev also worked on passenger planes. In total he was involved in over 100 aircraft projects. His life's work was continued by his son Alexei Andreyevich Tupolev.

Andrei N. Tupolev.

TU-154

TUPOLEV 154

	TU-154M
Length	47.9 m/157 ft 2 in
Wingspan	37.55 m/123 ft 2 in
Wing area	201.5 sq m/2169 sq ft
MTOW	100 000 kg/220 462 lb
Maximum speed	950 km/h /590 mph
Cruising speed	900 km/h /559 mph
Range	4000 km/2485 miles
Service ceiling	11000 m/36 089 ft
Crew	3–4
Passengers	160–180
Engines	3
Maiden flight	1968

A Tupolev-154B-2 of the North Korean airline Air Koryo after landing at Beijing in 1983.

Over 1,000 of Tupolev's most important model, the Tu-154 trijet, have been produced. In its early years it was widely flown by the airlines of Eastern Europe – whether they liked it or not. The last model, the Tu-154M, meets the requirements of category III ICAO noise regulations and is likely to be around for some time yet.

TU-204K

TU-204

With the Tu-204, a successor to the Tu-154, free market economy has made its entrance into Russian aviation. The Tu-204 is more economical than earlier models and features a two-crew glass cockpit with six colour monitors, a transparent head-up display of the kind used in bombers, fly-by-wire, an automatic landing system and two quiet but powerful latest generation Rolls-Royce engines.

However, Air Koryo also operates the very latest Tupolev models. The example shown is a Tu-204-300 built in 2007.

The Tu-204K is a study for a Tu-204 derivative powered by liquefied gas and using cryogenic technology. The 204K can carry 210 passengers, has a range of 5,200 km/3,231 miles and burns barely 20 g per passenger per km/around 1 oz of fuel per passenger per mile. Since Russia has abundant supplies of natural gas, this could be the future.

TUPOLEV 204

	TU-204-100	TU-204-120	TU-214	TU-204-300
Length	46 m/150 ft 11 in	46 m/150 ft 11 in	46 m/150 ft 11 in	40 m/131 ft
Wingspan	42 m/137 ft 10 in	42 m/137 ft 10 in	42 m/137 ft 10 in	42 m/137 ft 10 in
Wing area	184.2 sq m/1983 sq ft	184.2 sq m/1983 sq ft	184.2 sq m/1983 sq ft	184.2 sq m/1983 sq ft
MTOW	103 000 kg/227 076 lb	103 000 kg/227 076 lb	110 750 kg/244 162 lb	107 500 kg/236 997 lb
Maximum speed	850 km/h /528 mph	850 km/h /528 mph	850 km/h /528 mph	850 km/h /528 mph
Cruising speed	810 km/h /503 mph	810 km/h /503 mph	810 km/h /503 mph	810 km/h /503 mph
Range	6500 km/4039 miles	6500 km/4039 miles	6670 km/4144 miles	7500 km/4660 miles
Service ceiling	12 600 m/41 339 ft	12 600 m/41 339ft	12 600 m/41 339 ft	12 600 m/41 339ft
Crew	2	2	2	2
Passengers	210	210	210	157
Engines	2	2	2	2
Maiden flight	1989	1998	1996	2003

DORNIER

In 1929, this Do-X flew into a brave new world. Its 12 water-cooled Jupiter-Curtiss-Conqueror engines, each with 12 cylinders, developed a total of 7,320 hp. The Do-X had a top speed of 211 km/h /131 mph and a range of 1,700 km/1,056 miles.

Claude Honoré Desiré Dornier, whose father was French, was born in Kempten, Germany, in 1884. In 1912, Count Ferdinand von Zeppelin intervened personally to ensure that the gifted engineer and employee of the Zeppelin works in Friedrichshafen was granted German citizenship. Count Zeppelin entrusted Dornier with the running of an ancillary plant that eventually became Dornier Flugzeugwerke, which in turn went on to produce a number of epoch-defining aircraft including the 12-engined Do-X – in its day the largest aeroplane in the world. During its maiden flight over Lake Constance in October 1929, the Do-X

carried 159 passengers and ten crew, a record that remained unbroken until 1949 (by the Lockheed Constellation).

In addition to the manufacture of military equipment and the development of aviation and space technology, the Dornier works also designed a number of short-distance aircraft that proved their worth thanks to their short take-off and landing capability.

Had Dornier not been thrown into confusion by succession-related disputes and complexities, taken over by the Daimler-Benz group (which subsequently acquired MBB to form DASA) and

later merged with the near-bankrupt Fokker of Holland, it might have achieved Boeing-like success in Germany.

In the end, the company was split up and parts of it subsumed into EADS,

while other parts were sold to Fairchild Aircraft of America. The end of the road for Dornier came with the insolvency of Fairchild-Dornier in 2002. Its remaining assets were auctioned off in 2005.

The Do-228 has STOL (short take-off and landing) capabilities.

The Do-328JET is regarded as the Rolls-Royce of regional aircraft. However, it was so expensive that commercial success eluded it.

The Do-328 is extremely comfortable but very expensive. It is capable of carrying 33 passengers and is available in turboprop and jet versions. Despite first flying in 1991, the Do-328 incorporates sophisticated technology that was not seen again until the development of the Boeing 787. Production was terminated due to Dornier's complex ownership situation.

DORNIER

	DO-228	DO-328	DO-328JET
Length	15.03 m/49 ft 4 in	21.28 m/69 ft 10 in	21.22 m/69 ft 7 in
Wingspan	16.97 m/55 ft 8 in	20.98 m/68 ft 10 in	20.98 m/68 ft 10 in
Wing area	32 sq m/344 sq ft	40 sq m/430 sq ft	40 sq m/430 sq ft
MTOW	5700 kg/12 566 lb	13 990 kg/30 843 lb	13 990 kg/30 843 lb
Maximum speed	433 km/h /269 mph	650 km/h /404 mph	756 km/h /470 mph
Cruising speed	315 km/h /196 mph	620 km/h /385 mph	740 km/h /460 mph
Range	1343 km/834 miles	1350 km/839 miles	1850 km/1150 miles
Service ceiling	8535 m/28 002 ft	10 670 m/35 007 ft	10 670 m/35 007 ft
Crew	2	2	2
Passengers	15	30–33	30–33
Engines	2	2	2
Maiden flight	28 March 1981	6 December 1991	20 January 1998

The Do-328JET achieved a major triumph when a Chinese airline placed an order for the aircraft.

SAAB

The Saab 340 was developed by the Swedish firm in conjunction with Fairchild Aircraft of the United States, although Fairchild withdrew from the project in 1985. Production ceased in 2005.

The Swedish company SAAB was founded in 1937 to manufacture, under licence, aircraft such as the German Ju-86 bomber. In 1940, it began to develop its own models, albeit mainly for the Swedish military. However, the company has also achieved two major successes in the civil medium-range market with its 340 and 2000 models. Saab is also an important subcontractor for Airbus.

SAAB 340
Between 1983 and 1999, 459 of this 30-seat aircraft were produced. The Saab 340 has a range of 1,490 km/926 miles.

SAAB 2000
A total of just 64 of this 50-seater were built between 1994 and 1999. It has a range of 2,868 km/1,782 miles.

SAAB

	SAAB 340	SAAB 2000
Length	19.73 m/64 ft 9 in	27.2 m/89 ft 3 in
Wingspan	21.44 m/70 ft 4 in	24.76 m/81 ft 3 in
Wing area	41.8 sq m/450 sq ft	55.7 sq m/600 sq ft
MTOW	13 000 kg/28 660 lb	22 800 kg/50 265 lb
Maximum speed	525 km/h /326 mph	682 km/h /424 mph
Cruising speed	463 km/h /288 mph	594 km/h /369 mph
Range	1490 km/926 miles	2868 km/1782 miles
Service ceiling	8200 m/26 903 ft	9448 m/30 997 ft
Crew	2	2
Passengers	33–37	50–58
Engines	2	2
Maiden flight	26 March 1983	25 January 1992

The Saab 2000 is a derivative of the Saab 340 with a stretched fuselage.

Embraer is rapidly catching up its bigger competitors and penetrating the regional aircraft market with ever larger models.

Embraer (*Empresa Brasiliera de Aeronáutica*) is the world's third-largest aircraft manufacturer. The Brazilian company specializes in military aircraft and also regional airliners that are steadily growing in size. Many of its models are even built under licence in China. Embraer's range covers both turboprops and jets:

TURBOPROPS:
EMB110: 19 seats
EMB120: 30 seats

JETS: ERJ-135: 37 seats
ERJ-140: 44 seats
ERJ-145: 50 seats
Embraer 170: 78 seats
Embraer 175: 86 seats
Embraer 190: 106 seats
Embraer 195: 118 seats

EMBRAER-170-SERIES / ERJ-FAMILY

	170	175	190	195	ERJ-135	ERJ-140	ERJ-145
Length	29.9 m/98 ft 1 in	31.68 m/103 ft 11 in	36.24 m/118 ft 11 in	38.65 m/126 ft 10 in	26.3 m/86 ft 3 in	28.45 m/93 ft 4 in	29.87 m/98 ft
Wingspan	26 m/85 ft 4 in	26 m/85 ft 4 in	26 m/85 ft 4 in	28.72 m/94 ft 3 in	20 m/65 ft 7 in	20.4 m/66 ft 11 in	20.4 m/66 ft 11 in
Wing area	51.18 sq m/551 sq ft	51.18 sq m/551 sq ft	51.18 sq m/551 sq ft	95.5 sq m/1028 sq ft	49 sq m/527 sq ft	49 sq m/527 sq ft	49 sq m/527 sq ft
MTOW	35990 kg/79344 lb	37500 kg/82673 lb	50300 kg/110893 lb	50790 kg/111973 lb	22500 kg/49604 lb	21100 kg/46517 lb	21900 kg/48281 lb
Maximum speed	870 km/h /540 mph	870 km/h /540 mph	870 km/h /540 mph	870 km/h /540 mph	850 km/h /528 mph	834 km/h /518 mph	833 km/h /518 mph
Cruising speed	850 km/h /528 mph	850 km/h /528 mph	850 km/h /528 mph	850 km/h /528 mph	800 km/h /497 mph	830 km/h /516 mph	790 km/h /491 mph
Range	3889 km/2417 miles	3889 km/2417 miles	4260 km/2647 miles	3334 km/2072 miles	3241 km/2014 miles	3019 km/1876 miles	2870 km/1783 miles
Service ceiling	12500 m/41010 ft	12500 m/41010 ft	12500 m/41010 ft	12500 m/41010 ft	11200 m/36745 ft	11200 m/36745 ft	11200 m/36745 ft
Crew	2	2	2	2	2	2	2
Passengers	70–78	78–86	98–106	108–118	37	44	48–50
Engines	2	2	2	2	2	2	2
Maiden flight	19 February 2003	23 December 2004	30 August 2005	3 July 2006	4 July 1998	27 June 2000	11 August 1995

BOMBARDIER

The DHC-6 Twin Otter is perfect for short-distance operations in remote regions. Large enough to carry 20 passengers over distances of 1,000 km/600 miles and more, the Twin Otter is used to service offshore drilling platforms and isolated spots in northern Canada and the Pacific islands, and also serves Antarctic scientists as a transport plane. The above example is pictured at Vancouver's Waterfront Airport.

Bombardier Aerospace is the home of a number of aviation legends. It started in 1911 with the founding of Canadian Vickers to manufacture military equipment under licence from the British armaments firm Vickers. In 1944, the company was split into two: Canadian Vickers concentrated on shipbuilding while Canadair developed aircraft and produced variants of the DC-3 and DC-4 under licence. Canadair eventually became Bombardier Aerospace, which later took over another company with its roots in British industrial history: de Havilland Canada (DHC). Having acquired Avro Canada in 1962, DHC became a subsidiary of Boeing in the 1980s before being acquired by Bombardier in 1992.

Bombardier recently sold the exclusive rights to manufacture the DHC-6 to the Canadian firm Viking. While Viking continues to use the original de Havilland Canada designs, it is soon to launch a brand-new aircraft named the DHC-400.

DHC-6 TWIN OTTER

Length	12,566 m/51 ft 9 in
Wingspan	19.81 m/65 ft
Wing area	39 sq m/420 sq ft
MTOW	5700 kg/12 566 lb
Maximum speed	360 km/h /224 mph
Cruising speed	338 km/h /210 mph
Range	1300 km/809 miles
Service ceiling	3400 m/11 154 ft
Crew	2
Passengers	20
Engines	2
Maiden flight	20 May 1965

With its CRJ series, Bombardier has been competing for some time in the medium-distance segment.

DHC-6

Probably the most famous de Havilland Canada passenger plane is the DHC-6 Twin Otter, which is at home on every desert, rainforest and ice strip between the North and South Poles. Equipped with floats, it is also used to fly between the islands of the South Pacific or Maldives, and to link up the isolated lakes of the Arctic tundra.

DHC-8

The DHC-8 (or Dash 8) is also known as the Q Series. There are four different models available, from the Dash 8Q-100 to the Dash 8Q-400, which is the largest, capable of carrying 78 passengers.

CANADAIR REGIONAL JET CRJ

The CRJ series has achieved enormous success.

Q SERIES

	DASH 8Q-100	DASH 8Q-200	DASH 8Q-300	DASH 8Q-400
Length	22.3 m/73 ft 2 in	22.3 m/73 ft 2 in	25.7 m/84 ft 4 in	32.84 m/107 ft 9 in
Wingspan	25.9 m/85 ft	25.9 m/85 ft	27.4 m/89 ft 11 in	28.42 m/93 ft 3 in
Wing area	54.3 sq m/584 sq ft	54.3 sq m/584 sq ft	54.3 sq m/584 sq ft	63.1 sq m/679 sq ft
MTOW	16 465 kg/36 299 lb	16 465 kg/36 299 lb	19 505 kg/43 001 lb	29 257 kg/64 501 lb
Maximum speed	490 km/h /304 mph	500 km/h /312 mph	560 km/h /348 mph	648 km/h /403 mph
Cruising speed	440 km/h /273 mph	446 km/h /277 mph	532 km/h /331 mph	629 km/h /391 mph
Range	2000 km/1243 miles	2000 km/1243 miles	1600 km/994 miles	2825 km/1755 miles
Service ceiling	7620 m/25 000 ft	7620 m/25 000 ft	7620 m/25 000 ft	7620 m/25 000 ft
Crew	2	2	2	2
Passengers	39	39	56	78
Engines	2	2	2	2
Maiden flight	20 June 1983	2 April 1995	15 May 1987	31 January 1998

CANADAIR REGIONAL JET

	CRJ-100	CRJ-200	CRJ-700	CRJ-900	CRJ-1000
Length	26.77 m/87 ft 10 in	26.77 m/87 ft 10 in	32.51 m/106 ft 8 in	36.4 m/119 ft 5 in	39.13 m/128 ft 5 in
Wingspan	21.23 m/69 ft 8 in	21.23 m/69 ft 8 in	23.24 m/76 ft 3 in	24.85 m/81 ft 6 in	26.18 m/85 ft 11 in
Wing area	48 sq m/517 sq ft	48 sq m/517 sq ft	68.83 sq m/741 sq ft	70.61 sq m/760 sq ft	n/a
MTOW	23 134 kg/51 002 lb	23 995 kg/52 900 lb	33 995 kg/74 946 lb	36 515 kg/80 502 lb	41 050 kg/90 500 lb
Maximum speed	880 km/h /547 mph	880 km/h /547 mph	876 km/h /544 mph	881 km/h /547 mph	900 km/h /559 mph
Cruising speed	860 km/h /534 mph	860 km/h /534 mph	829 km/h /515 mph	850 km/h /528 mph	870 km/h /541 mph
Range	1850 km/1150 miles	3713 km/2307 miles	3676 km/2284 miles	2472 km/1536 miles	2761 km/1716 miles
Service ceiling	12 496 m/40 997 ft	12 496 m/40 997 ft	12 496 m/40 997 ft	12 496 m/40 997 ft	12 496 m/40 997 ft
Crew	2	2	2	2	2
Passengers	50	50	75	86	104
Engines	2	2	2	2	2
Maiden flight	10 May 1991	10 May 1991	27 May 1999	21 February 2001	3 November 2008

ATR

The ATR-42 regional airliner is popular all over the world. Total production to date is over 400 and the aircraft performs equally well in the Caribbean, in Oceania or in the rainforests of South America.

The three initials of this company's name stand for *Avions de Transport Régional* in French and *Aerei da Transporto Regionale* in Italian. ATR is a binational aircraft manufacturer whose precursors were Aérospatiale of France and Alenia of Italy. In the mid-1980s, ATR unveiled two highly successful aircraft, the 50-seat ATR-42 and the 72-seat ATR-72, which have achieved combined sales of around 1,000.

The larger ATR-72 has been the most successful. American Eagle Airlines has 45 in its fleet and the Indian airline Kingfisher has ordered 32. The French-Italian consortium is continually bringing new models onto the market.

ATR-42/-72

	ATR 42-300	ATR 42-500	ATR 72-200	ATR 72-500
Length	22.67 m/74 ft 5 in	22.67 m/74 ft 5 in	27.16 m/89 ft 1 in	27.16 m/89 ft 1 in
Wingspan	24.57 m/80 ft 7 in	24.57 m/80 ft 7 in	27.06 m/88 ft 9 in	27.06 m/88 ft 9 in
Wing area	55 sq m/592 sq ft	55 sq m/592 sq ft	61 sq m/657 sq ft	61 sq m/657 sq ft
MTOW	16 700 kg/36 817 lb	18 600 kg/41 006 lb	22 000 kg/48 502 lb	22 500 kg/49 604 lb
Maximum speed	491 km/h /305 mph	556 km/h /345 mph	510 km/h /317 mph	510 km/h /317 mph
Cruising speed	470 km/h /292 mph	560 km/h /348 mph	490 km/h /304 mph	490 km/h /304 mph
Range	1150 km/715 miles	1550 km/963 miles	1400 km/870 miles	1330 km/826 miles
Service ceiling	8800 m/28 871 ft	8800 m/28 871 ft	8000 m/26 247 ft	8000 m/26 247 ft
Crew	2	2	2	2
Passengers	50	50	72	74
Engines	2	2	2	2
Maiden flight	16 August 1984	16 September 1994	27 October 1988	1 June 1997

Anton Herman Gerard Fokker, also known as Anthony Fokker, was born in the Dutch colony of Batavia (now Java, Indonesia) in 1890. He studied automotive and aviation engineering in Germany and established an aircraft factory in Schwerin. During World War I, the factory thrived. He provided Manfred von Richthofen with the fighters in which the 'Red Baron' scored his first victories. After the war, the Treaty of Versailles proscribed aircraft building in Germany. Turning to his Dutch roots, Fokker transported his entire factory to Holland by railway within the space of six weeks.

After World War II, the company started to develop passenger planes and achieved enormous success with the Fokker F-27 'Friendship', selling 786 throughout the world. Another hit was the Fokker 100, a twinjet airliner whose sales totalled 283.

However, not all was well with the company. Fokker's joint venture with VFW of Bremen resulted in sales of just 19 of the VFW 614 regional jetliner. Even a collaboration with DASA and Daimler-Benz was unable to stave off bankruptcy in 1996.

Nevertheless, many Fokker aircraft continue to fly, with maintenance services and spare parts provided by a recipient company.

FOKKER

	F-27	F-27-500	F-28-1000	F-28-4000	FOKKER 70	FOKKER 100
Length	23.5 m/77 ft 1 in	25.5 m/83 ft 8 in	27.4 m/89 ft 11 in	29.61 m/97 ft 2 in	30.91 m/101 ft 5 in	35.53 m/116 ft 7 in
Wingspan	29 m/95 ft 2 in	29 m/95 ft 2 in	23.58 m/77 ft 4 in	25.07 m/82 ft 3 in	28.08 m/92 ft 1 in	28.08 m/92 ft 1 in
Wing area	70 sq m/753 sq ft	70 sq m/753 sq ft	76.4 sq m/822 sq ft	78.97 sq m/850 sq ft	93.5 sq m/1006 sq ft	93.5 sq m/1006 sq ft
MTOW	19 050 kg/41 998 lb	20 410 kg/44 996 lb	29 485 kg/65 003 lb	33 110 kg/72 995 lb	36 740 kg/80 998 lb	45 810 kg/100 994 lb
Maximum speed	483 km/h /300 mph	480 km/h /298 mph	849 km/h /527 mph	843 km/h /524 mph	856 km/h /532 mph	845 km/h /525 mph
Cruising speed	450 km/h /280 mph	473 km/h /294 mph	820 km/h /509 mph	815 km/h /506 mph	734 km/h /456 mph	755 km/h /469 mph
Range	1468 km/912 miles	1315 km/817 miles	2090 km/1299 miles	2590 km/1609 miles	2000 km/1243 miles	3167 km/1968 miles
Service ceiling	9935 m/32 595 ft	8991 m/29 498 ft	10 675 m/35 023 ft	10 675 m/35 023 ft	10 600 m/34 777 ft	11 900 m/39 042 ft
Crew	2	2	2	2	2	2
Passengers	44	52	65	85	80	85–107
Engines	2	2	2	2	2	2
Maiden flight	24 November 1955	1 November 1957	9 May 1967	20 October 1978	1 July 1994	30 November 1986

HOW TO LAUNCH AN AIRCRAFT

How is a new aircraft developed?

Demand analysis
- What is the market?
- How many passengers?
- Range?
- Short take-off characteristics?
- Hot and high?
- Competing products?
- Usage and acceptance levels achieved by the competition?
- Popular with pilots?

Power plant and weights
- Which new materials?
- Weight savings?
- Heavy, powerful engines?
- Lighter, less powerful engines?
- Thrust/weight ratio
- Desired cruising altitude
- Maintenance and running costs

Positioning of engines
- Rear of fuselage
  - Simplified wing and flap design
  - Lower stall speed*
  - Increased airfoil lift
  - Greater bending moment
  - Stronger construction
- Beneath the wings
  - Weight reduces bending moment
  - Less efficient airflow
  - More complicated flap design

Wing design
- Dependent on payload and MTOW
  - Ideal wing area
- Take-off and landing speed
  - Wingspan

Test series
- Compromise
  - Cost effectiveness?
  - Differentiation to the competition?
  - Sales prospects?
  - Profit expectation?

* Stall speed = the speed below which an aircraft stalls due to an excessively high angle of attack relative to the airflow.

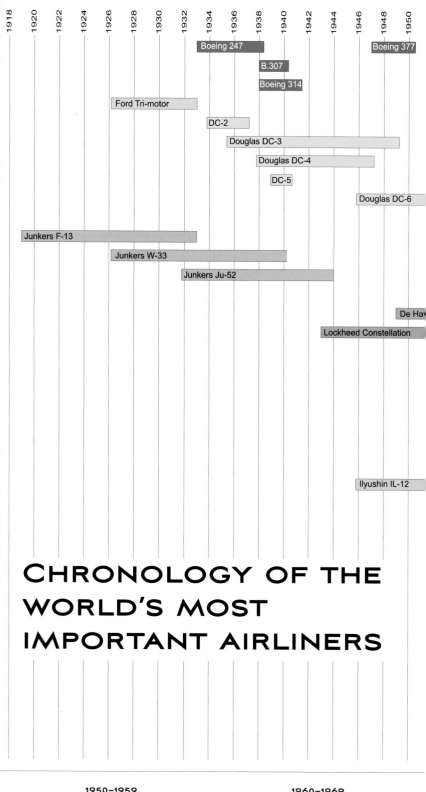

CHRONOLOGY OF THE WORLD'S MOST IMPORTANT AIRLINERS

1950–1959

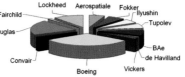

1960–1969

Boeing 720
Boeing 717

Boeing 727
McDonnell Douglas MD-11

Boeing 737 - 2016

Boeing 747 - 2014

nt
Vickers VC10
Boeing 757

Douglas DC-8
Boeing 767 - 2012

De Havilland Trident (Hawker Siddeley)
Boeing 777 - 2015

Douglas DC-9
Boeing 787

Airbus A300

Convair 880
Concorde
Airbus A310

40 Series
Douglas DC-10
Airbus A318 - 2013

le
BAC 1-11
Airbus A319 - 2014

Airbus A320 - 2017

Fokker F-28
Airbus A321 - 2015

Fokker F-27
L-1011 TriStar
Airbus A330 - 2014

ckh. Electra
Yakovlev Yak-40
Airbus A340 - 2010

Tu-104
Dornier Do328Jet
Airbus A380

upolev Tu-114
BAe-146/Avro RJ

Tupolev Tu-124
Yakovlev Yak-42

Tupolev Tu-134
Tupolev Tu-214 - 2011

Tupolev Tu-144
Tupolev Tu-204 - 2011

Tupolev Tu-154

Ilyushin IL-62

Ilyushin IL-14
Ilyushin IL-86

Ilyushin IL-18
Ilyushin IL-96 - 2010

Ilyushin IL-114 - 2010

Fokker 100 - 2019

Bombardier CRJ - 2012

ATR-42 - 2010

ATR-72 - 2012

DHC-8 - 2011

Saab 2000

Saab 340

Raytheon Beech 1900 D

Embraer EMB 110
Embraer EMB 120

Embraer ERJ - 2015

0–1979

1980–1989

1990–1999

2000–2009

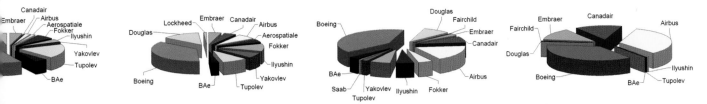

CONCORDE

To come straight to the point: Concorde is no longer flying. The star of passenger planes, which will probably remain for all time the most elegant, beautifully proportioned and fastest airliner ever to have flown passengers across the Atlantic, is now on display in various museums. However, Concorde was also loud, uneconomical and susceptible to faults. Nevertheless, were it not for the tragic accident that occurred in Paris on 25 July 2000, Concorde would probably still be flying today.

A return flight from London to New York cost almost 7,000 euros and took around 3.5 hours each way. It mattered less to the passengers that it was almost impossible to stand up straight in the plane, that the seats were narrower than the current economy class of an A320 and that there was barely enough room in the overhead lockers for their hand luggage: what mattered was the speed. Even the repeated loss of parts of the rudder or elevators over the ocean caused few public misgivings.

Production started in 1969. A total of just 20 aircraft were produced, 16 going into operation with Air France and British Airways. Over the years, the elegant bird aged imperceptibly, although on-board comfort lagged far behind what passengers could expect on a new Airbus A340 or a Boeing 777, not to mention the A380 or keenly anticipated Boeing 787.

Yet Concorde had its *raison d'être*. It allowed people to leave London or Paris in the morning for a meeting in New York or Washington – to arrive at the start of office hours and get home the same day.

Of course, it is now impossible for ordinary mortals to experience two sunrises on the same day.

CONCORDE

Length	61.66 m/202 ft 1 in
Wingspan	25.6 m/84 ft
Wing area	358 sq m/3853 sq ft
MTOW	186 800 kg/412 000 lb
Maximum speed	2330 km/h /1448 mph
Cruising speed	1320 km/h /820 mph
Range	7250 km/4505 miles
Service ceiling	18 300 m/60 039 ft
Crew	3
Passengers	100
Engines	4
Maiden flight	2 March 1969

The Active World Fleet

Seating category	Aircraft model	Seats	Classes	Manufacturer	Engines	Typical cruising speed km/h	KTS	Maximum range km	NM	Maximum take-off weight kg	lbs	Wingspan m	ft	Length m	ft	Entered service	Number produced

TURBOPROP

The turboprop category consists of narrowbody, propeller-driven regional airliners holding between 10 and 80 passengers.

Seating category	Aircraft model	Seats	Classes	Manufacturer	Engines	km/h	KTS	km	NM	kg	lbs	m	ft	m	ft	Entered service	Number produced
15–19	AN-12	14	1	ANTONOV	4	777	420	5700	3078	61000	134481	38.0	124.7	33.1	108.6	1960	835
	BE1900D	19	1	RAYTHEON	2	495	267	2900	1566	7530	16601	16.6	54.5	17.63	57.8	1982	438
	EMB110	19	1	EMBRAER	2	460	248	2000	1080	5900	13007	15.33	50.3	15.1	49.5	1972	500
20–39	AN-38	26	1	ANTONOV	2	405	219	2200	1188	8800	19400	15.67	51.4	22.06	72.4	1991	
	DHC8-100	30	1	BOMBARDIER	2	490	265	2040	1102	16465	36299	25.91	85.0	22.25	73.0	1983	291
	EMB120	30	1	EMBRAER	2	550	297	1500	810	11990	26433	19.78	64.9	20.0	65.6	1983	
40–59	ATR-42	42	1	ATR	2	490	265	5040	2721	18600	41006	24.57	80.6	22.67	74.4	1984	417
	AN-24	50	1	ANTONOV	2	500	270	2400	1296	21000	46297	29.2	95.8	25.53	83.8	1965	1114
	DHC8-300	50	1	BOMBARDIER	2	532	287	1612	870	19505	43001	27.43	90.0	25.68	84.3	1985	215
	Fokker 50	50	1	FOKKER	2	532	287	2055	1110	20820	45900	29.0	95.1	25.25	82.8	1983	205
	AN-140	52	1	ANTONOV	2	575	310	2100	1134	19150	42218	24.51	80.4	22.61	74.2	1997	32
60–79	IL-114	64	1	ILYUSHIN	2	500	270	4800	2592	23500	51808	30.0	98.4	26.88	88.2	1990	27
	ATR-72	70	1	ATR	2	526	284	2665	1439	22000	48501	27.05	88.7	27.17	89.1	1988	551
	DHC8-400	70	1	BOMBARDIER	2	648	350	2400	1296	28690	63250	28.24	92.7	32.34	106.1	1998	302

NARROWBODY JET

Narrowbody jets commonly seat four to six passengers abreast with a single, central aisle.

Seating category	Aircraft model	Seats	Classes	Manufacturer	Engines	km/h	KTS	km	NM	kg	lbs	m	ft	m	ft	Entered service	Number produced
20–39	328JET	30	1	DORNIER	2	756	408	1850	999	13990	30842	20.98	68,8	21,22	69,6	1998	113
	ERJ-135	37	1	EMBRAER	2	834	450	3138	1694	20000	44092	20.04	65.7	26.34	86,4	1998	331
40–59	ERJ-140	44	1	EMBRAER	2	834	450	3019	1630	21100	46517	20.04	65.7	28.45	93.3	2000	74
	CRJ-200	50	1	BOMBARDIER	2	860	464	3713	2005	23995	52899	21.23	69.7	26.77	87.8	1991	900
	ERJ-145	50	1	EMBRAER	2	833	450	2870	1550	22000	48501	20.04	65.7	29.87	98.0	1995	700
60–79	ERJ-170	70	1	EMBRAER	2	870	470	3889	2100	37200	82011	26.0	85.3	29.9	98.1	2002	754
	CRJ-700	78	1	BOMBARDIER	2	876	473	3676	1985	33995	74945	23.24	76.2	32.51	106.7	1999	322
	ERJ-175	78	1	EMBRAER	2	870	470	3889	2100	38790	85516	26.0	85.3	31.68	103.9	2003	178
	B737-100	85	2	BOEING	2	917	495	3440	1857	49940	110098	28.35	93.0	28.65	94.0	1967	30
	CRJ-900	86	1	BOMBARDIER	2	881	476	3660	1976	37995	83764	24.85	81.5	36.4	119.4	2001	252
80–99	BAe-146-100	94	1	BRITISH AEROSPACE	4	767	414	3000	1620	38100	83995	26.21	86.0	26.2	86.0	1982	30
	B737-200	96	2	BOEING	2	917	495	4200	2268	58100	128087	28.35	93.0	30.53	100.2	1967	982
	ERJ-190	98	1	EMBRAER	2	870	470	4260	2300	51800	114198	28.72	94.2	36.24	118.9	2004	334
	RRJ-95	98	1	SUKHOI	2	964	521	4420	2387	45880	101147	27.8	91.2	29.82	97.8	2008	
	ERJ-195	108	1	EMBRAER	2	870	470	3334	1800	52290	115279	28.72	94.2	38.65	126.8	2004	63
100–119	B737-500	103	2	BOEING	2	907	490	5200	2808	53400	117726	28.35	93.0	31.01	101.7	1990	389
	Fokker 100	103	2	FOKKER	2	845	456	3167	1710	45810	100993	28.08	92.1	35.53	116.6	1967	279
	CRJ-1000	104	1	BOMBARDIER	2	870	470	3131	1691	41050	90499	26.18	85.9	39.13	128.4	2008	24
	B717	106	2	BOEING	2	811	438	2545	1374	49899	110007	28.45	93.3	37.81	124.0	1998	156
	B737-600	108	2	BOEING	2	852	460	7200	3888	65150	143630	34.3	112.5	31.24	102.5	1998	69
	BAe-146-200	112	1	BRITISH AEROSPACE	4	767	414	2910	1571	42185	93001	26.21	86.0	28.6	93.8	1982	98
	A318	115	2	AIRBUS	2	840	454	5950	3213	68000	149913	34.1	111.9	31.45	103.2	2002	70
	BAe-146-300	116	1	BRITISH AEROSPACE	4	790	427	2817	1521	42185	93001	26.21	86.0	30.99	101.7	1981	61

Seating category	Aircraft model	Seats	Classes	Manufacturer	Engines	Typical cruising speed km/h	KTS	Maximum range km	NM	Maximum take-off weight kg	lbs	Wingspan m	ft	Length m	ft	Entered service	Number produced
120–169	B737-300	123	2	BOEING	2	907	490	4400	2376	61250	135032	28.88	94.8	33.4	109.6	1984	1114
	A319	124	2	AIRBUS	2	840	454	6800	3672	75500	166447	34.1	111.9	33.84	111.0	1996	1520
	DC-9	125	2	McDONNELL DOUGLAS	2	898	485	2880	1555	54885	120999	28.47	93.4	40.72	133.6	1965	1077
	MD-90	163		McDONNELL DOUGLAS	2	809	437	4425	2389	70760	155997	32.87	107.8	46.51	152.6	1993	117
	B737-700	128	2	BOEING	2	852	460	7630	4120	69400	152999	34.3	112.5	33.63	110.3	1997	1273
	B727-200	145	2	BOEING	2	990	535	4450	2403	95030	209503	32.92	108.0	46.49	152.5	1963	876
	B737-400	146	2	BOEING	2	907	490	5000	2700	62820	138493	28.88	94.8	36.4	119.4	1988	486
	B707-320	147	2	BOEING	2	990	535	9256	4998	116575	257001	44.42	145.7	46.61	152.9	1958	540
	A320	150	2	AIRBUS	2	840	454	5700	3078	77000	169754	34.1	111.9	37.57	123.3	1987	3245
	B737-800	162	2	BOEING	2	852	460	6650	3591	79010	174185	34.3	112.5	39.47	129.5	1998	2326
	TU-154M	164	2	TUPOLEV	3	950	513	4000	2160	100000	220460	37.55	123.2	47.9	157.2	1968	921
170–229	B737-900	177	2	BOEING	2	852	460	6660	3596	79016	174199	34.3	112.5	42.11	138.2	2001	279
	B757-200	178	2	BOEING	2	900	486	7870	4249	115665	254995	38.05	124.8	47.32	155.2	1982	997
	A321	180	2	AIRBUS	2	840	454	5600	3024	93500	206130	34.1	111.9	44.51	146.0	1994	664
	DC-8	189	2	DOUGLAS	2	887	479	8950	4833	162025	357200	45.23	148.4	57.12	187.4	1959	556
	TU-204-100	212	2	TUPOLEV	2	850	459	6500	3510	103000	227074	42.0	137.8	46.0	150.9	1989	26

WIDEBODY JET

In economy class, widebody jets generally have rows of seven to ten seats with twin aisles.

Seating category	Aircraft model	Seats	Classes	Manufacturer	Engines	Typical cruising speed km/h	KTS	Maximum range km	NM	Maximum take-off weight kg	lbs	Wingspan m	ft	Length m	ft	Entered service	Number produced
230–309	B767-200/ 200ER	181	3	BOEING	2	851	460	12223	6600	179170	394998	47.6	156,2	48.5	159,1	1981	250
	B767-300/ 300ER	218	3	BOEING	2	851	460	11306	6105	186880	411996	47.6	156,2	54.9	180.1	1986	724
	A310-300	220	3	AIRBUS	2	897	484	9580	5173	157000	346122	43.9	144.0	46.66	153.1	1983	170
	A300-600	231	3	AIRBUS	2	890	481	6968	3762	165000	363759	44.84	147.1	54.08	177.4	1984	317
	B757-300	240	3	BOEING	2	989	534	6455	3485	122470	269997	38.05	124.8	54.47	178.7	1999	55
	B767-400ER	245	3	BOEING	2	851	460	10454	5645	204120	450003	51.9	170.3	61.4	201.4	1999	37
	DC-10 (MD-10)	250	2	McDONNELL DOUGLAS	3	982	530	12055	6509	263085	579997	50.4	165.4	55.5	182.1	1971	446
	A330-200	256	3	AIRBUS	2	913	493	12500	6749	230000	507058	60.3	197.8	45.0	147.6	1998	461
	L-1011	256	2	LOCKHEED	2	973	525	6820	3683	211375	465997	47.34	155.3	54.17	177.7	1970	200
	A350-900	285	3	AIRBUS	2	900	486	13890	7500	245100	540347	61.1	200.5	65.2	213.9	2012	169
	A330-300	295	3	AIRBUS	2	989	534	10500	5670	230000	507058	60.3	197.8	63.6	208.7	1993	347
	MD-11(ER)(P)	298	2	McDONNELL DOUGLAS	3	945	510	13408	7240	285989	630491	51.66	169.5	61.21	200.8	1990	33
	B787	296	2	BOEING	2	993	536	15200	8207	233000	513672	58.8	192.9	55.5	182,1	2009	
310–399	A340-300	295	3	AIRBUS	4	880	475	13350	7208	271000	597447	60.3	197.8	63.6	208.7	1992	219
	B777-200/ER	305	3	BOEING	2	896	484	14300	7721	297560	656001	60.9	199.8	63.7	209.0	1995	568
	A340-500	313	3	AIRBUS	4	905	489	16050	8666	368000	811293	60.3	197.8	67.9	222.8	2003	33
	B777-300/ER	368	3	BOEING	2	896	484	11029	5955	297560	656001	60.9	199.8	73.9	242.5	1998	347
	A340-600	380	3	AIRBUS	4	905	489	13900	7505	368000	811293	63.45	208.2	75.3	247.0	2001	103
400–499	B747-400/ER	416	3	BOEING	4	913	493	14205	7670	412775	910004	64.4	211.3	70.6	231.6	1988	528
	B747-8	430	3	BOEING	4	920	497	14815	7999	439985	969991	68.5	224.7	76.4	250.7	2009	21
Over 500	A380-800	555	3	AIRBUS	4	995	537	15200	8207	560000	1234576	79.8	261.8	73.0	239.5	2008	187
																	32368

This table covers only the main aircraft types.

The World's Commercial Airports

Airports of the World

There are an estimated 49,000 airports throughout the world, handling some 40 million commercial flights a year. This equates to an average of around two flights per day per airport. However, a front-runner like Atlanta handles nearly a million flights each year – the equivalent of nearly 3,000 flights a day, or two to three flights per minute. Bringing up the rear of the table of statistics for the major intercontinental passenger airports are Montreal's Mirabel Airport, a prime example of bad planning, and the Easter Island airport, each of which handle just one or two flights a day.

The earliest airports were built close to city centres. They often have difficult landing procedures, such as Hong Kong's Kai Tak Airport, and are a source of significant noise pollution for the local residents. By the 1980s, if not before, these old airports were starting to reach capacity. Today's major airports are generally built at a certain distance from the cities they serve, on enormous sites offering potential for rapid expansion. Their architecture is often breathtaking, as is the design and construction of the runways, which are more and more frequently built on land reclaimed from the sea.

Where do Airports Get Their Names?

Originally, airports took their names from their location. Currently, there is an increasing trend for (important) personalities to be honoured in the names of airports, although aviation pioneers are not well represented. The Wright brothers have lent their name to a small airport in Dayton, Ohio, while San Diego's airport is named after Lindbergh. Elly Beinhorn and the Montgolfier brothers remain unrecognized, while the Australian aviation pioneer Kingford Smith (Sydney) and the relatively unknown naval airman O'Hare (Chicago) have been immortalized.

Galileo and Copernicus have given their names to the airports of Pisa, Italy, and Wroclaw, Poland, respectively, and Leonardo da Vinci has lent his to Rome's Fiumicino airport.

Writers and thinkers are thin on the ground, with no airports as yet named after Shakespeare, Dickens or Victor Hugo, and musicians are doing little better. There is John Lennon in Liverpool, Wolfgang Amadeus Mozart in Salzburg, Chopin in Warsaw and Louis Armstrong in New Orleans, but Bach, Beethoven, Handel and Vivaldi are still absent from the arrival and departure boards. Philosophers and natural scientists are faring no better.

British Airways' intercontinental network showing routes to the world's major conurbations.

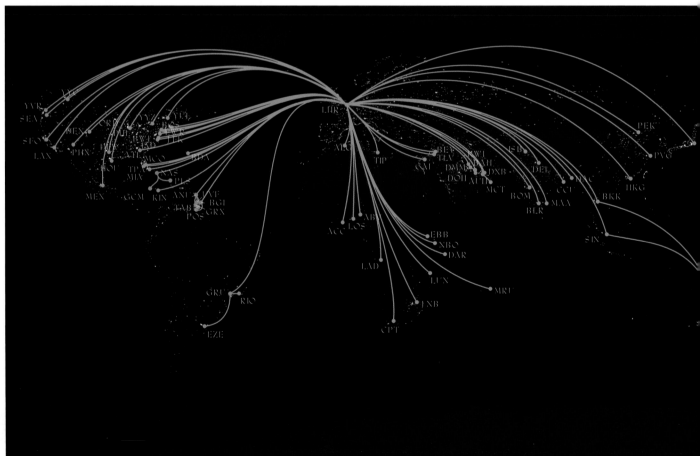

The few film stars that have made it include John Wayne (Orange County, California) and Ronald Reagan (Washington DC), the latter probably in his capacity as president rather than as an actor.

The reason for this is that airports are the province of local politicians. How many passengers have ever heard of Mayors Hartsfield and Jackson, who gave their names to Atlanta Airport? Or Ebert Douglas, Senator McCarran and Franz Josef Strauß, former minister-president of Bavaria, who have given their names to airports in Charlotte in North Carolina, Las Vegas and Munich respectively?

For national leaders, the outlook is varied. There is (understandably) no Stalin Airport, but there is no Winston Churchill Airport either. F. D. Roosevelt has lent his name only to a mini-airport in the Netherlands Antilles, while Charles de Gaulle airport in Paris is now better known than General Charles de Gaulle, after whom it is named.

In America, it would seem to be easier for Republican presidents to be honoured by the world of aviation than it is for Democrat presidents. George Bush Senior basks in the limelight in Houston, but Jimmy Carter and Bill Clinton are still in the holding pattern.

Sometimes name changes are brought about by evolving political situations. In South Africa, the apartheid politician Jan Smuts has given way to Oliver Tambo in Johannesburg.

However, there is a new idea on the table. Like football stadia, airports could rent out their names. A stadium with 1.6 million visitors per year earns some five million euros in advertising revenue – around three euros per visitor. So let's wait and see what the future brings.

Rank	Country	City (airport)	Airport name	Total passengers	Origin of the name
1	USA	ATLANTA GA	Hartsfield-Jackson	90039280	Named after two former mayors of Atlanta.
2	USA	CHICAGO IL	O'Hare	69353876	Named after an American World War II flying ace.
3	UK	LONDON	Heathrow	67056379	Named after the village of Hetherow, as recorded in 1675.
4	Japan	TOKYO	Narita	66754829	Named after the city of Narita, which has 90,000 inhabitants.
5	France	PARIS	Charles de Gaulle	60874681	Named after General Charles de Gaulle.
6	USA	LOS ANGELES CA	Los Angeles International	59497539	
7	USA	DALLAS/FORT WORTH TX	Dallas Fort Worth	57093187	
8	China	BEIJING	Capital Airport	55937289	
9	Germany	FRANKFURT	Rhein-Main Airport	53467450	The airport lies at the confluence of the Rhine and Main rivers.
10	USA	DENVER CO	Denver International	51245334	
11	Spain	MADRID	Madrid Barajas	50824435	Named after the nearby town Barajas.
12	China	HONG KONG	Chek Lap Kok	47857746	Name of the island on which the airport was built.
13	USA	NEW YORK NY	JFK	47807816	Named after the assassinated president John Fitzgerald Kennedy.
14	Netherlands	AMSTERDAM	Schiphol	47430019	Prior to the land reclamation, there was a bay here. A number of shipping disasters led to the place name 'Ship Hole'.
15	USA	LAS VEGAS NV	McCarran	43208724	Named after Senator McCarran.
16	USA	HOUSTON TX	George Bush Intercontinental	41709389	Named after president George Bush Senior.
17	USA	PHOENIX AZ	Sky Harbor	39891193	The United States has five airports with the same name.
18	Thailand	BANGKOK	Suvarnabhumi	38603490	Named in memory of the golden kingdom of Suvarnabhumi.
19	Singapore	SINGAPORE	Changi	37694824	Name of the region.
20	UAE	DUBAI	Dubai International	37441440	
21	USA	SAN FRANCISCO CA	San Francisco International	37234592	
22	USA	ORLANDO FL	Orlando International	35660742	
23	USA	NEWARK NJ	Liberty International	35360848	Named in response to the terrorist attacks of 11 September 2001.
24	USA	DETROIT MI	Metropolitan Wayne County	35135828	Named after the county in which it is located.
25	Italy	ROME	Leonardo da Vinci	35132224	Named after the great scientist and artist.
26	USA	CHARLOTTE NC	Douglas International	34739020	Named after mayor Ben Elbert Douglas.
27	Germany	MUNICH	Franz Josef Strauß Airport	34530593	Long-serving minister-president of Bavaria.
28	UK	LONDON	Gatwick	34214740	In 1241 a goat farm stood on the site. The name is derived from 'goat wik'.
29	USA	MIAMI FL	Miami International	34063531	
30	USA	MINNEAPOLIS MN	Minneapolis-Saint Paul International	34056443	

Country	IATA	ICAO	Airport Name	Pax (2008)	Terminals	Runways	Longest Runway m	ft	Opening
Canada									
	YEG	CYEG	**Edmonton** International Airport	6 437 334	2	2	3353	11001	1960
	YHZ	CYHZ	**Halifax** Stanfield International	3 578 931	1	2	2682	8799	1942
	YLW	CYLW	**Kelowna** International	1 389 883	1	1	2713	8901	1946
	YMX	CYMX	**Montreal**-Mirabel International	200 000	1	1	3658	12001	1975
	YOW	CYOW	**Ottawa** Macdonald-Cartier International	4 339 225	2	3	3050	10007	1950
	YQB	CYQB	**Quebec** Jean Lesage International	1 026 090	1	2	2743	8999	1939
	YQR	CYQR	**Regina** International	1 005 270	1	2	2408	7900	1930
	YQT	CYQT	**Thunder Bay** International	626 351	1	2	1890	6201	1939
	YQX	CYQX	**Gander** International	n/a	1	3	3109	10200	1938
	YUL	CYUL	**Montreal**-Trudeau International	12 813 199	3	3	3353	11001	1941
	YVR	CYVR	**Vancouver** International	17 852 459	4	4	3505	11499	1930
	YWG	CYWG	**Winnipeg** James Armstrong Richardson International	3 570 033	1	2	3353	11001	1928
	YXE	CYXE	**Saskatoon** John G. Diefenbaker International	1 135 113	2	2	2530	8301	1929
	YXS	CYXS	**Prince George**	417 484	1	3	3490	11450	1941
	YXU	CYXU	**London** International	449 745	1	2	2682	8799	1939
	YXY	CYXY	Erik Nielsen **Whitehorse** International	n/a	1	3	2895	9498	n/a
	YYC	CYYC	**Calgary** International Airport	12 500 000	1	3	3863	12674	1939
	YYJ	CYYJ	**Victoria** International	1 538 417	1	3	2134	7001	1914
	YYZ	CYYZ	**Toronto** Pearson International	32 334 831	3	5	3389	11119	1939
USA									
	ABQ	KABQ	**Albuquerque** International Sunport	6 467 263	1	4	3048	10000	1939
	ALB	KALB	**Albany** International	3 100 000	1	2	2591	8501	1910
	ANC	PANC	Ted Stevens **Anchorage** International	523 500	2	3	3531	11585	1951
	ATL	KATL	Hartsfield-Jackson **Atlanta** International	90 039 280	2	5	3624	11890	1926
	AUS	KAUS	**Austin**-Bergstrom International	8 261 310	1	2	3733	12247	1999
	BHM	KBHM	**Birmingham**-Shuttlesworth International	322 689	1	2	3658	12001	1931
	BNA	KBNA	**Nashville** International (Berry Field)	10 000 000	1	4	3362	11030	1937
	BOI	KBOI	**Boise**	3 158 000	1	2	3048	10000	1926
	BOS	KBOS	Gen. Edward Lawrence Logan International **(Boston)**	26 102 651	4	6	3073	10082	1923
	BUF	KBUF	**Buffalo** Niagara International	5 526 301	2	2	2690	8825	1926
	BUR	KBUR	Bob Hope **(Burbank)**	6 000 000	1	2	2099	6886	1930
	BWI	KBWI	Thurgood Marshall **(Baltimore-Washington)**	20 488 881	1	4	3201	10502	1947
	CLE	KCLE	**Cleveland**-Hopkins International	11 106 194	1	3	3034	9954	1925
	CLT	KCLT	**Charlotte**/Douglas International	34 732 584	2	4	3048	10000	1936
	CMH	KCMH	**Port Columbus** International	7 719 000	1	2	3086	10125	1929
	CVG	KCVG	**Cincinnati**/Northern Kentucky International	17 000 000	3	4	3658	12001	1947
	DAL	KDAL	**Dallas** Love Field	7 500 000	2	3	2682	8799	1917
	DCA	KDCA	Ronald Reagan **Washington** National	18 600 000	3	3	6869	22536	1941
	DEN	KDEN	**Denver** International	51 435 575	1	6	4877	16001	1995
	DFW	KDFW	**Dallas**-Fort Worth International	57 093 000	5	7	4085	13402	1953
	DTW	KDTW	Coleman A. Young International **(Detroit)**	35 144 841	4	6	3659	12005	1929
	ELP	KELP	**El Paso** International	3 302 764	1	3	3664	12021	1929
	EWR	KEWR	**Newark** Liberty International	35 299 719	3	3	3353	11001	1928
	FLL	KFLL	**Fort Lauderdale**-Hollywood International	22 621 500	6	3	2743	8999	1953
	GEG	KGEG	**Spokane** International (Geiger Field)	3 400 000	1	2	2744	9003	1941
	HNL	PHNL	**Honolulu** International	21 505 855	3	6	3749	12300	1927
	HOU	KHOU	William P. Hobby **(Houston)**	9 000 000	1	4	2317	7602	1927
	IAD	KIAD	**Washington** Dulles International	23 876 780	3	5	3505	11499	1962
	IAH	KIAH	George Bush Intercontinental **(Houston)**	41 698 832	5	5	3658	12001	1969
	IND	KIND	**Indianapolis** International	8 150 000	1	3	3414	11201	1931
	JAX	KJAX	**Jacksonville** International	6 002 698	1	2	3048	10000	1968
	JFK	KJFK	John F. Kennedy International **(New York)**	47 790 485	8	4	4442	14573	1942
	KOA	PHKO	**Kona** International	3 216 642	1	1	3353	11001	1970
	LAS	KLAS	McCarran International **Las Vegas**	44 074 707	3	4	4423	14511	1942
	LAX	KLAX	**Los Angeles** International	59 542 151	9	4	3685	12090	1930
	LGA	KLGA	La Guardia **(New York)**	25 300 000	4	2	2135	7005	1929
	LIH	PHLI	**Lihue** (Lihu'e)	2 955 394	1	2	1981	6499	1949
	MCI	KMCI	**Kansas City** International	10 469 892	3	3	3292	10801	1956
	MCO	KMCO	**Orlando** International	35 622 252	4	4	3659	12005	1974
	MDW	KMDW	**Chicago** Midway International	18 868 388	1	5	1988	6522	1923
	MEM	KMEM	**Memphis** International	10 532 095	1	4	3389	11119	1929
	MHT	KMHT	**Manchester**-Boston Regional	4 100 000	1	2	2819	9249	1927
	MIA	KMIA	**Miami** International	34 063 531	1	4	3962	12999	1928

USA/CANADA

⊛ *intercontinental airports*

MKE	KMKE	General Mitchell International **(Milwaukee)**	7 956 968	1	5	3258	10 689	1920
MSP	KMSP	Minneapolis-St. Paul International	34 056 443	2	4	3354	11 004	1921
MSY	KMSY	Louis Armstrong **New Orleans** International	7 944 397	1	3	3080	10 105	1910
OAK	KOAK	Metropolitan **Oakland** International	11 500 000	2	4	3048	10 000	1928
OGG	PHOG	**Kahului**	6 517 710	1	2	2132	6995	1919
OKC	KOKC	Will Rogers World **(Oklahoma City)**	3 740 000	1	4	2988	9803	1930
OMA	KOMA	Eppley Airfield **(Omaha)**	4 300 000	1	3	2896	9501	1959
ONT	KONT	**Ontario** International	6 200 000	3	2	3718	12 198	1923
ORD	KORD	**Chicago** O'Hare International	69 353 654	5	7	3962	12 999	1943
ORF	KORF	**Norfolk** International	3 800 000	1	2	2744	9003	1920
PBI	KPBI	**Palm Beach** International	6 476 303	1	3	3050	10 007	1936
PDX	KPDX	**Portland** International	14 654 222	1	3	3353	11 001	1940
PHL	KPHL	**Philadelphia** International	31 768 000	7	4	3202	10 505	1925
PHX	KPHX	**Phoenix** Sky Harbor International	39 891 193	4	3	3139	10 299	1930
PIT	KPIT	**Pittsburgh** International	8 710 291	2	4	3505	11 499	1923
PVD	KPVD	Theodore Francis Green State **(Providence)**	4 692 974	1	2	2184	7165	1931
RDU	KRDU	**Raleigh**-Durham International	10 000 000	2	3	3048	10 000	1929
RIC	KRIC	**Richmond** International	3 634 544	1	3	2744	9003	1927
RNO	KRNO	**Reno**-Tahoe International	4 430 000	1	3	3353	11 001	1929
RSW	KRSW	Southwest Florida International **(Fort Myers)**	7 603 845	1	2	3658	12 001	1973
SAN	KSAN	**San Diego** International	18 125 633	3	1	2865	9400	1928
SAT	KSAT	**San Antonio** International	8 031 405	2	3	2591	8501	1941
SDF	KSDF	**Louisville** International (Standiford Field)	4 000 000	1	3	3624	11 890	1941
SEA	KSEA	**Seattle**-Tacoma International	32 196 528	3	3	3627	11 900	1944
SFO	KSFO	**San Francisco** International	37 405 467	4	4	3618	11 870	1927
SJC	KSJC	Norman Y. Mineta **San José** International	9 717 717	3	3	3353	11 001	1940
SLC	KSLC	**Salt Lake City** International	20 790 400	2	4	3659	12 005	1911
SMF	KSMF	**Sacramento** International	10 400 000	4	2	2622	8602	1967
SNA	KSNA	John Wayne – Orange County **(Santa Ana)**	8 989 603	2	2	1738	5702	1923
STL	KSTL	Lambert-**St. Louis** International	14 431 471	2	4	3359	11 020	1920
TPA	KTPA	**Tampa** International	18 867 541	1	3	3353	11 001	1914
TUL	KTUL	**Tulsa** International	3 261 560	1	3	3048	10 000	1928
TUS	KTUS	**Tucson** International	4 429 905	2	3	3352	10 997	1919

ANCHORAGE ANC

ANCHORAGE

During the Cold War, Anchorage was a busy transfer hub for passengers bound for the Far East. The shortest route from Europe to East Asia was via the Soviet Union, which refused to grant overflying rights. The roundabout route via South East Asia meant up to 24 hours flying time and the Aeroflot option (hated by business travellers at that time) meant spending a night in Moscow's airport hotel. The best alternative was to fly via Alaska, for which the airlines charged handsomely. This particular source of income dried up in the 1990s. Today the airport is counting on new connections with Sakhalin and commodity-rich Siberia.

CALGARY

One of the eight Canadian airports with US border preclearance. This allows US passport control and customs to be located at a small number of airports in the country of departure rather than at each of the hundreds of airports in America. The United States also operates this system in Ireland, the Bahamas and Bermuda.

CALGARY YYC

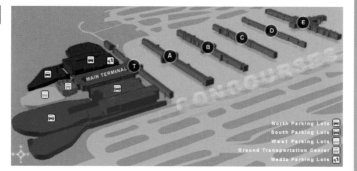
ATLANTA ATL

ATLANTA HARTSFIELD-JACKSON AIRPORT

Hartsfield-Jackson Airport has six concourses, 176 gates and is the world's biggest and busiest airport. It handles nearly a million flights per year and offers waiting passengers a bewildering array of entertainment. In spite of this, between December 2006 and March 2007, 30 people, including a number of well-known figures, were arrested for 'indecent exposure involving reported sex acts in airport bathrooms'. It boasts a highly efficient transport system.

BOSTON

Enjoying a spectacular peninsula location, Boston is New England's most important airport. Nobody could have imagined that from this aeronautical haven two airliners bound for Los Angeles would be hijacked and shortly afterwards destroy the World Trade Center.

BOSTON BOS

CHICAGO O'HARE

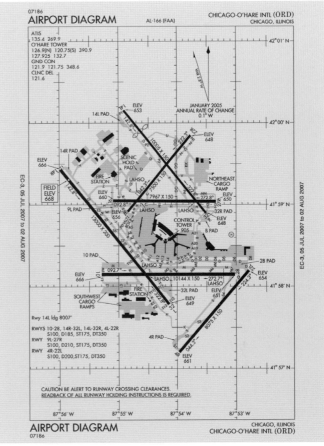

For the last ten years, passengers have voted the main airport of the 'Windy City' (so named because of political, rather than meteorological, turbulence) 'best airport in North America' . Nevertheless, delays are not infrequent at United Airlines' main hub. Six billion dollars and four new runways (bringing the total to 11) should help raise O'Hare's capacity to over 100 million passengers per year .

CHICAGO ORD

DALLAS FORT WORTH

In terms of area, DFW is the world's second-largest airport. It is also like a city in its own right (DFW Airport, TX) with its own postcode and public services. It opened in 1974 as the most expensive commercial airport in the world. DFW benefited from the controversial Wright Amendment of 1979, which drastically curtailed the range of flights allowed to take off from competing Love Field, the base of American Airlines.

VANCOUVER YVR

VANCOUVER

Vancouver owes its airport to Charles Lindbergh. In 1927, the aviation pioneer refused to fly to the city because of its lack of an adequate airport. Construction began two years later.

On 11 September 2001, numerous intercontinental flights had to be diverted to Canada (Operation Yellow Ribbon). Virtually all the flights arriving from Asia had to land in Vancouver because nowhere else on Canada's west coast had a suitable runway.

DALLAS/FORT WORTH DFW

NEW YORK
JOHN F. KENNEDY

Originally inaugurated in 1948, the airport was renamed in 1963 after the assassination of the US president in Dallas. Ever since, JFK has been synonymous with the glamour of international air travel. It might be said that those who travel to New York via JFK are entering the city through the front door, whereas Newark (until 1980 busier than JFK) is more of a tradesmen's entrance. JFK adorns the route map of almost every international airline of renown. It handles less than half the number of flights that Atlanta does, but it has plenty of flair.

JFK also leads the way where architecture is concerned. Skidmore, Owings & Merrill (Sears Tower, Jin Mao Tower) were responsible for the arrivals hall, while the TWA terminal was the work of Finn Eero Saarinen.

Around a million travellers enjoyed the experience of arriving in New York by Concorde. Indeed London–JFK and Paris–JFK proved to be the supersonic jet's only profitable routes.

The Mafia has also been fascinated by JFK. In 1978, a heist on a Lufthansa cargo terminal yielded the sum of 5 million dollars. When it came to dividing up the spoils, those involved had differing ideas and by 1984, 13 members of the Mafia had been liquidated by the Lucchese clan. The story later featured in a film (Goodfellas) by Martin Scorsese.

A dozen serious crashes have overshadowed the history of the airport.

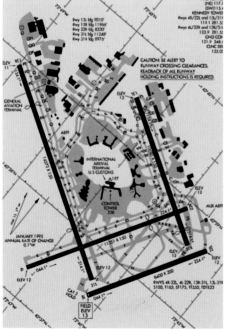

NEW YORK JFK

LAX
LOS ANGELES
INTERNATIONAL

This gateway to the movie metropolis possesses a spectacular architectonic landmark in the form of the Theme Building, a flying saucer in the Populux style of the 1960s. Due to enormous

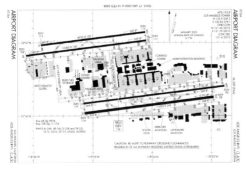

running costs, its 360 degree revolving restaurant ceased to turn shortly after it opened in 1961. In 1997 the interior was lavishly redesigned by Disney Engineering. Sadly, the rooftop viewing platform was closed for security reasons after the terrorist attacks of 11 September 2001.

The X in LAX has no real significance. Originally, airport codes consisted of two rather than three letters. When a third letter was needed, the X was simply tacked onto the end.

LOS ANGELES LAX

LOS ANGELES LAX

SAN
FRANCISCO
INTERNATIONAL

The positioning of SFO's two parallel runways, with less than 250 m/820 ft between them, is not unproblematic. Often during bad weather only one runway can be used, which can cause lengthy delays. For this reason many low-cost airlines have

switched to other airports in the surrounding region. A further extension to the airport in San Francisco Bay is in the pipeline, but to date plans have failed due to the opposition of environmentalists.

SAN FRANCISCO SFO

SAN FRANCISCO SFO

SAN FRANCISCO INTERNATIONAL

MIAMI MIA

MIAMI INTERNATIONAL

From Panama to Sao Paulo via Miami. For a long time MIA was a transfer hub for travellers in Central or South America. Very often, passengers wanting to make this journey were forced to make a 1,610-km/1,000-mile detour via Miami in the north. More recently, though, flight connections in the southern part of the continent have improved.

Following the terrorist attacks of 11 September 2001, visa requirements have been substantially tightened for those travelling to the United States. As a result, many European airlines have also moved their hubs away from Miami, whose importance as an international airport has declined considerably.

PHOENIX

An important transfer hub in Arizona. Owing to the stable weather conditions, Phoenix is one of the largest airports in the world to have parallel runways only.

PHOENIX PHX

TORONTO

The biggest airport in Canada was opened in 1939. After its expansion in 1960 as Toronto International Airport, it quickly became the most important airport in the country. Yet even today there is still no train connection between the city and the airport – a fact that apparently will be altered in the near future.

This huge airport appears again and again throughout aviation history. In 1980, a DC-8 broke up during a failed attempt at a go-around. In 1985, a suitcase bomb was loaded in Toronto onto an Air India Boeing 747, which then exploded over the Atlantic, killing 329 people. In 2001, Air Transat Flight 236 to Lisbon took off here, only to suffer a

TORONTO YYZ

fuel leak on the way; after the longest flight with no power in history, it landed safely in the Azores. Finally, in 2005, an A340 overshot the runway in wet conditions and burst into flames. All 309 people on board evacuated the plane via the emergency chutes and escaped unharmed.

TORONTO YYZ

WASHINGTON DULLES

The main terminal building is another masterpiece by Eero Saarinen and was subsequently copied at Taiwan Taoyuan International Airport, Taiwan. Now an important international airport, in the 1960s and 1970s there was only a handful of destinations IAD could profitably serve, due to its inconvenient location 42 km/26 miles from the city centre. Back then, it was regarded by the people of Washington as a white elephant.

WASHINGTON DULLES IAD

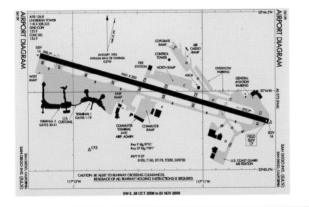

SAN DIEGO

With one runway in the heart of the city, serving nearly 20 million passengers per year, San Diego is the United States' busiest single-runway airport. However, planes are only allowed to take off and land between 6.30 am and 11.30 pm. With around 230,000 flight movements a year, this means a plane takes off or lands every 98 seconds. Passengers are astonished to see aircraft landing in such close succession.

In 1978, there was a serious collision (which was filmed) between an approaching Boeing 727 and a small Cessna. Tragically, 144 people lost their lives.

SAN DIEGO
SAN

Miami International Airport is one of the most important hubs in the southeast of the United States. It is also the gateway to the Caribbean from the United States.

SEATTLE

Seattle-Tacoma International Airport is located 19 km/ 12 miles south of Seattle and 19 km/12 miles north of Tacoma. It was expanded into an intercontinental airport for the 1962 World's Fair. The city of Tacoma contributed 100,000 dollars to its cost on condition that its name be linked forever with the airport. When, in 1983, the airport was due to be renamed after the deceased senator Henry Jackson, the citizens of Tacoma regarded this as an affront and initiated a successful court action to prevent the name change.

SEATTLE SEA

DENVER DEN

DENVER

Denver airport is constructed on 'eternal hunting grounds' where the local Native Americans buried their dead. Out of a desire not to hold up progress, a compromise was agreed upon whereby Native American funerary music is played 24 hours a day on the bridge linking the two terminals. The 34 pinnacles of the coated canvas roof are reminiscent of tepees or the Rocky Mountains.

Covering some 140 sq km/54 sq miles, Denver is the largest airport in the United States by area. It possesses a solar farm that can generate up to 3.5 million kilowatt hours of energy per year, saving over 2,000 tonnes of CO_2 emissions. Located at an altitude of 1,600 m/5,249 ft, the airport also boasts the longest runway in the United States. This allows fully laden jumbos and A380s to take off and land in the thinner air, even in the summer months.

LAS VEGAS LAS

LAS VEGAS MCCARRAN

Some 44 million gamblers a year can begin their Vegas experience on the airport's one-armed bandits. Whether the turnover from the 1,300 or so gaming machines of 'Michael Gaughan Airport Slots' is higher than that of the airport itself (not unlikely) could not be ascertained.

DETROIT

Detroit was the main hub of Northwest Airlines, which had its own terminal (the Edward McNamara terminal) here. The *ExpressTram* conveys passengers through the 1.6-km/1-mile long building.

The underground *Light Tunnel* links the two concourses.

Detroit was the scheduled final destination of Pan Am Flight 103, which was blown up over Lockerbie in Scotland in 1988. It was also the scene of an attempted bombing in December 2009.

EDMONTON YEG

DETROIT DTW

EDMONTON

Like many Canadian airports, Edmonton has a United States preclearance facility, meaning that United States customs are cleared by passengers prior to departure from Canada. This allows the aircraft and its passengers to be treated as a domestic flight upon arrival in the United States. For Canadian Airlines, this offers the advantage that it is not restricted to United States customs airports but can fly to other destinations too.

HONOLULU

Honolulu International is one of the United States' busiest airports and has four runways. The first, known as the Reef Runway, was the world's first offshore runway. Today, A380s and 747s can also land here. In addition, there are two water runways for seaplanes.

In 1988, Aloha Airlines Flight 243, with 95 passengers on board, was making the short flight from Hilo, Hawaii, to Honolulu. At a height of 7,500 m/24,000 ft a small section of the fuselage roof ruptured due to metal fatigue. The sudden decompression caused the hole to grow to a length of 5.5 m/18 ft, leaving six rows of seats completely exposed. Despite this, the 737 managed to land safely. A flight attendant was sucked out of the aircraft but all of the passengers survived. Pictures of the damaged aircraft were shown around the world.

HONOLULU HNL

HONOLULU HNL

The so-called Aloha Airlines 'cabrio' was one of the most dramatic incidents in the history of aviation. Even the pilots could not believe their eyes when they stepped into the cabin after landing.

Country	IATA	ICAO	Airport Name	Pax (2008)	Terminals	Runways	Longest Runway m	Longest Runway ft	Opening
Mexico & Central America									
Belize									
	BZE	MZBZ	Philip S.W.Goldson International (Belize)	n/a	1	1	2957	9701	n/a
Costa Rica									
	SJO	MROC	Juan Santamaría International (San José)	3300000	3	1	3012	9882	1923
El Salvador									
	SAL	MSLP	Cuscatlan International (San Salvador)	2000000	1	2	3200	10499	1976
Guatemala									
	GUA	MGGT	La Aurora International (Guatemala City)	n/a	2	1	3000	9843	1944
Honduras									
	TGU	MHTG	Toncontin International (Tegucigalpa)	n/a	1	1	2163	7096	1921
Mexico									
	ACA	MMAA	General Juan N. Álvarez International (Acapulco)	1088000	1	2	3302	10833	n/a
	CUN	MMUN	**Cancún** International	12646451	3	2	3500	11483	n/a
	CZM	MMCZ	**Cozumel** International	511043	1	2	3098	10164	n/a
	GDL	MMGL	Don Miguel Hidalgo y Costilla International (Guadalajara)	7193200	2	2	4000	13123	1966
	MEX	MMMX	**Mexico City** International	26210217	2	2	3952	12966	n/a
	MID	MMMD	Manuel Crescencio Rejón International (Mérida)	1000000	1	2	3200	10499	n/a
	MZT	MMMZ	General Rafael Buelna International (Mazatlàn)	819200	1	1	2700	8858	n/a
	NTR	MMAN	General Mariano Escobedo International (Monterrey)	5250000	3	2	3000	9843	n/a
	PVR	MMPR	Licenciado Gustavo Díaz Ordaz Int (Puerto Vallarta)	3139100	2	1	3100	10171	n/a
	SJD	MMSD	**Los Cabos** International (San José del Cabo)	2901200	4	1	3000	9843	n/a
	TIJ	MMTJ	General Abelardo L. Rodríguez International (Tijuana)	3968700	2	1	2960	9711	n/a
Nicaragua									
	MGA	MNMG	Augusto Sandino International (Managua)	n/a	1	1	2442	8012	1968
Panama									
	PTY	MPTO	Tocumen International (Panama City)	4549170	1	2	3050	10007	1947
Caribbean Islands & Bermuda									
Antigua & Barbuda									
	ANU	TAPA	**St. John's** V.C. Bird International, Antigua	1100000	1	1	2744	9003	1949
Bahamas									
	FPO	MYGF	Grand Bahama International Airport (Freeport)	n/a	1	1	3359	11020	n/a
	NAS	MYNN	Lynden Pindling International Airport (Nassau)	n/a	1	2	3358	11017	n/a
Barbados									
	BGI	TBPB	**Bridgetown** Adams International, Barbados	n/a	2	1	3361	11027	1939
Bermuda									
	BDA	TXKF	L.F. Wade International Airport (Hamilton)	1000000	1	1	2961	9715	1948
Cayman Islands									
	GCM	MWCR	**Cayman** Owen Roberts International	n/a	1	1	2139	7018	1954
Cuba									
	HAV	MUHA	José Martí International Airport (Havana)	3471920	5	1	4000	13123	1930
	VRA	MUVR	Juan Gualberto Gómez Airport (Varadero)	n/a	1	1	3502	11490	1989
Dominican Republic									
	POP	MDPP	Gregoria Luperon International (Puerto Plata)	1600000	1	1	3081	10108	n/a
	PUJ	MDPC	**Punta Cana** International	3500000	1	1	3100	10171	n/a
	SDQ	MDSD	Las Américas International (Santo Domingo)	3500000	3	1	3355	11007	1959
Haiti									
	PAP	MTPP	Toussaint Louverture **Port-au-Prince** International	n/a	1	1	3040	9974	1965
Jamaica									
	KIN	MKJP	Norman Manley **Kingston** International	1730000	1	1	2713	8901	n/a
	MBJ	MKJS	**Montego Bay** Sangster International	3378000	1	1	2662	8734	1947
Martinique									
	FDF	TFFF	Martinique Aimé Césaire International (Fort-de-France)	n/a	1	1	3300	10827	1950
	PTP	TFFR	Pointe-à-Pitre International (Guadalupe)	2500000	1	1	3505	11499	n/a
Netherlands Antilles									
	AUA	TNCA	Queen Beatrix International (Aruba)	n/a	1	1	2814	9232	1933
	BON	TNCB	Flamingo International (Bonaire)	650000	1	1	2880	9449	1936
	CUR	TNCC	Hato International (Curaçao)	n/a	1	1	3410	11188	1945
Puerto Rico									
	SJU	TJSJ	Luis Muñoz Marín International (San Juan)	10500000	2	2	3049	10003	1955
Saint Martin									
	SXM	TNCM	Princess Juliana International (St. Maarten)	1662226	1	1	2180	7152	1943
Trinidad & Tobago									
	POS	TTPP	Piarco International (Port of Spain)	2566200	1	1	3200	10499	1931
	TAB	TTCP	Crown Point International (Tobago)	n/a	1	1	2744	9003	1940

MEXICO, CENTRAL AMERICA, CARIBBEAN ISLANDS & BERMUDA

Tijuana
TIJ

Bermuda
BDA

Mazatlàn
MZT

Monterrey
NTR

San José del Cabo
SJD

Puerto Vallarta
PVR

Mexico City
MEX

Guadalajara
GDL

Acapulco
ACA

Mérida
MID

Cancún
CUN

Cozumel
CZM

Belize
BZE

Guatemala City
GUA

Tegucigalpa
TGU

San Salvador
SAL

Managua
MGA

San José
SJO

Panama City
PTY

Freeport
FPO

Nassau
NAS

Havana
HAV

Varadero
VRA

Cayman
CGM

Port-au-Prince
PAP

Montego Bay
MBJ

Kingston
KIN

Puerto Plata
POP

Punta Cana
PUJ

Santo Domingo
SDQ

San Juan
SJU

Guadalupe
PTP

Aruba
AUA

Curaçao
CUR

Bonaire
BON

St. Maarten
SXM

St. John's
ANU

Fort-de-France
FDF

Bridgetown
BGI

Tobago
TAB

Port of Spain
POS

⊛ intercontinental airports

The skies of Central and South America are far less busy than those of North America. This is corroborated by the passengers to inhabitants ratio. The figure in the United States is generally above ten (ten passenger movements per inhabitant); in Central and South America (excluding the tourist regions) it is around one.

Connections between the main cities and the major European and North American airports have always been good, and Iberia and American Airlines currently offer direct flights from Europe and the United States respectively to all the Latin American countries. Flying within Central and South America, meanwhile, has traditionally been difficult, and passengers often had to fly via Miami. The airlines TAM, TACA and LAN are expanding their Latin American networks, however, while Copa Airlines, with its main hub in Panama, is an economical alternative.

HAVANA

In 1961, Cuban exiles (and some Americans) bombed Havana Airport in advance of the Bay of Pigs invasion. Using every possible pretext and an assortment of tricks, the CIA had come up with a political reason to retake Cuba following the revolution. The invasion was led by unscrupulous CIA man E. Howard Hunt, one of the main initiators of the Watergate affair and an advocate of the assassination of Fidel Castro.

HAVANA HAV

The invasion failed miserably and a number of United

HAVANA HAV

States firms in Cuba were expropriated in the aftermath.

The Americans were unforgiving. Since 1962, the embargo against Cuba has prevented any United States aircraft from landing in Havana and Americans can only travel to the island by making complicated stopovers in Toronto or Mexico. Other countries have carved up the business between them. José Martí is one of the largest airports in the Caribbean.

MEXICO CITY

The largest 'hot and high' airport in the world, Mexico City lies at an altitude of 2,240 m/7,349 ft. The air is thinner at higher elevations and lift is therefore reduced. This means that large aircraft need a longer runway to take off. Many widebody jets therefore take off during the cooler night hours. Mexico City has two runways of

nearly 4,000 m/13,000 ft each, positioned far too closely together in a densely populated residential area. Lack of space is the main problem for Latin America's largest airport. MEX has almost reached its maximum capacity of 32 million passengers and expansion is well-nigh impossible. There are, however, no concrete plans to build an alternative airport at present.

MEXICO CITY MEX

SAN JOSÉ SJO

SAN JOSÉ JUAN SANTA-MARÍA

After Panama City, this is Central America's largest airport, currently in the throes of a somewhat turbulent modernization. Alterra Partners had been struggling with the expansion of Juan Santamaría (leading to delays, unsatisfactory results and considerable financial strain) for a many years until Costa Rica ran out of patience and handed the project to the Houston Airport System in July 2009.

TEGUCIGALPA

Toncontin is an airport with a long history and a very short runway that can just about handle the 757. In bad weather many flights are diverted to San Salvador.

In 2008, an A320 overshot the runway with the loss of five lives. In addition to a tail wind and a wet runway, human error (late touch-down) was blamed for the accident.

TEGUCIGALPA TGU

PANAMA CITY

Tocumen is Central America's largest airport and the main hub of Copa Airlines. Passenger figures have been rising by double-figure percentages for years and, with the second phase of expansion, dubbed 'Muelle Norte', capacity is set to rise to ten million passengers (mostly transit) per year.

PANAMA CITY PTY

NASSAU NAS

NASSAU BAHAMAS LYNDEN PINDLING

From here, passengers can connect to the 20 regional airports of this island paradise. However, a degree of patience is called for. Problems with lost luggage and frequent delays have given rise to the saying: 'If you have time to spare, welcome to Bahamasair.'

BERMUDA L.F. WADE

Named after Frederick Wade and not, as many German passengers seem to think, the naked portion of the legs beneath Bermuda shorts (*Wade* is German for 'calf'). Bermuda is also an emergency landing site for the Space Shuttle.

MONTEGO BAY

One of the most modern airports in the Caribbean, Montego Bay in Jamaica has a capacity of nine million passengers per year and is the Caribbean hub of numerous airlines. It outdoes the airport of the capital Kingston.

MONTEGO BAY MBJ

BERMUDA BDA

Country	IATA	ICAO	Airport Name	Pax (2008)	Terminals	Runways	Longest Runway m	Longest Runway ft	Opening
Argentina									
	AEP	SABE	Aeroparque Jorge Newbery (**Buenos Aires**)	5 665 808	1	1	2100	6890	1947
	BRC	SAZS	Teniente Luis Candelaria International (**Bariloche**)	724 010	1	1	2200	7218	n/a
	COR	SACO	Ingeniero Taravella International (**Córdoba**)	981 143	2	2	3200	10 499	n/a
	EZE	SAEZ	Ministro Pistarini International (**Buenos Aires**)	8 012 794	3	3	3300	10 827	1949
	USH	SAWH	Malvinas Argentinas International (**Ushuaia**)	n/a	1	1	2800	9186	1995
Bolivia									
	CBB	SLCB	Jorge Wilstermann International (**Cochabamba**)	800 000	1	2	3798	12 461	n/a
	LPB	SLLP	El Alto International (**La Paz**)	833 212	1	1	4000	13 123	n/a
	VVI	SLVR	Viru Viru Internacional (**Santa Cruz**)	985 794	1	1	3500	11 483	1984
Brazil									
	BSB	SBBR	**Brasília** International – President Juscelino Kubitschek	10 443 393	1	2	3200	10 499	1960
	CGH	SBSP	Congonhas Airport (**Sao Paulo**)	13 672 301	1	2	1940	6365	1936
	FOR	SBFZ	Pinto Martins International (**Fortaleza**)	3 613 634	1	1	2545	8350	n/a
	GIG	SBGL	Antonio Carlos Jobim International (**Rio de Janeiro**)	10 352 616	2	2	4000	13 123	1923
	GRU	SBGR	Governor André Franco Montoro International (**Sao Paulo**)	20 400 304	2	2	3700	12 139	1985
	MAO	SBEG	Eduardo Gomes International (**Manaus**)	2 021 668	1	1	2700	8858	1976
	REC	SBRF	Guararapes International (**Recife**)	4 679 457	1	1	3315	10 876	n/a
	SDU	SBRJ	Santos Dumont Airport (**Rio de Janeiro**)	1 600 000	1	1	1323	4341	1944
Chile									
	ANF	SCFA	Cerro Moreno International (**Antofagasta**)	n/a	1	1	2599	8527	1954
	IPC	SCIP	Mataveri International Airport (**Easter Island**)	n/a	1	1	3318	10 886	1967
	PUQ	SCCI	Carlos Ibanez Del Campo International (**Punta Arenas**)	n/a	1	3	2790	9154	1950
	SCL	SCEL	Comodoro Arturo Merino Benítez International (**Santiago de Chile**)	9 017 718	2	2	3800	12 467	1967
Colombia									
	BAQ	SKBQ	Ernesto Cortissoz International (**Barranquilla**)	1 207 115	2	1	3000	9843	1920
	BOG	SKBO	Aeropuerto Internacional El Dorado (**Bogotá**)	6 000 000	2	2	3800	12 467	1959
	EOH	SKMD	Aeropuerto Enrice Olaya Herrera (**Medellín**)	1 125 253	1	1	2510	8235	1923
	MDE	SKRG	José María Córdova International (**Medellín**)	2 367 555	2	1	3557	11 670	n/a
Ecuador									
	GPS	SEGS	Seymour Airport (**Galapagos**)	n/a	1	1	2401	7877	1942
	GYE	SEGU	José Joaquin de Olmedo International (**Guayaquil**)	3 477 800	1	1	2790	9154	n/a
	UIO	SEQU	Mariscal Sucre International (**Quito**)	3 900 000	1	1	3120	10 236	1960
French Guyana									
	CAY	SOCA	**Cayenne**-Rochambeau Airport	600 000	1	1	3200	10 499	n/a
Guyana									
	GEO	SYCJ	Cheddi Jagan International (**Georgetown**)	n/a	1	2	2270	7448	1945
Paraguay									
	ASU	SGAS	Silvio Pettirossi International (**Asunción**)	593 911	1	1	3353	11 001	n/a
Peru									
	CIX	SPHI	Capitan José Quinones Gonzales International (**Chiclayo**)	n/a	1	1	2519	8264	n/a
	CUZ	SPZO	Alejandro Velasco Astete International (**Cuzco**)	1 252 478	1	1	3397	11 145	n/a
	LIM	SPIM	Jorge Chávez International (**Lima**)	8 285 688	1	1	3507	11 506	1960
Uruguay									
	MVD	SUMU	Carrasco General Cesáreo L. Berisso International (**Montevideo**)	2 000 000	1	2	3200	10 499	1947
Surinam									
	PBM	SMJP	Johan Adolf Pengel International (**Paramaribo**)	100 000	1	1	3480	11 417	1941
Venezuela									
	CCS	SVMI	Simón Bolívar International (**Caracas**)	8 357 446	3	2	3500	11 483	1945
	MAR	SVMC	La Chinita International (**Maracaibo**)	2 384 856	1	2	3000	9843	1969
	PMV	SVMG	Del Caribe International General Santiago Marino Airport (**Porlamar**)	1 005 377	2	2	3200	10 499	1974
	VLN	SVVA	Arturo Michelena International (**Valencia**)	n/a	1	1	3300	10 827	1991

⊛ *intercontinental airports*

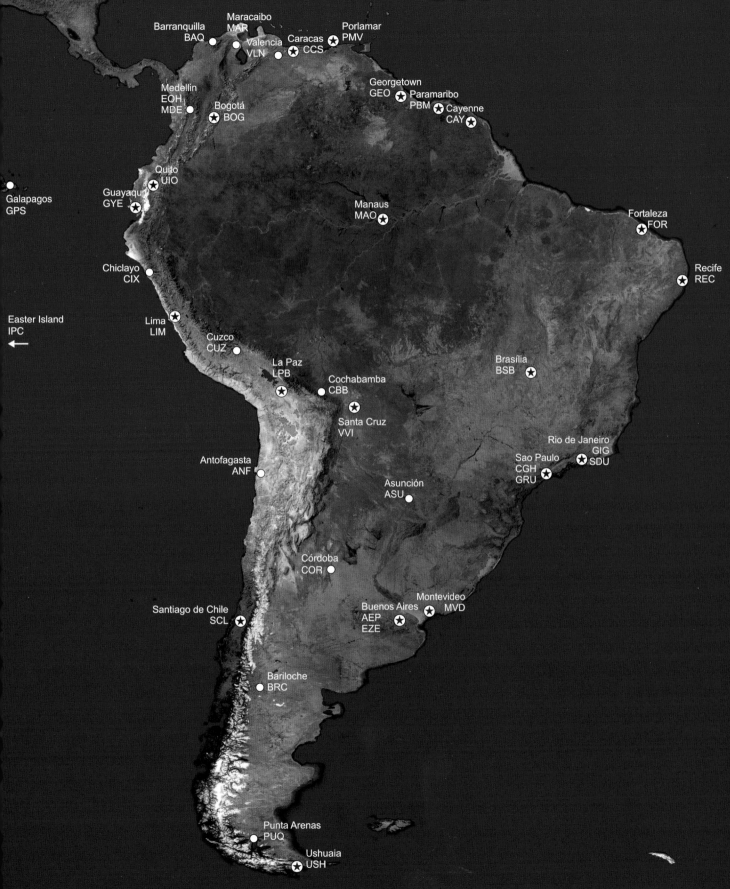

SOUTH AMERICA

Barranquilla
BAQ

Maracaibo
MAR

Valencia
VLN

Caracas
CCS

Porlamar
PMV

Medellín
EOH
MDE

Bogotá
BOG

Georgetown
GEO

Paramaribo
PBM

Cayenne
CAY

Quito
UIO

Guayaquil
GYE

Manaus
MAO

Galapagos
GPS

Fortaleza
FOR

Chiclayo
CIX

Recife
REC

Easter Island
IPC
←

Lima
LIM

Cuzco
CUZ

La Paz
LPB

Cochabamba
CBB

Brasília
BSB

Santa Cruz
VVI

Antofagasta
ANF

Rio de Janeiro
GIG
SDU

Sao Paulo
CGH
GRU

Asunción
ASU

Córdoba
COR

Montevideo
MVD

Buenos Aires
AEP
EZE

Santiago de Chile
SCL

Bariloche
BRC

Punta Arenas
PUQ

Ushuaia
USH

CARACAS CCS

CARACAS

One of the few airports that was served (at least for a time) by both Concorde operators British Airways and Air France. In the end, the idea of a fast connection to a South American hub failed to catch on.

LIMA

The newly built airport with a passenger terminal designed by architects Arquitectonica has been voted South America's best airport several times since 2005.

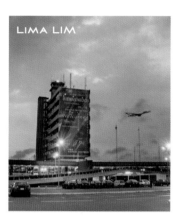

LIMA LIM

SAO PAULO CONGONHAS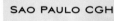

In order to relieve some of the strain on Congonhas, Brazil's largest airport, Guarulhos, was built in 1985. Guarulhos serves international destinations while Congonhas handles domestic flights. After the 2007 TAM accident at Congonhas, in which 199 people lost their lives, the airport has been the target of heavy criticism. Should an airport be allowed in the middle of a densely populated city?

SAO PAULO CGH

RIO DE JANEIRO SDU

RIO DE JANEIRO

Rio's main international airport is Antonio Carlos Jobim, which has a capacity of 15 million passengers per year. More spectacularly sited is the city airport, Santos Dumont: with a tricky approach to an extremely short runway and Sugar Loaf Mountain as an added complication, pilots have to come in close to the mountains, decelerate, descend and eventually land skilfully on the 1,323-m/4,341-ft runway.

LA PAZ

Until El Alto airport ('the heights' or 'the high one') was renamed in 1999, it was possible to fly from JFK to JFK (Aeropuerto John F. Kennedy). Situated at an altitude of 4,061 m/13,323 ft, El Alto is one of the highest airports in the world. The rusting wrecks of aircraft that line the runway make for a particularly arresting sight.

SANTIAGO DE CHILE

For a long time discussions have been in progress over whether to change the name of Comodoro Arturo Merino Benítez Airport (named after the first commander-in-chief of the Chilean air force) to Pablo Neruda Airport, after the Chilean winner of the 1971 Nobel Prize for Literature. Passengers are greeted by a functional modern airport with breath-taking views of the Andes.

USHUAIA

The southernmost airport in the world and a setting-off point for those travelling to the Antarctic, Ushuaia can handle large aircraft such as the 747. However, there is one destination that cannot be reached from Ushuaia (also known as Malvinas Argentinas International Airport): the Malvinas Islands. Passengers for the Falklands have to travel from Rio Gallegos, or Punta Arenas in Chile.

MATAVERI EASTER ISLAND

The world's most remote airport is located in the South Pacific Ocean 3,760 km/2,336 miles from Santiago, Chile. Since 1984 Mataveri has been equipped to handle an emergency landing of the Space Shuttle. The runway divides the southwestern tip of this tiny island into two. When it was opened in 1967, Mataveri handled one flight a month. In the 1970s, this increased to one a week and today it is one a day. Working hours at the airport are 'convenient' to say the least. The airport staff, including customs and security, arrive from the nearby town of Hanga Roa at around 10 am and knock off just before 2 pm.

BUENOS AIRES

Extremely well-equipped pickpockets were in operation here: in 2007, it was discovered that security staff had been purloining mobile phones, laptops and jewellery after x-raying passengers' luggage with a little more care than usual. However, it would appear that a number of Ezeiza's workers were only after chocolate.

Country	IATA	ICAO	Airport Name	Pax (2008)	Terminals	Runways	Longest Runway m	ft	Opening
Albania									
	TIA	LATI	**Tirana** International Airport Nënë Tereza	250000	1	1	2734	8970	1958
Armenia									
	EVN	UDYZ	**Zvartnots** International Airport **(Yerevan)**	1500000	1	1	3840	12598	1961
Austria									
	INN	LOWI	**Innsbruck**-Kranebitten	969474	1	1	2000	6562	1948
	VIE	LOWW	**Vienna** International Schwechat	19747289	3	2	3600	11811	1938
Azerbaijan									
	GYD	UBBB	**Heydar Aliyev** International Airport **(Baku)**	n/a	2	2	3200	10499	n/a
Belarus									
	MSQ	UMMS	**Minsk** International Airport	1010695	1	1	3641	11946	1982
Belgium									
	BRU	EBBR	**Brussels** Zaventem	19000000	1	3	3638	11936	1940
Bosnia & Herzegovina									
	SJJ	LQSA	**Sarajevo** International	506398	2	1	2641	8665	1969
Bulgaria									
	BOJ	LBBG	**Burgas**	1936853	1	1	3200	10499	1927
	SOF	LBSF	**Sofia**-Vrazhdebna	3000000	2	1	3600	11811	1935
	VAR	LBWN	**Varna**	1432703	1	1	2500	8202	1916
Croatia									
	ZAG	LDZA	Pleso Airport **(Zagreb)**	2192453	1	1	3252	10669	1928
Cyprus									
	LCA	LCLK	**Larnaca** International	5500000	1	1	2980	9777	1974
Czech Republic									
	PRG	LKPR	Ruzyně International **(Prague)**	13000000	4	3	3715	12188	1937
Denmark									
	CPH	EKCH	**Copenhagen** Airport	22000000	3	3	3600	11811	1925
Estonia									
	TLL	EETN	**Tallinn** Ülemiste	1800000	1	1	3070	10072	1936
Finland									
	HEL	EFHK	**Helsinki**-Vantaa	13500000	2	3	3440	11286	1952
France									
	CDG	LFPG	**Paris**-Charles de Gaulle	60851998	3	4	4215	13829	1974
	ORY	LFPO	**Paris**-Orly	26000000	2	2	3650	11975	1932
Georgia									
	TBS	UGTB	**Tbilisi** International	650000	1	2	3000	9843	1995
Germany									
	FRA	EDDF	**Frankfurt** Rhein-Main Airport	53472915	2	4	4000	13123	1936
	MUC	EDDM	**Munich** Franz Josef Strauß Airport	34552189	2	2	4000	13123	1992
Greece									
	ATH	LGAV	**Athens** International 'Elefthérios Venizélos'	16466491	2	2	4000	13123	2001
Hungary									
	BUD	LHBP	**Budapest** Ferihegy International	8443053	3	2	3707	12162	1950
Iceland									
	KEF	BIKF	**Keflavík** International	1991338	1	2	3065	10056	1943
Ireland									
	DUB	EIDW	**Dublin** Airport	24000000	2	2	2637	8652	1940
Italy									
	CIA	LIRA	**Rome**-Ciampino Airport	5500000	1	1	2207	7241	1916
	FCO	LIRF	Aeroporto internazionale Leonardo da Vinci **(Rome)**	35226351	5	4	3900	12795	1961
	LIN	LIML	**Milan** Linate Airport	10000000	1	2	2442	8012	1937
	MXP	LIMC	**Milan** Malpensa Airport	24000000	2	2	3920	12861	1919
Latvia									
	RIX	EVRA	**Riga** International	3690549	1	1	2550	8366	1993
Lithuania									
	VNO	EYVI	**Vilnius** International 'Tarptautinis Vilniaus Oro Uostas'	2048439	2	1	2515	8251	1991
Luxembourg									
	LUX	ELLX	**Luxembourg**-Findel	1696011	2	1	4000	13123	1945
Macedonia									
	SKP	LWSK	**Skopje** Airport 'Alexander the Great'	652815	1	1	2450	8038	1928
Moldova									
	KIV	LUKK	**Chişinău** International Airport	847900	1	1	3590	11778	1926
Netherlands									
	AMS	EHAM	**Amsterdam** Airport Schiphol	48000000	1	6	3800	12467	1920
Norway									
	OSL	ENGM	**Oslo** Airport, Gardermoen	19344459	1	2	3600	11811	1920

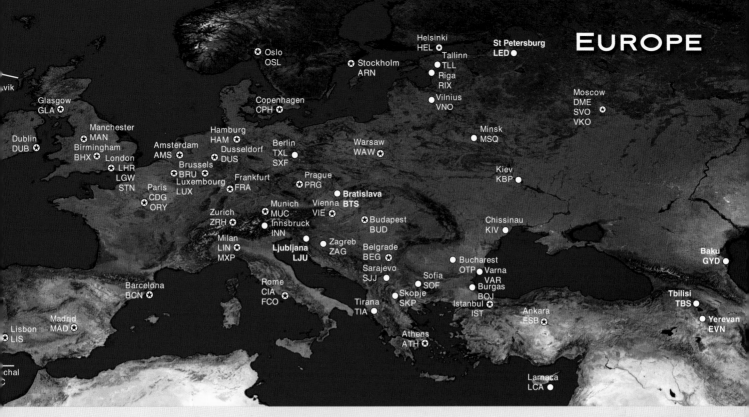

⊛ *intercontinental airports*

Poland								
	WAW	EPWA	Frédéric-Chopin-Airport (**Warsaw**)	9600000	4	2	3690	12106	1910
Portugal								
	FNC	LPMA	Madeira Airport (**Funchal**)	2446924	1	1	2781	9124	1964
	LIS	LPPT	**Lisbon** Portela Airport	14000000	2	2	3805	12484	1942
Romania								
	OTP	LROP	Henri Coandă International (**Bucharest**)	5064230	1	1	3500	11483	1968
Russia								
	DME	UUDD	**Moscow** Domodedovo	18755098	2	3	3794	12448	1964
	LED	ULLI	**St. Petersburg** Pulkovo	5121222	2	2	3780	12402	1932
	SVO	UUEE	**Moscow** Sheremetyevo	15213979	2	2	3700	12139	1959
	VKO	UUWW	**Moscow** Vnukovo	5117000	1	2	3000	9843	1941
Serbia								
	BEG	LYBE	**Belgrade** Nikola Tesla Airport	2650048	2	1	3400	11155	1927
Slovakia								
	BTS	LZIB	M.R. Štefánik Airport (**Bratislava**)	2218545	1	2	3190	10466	1951
Slovenia								
	LJU	LJLJ	**Ljubljana** Jože Pučnik Airport	1673050	2	1	3300	10827	1963
Spain								
	MAD	LEMD	**Madrid**-Barajas Airport	50846104	4	4	4470	14665	1928
	BCN	LEBL	**Barcelona** Airport	30208134	4	3	3352	10997	1918
Sweden								
	ARN	ESSA	**Stockholm**-Arlanda Airport	18136105	4	3	3301	10830	1960
Switzerland								
	ZRH	LSZH	**Zurich** Kloten	22100000	2	3	3700	12139	1953
Turkey								
	ESB	LTAC	Esenboğa International (**Ankara**)	5692133	1	2	3750	12303	1955
	IST	LTBA	Atatürk International (**Istanbul**)	28500000	2	3	3000	9843	1912
Ukraine								
	KBP	UKBB	Boryspil International (**Kiev**)	6700000	5	2	4000	13123	1959
United Kingdom								
	BHX	EGBB	**Birmingham** International	9627600	3	1	2599	8527	1939
	GLA	EGPF	**Glasgow** International	8178900	1	2	2658	8720	1932
	LGW	EGKK	**London**-Gatwick Airport	34178600	2	2	3159	10364	1958
	LHR	EGLL	**London**-Heathrow Airport	66909900	5	2	3901	12799	1930
	MAN	EGCC	**Manchester** Airport	21219500	3	2	3200	10499	1938
	STN	EGSS	**London**-Stansted Airport	22337500	1	1	3048	10000	1942

REYKJAVIK KEFLAVIK

Keflavik, which boasts a picturesque setting, was built by the United States military during World War II. In the 1960s and 1970s there were marathon demonstrations here. Each year an annual protest march would set off from Reykjavik for the air base 50 km/31 miles away, with the people chanting 'Iceland out of NATO'. One of the more prominent marchers was Vidgis Finnbogadóttir, later president of Iceland.

REYKJAVIK/KEFLAVIK KEF

COPENHAGEN CPH

COPENHAGEN

Scandinavia's busiest airport by passenger numbers and the main hub of SAS, Copenhagen boasts an impressive duty-free shopping mall, containing specialist shops selling everything from Lego to bed springs.

STOCKHOLM ARLANDA

Sweden's largest airport is some 40 km/25 miles from Stockholm but benefits from a fast and efficient train connection. It is one of Scandinavian Airline Systems' three hubs.

Over the last 25 years, Arlanda has been the scene of a number of serious accidents in which passengers have narrowly escaped. Perhaps the most spectacular occurred in 1991 when both engines of an MD-81 failed after take-off due to inadequate de-icing. The aircraft could not make it back to the airport and brushed treetops before crashing in a clearing, where it broke up into three parts. All 129 people on board survived the crash.

STOCKHOLM ARN

DUBLIN

The headquarters of Aer Lingus and Europe's biggest no-frills carrier Ryanair, Dublin was given a major boost by a new Irish–American agreement in 1993. In 1945 it had been agreed that flights from Ireland to the United States had to depart from Shannon (the last stop before the Atlantic) and could only land in Boston, Chicago and New York. In 1971, the United States threatened Aer Lingus with withdrawal of its New York landing rights unless it allowed US Airlines to land in Dublin. The 1993 agreement stipulated that

DUBLIN DUB

only 50 per cent of all flights from Ireland had to leave from Shannon. Since 2007 (the Open Skies agreement), US-bound flights can depart from anywhere in Ireland – to Dublin's enormous benefit and Shannon's great disadvantage.

HEATHROW

When talk turns to badly organized international airports, Heathrow is never far from people's lips – and not only since the disastrous opening of Terminal Five. Long treks in narrow corridors, lost luggage, missed connections… Many consider that Heathrow is the benchmark.

One passenger describes his personal flying experience and statistics as follows: 'I've flown around 5,000 times in my life; around 200 times to Heathrow. My luggage has been lost 15 times, 11 of these at Heathrow (the busiest lost property office in the world). I've missed a connection despite leaving adequate transfer time and had to spend the night in a 'charming' airport hotel on four occasions, three of these at Heathrow. Once I was arriving from Singapore first class. I had 70 minutes in which to transfer. A helpful member of Singapore Airlines' staff took me by the hand and said: "We need to rush."

He led me the entire way, taking me past queues and the various other hurdles that Heathrow strews in people's path. We finally arrived utterly exhausted 75 minutes later, only to find that the gate had already closed.' Not a great welcome to Britain.

AMSTERDAM

Schiphol, meaning 'ship's hole', is located in Harlemmermeer, a polder that was drained in 1848. At around 3 m/10 ft below sea level, Schiphol is Europe's lowest-lying airport. During World War II the airport was bombed and largely destroyed by the German invaders. Today Schiphol is Europe's fifth-largest airport by passenger volume. In 2008, its founding was included alongside Rembrandt's *Night Watch*, the assassination of film-maker Theo van Gogh and the Bijlmermeer residential development as one of the 50 'windows' in the Canon of Amsterdam, a list detailing the city's key historical events.

In 1992, Bijlmermeer came to international attention when an EL AL freighter crashed into a housing block there. Two of its engines had broken away shortly after taking off from Schipol. The crew and 43 residents, mostly immigrants, died in the disaster. Despite assurances given at the time, it was subsequently revealed that as well as flowers and perfume, the 747 was carrying over 200 kg/440 lb of a chemical used in the manufacture of the nerve gas sarin. Following the accident, a higher than average number of children were born in this region with deformities.

BRUSSELS ZAVENTEM

During World War I, the German occupation force established a Zeppelin airfield here which was transformed into Melsbroeck military airfield during World War II. After the cessation of hostilities it was gradually expanded into Belgium's largest civil airport. When Sabena went bankrupt in 2001, Zaventem suffered a dramatic collapse in its fortunes. Passenger numbers plummeted from almost 22 million in 2000 to a little over 14 million in 2001, and by 2008 had still only recovered to around 18.5 million per annum.

ZURICH KLOTEN

After a number of difficult years following Swissair's bankruptcy in 2001, Kloten has recovered over the last few years and is now Lufthansa's third most important hub following its take-over of the Swiss airline.

VIENNA SCHWECHAT

An airport serving Austria, Slovakia and Hungary. Thanks to a new motorway, Bratislava (which also has its own airport) is now just 20 minutes away. For a long time Vienna Schwechat was the main transfer airport for flights to Eastern Europe. In 1985, terrorists with ties to Abu Nidal attacked a queue of EL AL passengers with hand grenades, taking four lives and leaving 40 people injured.

FRANKFURT MAIN

The first Rhine-Main airport was opened at Griesheim, near Darmstadt, in 1907. In 1933, the Nazis began to clear the municipal forest for a Zeppelin and military airfield just outside Frankfurt from which bombers took off for France during World War II. After being captured and repaired by the Americans, Frankfurt became one of the airports used during the Berlin Airlift in 1948–49. Between 1950 and 1970, passenger traffic increased a hundredfold. Due to massive environmental protests, the planned new West Runway was not opened until 1984. With over 70,000 staff, Frankfurt airport is today Germany's largest local employer and has all the trappings of a city. Between 1978 and 2000, there was even a nightclub at the airport. It was called the Dorian Gray and took its inspiration from Studio 54 in New York. In order to make way for the new North Runway, an entire chemical works is to be moved.

FRANKFURT MAIN FRA

FRANKFURT MAIN FRA

MUNICH

Prior to the opening of the new airport at Erding, the luggage-handling system was tested for two years. Six months before the big day the airport was subjected to continuous 24-hour testing. The entire airport operation was simulated using vehicles and transport aircraft. Each aircraft ramp and loading station was thoroughly tested. When the airport finally opened in 1992, everything went off without a hitch. Munich–Riem airport closed at midnight and the new Franz Josef Strauß Airport, some 30 km/20 miles away, opened at 5 am the next morning.

Since then, Munich Airport has enjoyed an enviable reputation as a consultant in matters relating to organization and operational readiness.

MUNICH MUC

MUNICH MUC

Franz Josef Strauß Airport in Munich is notorious for its foggy conditions.

PARIS CDG

PARIS CHARLES DE GAULLE

Futurism *à la française.*
Even Terminal One, dating
from the early 1970s, was
highly innovative for its time,
resembling a multi-storey
spaceship with internal
escalators and surrounding
satellite buildings that provided
easy access to the gates. Even
the somewhat comical chime
preceding the airport's public
announcements was unique.
Terminal Two was started in the
1980s and gradually extended
in blocks A to G along either
side of a central street. Its
architectural qualities were
sadly overshadowed by the
collapse of Terminal 2E in 2004
(re-opened in 2008) with the
loss of four lives.

Indeed the airport's entire
history has been marked by
dramatic incidents, and even

its opening in 1974 was marred
by the crash of a Turkish
Airlines jet. In 2000, Concorde
crashed with the loss of all 113
passengers on board shortly
after striking a piece of metal
on the runway. In 2009, the
pitot tube (airspeed measuring
device) of an A330 failed during
an Air France flight from Rio de
Janeiro to CDG. The flight deck
received a number of different
readings and the plane
crashed into the sea with 229
people on board. Airbus had
recommended the replacement
of the faulty part some time
before. After the accident the
devices were replaced, but
by others of the same French
make. Only after a further
incident did Air France decide
to use a reliable alternative –
this time from an American
competitor.

Use of the French language
in aviation is widely regarded
as problematic and even

dangerous. In May 2000, a
freighter and a passenger plane
crashed as they both prepared
for take-off. The control tower
had given clearance for take-off
to the airliner in French and
instructions to taxi towards
the runway to the freighter in
English. Among other errors
which contributed to the
accident, the co-pilot of the
freighter, who was killed in the
accident, did not understand
the instructions given to the
French plane, clearing it to
depart. Following the incident

there was a move to prohibit
the use of French at French
airports in communications
between the tower and pilots.
The political outcry that
ensued, based on the argument
that pilots could be alienated
from their own language,
prevented the introduction of
this sensible initiative and, as
of 2009, the danger to aviation
safety from the use of French
in international air traffic
remains. In air traffic control
communications, the default
language worldwide is English.

PARIS CDG

PARIS CDG

BARCELONA

Barcelona serves mainly Europe and North America. Until 2008, the 'air bridge' (*Puente Aeró*) with Madrid was the world's busiest airway. Now the two cities are also linked by a high-speed train that carries people from city centre to city centre in just 2 hours and 35 minutes. Taking into account the journey to the airport and check-in time, this is faster than the plane. The train is also more environmentally friendly, with CO_2 emissions of 13.8 kg/30.4 lb per passenger compared to 71 kg/157 lb by air.

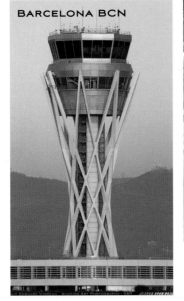

BARCELONA BCN

MADRID MAD

MADRID MAD

MADRID

Barajas is currently Europe's fourth biggest airport with a capacity of just over 50 million passengers. Its fourth terminal, designed by star British architect Richard Rogers, extends over an area of more than 1.1 million sq m/3.6 million sq ft and cost over seven billion euros. It opened in 2006 to the envy of the British: Richard Rogers also designed Heathrow's Terminal Five, but Madrid's new terminal was the greater success. On 30 December 2006, ETA exploded a bomb in one of the airport's car parks and two Columbians were killed. Perversely, ETA later blamed the Spanish authorities for the deaths, claiming they had failed to evacuate the building despite receiving a bomb warning.

FUNCHAL FNC

FUNCHAL MADEIRA

Until 2000, Madeira, with its short runway perching on a steep and dangerous coastline, was dreaded by pilots. In 1977, a Portuguese TAP flight crashed here with the loss of 131 lives. The runway has now been extended to a length of 2,777 m/9,111 ft. The new section rests on concrete pillars up to 59 m/ 194 ft high.

FUNCHAL FNC

MILANO MXP

MILAN MALPENSA

Until 1998, this international airport, which is situated at a considerable distance from Milan, handled mainly intercontinental flights. Nearby Linate airport, which is closer to the centre of Milan, was preferred for European flights. Even after the Scandinavian Airlines System disaster, which resulted in the loss of 114 lives, operators had to be forced to move to Malpensa. A third runway is currently planned, due for completion by the time of EXPO 2015. However, it is facing fierce resistance from local residents.

ROME FIUMICINO

From the 1960s to the 1970s, Italy's busiest airport was a favoured hunting ground for terrorists and hijackers due to its lax security. In 1973, Palestinian terrorists killed 30 passengers here when they threw 30 phosphorous bombs into a Pan Am aircraft. In 1985, another group of Palestinians shot 16 passengers dead in the airport building. In 1986, plastic explosives were detonated during a flight from Rome to Athens. The captain succeeded in making an emergency landing, but four passengers fell to their deaths through the damaged outer skin of the plane.

ROME FCO

ISTANBUL ESB

ISTANBUL

An impressive 220 check-in desks, 74 passport control positions and a total area of 250,000 sq m/2,690,978 sq ft: these statistics give an idea of the scale of the latest terminal to be completed at this enormous airport. Atatürk was designed to handle 27 million passengers a year, but following the recent expansion, this figure is expected to rise to around 50 million.

ATHENS

Eleftherios Venizelos airport is regarded as one of the most modern and efficient in southeastern Europe, but also one of the most expensive as far as shop rents and landing fees are concerned. Its best-known security workers are Hercules and Ulysses, two robots used to remove suspect objects. As an example of how seriously Greek authorities take their aviation security, in 2001, 12 British and two Dutch plane spotters were arrested and charged with espionage after allegedly taking photos of a military air base near Kalamata. They were sentenced to up to three years in prison but were aquitted in 2003.

ATHENS ATH

BUDAPEST BUD

PRAGUE

Ruzyně Airport has had many ups and downs during its 70-year history. Ten different airport operators have overseen either stagnation or development; airlines have come and gone. Not until the turn of the millennium did the airport acquire a more modern face. In the James Bond film *Casino Royale* there is an episode that supposedly takes place in Miami Airport, but was actually filmed in Prague. A Virgin Atlantic plane is clearly in shot in the film and so, for its in-flight version, British Airways cut out every scene in which its competitor's aircraft is shown.

PRAGUE PRG

BUDAPEST

Ferihegy Airport dates from the same era as all the other airports in this region. In 1977, it was given a new tower closely resembling the one in Boston, Massachussets. Budapest played a special political role during the Cold War: as well as serving as a transfer hub for flights within the Eastern Bloc, it was also used for informal meetings between politicians from the different sides of the Iron Curtain. After 1989, traffic dropped off sharply and the airport's fortunes only improved with the emergence of the low-cost carriers. In 2005, the airport was privatized. The major shareholder is Hochtief AirPort of Germany.

ST. PETERSBURG LED

MOSCOW

Moscow Sheremetyevo opened in 1959. State-operated, for several decades it was the main port of entry for foreign visitors to the Soviet Union. Since it was built during the Cold War, it was equipped with secret rooms and corridors, and hidden doors. Furthermore, all its gates were bugged in the hope of extracting confidential information from passengers as they prepared for departure. In 1996, Domodedovo, Moscow's other main airport, was expanded by a private consortium. Within a few years it had overtaken Sheremetyevo as Russia's largest airport. Domodedovo is state-of-the-art and has possessed whole-body scanners, which are now being selectively introduced elsewhere, since 2005.

ST. PETERSBURG

Until the 1930s, Pulkovo Airport was still known as Shosseynaya, after the nearby village of the same name. While it is a punishable offence to take photographs of Russian airports, railway stations and various other buildings and installations, Pulkovo has recently started to hold plane-spotting festivals in high summer, inviting photographers from all over the world to attend. These events take place under the name 'White Nights', referring to the bright northern nights during which St. Petersburg is shown off in a strange and splendid light.

MOSCOW SVO

Country	IATA	ICAO	Airport Name	Pax (2008)	Terminals	Runways	Longest Runway m	Longest Runway ft	opening
Algeria	ALG	DAAG	Houari Boumedienne (Algiers)	7183340	2	2	3500	11483	1940
	TMR	DAAT	Tamanrasset – Hadj Bey Akhamok	n/a	1	2	3600	11811	n/a
Angola	LAD	FNLU	Aeroporto Quatro de Fevereiro (Luanda)	1000000	1	2	3716	12192	n/a
Benin	COO	DBBB	Cotonou Cadjehoun Airport	500000	1	1	2400	7874	n/a
Botswana	GBE	FBSK	Sir Seretse Khama International Airport (Gaborone)	300000	1	1	3000	9843	n/a
Burkina Faso	OUA	DFDD	Ouagadougou Airport	500000	1	2	3028	9934	n/a
Burundi	BJM	HBBA	Aéroport International de Bujumbura	100000	1	1	3600	11811	n/a
Cameroon	DLA	FKKD	Douala International Airport	n/a	1	1	2853	9360	n/a
	NSI	FKYS	Yaoundé Nsimalen International Airport	220000	1	1	3400	11155	n/a
Cape Verde	RAI	GVNP	Praia International Airport	n/a	1	1	2096	6877	2005
	SID	GVAC	Amílcar Cabral International Airport (Sal International)	n/a	1	2	3272	10735	1949
Central African Republic	BGF	FEFF	Bangui M'Poko International Airport	70000	1	1	2600	8530	n/a
Chad	NDJ	FTTJ	N'Djamena International	n/a	1	1	2800	9186	n/a
Comoros	HAH	FMCH	Prince Said Ibrahim International (Moroni)	n/a	1	1	2900	9514	n/a
Egypt	CAI	HECA	Cairo International	14360175	3	4	4000	13123	n/a
	HRG	HEGN	Hurghada International	6743199	1	1	4000	13123	n/a
	LXR	HELX	Luxor International	2168700	1	1	3000	9843	n/a
	SSH	HESH	Sharm el-Sheikh International	7758859	3	2	3081	10108	1968
Equatorial Guinea	SSG	FGSL	Malabo International Airport	n/a	1	1	2940	9646	n/a
Ethiopia	ADD	HAAB	Bole International (Addis Ababa)	6295713	2	2	3800	12467	n/a
Gabon	LBV	FOOL	Libreville Leon M'ba International Airport	n/a	1	1	3000	9843	n/a
Gambia	BJL	GBYD	Yundum International (Banjul International)	1000000	1	1	3600	11811	n/a
Ghana	ACC	DGAA	Kotoka International Airport (Accra)	1100000	1	1	3403	11165	n/a
Guinea	CKY	GUCY	Gbessia International (Conakry International)	n/a	1	1	3300	10827	n/a
Guinea-Bissau	OXB	GGOV	Osvaldo Vieira International Airport (Bissau)	n/a	1	1	3200	10499	n/a
Ivory Coast	ABJ	DIAP	Felix Houphouet Boigny International (Abidjan)	n/a	2	1	3000	9843	n/a
Kenya	NBO	HKJK	Jomo Kenyatta International (Nairobi)	5104791	1	1	4117	13507	1958
	MBA	HKMO	Moi International (Mombasa)	n/a	1	2	3350	10991	1942
Congo DR	FIH	FZAA	N'Djili International Airport (Kinshasa)	800000	1	1	4700	15420	n/a
Congo (Republic of Congo)	BZV	FCBB	Maya-Maya Airport (Brazzaville)	451000	1	1	3300	10827	n/a
Liberia	MLW	GLMR	James Spriggs Payne Airport (Monrovia)	n/a	1	1	1829	6001	n/a
Libya	BEN	HLLB	Benina International (Benghazi)	n/a	1	2	3576	11732	n/a
	TIP	HLLT	Tripoli International	3070200	2	2	3600	11811	1952
Madagascar	TNR	FMMI	Ivato International (Antananarivo)	750000	1	1	3100	10171	n/a
Malawi	LLW	FWKI	Lilongwe International	n/a	1	1	3391	11125	n/a
Mali	BKO	GABS	Bamako Senou International	700000	1	1	2706	8878	1974
Mauritania	NKC	GQNN	Nouakchott International	n/a	1	1	3010	9875	n/a
Mauritius	MRU	FIMP	Sir Seewoosagur Ramgoolam International (Mauritius)	2609805	1	1	3370	11056	1945
Morocco	AGA	GMAD	Al Massira International (Agadir)	1455194	1	1	3200	10499	n/a
	CMN	GMMN	Mohammed V International (Casablanca)	6209711	3	2	3720	12205	1943
	RAK	GMMX	Marrakech – Menara Airport	3100495	1	1	3100	10171	1943
Mozambique	MPM	FQMA	Maputo International Airport	n/a	1	2	3660	12008	n/a
Namibia	WDH	FYWH	Windhoek Hosea Kutako International	700000	1	2	4673	15331	n/a
Niger	NIM	DRRN	Diori Hamani International (Niamey)	150000	1	2	3000	9843	1963
Nigeria	ABV	DNAA	Nnamdi Azikiwe International (Abuja)	2746300	1	1	3609	11841	n/a
	LOS	DNMM	Murtala Muhammed International (Lagos)	5136697	3	2	3900	12795	1979
	PHC	DNPO	Port Harcourt International	n/a	1	1	3001	9846	n/a
Rwanda	KGL	HRYR	Kigali International Airport	250000	1	1	3500	11483	n/a
São Tomé & Principe	TMS	FPST	São Tomé International Airport	n/a	1	1	2220	7283	n/a
Senegal	DKR	GOOY	Dakar-Yoff/Léopold Sédar Senghor International	2205000	1	2	3490	11450	1942
Seychelles	SEZ	FSIA	Seychelles International Airport (Victoria)	n/a	1	1	2987	9800	1972
Sierra Leone	FNA	GFLL	Freetown-Lungi International Airport	n/a	1	1	3200	10499	n/a
Somalia	MGQ	HCMM	Aden-Adde International Airport (Mogadishu)	n/a	1	1	3018	9902	n/a
South Africa	BFN	FABL	Bloemfontein Airport	n/a	1	2	2559	8396	n/a
	CPT	FACT	Cape Town International	8970000	5	2	3201	10502	n/a
	DUR	FADN	Durban International	4458715	1	1	2439	8002	n/a
	JNB	FAJS	OR Tambo International (Johannesburg)	18501628	3	2	4418	14495	1952
	PLZ	FAPE	Port Elizabeth Airport	1491591	1	3	1980	6496	1929
Sudan	KRT	HSSS	Khartoum International Airport	n/a	1	1	2980	9777	n/a
Tanzania	DAR	HTDA	Julius Nyerere International Airport (Dar-es-Salaam)	n/a	1	2	3000	9843	n/a

AFRICA

Monastir MIR
★ Tunis TUN
Algiers
★ ALG
Djerba DJE
Casablanca
CMN
Tripoli ★
TIP
Benghazi
BEN
Cairo
CAI ★
Sharm el-Sheikh
SSH
Agadir
AGA
Marrakech
RAK
Hurghada
HRG
Luxor
LXR
Tamanrasset
TMR
Nouakchott
NKC
Khartoum
★ KRT
Dakar DKR
Banjul BJL
Niamey
NIM
Bissau OXB
Bamako
BKO
Ouagadougou
OUA
N'Djamena
NDJ
Addis Ababa
★ ADD
Monrovia MLW
Conakry CKY
Freetown FNA
Abuja
ABV
Cotonou
COO
Port Harcourt
PHC
Praia RAI
Sal SID
Accra
ACC
Lagos
LOS
Douala
DLA
Bangui
BGF
Lomé
LFW
Abidjan
ABJ
Yaoundé
NSI
Mogadishu
MGQ
Malabo
SSG
Libreville
LBV
Entebbe
EBB
São Tomé
TMS
Kigali
KGL
Nairobi
NBO
Mombasa
MBA
Brazzaville
BZV
Kinshasa
FIH
Bujumbura
BJM
Dar-es-Salaam
DAR
Victoria SEZ
Luanda
LAD
Lilongwe
LLW
Moroni
HAH
Lusaka
LUN
Antananarivo
TNR
Harare
HRE
Windhoek
WDH
Mauritius MRU
Gaborone
GBE
Maputo
MPM
Bloemfontein
BFN
Johannesburg
JNB
Durban
DUR
Cape Town
CPT
Port Elizabeth
PLZ

★ intercontinental airports

Togo	LFW	DXXX	**Lomé**-Tokoin Airport – (Gnassingbé Eyadéma International)	350000	1	1	3001	9846	n/a
Tunisia	DJE	DTTJ	**Djerba** – Zarzis International	2626742	1	1	3100	10171	n/a
	MIR	DTMB	Habib Bourguiba International (**Monastir**)	4314040	1	1	2903	9524	1942
	TUN	DTTA	**Tunis** – Carthage International	4068233	1	2	3200	10499	1941
Uganda	EBB	HUEN	**Entebbe** International Airport	720000	2	2	3658	12001	n/a
Zambia	LUN	FLLS	**Lusaka** International Airport	n/a	1	2	3692	12113	n/a
Zimbabwe	HRE	FVHA	**Harare** International Airport	600000	2	1	4725	15502	n/a

CASABLANCA CMN

CASABLANCA

Morocco's largest airport was built by the Americans in 1943, during World War II. After the end of French rule, King Mohammed V insisted that America withdraw its troops from the country. Since 1963, therefore, the airport has been under exclusive Moroccan control.

CAIRO

Cairo is the main hub of Egypt Air (Star Alliance) and is Africa's second-largest airport. Since 2004, it has been operated by Fraport of Germany. The geographical location of the city makes Cairo a natural hub between Europe, Africa and the Middle East.

CAIRO CAI

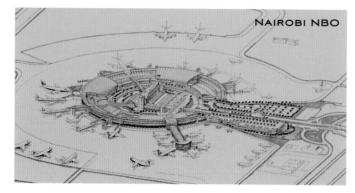

NAIROBI NBO

NAIROBI

In 1974, Central Africa's busiest airport was the scene of Lufthansa's most serious accident. The failure to carry out all the actions on a checklist led to the malfunction of the Krueger flaps on the leading edges of the wings of a four-year-old first-series jumbo. The aircraft was unable to achieve sufficient lift and crashed shortly after take-off, breaking up into three sections. Of the 157 people on board, 98 survived. Following the crash, the first ever by a jumbo jet, Boeing incorporated acoustic and optical signals to warn the crew of defective configurations.

TRIPOLI

Tensions between the United States and Libya came to a head in the 1980s with the bombing of Pan Am Flight 103 over Lockerbie in Scotland. Europe and the United States imposed sanctions that had a major impact on Tripoli Airport. In 2003, Libya embarked on a radical change of direction, destroying its weapons factories and paying compensation of three billion dollars to the families of the Lockerbie victims. This new stance should also help to improve the fortunes of the international airport.

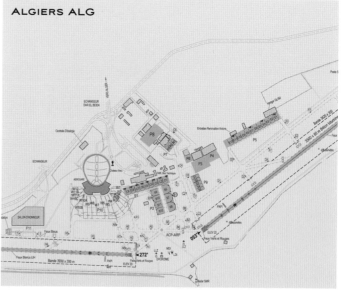

ALGIERS ALG

TRIPOLI TIP

ALGIERS

One of Africa's most modern airports in a country with a history of instability. On Christmas Eve 1994, an Airbus A300 was hijacked by four Islamic terrorists who shot dead three passengers. Upon landing in Marseille, the plane was stormed by the GIGN – the French police's elite counter-terrorism unit – and all the hijackers were killed.

LAGOS LOS

LAGOS

For many years, this was one of the most corrupt airports in the world. Planes were ambushed on the ground, bribes had to be paid for customs stamps and additional fees were fabricated.

Finally, in 1993, the FAA ran out of patience and suspended all flights between Lagos and the United States. Following the 1999 election of Olusegun Obasanjos as president of Nigeria, the situation improved markedly.

MOGADISHU

In 1977, Hans-Martin Schleyer, president of the West German Employers' Federation, was kidnapped by the Red Army Faction (also known as the Baader-Meinhof gang). In order to reinforce the kidnappers' demands, Palestinian terrorists hijacked a Lufthansa flight from Majorca to Frankfurt. The aircraft was forced to make a number of landings after the last of which the captain, Jürgen Schumann, was shot dead. The final stop was Mogadishu. The Somali government gave permission for what turned out to be a dramatic but successful rescue operation by German special forces. Three of the four hijackers were killed but all of the passengers survived. A group of jailed RAF terrorists, whose release the hijackers were trying to obtain, committed suicide in prison the same night. Schleyer was killed the next day and his body found in the boot of a car.

MOGADISHU MGQ

JOHANNESBURG JNB

JOHANNES-BURG

Another hot and high airport, Johannesburg is located at an altitude of 1,700 m/5,577 ft above sea level. This restricts maximum take-off weight and, therefore, the amount of fuel the aircraft can hold. Since it cannot carry enough fuel to fly direct from Johannesburg to Washington, DC, a stopover is made in Dakar, Senegal. In Washington, on the other hand, take-off is at a height not much above sea level and so the 15-hour return flight is technically unproblematic. During the 1980s, many airlines suspended their services to South Africa because of apartheid. Furthermore, South African Airlines was prohibited from overflying most African countries and had to make long detours using special 747SPs. The airport has been expanded and its capacity increased in preparation for the 2010 Football World Cup.

CAPE TOWN

By 2017, the capacity of Cape Town Airport is expected to increase to around 15 million passengers per year. So far, only the international terminal has been provided with jetways. Eight domestic and 16 international airlines fly to the city. Cape Town is one of a small number of airports to have imposed a 3-m/10-ft wide no-standing zone around its luggage carousels. This area may only be entered when passengers spot their own luggage.

CAPE TOWN CPT

Middle East

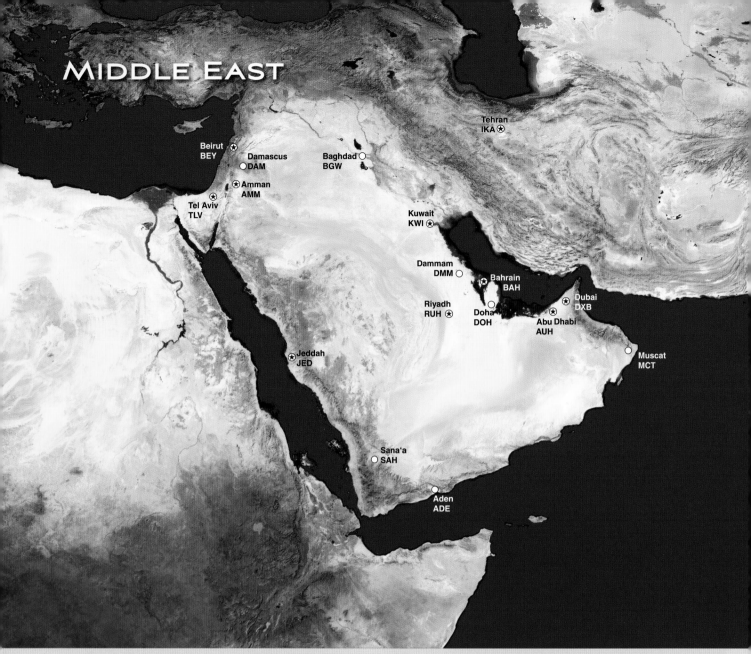

⊛ intercontinental airports

Country	IATA	ICAO	Airport Name	Pax (2008)	Terminals	Runways	Longest Runway m	ft	Opening
Bahrain	BAH	OBBI	**Bahrain** International	7 000 000	1	2	3956	12 979	1932
Iran	IKA	OIIE	Imam Khomeini International **(Tehran)**	n/a	1	1	4249	13 940	2004
Iraq	BGW	ORBI	**Baghdad** International	n/a	2	2	4000	13 123	1982
Israel	TLV	LLBG	Ben Gurion International **(Tel Aviv)**	11 081 231	4	3	3657	11 998	1936
Jordan	AMM	OJAI	Queen Alia International **(Amman)**	4 000 000	2	2	3660	12 008	1983
Kuwait	KWI	OKBK	**Kuwait** International	7 226 345	2	2	3500	11 483	n/a
Lebanon	BEY	OLBA	**Beirut** Rafic Hariri International	4 004 972	1	3	3800	12 467	1954
Oman	MCT	OOMS	**Muscat** International (Masqat)	4 002 121	1	1	3589	11 775	1972
Qatar	DOH	OTDB	**Doha** International	15 000 000	1	1	4572	15 000	1960
Saudi Arabia	DMM	OEDF	King Fahd International **(Dammam)**	3 900 000	2	2	4000	13 123	1999
	JED	OEJN	King Abdulaziz International **(Jeddah)**	13 000 000	4	3	3800	12 467	1981
	RUH	OERK	King Khalid International **(Riyadh)**	20 000 000	4	2	4205	13 796	1990
Syria	DAM	OSDI	**Damascus** International	3 500 000	1	2	3600	11 811	1973
UAE	AUH	OMAA	**Abu Dhabi** International	9 026 000	3	1	4100	13 451	1982
	DXB	OMDB	**Dubai** International	36 592 307	4	2	4000	13 123	1960
Yemen	ADE	OYAA	**Aden** International	n/a	1	1	3100	10 171	n/a
	SAH	OYSN	El Rahaba Airport (**Sana'a** International)	n/a	2	1	3252	10 669	n/a

For the last 50 years or so, the Middle East has been trying to maintain normal air traffic operations against a background of Islamic fundamentalism. Prolonged security checks in Israel, 'corkscrew manoeuvres' in Iraq, bombs and kidnappings terrify passengers and present challenges to security personnel and the intelligence services. At the same time, luxury tourist paradises are being created (for example in the Emirates), with an exponential increase in flights and levels of service. As a result of its strategic position between Europe and South-East Asia/Australia, the airlines in the Gulf region are marketing themselves to travellers who want to break long flights with a short luxury stay in one of the Emirates. Dubai is competing for customers with Abu Dhabi, Bahrain, Dammam and Doha through an array of new attractions, higher and higher levels of luxury and extensive duty-free offers. Meanwhile, the airlines are undercutting each other and attempting to lure European customers with attractive prices and increased levels of in-flight comfort.

TEL AVIV TLV

welcome to israel ברוכים הבאים לישראל

TEL AVIV

Amazingly, this is now one of the safest airports in the world. Despite numerous attempts, no hijackings or other terrorist incidents have taken place at Ben Gurion International Airport and passengers are protected by a cleverly devised security system.

However, in 1972, before the airport changed its name, a massacre occurred when members of the Japanese Red Army, arriving from Paris, removed machine guns from their bags and opened fire on a group of pilgrims from Puerto Rico (the Lod Airport Massacre). One of the terrorists was released in an exchange of prisoners with Israel in 1985 and today has political asylum under Lebanese law by virtue of having taken part in 'resistance operations' against Israel.

While most of the world's airports have terminal buildings resembling glass palaces, Tel Aviv's airport is more like a bunker. The observation slits in its tower are akin to embrasures glazed with bullet-proof glass.

TEL AVIV TLV

BEIRUT BEY

BEIRUT

In 1968, an EL AL aircraft was hijacked in Rome and forced to land in Algiers. It was 40 days before all the passengers were released. In December of the same year there was an attack on an EL AL plane in Athens. In retaliation for the open Lebanese support of the Palestinian terror plot Israel responded with an air assault on Beirut Airport that destroyed 14 civil aircraft. This was a heavy blow for Lebanese aviation and drove Lebanese International Airways into bankruptcy. Today the airport is named in honour of the politician Rafic Hariri, who was killed in a bomb attack.

TEHRAN IKA

TEHRAN

The revolutionary mills grind slowly. The planning of Tehran Airport began before 1979 with a design based on Dallas Fort Worth. After the revolution, the American team of architects was replaced by an Iranian one – periodically consulting with French experts. Not long afterwards, a Turkish-Austrian consortium was called in and some 25 years later the airport was ready to open.

BAGHDAD

Travelling to or from the former Saddam Airport is still a strange experience. In order to avoid the fire of short-range weapons, crews perform 'corkscrew manoeuvres' (flying in a spiral) when taking off from, or landing at, the airport.

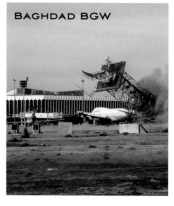
BAGHDAD BGW

JEDDAH

This airport near Mecca is famous for its tent-like Hajj Terminal, the fourth-largest terminal in the world. It was built for foreign travellers on the pilgrimage to Mecca and was designed by Skidmore, Owings and Merrill. The area around Mecca and Medina is sacred to Muslims, meaning that non-Muslim aircraft crews are subject to stringent controls: they are denied freedom of movement and are required to submit their passports while on the ground. Since the pilgrims carry so much hand luggage on their return flights – everything from

RIYADH RUH

water canisters to televisions bought from Jeddah's huge duty-free warehouse – crews always allow for a 25 per cent increase in weight.

RIYADH

Saudi Arabia's largest airport, handling over 20 million passengers, also provides landing facilities for the Space Shuttle.

The focal point of the airport is an enormous mosque able to accommodate 5,000 believers. Its minarets are 39 m/128 ft high, soaring above the airport buildings – except for the control tower, which stands at 81 m/277 ft.

BAHRAIN

The island kingdom's international airport is now the main hub of Gulf Air. In the 1930s, Empire seaplanes landed off Bahrain on their way from Britain to the colonies. In the 1950s, British Airways precursor BOAC flew to the Far East and Australia via Bahrain. In 1976 a regular Concorde service to London was launched.

BAHRAIN BAH

JEDDAH JED

Dubai

Dubai loves superlatives. This international airport, which has one of the most impressive duty-free shops in the world, has almost quadrupled its passenger figures from 10 million in 1999 to nearly 40 million in 2008. It is planning to raise this to 80 million by 2011. Yet another airport, Al Maktoum International (Dubai World Central), with its five 4,500-m/1,4764-ft runways and a capacity of – believe it or not – 120 million passengers, is currently under construction. Dubai is a residential city of 800,000 with a combined air and sea freight six times larger than Frankfurt's total freight volume – and all in a country with just 1.3 million inhabitants.

Country	IATA	ICAO	Airport Name	Pax (2008)	Terminals	Runways	Longest Runway m	ft	Opening
Afghanistan	KBL	OAKB	**Kabul** International Khwaja Rawash	n/a	1	1	3500	11483	1960
Armenia	EVN	UDYZ	Zvartnots International Airport **(Yerevan)**	1500000	1	1	3840	12598	1961
Azerbaijan	GYD	UBBB	Heydar Aliyev International **(Baku)**	n/a	2	2	3200	10499	1980
Bangladesh	DAC	VGZR	Zia International **(Dhaka)**	5000000	2	1	3200	10499	1981
Bhutan	PBH	VQPR	**Paro** Airport	50000	1	1	1985	6512	n/a
Brunei	BWN	WBSB	Brunei International **(Bandar Seri Begawan)**	1300000	1	1	3658	12001	1953
Cambodia	PNH	VDPP	**Phnom Penh** International	1700000	2	1	3000	9843	2003
	REP	VDSR	Siem Reap-**Angkor** International	1500000	2	1	2550	8366	2006
PR China	CAN	ZGGG	**Guangzhou** Baiyun International	33435472	1	2	3800	12467	2004
	HGH	ZSHC	**Hangzhou** Xiaoshan International	12673198	1	1	3600	11811	2000
	HKG	VHHH	**Hong Kong** International	47898000	2	2	3800	12467	1998
	KMG	ZPPP	**Kunming** Wujiaba International	15877814	1	1	3400	11155	1923
	PEK	ZBAA	**Beijing** Capital International	55938136	3	3	3800	12467	1958
	PVG	ZSPD	**Shanghai** Pudong International	28235691	2	3	4000	13123	1999
	SHA	ZSSS	**Shanghai** Hongqiao International	22877404	n/a	n/a	n/a	n/a	n/a
	SZX	ZGSZ	**Shenzhen** Bao'an International	21400509	3	1	3400	11155	1991
	TSN	ZBTJ	**Tianjin** Binhai International	4637299	1	2	3600	11811	n/a
	XIY	ZLXY	**Xi'an** Xianyang International	11921919	1	1	3000	9843	1991
Georgia	TBS	UGTB	**Tbilisi** International	650000	1	1	3000	9843	1995
India	BLR	VOBL	**Bengaluru** International	10120000	1	1	4000	13123	2008
	BOM	VABB	Chhatrapati Shivaji International **(Mumbai)**	25860000	4	2	3445	11302	n/a
	CCU	VECC	Netaji Subhash Chandra Bose International **(Kolkata)**	7460000	2	2	3627	11900	1924
	DEL	VIDP	Indira Gandhi International **(Delhi)**	23970000	5	3	4430	14534	1945
	MAA	VOMM	**Chennai** International	10600000	2	2	3658	12001	1954
	TRV	VOTV	**Trivandrum** International	2100000	2	1	3398	11148	1932
Indonesia	DPS	WADD	Ngurah Rai International **(Denpasar, Bali)**	5500000	2	1	3000	9843	1931
	JGK	WIII	Soekarno-Hatta International **(Jakarta)**	32172114	3	2	3660	12008	1985
	JOG	WARJ	Adisucipto (or Adisutjipto) International **(Yogyakarta)**	n/a	1	1	2200	7218	1945
	SUB	WARR	Juanda International **(Surabaya**, Java)	10000000	2	1	3000	9843	1964
Japan	HND	RJTT	Haneda Airport **(Tokyo)**	66000000	2	3	2999	9839	1931
	KIX	RJBB	Kansai International **(Osaka)**	17000000	2	2	4000	13123	1994
	NGO	RJGG	Chūbu Centrair International **(Nagoya)**	10800000	2	1	3500	11483	2000
	NRT	RJAA	Narita International **(Tokyo)**	36000000	2	2	4000	13123	1978
Kazakhstan	ALA	UAAA	**Almaty** International	1250000	2	2	4000	13123	1935
Korea, North	FNJ	ZKPY	Sunan International **(Pyongyang)**	n/a	1	2	3802	12474	n/a
Korea, South	ICN	RKSI	Incheon International **(Seoul)**	30000000	1	3	4000	13123	2001
Kyrgyzstan	FRU	UAFM	Manas International **(Bishkek)**	226000	1	1	4200	13780	1974
Laos	LPQ	VLLB	**Luang Prabang** International	n/a	1	1	2200	7218	n/a
	VTE	VLVT	Wattay International **(Vientiane)**	n/a	n/a	1	3000	9843	n/a
Macau	MFM	VMMC	**Macau** International	5000000	1	1	3360	11024	1995
Malaysia	BKI	WBKK	**Kota Kinabalu** International	4300000	2	1	2987	9800	1943
	KUL	WMKK	**Kuala Lumpur** International	25000000	2	2	4050	13287	1998
Maldives	MLE	VRMM	**Malé** International	2100000	1	1	3200	10499	1966
Mongolia	ULN	ZMUB	Chinggis Khaan International **(Ulan Bator)**	n/a	1	2	3100	10171	1961
Myanmar	RGN	VYYY	**Yangon** International Airport	n/a	1	1	3414	11201	1947
Nepal	KTM	VNKT	Tribhuvan International **(Kathmandu)**	2300000	2	1	3050	10007	1949
Pakistan	ISB	OPRN	Benazir Bhutto International **(Islamabad)**	4800000	2	1	3287	10784	1960
	KHI	OPKC	Jinnah International Airport **(Karachi)**	27000000	2	2	3400	11155	1929
	LHE	OPLA	Allama Iqbal International **(Lahore)**	3100000	2	2	3310	10860	2003
Philippines	MNL	RPLL	Ninoy Aquino International **(Manila)**	22253158	3	2	3737	12260	1937
Russia	AER	URSS	**Sochi** International	1800000	1	2	2890	9482	1945
	IKT	UIII	**Irkutsk** Airport	1100000	2	1	3565	11696	1928
	KJA	UNKL	Yemelyanovo International **(Krasnojarsk)**	n/a	2	1	3700	12139	1980
	OMS	UNOO	Tsentralny Airport **(Omsk)**	600000	1	3	2876	9436	n/a
	OVB	UNNT	**Novosibirsk** Tolmachevo Airport	2100000	2	3	3605	11827	1957
Singapore	SIN	WSSS	**Singapore** Changi Airport	36000000	4	3	4000	13123	1981
Sri Lanka	CMB	VCBI	Bandaranaike International/Katunayake International **(Colombo)**	5000000	1	1	3350	10991	1934
Taiwan	TPE	RCTP	Taiwan Taoyuan International **(Taipei)**	23000000	2	2	3660	12008	1979
Tajikistan	DYU	UTDO	**Dushanbe** Airport	n/a	1	1	3100	10171	1964
Thailand	BKK	VTBS	Suvarnabhumi International **(Bangkok)**	43000000	1	2	4000	13123	2006
Turkmenistan	ASB	UTAA	**Ashgabat** Airport (Saparmurat Turkmenbashy International)	n/a	1	3	3800	12467	1994
Uzbekistan	TAS	UTTT	**Tashkent** International (Yuzhniy)	2000000	2	2	4000	13123	2001
Vietnam	HAN	VVBN	Noi Bai International **(Hanoi)**	5500000	1	2	3800	12467	1965
	SGN	VVTS	Tan Son Nhat International **(Ho Chi Minh City)**	7000000	2	2	3800	12467	1930

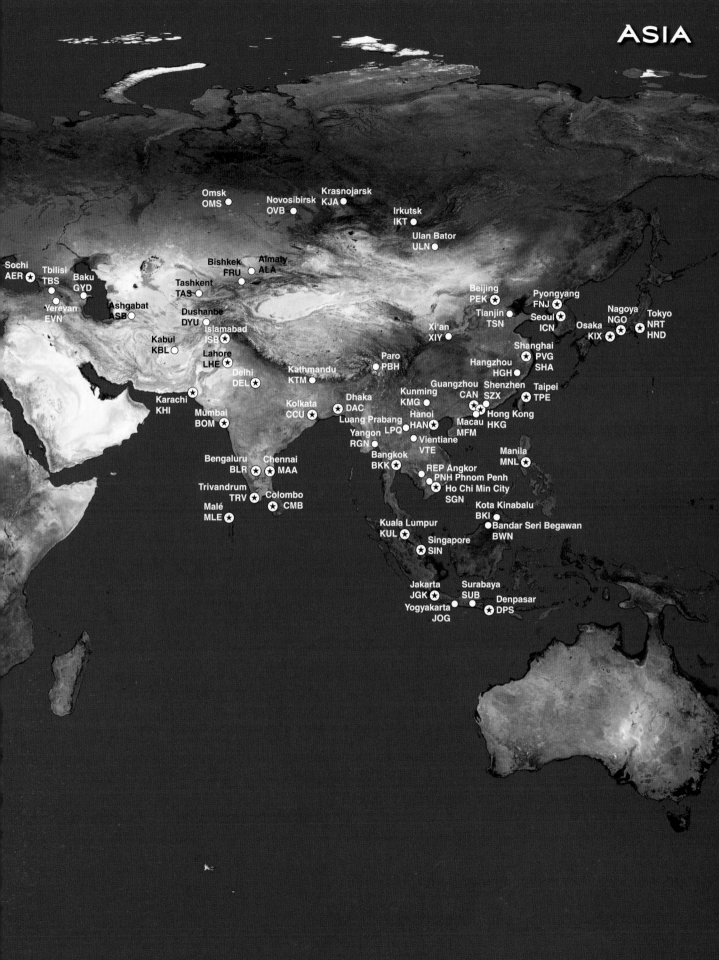

ASIA

Sochi
AER ✪

Tbilisi
TBS ●

Baku
GYD ●

Yerevan
EVN ●

Ashgabat
ASB ●

Omsk
OMS ●

Novosibirsk
OVB ●

Krasnojarsk
KJA ●

Irkutsk
IKT ●

Ulan Bator
ULN ✪

Bishkek
FRU ●

Almaty
ALA ✪

Tashkent
TAS ●

Dushanbe
DYU ●

Beijing
PEK ✪

Tianjin
TSN ●

Pyongyang
FNJ ✪

Seoul
ICN ✪

Nagoya
NGO ✪

Tokyo
NRT ✪
HND

Osaka
KIX ✪

Kabul
KBL ●

Islamabad
ISB ✪

Xi'an
XIY ●

Shanghai
PVG ✪
SHA

Lahore
LHE ✪

Delhi
DEL ✪

Kathmandu
KTM ●

Paro
PBH ●

Hangzhou
HGH ●

Karachi
KHI ✪

Dhaka
DAC ●

Kunming
KMG ●

Guangzhou
CAN ●

Shenzhen
SZX ●

Taipei
TPE ✪

Mumbai
BOM ✪

Kolkata
CCU ✪

Luang Prabang
LPQ

Hanoi
HAN ✪

Macau
MFM ●

Hong Kong
HKG ●

Yangon
RGN ●

Bengaluru
BLR ✪

Chennai
MAA ✪

Vientiane
VTE ●

Manila
MNL ✪

Trivandrum
TRV ✪

Colombo
CMB ✪

Bangkok
BKK ✪

REP Angkor
PNH Phnom Penh

Kota Kinabalu
BKI ●

Malé
MLE ✪

Ho Chi Min City
SGN ●

Bandar Seri Begawan
BWN ●

Kuala Lumpur
KUL ✪

Singapore
SIN ✪

Jakarta
JGK ✪

Surabaya
SUB ●

Denpasar
DPS ✪

Yogyakarta
JOG

143

KABUL

During Afghanistan's brief 'golden age', when it opened up to the West, Kabul Airport, built by the Soviets in 1960, was served by numerous international airlines. After the Soviet invasion of 1979, the country descended into terror and civil war. Today NATO, the ISAF and the United States are trying to stabilize the country and keep Kabul open as portal to the rest of the world.

KARACHI KHI

KABUL KBL

KARACHI

In the days when aircraft had a limited range and it was forbidden to overfly the Soviet Union, all the major airlines stopped over at Karachi on their way to the Far East.

On 12 October 1999, a pilot named Captain Hussein was carrying Pervez Musharraf, the recently dismissed chief of staff of the Pakistani army and sworn political enemy of Prime Minister Nawaz Sharif, on a flight from Colombo to Karachi. As the PIA A300 approached for landing, Sharif denied permission to land and the captain was forced to make for nearby Nawabshah with what little fuel remained.

As the plane came in to land, airport security notified him that the airport was closed to Musharraf and that the captain should 'go and find another country to land in'. Captain Hussein explained that he must land or else the plane would crash with 190 passengers on board. In the meantime, troops loyal to Musharraf had seized Karachi Airport. They ordered Captain Hussein to return to the capital, which he duly did, landing successfully on the aircraft's last remaining drops of fuel. General Musharraf immediately assumed power. Nawaz Sharif was tried for hijacking and terrorism before subsequently being pardoned and sent into exile.

Karachi is suffering under Taliban terror and a 'normal life' is unlikely to be possible there for the foreseeable future.

DELHI

Delhi, previously a nightmare of disorganization and bureaucracy, is today on the road to becoming a modern airport conforming to international standards. During the Muslim pilgrimage season, a separate Hajj Terminal is opened in order to regulate passenger traffic. In 2008, a new 4,500-m/1,764-ft runway opened, making it the longest in Asia. However, modernity has not yet penetrated everywhere. Anyone leaving the airport through the door marked 'Private Taxis' will end up paying three times the going rate plus tip.

MUMBAI BOM

DELHI DEL

MUMBAI

Mumbai is India's most modern airport and also has impressive plans for the future. However, according to Forbes, it also has more delays than any other airport in the world. Travellers needing to transfer in Mumbai should allow ample time.

The airport was formed from the merger of two neighbouring aerodromes, Sahar and Santa Cruz. During the monsoon season, it is invaded by countless birds. There are 12 specially appointed bird protectors, who work in shifts. Alongside two high-tech scarecrows, they have their work well and truly cut out.

KUALA LUMPUR

Kuala Lumpur's prestige airport – located at Sepang, 60 km/37 miles from the city – opened in 1998. Enthusiasm for the chic new airport evaporated rapidly, however, due to the length of the journey to get there from the city. Domestic customers continued to favour the old Sultan Abdul Aziz Shah Airport in the Subang district, just 16 km/10 miles from the city centre.

In order to stem the loss of customers on its domestic flights, Malaysia Airlines was forced to operate its domestic network from both airports on the premise that international flights need domestic connections. A loss of 100 million euros was the consequence. However, worse was to come for both the airline and the airport when a live rat was discovered in the first class area of a Perth-bound Boeing 777 (ticket price 2,400 euros). The captain immediately returned to Sepang, where the crew, passengers and luggage were transferred to another plane, making the plane hours late for its arrival in Australia. The airport was subsequently found to be populated by hundreds of the rodents.

SINGAPORE SIN

SINGAPORE

Singapore's Changi Airport has been setting new standards ever since it opened. Whereas elsewhere passengers usually try to minimize the time they spend at the airport, Changi encourages travellers to add an extra day to their stay. It offers swimming pools, showers, fitness studios, quiet zones for those who wish to sleep, bars, themed restaurants, waterfalls, bamboo gardens and even a tropical butterfly garden. Naturally, there is also free internet access (wireless LAN), and meeting rooms are available. An excellent local transport system connects the airport to the city. Extremely well-appointed, Changi has provided a consistently high level of quality over many decades and is widely regarded as the best airport in the world.

JAKARTA

Designed by architect Paul Andreu (also responsible for Charles de Gaulle, Paris), Jakarta Airport is Indonesian in inspiration and has numerous gardens. Today the airport is hopelessly overloaded. Designed for 18 million passengers, it now handles over 30 million per year. As well as the long treks necessary to get from place to place within the airport, a major problem is the occasional flooding of the airport access road, which lies just 1 m/3 ft above sea level and runs through marshland.

BEIJING PEK

JAKARTA JGK

BEIJING

The size and quality of China's largest airport is impressive. Good signage makes it easy for passengers to find their way around the three marble-clad terminals, which are linked by a train that passes through an underground garden. Since the 2008 Olympics, the airport has also had an express train link into Beijing.

There are currently 147 airports in China and by 2020 this number is set to increase to 244 at a cost of 64 billion dollars. This will mean that 81 per cent of the population will then be living within 100 km/62 miles of an airport.

BANGKOK

Although regarded for a long time as a gigantic design failure, in terms of its overall concept, Suvarnabhumi is one of Asia's best airports. Due to the high groundwater level, however, continual repairs need to be made to its earth banks and concrete surfaces.

In 2008, the airport was occupied for weeks by angry demonstrators, leaving some 350,000 tourists stranded in the country.

Duty-free shops are not clearly demarcated from other areas and the Irish foreign ministry has warned that customers holding an unpaid item who take a few steps to the side, for example to make way for someone, run the risk of being arrested as shoplifters. Denmark issued similar travel advice that reads: 'Anyone found during checks with new goods on them and no till receipt is in danger of being imprisoned for weeks in a Thai jail unless they own up to theft and pay a hefty fine'.

BANGKOK BKK

BANGKOK BKK

SHANGHAI PUDONG

SHANGHAI PVG

Shanghai Pudong was built at a considerable distance from the city centre. Arriving passengers are hardly aware of this, however, thanks to the German-built Maglev (magnetic levitation) train, the pride of the city, which whisks them to downtown Shanghai in 7 minutes and 20 seconds. Unfortunately, the walk from baggage reclaim to the platform takes about the same time.

HONG KONG CLK

HONG KONG

Who could forget the old airport, Kai Tak, which boasted the world's most breathtaking approach. Aircraft would follow the line of the mountains before descending seemingly to the level of the skyscrapers and residential towers. They would then fly towards a cliff before executing a 45 degree turn at the last moment and setting down on the single narrow runway that extended into the sea. Jumbos were flown like Cessnas – and more than one plane ended up in the harbour.

Costing 20 billion dollars, the new Hong Kong International (Chek Lap Kok) Airport was due to open in 1998 as a logistical tour de force. From the flight information system to baggage handling, everything was to be controlled by a central computer costing 600 million euros. The airport's system included the capacity to handle 20,000 items of luggage each hour and an air safety system that recommended priorities to the air traffic controllers based on ground movements and wake turbulence, and allocated gates to incoming aircraft according to the cost of the waiting room air-conditioning.

When the airport opened, everything that could go wrong did go wrong. Gates were mixed up, helpless pilots blocked the ramps and flights took off either without passengers or without luggage. The resource planners had to push pieces of plastic around a model of the airport in order to gain any kind of overview of who was where at any given time. Tankers drove around the apron asking mystified cockpit crews which of them had ordered fuel. Valuable perishable freight was left on the taxiway in the humid heat after an input mistake deleted the cargo lists. The counter staff panicked when the system refused to print any more boarding cards and made even more input errors, finally causing all the airport's computers, including the air safety computer, to crash. In the end, extra staff were drafted in to issue manual boarding cards and carry luggage to aircraft that had been delayed by hours. It was six months before the final problems were remedied.

HONG KONG KAI TAK

TAIPEI

Taiwan Taoyuan International Airport used to be called Chiang Kaishek International. In order to help improve diplomatic relations, the old name, which the Chinese had regarded as a constant provocation, was dropped. A total ban on photography has been imposed at the airport, meaning that many international visitors, whether politicians or industrialists, can go unnoticed on their visits to Taiwan.

SEOUL

In 2009, Seoul Incheon was voted the world's best airport in Skytrax's annual awards. It was only built after the 1988 Olympics, when the world discovered South Korea as a travel destination. Building work continues at the airport, with a fourth runway currently being planned. Incheon is located 70 km/44 miles from the city, on an island in the sea. Seoul's domestic airport, Gimpo, is half this distance from the city.

SEOUL ICN

TAIPEI TPE

HO CHI MINH CITY SGN

HO CHI MINH CITY

Between 1975 and 2006, no American airline would fly to Ho Chi Minh City (formerly Saigon) in Vietnam. No doubt the pain was too intense on both sides. Europeans, on the other hand, discovered Vietnam as a travel destination long ago. In response to a boom in passenger numbers a new airport, Long Thanh International, will take over as Vietnam's International hub in 2011.

OSAKA

The Osaka conurbation is densely populated and it was impossible to expand the old Itami airport because it had long been encircled by the city. The new Kansai International mega-airport was therefore built out at sea on an artificial island. Pessimists feared that the heavy materials necessary for its construction would cause it to sink. In actual fact, it is sinking at an increasingly slower rate than anticipated: 50 cm/20 inches per year initially has fallen to under 7 cm/3 inches per year. This process is compensated for by hydraulic pillars on which the terminal buildings rest. The Kobe earthquake, which measured 7 on the Richter scale and whose epicentre was only 20 km/12 miles away in the sea, caused no damage to the airport thanks to its intelligent construction method using sliding joints. Not even the windows shattered.

Market forces, however, did threaten Kansai's success. High landing fees were supposed to recoup the cost of the airport, but all they did was put the airlines off flying to Osaka. Only when significant reductions were made was the airport accepted by the international carriers.

OSAKA KIX

TOKYO HANEDA

Due to its proximity to the city, Haneda airport remains more popular than Narita, and as well as serving domestic routes, flights have recently resumed from here to Japan's international neighbours. The plan was to close Haneda airport and replace it with Narita, but fierce resistance meant there was no alternative but to keep it open as Tokyo's second airport. However, it needed major improvement. Today, Haneda is more like a city railway terminal with a shopping centre attached. With its bright and colourful shops, restaurants and cantilever escalators, it's easy to forget that it is an airport. A fourth runway is now under construction on a site where the water, as at Kansai Airport in Osaka, is around 20 m/65 ft deep.

TOKYO HND

TOKYO NRT

TOKYO NARITA

Narita's unhappy history dates to the 1960s. Haneda was bursting at its seams, but there was no room in Tokyo Bay and land reclamation was too expensive. Located 60 km/37 miles from the city, Narita seemed the most suitable site for a new airport.

The construction phase felt at times like civil war. Local farmers were unhappy about the expropriation of their land and protested. The dispute escalated and resulted in a toll of five dead and 3,800 injured. Narita eventually opened in 1978 with a single runway. The second was not 'finished' until 2002. The only problem was that this new runway came to an end after just 2,100 m/6,890 ft in front of the fenced-off property of intransigent poultry farmer Shoji Shimamura. It was, therefore, too short to be used by long-haul aircraft. Haneda had to be expanded and Narita has gone down in history as one of the most expensive airport projects of all time. Even today, passengers are bewildered by the continuing demonstrations and the stringent controls they have to pass through even before they reach the terminal building.

On 1 December 1999, Shimamura and his comrades-in-arms received a written apology from the transport minister. The government is now planning a third international airport.

Country	IATA	ICAO	Airport Name	Pax (2008)	Terminals	Runways	Longest Runway m	Longest Runway ft	Opening
Australia	ADL	YPAD	**Adelaide** Airport	7 000 000	2	2	3100	10 171	1927
	BNE	YBBN	**Brisbane** Airport	18 523 979	2	2	3560	11 680	1928
	CBR	YSCB	**Canberra** International	2 600 000	1	2	3273	10 738	1927
	CNS	YBCS	**Cairns** Airport	3 856 418	2	2	3196	10 486	1942
	MCY	YBMC	**Sunshine Coast** Airport	910 000	1	2	1803	5915	1961
	MEL	YMML	Tullamarine Airport **(Melbourne)**	24 772 000	4	2	3657	11 998	1970
	OOL	YBCG	**Gold Coast** Airport	4 100 000	2	2	2342	7684	1939
	PER	YPPH	**Perth** Airport	7 116 194	2	2	3444	11 299	1944
	SYD	YSSY	Kingsford Smith **(Sydney)**	30 100 000	3	3	3962	12 999	1933
Australia – Christmas Island	XCH	YPXM	**Christmas Island** Airport	n/a	1	1	2103	6900	1974
Australia – Tasmania	HBA	YMHB	**Hobart** Airport	1 873 000	1	1	2251	7385	1956
Fiji	NAN	NFFN	**Nadi** International	1 400 000	1	2	3273	10 738	1939
Guam (Am.)	GUM	PGUM	Antonio B. Won Pat International **(Guam)**	2 870 000	1	2	3053	10 016	1943
Irian Jaya (West Papua)	DJJ	WAJJ	Sentani Airport **(Jayapura)**	n/a	1	1	2183	7162	1942
Kiribati	CXI	PLCH	**Cassidy** International	n/a	1	1	2103	6900	n/a
Marshall Islands	KWA	PKWA	Bucholz AAF **(Kwajalein)**	n/a	1	1	2032	6667	1945
	NAJ	PKMJ	Marshall Islands International **(Majuro)**	n/a	1	1	2407	7897	1945
Mariana Islands	YAP	PTYA	**Yap** International	n/a	1	1	1829	6001	1943
Mariana Islands (Am.)	SPN	PGSN	**Saipan** International (Mariana Ils.)	n/a	1	1	2652	8701	1934
Micronesia, Federated States of	PNI	PTPN	**Pohnpei** International	n/a	1	1	1829	6001	n/a
	TKK	PTKK	**Chuuk** International	n/a	1	1	1831	6007	n/a
Nauru	INU	ANAU	**Nauru** International	200 000	2	1	2150	7054	1943
New Caledonia (Fr.)	NOU	NWWW	La Tontouta International **(Noumea)**	460 000	1	1	3250	10 663	n/a
New Zealand	AKL	NZAA	**Auckland** Airport	13 202 772	2	2	3635	11 926	1965
	WLG	NZWN	**Wellington** International	5 177 634	1	1	2026	6647	1929
	CHC	NZCH	**Christchurch** International	6 037 729	1	3	3287	10 784	1950
	DUD	NZDN	**Dunedin** International	700 000	1	1	1900	6234	1962
New Zealand – Cook Islands	RAR	NCRG	**Rarotonga** International	n/a	1	1	2328	7638	1975
Palau	ROR	PTRO	Roman Tmetuchl International **(Palau)**	n/a	1	1	2195	7201	n/a
Papua New Guinea	POM	AYPY	Jacksons International **(Port Moresby)**	1 000 000	2	2	2750	9022	1940
Polynesia (Fr.)	PPT	NTAA	Tahiti Faa'a International **(Papeete)**	1 380 000	1	1	3463	11 362	1961
	BOB	NTTB	**Bora Bora** Airport /Motu Mute Airport	315 000	1	1	1500	4921	1943
Samoa	APW	NSFA	Faleolo International **(Apia)**	n/a	1	1	3000	9843	1984
Samoa (Am.)	PPG	NSTU	**Pago Pago** International/Tafuna International (Am. Samoa)	130 000	1	2	3048	10 000	1950
Solomon Islands	HIA	AYPY	**Honiara** International	n/a	1	1	2200	7218	1943
Tonga	TBU	NFTF	Fua'amotu International **(Nuku'alofa)**	200 000	1	2	2681	8796	1940
Tuvalu	FUN	NGFU	**Funafuti** International	n/a	1	1	1524	5000	1943
Vanuatu	VLI	NVVV	Bauerfield International **(Port Vila)**	260 000	1	1	2600	8530	1981

When people say that life in the southern hemisphere is more tranquil than elsewhere, it is surely Australasia/ Oceania they are thinking of. The name 'Pacific' was coined by Ferdinand Magellan after he sailed west through the southern tip of Chile and was struck by how calm the water was on the other side. Nevertheless, the region is subject to major hurricanes and typhoons that sometimes force aircraft to make lengthy detours. An abundance of alternative airports is therefore important in Oceania.

MELBOURNE MEL

MELBOURNE

Tullamareena was an Aborigine who resisted the British settlers. In 1838, he was arrested and locked up for the alleged theft of a sheep. The very next night, with the help of his brother, he escaped and the jail went up in flames. A little while later Tullamareena was recaptured, sent to Sydney by boat and tried in court. However, the trial had to be dropped because he spoke no English, and he was freed – 700 km/435 miles from home. Today, Melbourne's airport is named after him.

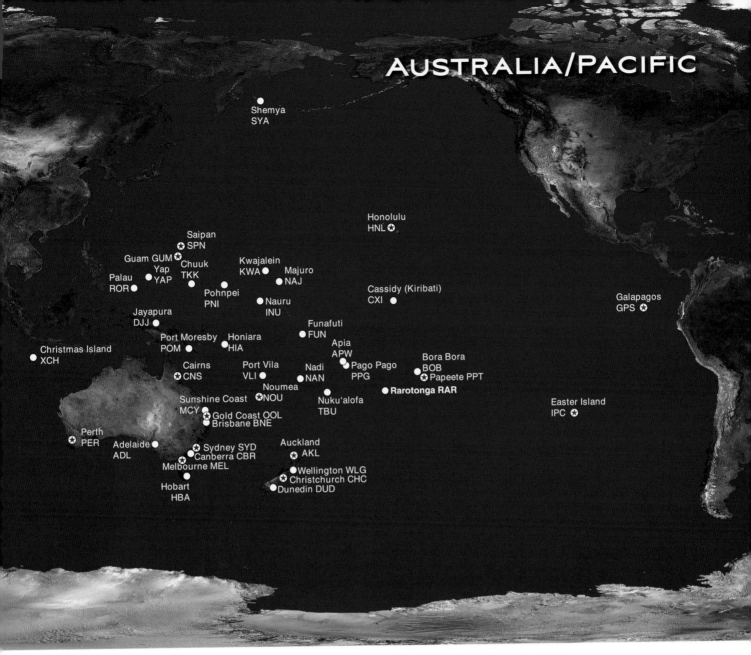

Shemya
SYA

Honolulu
HNL ✪

Saipan
✪ SPN

Guam GUM ✪ Chuuk
Yap TKK
Palau ● YAP
ROR ●

Kwajalein
KWA ● Majuro
● NAJ

Cassidy (Kiribati)
CXI ●

Galapagos
GPS ✪

Pohnpei
PNI

Nauru
INU

Jayapura
DJJ ●

Funafuti
● FUN

Apia
APW

Bora Bora
BOB ●
✪ Papeete PPT

Port Moresby
POM ● Honiara
● HIA

Christmas Island
● XCH

Cairns
✪ CNS

Port Vila
VLI ●

Nadi
● NAN

Pago Pago
PPG

● Rarotonga RAR

Easter Island
IPC ✪

Noumea
Sunshine Coast ✪ NOU
MCY ●
✪ Gold Coast OOL
● Brisbane BNE

Nuku'alofa
TBU

Perth
✪ PER

Adelaide
ADL ●

✪ Sydney SYD
● Canberra CBR

Auckland
✪ AKL

Melbourne MEL

Hobart
HBA

● Wellington WLG
✪ Christchurch CHC
● Dunedin DUD

SYDNEY

This airport is named after Australian aviation pioneer Sir Charles Edward Kingsford-Smith. During World War I, he served alongside troops from Britain, New Zealand and France in battles with Turkish troops during the Gallipoli campaign. In 1917, he was shot down, but survived. He later flew as one of the first airline pilots in Australia. His biggest achievement was probably his solo flight from California to Australia in 1928. The first leg of the journey – from Oakland to Hawaii – took him 27 hours. The second leg to

Fiji was 5,000 km/3,100 miles and took almost 35 hours. The final stretch to Brisbane took another 20 hours.

The most important airport in Australia has a strict ban on night flights (from 11 pm to 6 am). Since the weather conditions during the permitted times sometimes make take-off or landing impossible, it is sometimes the case that travellers cannot fly on their planned departure date. Infringements of the night-flying ban can incur a fine up to half a million Australian dollars.

SYDNEY SYD

GUAM GUM

NADI (FIJI)

Nadi International has been an important Pacific hub from the day it opened.

It is located 2,500 km/ 1,550 miles from Auckland, 3,500 km/2,175 miles from Australia, the same distance from Tahiti and 5,000 km/ 3,100 miles from Hawaii. In 2008, this airport, whose runway is 3,300 m/11,000 ft long, proved itself capable of coping with the emergency landing of a brand new Qantas A380 on its way from Los Angeles to Sydney. A passenger in diabetic shock urgently required medical treatment and needed to be taken to the nearest hospital. One of the on-board computers could not be restarted afterwards, meaning the onward flight was delayed for so long that the crew exceeded their maximum permitted work hours and the 337 passengers had to be put up in various hotels on Fiji. Worse things have happened!

GUAM

Guam's official status is that of 'non-incorporated organized US territory'. Passport control and security checks are the responsibility of the US Transport Security Agency (TSA). These checks can be painstaking, as the example of Continental Micronesia, a subsidiary of Continental Airlines, shows. This airline operates a daily flight from Guam to Honolulu with stopovers in Chuuk, Pohnpei, Kosrae, Kwajalein and Majuro. Each time the plane lands, passengers get on or off. The TSA then asks all the passengers on the left-hand side to exit the aircraft with their luggage while their half of the plane is searched. Afterwards the passengers on the right-hand side are made to move to the now empty left side while their area is searched. Eventually all the passengers are allowed to return to their own seats. This happens at each stop and the rationale behind it is difficult to grasp!

NADI NAN

PORT MORESBY

This is an important hub for New Guinea, the Solomon Islands and the island state of Papua New Guinea. There are also direct flights to Tokyo, Hong Kong, Singapore, Manila and Kuala Lumpur, as well as to some of the less distant destinations in Australia.

PORT MORESBY POM

TONGA TBU

TONGA

Fua'amotu International Airport serves the Tonga archipelago and is located on the main island of Tongatapu, some 35 km/22 miles from the capital Nuku'alofa. Although the airport offers direct flights to Sydney, Auckland, Samoa and Fiji, each flight has to be announced 24 hours in advance so that the staff rota can be drawn up as necessary.

AUCKLAND AKL

AUCKLAND

The airport of long treks. Auckland was once a trusting airport, with arriving and departing passengers sharing the same shops, restaurants and corridors. This came to an abrupt end after 11 September 2001. Additional screening areas were set up at every gate handling flights to the United States. Dividing walls were put up and the passenger flow had to be lengthily redirected, provoking massive criticism from frequent flyers.

A solution has now been devised in the form of a two-storey pier that is currently under construction. However, even after its completion, arriving passengers will need to take a long detour to get to passport control before continuing on their way to baggage reclaim. The idea behind this is to prevent passengers arriving before their luggage and overfilling the baggage reclaim hall.

TAHITI PPT

TAHITI

To avoid steep cliffs, the airport at Papeete was built on a coral reef just offshore. It offers direct flights to Santiago de Chile, Easter Island, Honolulu, Los Angeles, New York, Paris, Sydney, Auckland, Tokyo and also, of course, the surroundings islands and atolls.

TAHITI PPT

DISTANCES

Beijing
Tokyo
Shanghai
Hong Kong
Delhi
Bangkok
Singapore
Jakarta
Perth
Sydney
Auckland
Tahiti
Anchorage
Chicago · Toronto
San Francisco · Denver · New York
Los Angeles · Washington D.C.
Atlanta
Houston
Honolulu
Mexico City
Caracas
Santiago de Chile
Buenos A

statute miles
kilometers

		Amsterdam AMS	Anchorage ANC	Athens ATH	Atlanta ATL	Auckland AKL	Bangkok BKK	Beijing PEK	Buenos Aires EZE	Cairo CAI	Caracas CCS	Chicago ORD	Delhi DEL	Denver DEN	Dubai DXB	Frankfurt FRA	Hong Kong HKG	Honolulu HNL
Amsterdam	AMS		4489	1357	4401	11269	5727	4877	7107	2044	4873	4120	3961	4812	3215	228	5773	7256
Anchorage	ANC	7224		5595	3417	7047	6016	3961	8327	6142	5347	2846	5712	2405	6311	4677	5081	2777
Athens	ATH	2184	9004		5700	10846	4933	4738	7276	688	5826	5463	3103	6169	2035	1130	5293	8353
Atlanta	ATL	7083	5499	9173		8096	9158	7185	4999	6373	1933	606	7985	1199	7599	4614	8399	4502
Auckland	AKL	18136	11341	17455	13029		5933	6463	6421	10292	8212	8184	7764	7352	8824	11304	5688	4389
Bangkok	BKK	9217	9682	7939	14738	9548		2056	10490	4529	10565	8562	1832	8403	3050	5599	1049	6591
Beijing	PEK	7849	6375	7625	11563	10401	3309		11983	4691	8936	6579	2371	6348	3638	4853	1234	5062
Buenos Aires	EZE	11438	13401	11710	8045	10334	16882	19285		7360	3173	5603	9817	5922	8497	7132	11458	7558
Cairo	CAI	3289	9885	1107	10256	16563	7289	7549	11845		6352	6149	2741	6855	1503	1817	5042	8840
Caracas	CCS	7842	8605	9376	3111	13216	17003	14381	5106	10223		2505	8831	3063	7845	5020	10167	6020
Chicago	ORD	6630	4580	8792	975	13171	13779	10588	9017	9896	4031		7484	888	7246	4343	7794	4244
Delhi	DEL	6375	9193	4994	12851	12495	2948	3816	15799	4411	14212	12044		7721	1359	3811	2331	7416
Denver	DEN	7744	3870	9928	1930	11832	13523	10216	9531	11032	4929	1429	12426		7771	5039	7486	3365
Dubai	DXB	5174	10157	3275	12229	14201	4908	5855	13675	2419	12625	11661	2187	12506		3013	3684	8531
Frankfurt	FRA	367	7527	1819	7426	18192	9011	7810	11478	2924	8079	6989	6133	8109	4849		8310	7450
Hong Kong	HKG	9291	8177	8518	13517	9154	1688	1986	18440	8114	16362	12543	3751	12048	5929	13374		5568
Honolulu	HNL	11677	4469	13443	7245	7063	10607	8146	12163	14227	9688	6830	11935	5415	13729	11990	8961	
Houston	IAH	8066	5256	10200	1109	11933	14877	11579	8146	11294	3637	1489	13475	1387	13145	8420	13432	6283
Jakarta	CGK	11354	11315	9791	16753	7665	2285	5216	15215	8950	19167	15781	4978	15139	6544	11108	3243	10823
Johannesburg	JNB	8987	16110	7107	13581	12191	8995	11698	8129	6235	11047	14016	7995	13406	6389	8658	10672	19195
London	LHR	372	7224	2430	6775	18353	9588	8175	11111	3536	7472	6362	6743	7516	5506	655	9646	11647
Los Angeles	LAX	8977	3774	11150	3132	10467	13309	10060	9841	12241	5821	2808	12896	1387	13420	9344	11684	4113
Madrid	MAD	1460	8333	2383	6977	19594	10206	9226	10062	3355	7010	6761	7269	8061	5658	1419	10525	12667
Mexico City	MEX	9220	6082	11312	2140	10958	15754	12455	7377	12389	3579	2713	14677	2327	14346	9566	13073	6111
Moscow	SVO	2152	6997	2243	8658	16211	7107	5810	13481	2911	9917	7997	4366	8798	3710	2031	7147	11319
New York	JFK	5863	5448	7952	1223	14207	13964	11003	8501	9035	3394	1191	11777	2617	11022	6204	12991	8019
Paris	CDG	399	7545	2111	7071	18533	9460	8211	11076	3212	7635	6682	6577	7854	5245	449	9608	11978
Perth	PER	14146	13269	12266	18110	5348	5303	7974	12592	11254	17622	17632	7858	16285	9027	13850	6008	10889
Rio de Janeiro	RIO	9535	13106	9722	7630	12273	16100	17326	1989	9899	4521	8528	14069	9426	10329	9551	17683	13348
Rome	FCO	1297	8476	1088	8105	18430	8887	8167	11135	2152	8343	7762	5943	8953	4348	958	9299	12942
San Francisco	SFO	8808	3248	10956	3442	10486	12767	9516	10382	12027	6265	2971	12403	1556	13041	9172	11148	3861
Santiago de Chile	SCL	11982	12656	12567	7556	9674	17663	19022	1141	12825	4886	8528	16925	8829	14777	12080	18694	11034
Shanghai	PVG	8930	6933	8576	12326	9345	2894	1098	19595	8385	15290	11357	4300	10802	6460	8880	1254	7928
Singapore	SIN	10517	10726	9048	16034	8409	1410	4474	15884	8266	15059	4152	14595	5847	10285	2556	10800	15
Sydney	SYD	16653	11803	15305	14943	2165	7503	8935	11790	14402	15360	14857	10422	13435	12040	16494	7372	8153
Tahiti	PPT	15549	8727	17661	8935	4094	12519	11565	9012	18609	9598	9136	15121	7881	17308	15912	11384	4395
Tokyo	NRT	9342	5526	9555	11024	8806	4649	2140	18305	9613	14127	10097	5921	9313	7994	9392	2964	6146
Toronto	YYZ	6006	4880	8148	1189	13866	13652	10586	8953	9247	3864	702	11661	2116	11103	6360	12569	7482
Washington D.C.	IAD	6223	5401	8317	859	13845	14175	11138	8396	9402	3307	948	12080	15115	11376	6566	13121	7752

MAJOR
AIRLINES
OF THE WORLD

AIR CANADA

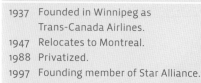 CANADA

1937 Founded in Winnipeg as Trans-Canada Airlines.
1947 Relocates to Montreal.
1988 Privatized.
1997 Founding member of Star Alliance.

2001 Merger with Canadian Airlines, the second largest Canadian airline
2003 Under bankruptcy protection due to financial difficulties.
2004 Modernization of fleet with Airbus aircraft.

Subsidiaries: Air Canada Cargo, Air Canada Jazz (one of the world's largest regional airlines) and Air Canada Jetz (flies businesspeople and professional sports teams in premium A320s with just 64 business class seats). The bulk of inland services are handled by Air Canada's subsidiaries. Focus of operations: Canada, the United States, the Caribbean and Europe.

www.aircanada.ca

AIR NORTH

 CANADA

Operates scheduled, charter and freight services out of Whitehorse in the Yukon. Flies predominantly robust classic aircraft that are exceptionally well maintained. Focus of operations: western Canada from Vancouver to Inuvik on the Arctic Ocean.

www.flyairnorth.com

CANADIAN NORTH

CANADA

NorTerra, a holding company owned by the Inuit, purchased the company in 1998 from Canadian Airlines. Its logo combines the polar bear, the midnight sun and the northern lights, all symbols of its remote destinations in northern Canada.

www.cdn-north.com

AIR TRANSAT

CANADA

1987 Founded by employees of Quebecair as a charter airline based in Montreal.
1991 Scheduled flights, mainly for tourists.
1993 Take-over of Nationair.
1996 Take-over of STAR Europe.
1999 Switches to Airbus aircraft.
2009 Carries three million passengers during the year.

Focus of operations: Florida, Mexico, the Caribbean and Europe (especially the Mediterranean region). Air Transat runs its own holiday resorts for package tourists.

KENN BOREK AIR

 CANADA

1970 Founded by Kenn Borek with one DHC-6 Twin Otter aircraft.
2001 Assists in the rescue of Dr Ron Shemenski from the Amundsen-Scott South Pole Station in temperatures as low as -67°C/-88.6°F.

www.borekair.com

FIRST AIR

 CANADA

1946 Founded as a charter operator under the name Bradley Air Services.
1958 Starts scheduled flight operations.
1971 Establishment of the world's most northerly base in Eureka, 1,000 km/ 620 miles from the North Pole.

www.firstair.ca

www.airtransat.com

WESTJET

🇨🇦 CANADA

1996 Founded as a successful low-cost carrier based in Calgary.

2004 Accused of espionage by Air Canada: a settlement is agreed in 2006, with WestJet having to pay Air Canada's legal costs and donate 10 million Canadian dollars to charities.

WestJet is the second-largest Canadian airline after Air Canada, focussing on flights between nearly all of Canada's cities, Mexico, the Caribbean and the United States, including Hawaii. WestJet controls a third of the Canadian air travel market.

www.westjet.com

AIR WISCONSIN

 UNITED STATES

1965 Founded. During the 1980s, becomes the largest US regional airline, codesharing with United Express.

1993 Purchased by private investors.

2006 New collaborative venture as an exclusive feeder for US Airways.

www.airwis.com

AirTran

🇺🇸 UNITED STATES *airTran.*

1993 Originally founded as a budget airline under the name ValuJet.

1996 Maintenance problems lead to withdrawal of operating licence.

1997 ValuJet executes a reverse merger with AirTran and adopts its name.

www.airtran.com

AMERICAN EAGLE AIRLINES

🇺🇸 UNITED STATES **AA** AmericanAirlines

Founded in 1984. Currently the largest regional carrier in the United States with around 270 aircraft (turboprops and small jets). Hubs in Chicago O'Hare, Dallas Fort Worth, Los Angeles LAX, Boston Logan and New York LaGuardia, among others.

www.aa.com

ATLANTIC SOUTHEAST AIRLINES

🇺🇸 UNITED STATES *ASA*

1979 Founded as a regional airline exclusively to serve Delta Air Lines.

2005 Sold to SkyWest. However, the contract with Delta Air Lines will run until 2020.

www.flyasa.com

ALASKA AIRLINES

🇺🇸 UNITED STATES *Alaska Airlines*

1932 Founded by Linius McGee for transporting trapper furs.

1934 Sold to Alaska Star Airlines.

1944 Government contracts for transporting troops and materials to support the construction of the Alaska Highway.

1948 Involved in the Berlin Airlift after World War II.

1961 First jets, Convair CV-880s.

1986 Acquisition of Horizon Air and Jet America Airlines.

1987 Merger of these companies with Alaska Airlines.

Since 2000, one of the largest airlines in the United States. Focus of operations: from Alaska to Florida, Mexico and Hawaii.

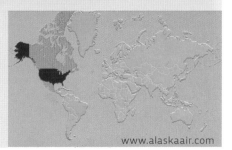

www.alaskaair.com

AMERICAN AIRLINES

 UNITED STATES

AmericanAirlines®

1970s Largest air carrier in the world.
1999 Founding member of Oneworld Alliance.
11 September 2001 Two aircraft hijacked and flown into the north tower of the World Trade Center and the Pentagon.
12 November 2001 Airbus A300 crashes in the New York borough of Queens.

1930s Amalgamation of a total of 82 small airlines, including Embry-Riddle Company, Colonial Airways, Colonial Air Transport, Colonial Western Airways, Canadian Colonial Airways, Universal Aviation Corporation, Northern Air Lines, Robertson Aircraft Corporation, Central Airlines, Southern Air Transport System, St. Tammany-Gulf Coast Airways, Gulf Air Lines and Standard Airlines, to form American Airways Corporation.

1934 American Airlines based at Midway Airport in Chicago, Illinois. Government contracts for transporting airmail is its major source of income initially.

1945 Merger with American Overseas Airlines (AOA), thereby gaining routes throughout the world.

Five hubs: Dallas, Chicago, Miami, St. Louis and San Juan (Puerto Rico). Focus of operations: the United States, South America and Europe.

www.aa.com

HAWAIIAN AIRLINES

UNITED STATES HAWAIIAN AIRLINES

1929 Founded by a ship-owner. Initially just scenic flights around the island, then inter-island flights.
Accident-free since it started.

In the 1980s, routes to all major destinations in the entire Pacific region.
Today, the leading airline in Hawaii.
The airline ranks at the top in the United States punctuality statistics. It is also one of the leaders in safety statistics and gains the highest national scores for customer service.

www.hawaiianair.com

CHAUTAUQUA AIRLINES

UNITED STATES CHAUTAUQUA AIRLINES
A REPUBLIC AIRWAYS COMPANY

1973 Company founded. Now operates under various 'flags' (e.g. US Airways Express, Delta Connection, United Express and Continental Express) as a regional commuter (feeder) airline.

www.flychautauqua.com

FRONTIER AIRLINES

 UNITED STATES

1994 First founded in Denver, Colorado; modest beginnings with two Boeing 737s and 180 employees.
2000 Already has 25 Boeings and 2,000 employees.
2000 Switches to Airbus A318 and A319.

Tail art: tailplanes repainted with images of native animals. Corporate identity: 'a whole different animal'.

Target group: the children of today are the customers of tomorrow. Core areas: United States, Canada, Mexico.

www.frontierairlines.com

JETBLUE AIRWAYS

UNITED STATES

1998 Established with a base in New York JFK. Orders 25 Airbus A320s for four billion dollars.
Options for a further 25.
First airline in the United States with satellite TV for every seat.
2007 German airline Lufthansa acquires 19 per cent of JetBlue shares.
2009 JetBlue acquires the TWA terminal in JFK.
2009 For one month only, JetBlue offers unlimited flying for a flat rate fee (599 dollars).

www.jetblue.com

CONTINENTAL AIRLINES

UNITED STATES

1934 Founded in El Paso, Texas.
1953 Merger with Pioneer Airways. Relocation of headquarters to Los Angeles.
During the Vietnam War, heavily involved in the transportation of troops.
Extensive network in the Pacific.
Offshoot: Continental Air Micronesia.
1983 Bankrupt.

1984 Works through bankruptcy and emerges profitable.
1990 Insolvent for the second time, but has bankruptcy protection.
1995 Successful once again.

Well-developed network in South America and the Caribbean. Continental now has nearly 400 jets in operation.

www.continental.com

HORIZON AIR

UNITED STATES *Horizon Air*

1981 Founded in Seattle.
Growth through acquisition of several airlines and forcing others out of the market.
1986 Alaska Airlines becomes new owner.
2007 Horizon Air is named 'Regional Airline of the Year' by Air Transport World magazine.

Focus of operations: primarily the northwestern United States.

www.horizonair.com

COMAIR

UNITED STATES   COMAIR ▲Delta Connection

1976 Established with bases in Orlando, Florida and Cincinnati, Ohio.

Comair operates as a regional feeder for Delta Air Lines. Hits the headlines in 1997 following a crash caused by ice build-up.

www.comair.com

DELTA AIR LINES

UNITED STATES

▲DELTA

1924 Founded as a crop-dusting company, 'Huff-Daland Dusters', in Macon, Georgia.
1926 Relocation to Monroe, Louisiana.
1927 Main source of income: government mail contracts.
1930 Switch to passenger transport in the Mississippi Delta area of the southern States.

1945 Relocation to Atlanta, Georgia.
1991 Purchase of ailing Pan Am.
2005 Bankruptcy protection; 9,000 employees laid off as part of restructuring.
2009 Take-over of Northwest Airlines.

www.delta.com

UNITED AIRLINES

 UNITED STATES

United Airlines headquarters in Chicago.

1926 United Airlines is founded, making it one of the oldest airlines in the world. It initially flies postal routes only from Washington state to Nevada, and for decades operates only domestic flights in the United States.

During World War II, over 5,700 aircraft are converted to bombers in United Airlines' works; 7,000 engineers train for the air force. United is one of Boeing's first customers for its 737s, 747s and 777s.

1983 First international routes.
1995 Growing financial problems.
1997 Founding member of Star Alliance.

11 September 2001 UA Flight 175 is flown into the World Trade Center, while UA Flight 93 crashes near Pittsburgh, Pennsylvania, following a courageous intervention by the passengers.
2002 Bankruptcy protection. Its 170 aircraft are put out of service and 20,000 employees laid off.

Rumours persist that in the light of the global wave of consolidations, United Airlines could one day merge with Continental Airlines. A first step in this direction is taken when Continental switches alliance in 2009 and co-ordinates its frequent flier programme with that of United Airlines.

www.united.com

VIRGIN AMERICA

UNITED STATES

2007 Is one of the newest low-cost carriers. The Virgin Group holds only 25 per cent of the shares because that is as much of a US airline as is allowed to be held in foreign hands under US law.

www.virginamerica.com

NORTHWEST AIRLINES

UNITED STATES

1926 Founded.
1939 Strong tradition of business in Asia.
1949–86 Relaunch as Northwest Orient Airlines.
1986 Expansion into Europe.
2005 Files for bankruptcy.
2008 Merger of Northwest with Delta.
2010 Further integration with Delta.

Northwest is the last major operator of DC-9s. According to Delta Air Lines, these will continue to fly after the integration process is complete. There is even the possibility that aircraft which have been out of service will be recommissioned.

www.delta.com

US AIRWAYS

☰ US AIRWAYS

▀▀ UNITED STATES

1990 Expansion into Europe.
1996 Renamed US Airways.
1996 Order for 400 Airbus aircraft.
2005 Take-over by America West Airlines, but US Airways brand retained.

1938 Founding of All American Airways, based in Pittsburgh, Pennsylvania, through the merger of numerous small regional carriers.
1953 Change of name to Allegheny Airlines.
1968 Take-over of Lake Central Airlines.
1972 Take-over of Mohawk Airlines.
1979 Renamed USAir, covering mainly the New England states.

1980 Purchase of Pacific Southwest and Piedmont Airlines.

www.usairways.com

SOUTHWEST AIRLINES

▀▀ UNITED STATES

Flight attendants have to clean the aircraft themselves after landing. Large passengers have to purchase two tickets. In terms of its fleet size, it is the second-largest airline in the world after American Airlines.

Founded in Dallas (Love Field) in 1971. Only one type of aircraft (Boeing 737). Business principle: internet bookings, fuel hedging, rapid turnaround times, no seat booking. Extras and services: either non-existent, minimal or only available at a charge.

www.southwest.com

SKYWEST AIRLINES

▀▀ UNITED STATES *SkyWest* AIRLINES

1972 Company established with a base in St. George, Utah.

Regional airline, flying for Delta, AirTran and United Airlines.

www.skywest.com

Aeromexico

 MEXICO    AeroMexico.

1934 Founded as Aeronaves de México.
1940 Buys out smaller rivals.
1959 Nationalization.
1971 Renamed Aeromexico.
1988 Bankruptcy and relaunch.
2005 Privatization.

www.aeromexico.com

Mexicana

 MEXICO   MEXICANA Ꜽ

Bandits were repeatedly attacking wagons transporting wages to Mexico's oilfields, so people started to fly the money in over their heads. This led to the formation of the airline in 1924. It is one of the oldest airlines in the world.

1924 Take-over of Compañía Mexicana de Aviación, founded in 1921.
1926 Mail delivery services.
1935 First connection to Los Angeles.
1976 Largest Boeing 727 operator outside the United States.
1989 Part-nationalized.

1990 Switch to Airbus aircraft.
2000 Member of Star Alliance.
2005 Reprivatized.

www.mexicana.com

MexicanaClick

 MEXICO   click

1975 Founded as Aerocaribe.
1990 Purchased by Mexicana.
2005 Aerocaribe becomes a low-cost airline and is renamed Click Mexicana. In 2009, its name becomes MexicanaClick.

www.mexicana.com

Cubana

CUBA   CUBANA

1929 Founding of Compañía Nacional Cubana de Aviación Curtiss, with backing from Pan Am.
1950 Flights to New York.
1959 Revolution and isolation from the West.
1962 Soviet aircraft replace Western ones. Cuba paid for seven aircraft with sugar cane.

Cubana has had just about every Russian aircraft type that has ever been built in its fleet.

www.cubana.cu

AIR JAMAICA

 JAMAICA

1968 Founded by Air Canada.
1974 Routes to Europe.
1981 Switches to Airbus aircraft.
1988 Partial destruction of the fleet by Hurricane Gilbert.
1994 Privatized.
1995 New corporate identity.
2004 Nationalized.
2009 US carrier Spirit Airlines buys Air Jamaica.

www.airjamaica.com

LIAT

 ANTIGUA

Founded in 1956, LIAT is operated by the governments of Dominica, St. Lucia, St. Vincent, Grenada, Antigua, St. Kitts/Nevis, Barbados, Guyana, Jamaica, and Trinidad and Tobago.

www.liat.com

TACA

EL SALVADOR **TACA**

1931 Founded in Tegucigalpa by New Zealander Lowell Yerex after his release from a German POW camp.
1937–41 World's largest cargo carrier: TACA carries more cargo than all the airlines in the United States combined. Numerous subsidiaries founded.
1945 Expropriation of many South American subsidiaries.
1947 Caught up in the struggle between TWA and Pan Am.
1951 Restructured.
1969 Suffers setback during civil war.
1970 Switches from BAC 1-11s to Boeing aircraft.
1989 Establishment of a multinational consortium.
1998 Switches to Airbus aircraft.

www.taca.com

COPA AIRLINES

PANAMA Copa Airlines

1944 Founded in Panama City.
1947 Commences flight operations.
1965 First international routes.
1984 Switches from Convair to Boeing aircraft.
1989 US invasion of Panama.
1990 Airline re-organized.
1998 Stake acquired by Continental Airlines.
2003 Routes as far as Argentina and Chile.
2005 Acquisition of Columbian air carrier AeroRepública.

www.copaair.com

AEROPERLAS REGIONAL

PANAMA AEROPERLAS REGIONAL

Panama's regional airline with hubs in Panama City and David.

www.aeroperlas.com

BAHAMASAIR

 BAHAMAS

1973 Founded. Bahamasair offers inter-island flights and connections to Florida.

www.bahamasair.com

SURINAM AIRWAYS

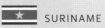 SURINAME

Surinam Airways connects the former Dutch islands to the Caribbean, Venezuela and Florida. It also still runs flights to the Netherlands.

www.slm.nl

AEROPOSTAL

 VENEZUELA AEROPOSTAL

Small Venezuelan airline with a long history (stretching back to 1929) and connections to the Caribbean, Peru, Colombia and the United States.

www.aeropostal.com

CONVIASA

VENEZUELA conViasa

Successor to VIASA, founded in 2004. State-owned. Apart from its domestic destinations, it also flies to Damascus in Syria and Tehran in Iran.

www.conviasa.aero

TAME

ECUADOR Tame

Ecuadorian domestic airline with connections to the Galapagos Islands.

www.tame.com.ec

SATENA

COLUMBIA SATENA

Servicio Aéreo a Territorios Nacionales SATENA is operated by the Colombian air force. This popular airline, which is considered to be reliable, offers a scheduled passenger service on domestic routes.

www.satena.com

AVIANCA

COLUMBIA Avianca

1919 Founded initially in Barranquilla as SCADTA.
1939 Stake acquired by Pan Am.
1940 Refounded in Barranquilla as Avianca.
1979–90 Several total losses due to terrorism and gang wars.
2001 Merger with rival ACES.
2004 Bankruptcy and relaunch.

www.avianca.com

AERO CONDOR

 PERU

Domestic charter flights, scenic flights, and cargo and air ambulance flights. Scheduled flights with 737s were suspended following several accidents due to maintenance problems.

www.aerocondor.com.pe

STAR PERU

PERU

Operates exclusively domestic flights and also has rainforest destinations in its schedule.
Artistic livery with ethnic scenes and cultural monuments depicted on tailplanes.

www.starperu.com

AeroSur

BOLIVIA  AeroSur

Extensive domestic network in Bolivia, with a number of destinations in neighbouring countries as well as flights to Miami. Lineas Aereas Canedo also provides nostalgia flights for tourists on a Douglas DC-3 for AeroSur.

www.aerosur.com.

GOL TRANSPORTES AEREOS

 BRAZIL

2000 Founded in São Paulo. Low-cost carrier offering minimal service. In ten years it has captured 50 per cent of the domestic market.
2004 Flotation.
2005 Major order with Boeing.
2006 International routes.
2006 Founding of low-cost subsidiary in Mexico.
2007 Acquisition of bankrupt airline VARIG. VARIG continues to fly routes under its own name, but for GOL's account.

www.voegol.com.br

TAM AIRLINES

BRAZIL

1961 Founded in São Paulo with four Cessnas.
1966 Switches to twin-engined aircraft.
1985 TAM purchases Fokker 27s.

1990 Switches to Fokker 100 jets.
1998 Switches to Airbus.
2008 Becomes member of Star Alliance.

Official business philosophy:
Rule 1: The customer is always right.
Rule 2: If the customer should ever not be right, see Rule 1.

www.tam.com.br

VARIG

 BRAZIL

VARIG has a long history and, following bankruptcy, has been rescued by low-cost airline GOL.
Now flies only in South America.

www.varig.com.br

PLUNA

 URUGUAY

1936 Airline founded.
1980 Has connections to Madrid.

It currently operates flights only to Uruguay's neighbouring countries.

www.flypluna.com

LAN ARGENTINA

ARGENTINA LAN

2005 Founded as a offshoot of the LAN group.

Provides strong competition to Aerolineas Argentinas.
Appears refreshingly efficient.

www.lan.com

AEROLINEAS ARGENTINAS

ARGENTINA **AEROLINEAS ARGENTINAS**

1950 Founding of airline in Buenos Aires.
1950 Purchase of 14 Comets.
By 1960 Series of losses of six Comet aircraft.
1960–70 Replacement with Boeing, BAC and Avro aircraft.
1975 Purchase of Boeing 747 aircraft.
1990 Privatization.
1998 Stake acquired by American Airlines.
2001 Bankruptcy threatens. Withdrawal of American Airlines. Suspension of all international flights.
2008 Renationalization.

www.aerolineas.com.ar

SKY AIRLINE

CHILE **SKY** Airline

2001 Founded in Santiago.
2005 Run by a German expat.

Domestic routes to 12 destinations. Also flies to La Paz, Bolivia, and Arequipa, Peru.

www.skyairline.cl

LAN AIRLINES

 CHILE LAN

1929 Founded as LAN Chile (Línea Aérea Nacional).
1989 Privatized.
2001 New name: LAN Airlines (Latin American Network).

Simultaneous expansion.
Member of Oneworld Alliance.
The former LAN Chile now operates subsidiaries in Ecuador, Peru and Argentina. In terms of livery, these subsidiaries cannot be distinguished from the parent company. This facilitates the deployment of aircraft from the pool to meet demand.

www.lan.com

AIR GREENLAND

GREENLAND   air greenland

Air Greenland's core business is the transportation of mail, cargo and people in the remotest, most inhospitable and coldest part of the world. In addition to its fixed-wing aircraft, the airline also operates helicopters.

www.airgreenland.com

ICELANDAIR

ICELAND   **ICELANDAIR**

1937   Founded as Flugfélag Akureyrar.
1940   Renamed Flugfélag Íslands
1973   Merger with Loftleidir.
New name Icelandair.
Cheap flights from Luxembourg to the United States with stopover in Iceland.
1999   Rather than from Luxembourg, now has direct flights between Iceland and many of Europe's capital cities.

www.icelandair.is

AIR ICELAND

ICELAND   *AIR ICELAND*
www.airiceland.is

Iceland's domestic airline. Merger in 1997 with Icelandair Domestic. Also maintains links to Greenland and the Faroe Islands. Maintenance and competence centre for Fokker 50s.

www.airiceland.is

AER LINGUS

IRELAND   Aer Lingus ☘

1936   Founded in Dublin.
1945   Exclusive rights to flights to United Kingdom.
1958   First transatlantic flights.
1965   Switches to jets.
1970   Purchase of Boeing 747s.

1994   Switches to Airbus.
2007   Exit from Oneworld Alliance.

www.aerlingus.com

RYANAIR

IRELAND   *RYANAIR*
THE LOW FARES AIRLINE

Founded in Dublin in 1985, becoming the largest low-cost airline in Europe and Europe's third-largest airline behind Air France-KLM and Lufthansa. Only Boeing 737s, with closely spaced seating. No adjustable seats. All extras and any services are charged extra, even check-in at the counter. All hold baggage carries an additional charge. Has 27 bases throughout Europe. Approximately 800 routes in approximately 25 countries.

Michael O'Leary has made a name for himself as a maverick with razor-sharp business acumen.

www.ryanair.com

AER ARANN

 IRELAND

1970 Founded as an island-hopper to the Aran Islands in Galway Bay off the west coast of Ireland, it now has connections to all major cities in Ireland, the United Kingdom and Brittany.

www.aerarann.com

FLYBE

 UNITED KINGDOM

1969 Launched in the Channel Islands and is now based in Exeter. Due to its large numbers of flight cancellations in the past, it has been given the nickname 'Flymaybe'.

www.flybe.com

VIRGIN ATLANTIC

 UNITED KINGDOM

The founder, Sir Richard Branson, is constantly in dispute with British Airways. When BA removed the Union Jack from their planes in 1997, Branson furnished all his aircraft with the flag instead as part of its 'British Flag Carrier' logo.

After Virgin Atlantic won another legal dispute with its rival, BA was sentenced to pay £611,000 to Branson and his airline. The billionaire shared this money out among his employees, calling it a 'BA bonus'.

www.virgin-atlantic.com

THOMAS COOK AIRLINES

UNITED KINGDOM

1999 Merger of Flying Colours Airlines and Caledonian Airways to form JMC Airlines, based in Manchester.
2003 Change of name to Thomas Cook UK.
2007 Merger of Thomas Cook and MyTravel.
2008 Integration of MyTravel Airways.

Thomas Cook Airlines operates charter flights mainly for Thomas Cook Tour Operations, from a number of UK bases to holiday destinations worldwide.

www.thomascookairlines.co.uk

EASYJET

UNITED KINGDOM

1995 Founded by Stelios Haji-Ioannou, son of a Cypriot ship-owner.

The world's third-largest low-cost airline after Southwest Airlines and Ryanair. Initially operated Boeing 737s only. Since 2002 has had Airbus A319s. Has 20 different hubs across Europe.

www.easyjet.com

An Airbus A330 being serviced in icy temperatures at Kangerlussuaq, Greenland.

Monarch Airlines

 UNITED KINGDOM **Monarch**

British holiday airline with destinations in Europe, the United States, Canada, the Caribbean, Mexico, Africa and India.

www.monarch.co.uk

Thomson Airways

UNITED KINGDOM **Thomsonfly**

1962 Founded in Luton as Euravia.
1964 Change of name to Britannia Airways.
1965 Taken over by Thomson Travel (TUI).
2005 Change of name to Thomsonfly.
2008 Shared fleet with First Choice Airways.
2009 Merger into Thomson Airways.

Alliance with TUI Airlines. This Group includes TUIfly, Thomson Airways, TUIfly Nordic, Jetairfly, Jet4you, Corsairfly and Arkefly. The entire fleet comprises some 160 aircraft.

http://flights.thomson.co.uk

British Airways

UNITED KINGDOM

BRITISH AIRWAYS

1924 Merger of the four British airlines Instone Air Line, Handley Page Transport, Daimler Airways and British Marine Air Navigation Co. Ltd. to form Imperial Airways.
1935 Merger of further airlines to form British Airways.
1939 Merger and nationalization of Imperial and British Airways to form British Overseas Airways Corporation (BOAC).
1946 Founding of British South American Airways (BSAA).

1946 Founding of British European Airways (BEA).
1949 Integration of BSAA.
1972 Merger of BOAC and BEA to form British Airways (BA).
1987 Privatization.
1988 Take-over of British Caledonian Airways.
1992 Founding of Deutsche BA.
1993 Acquisition of Brymon Airways.
1995 Founding of British Asia Airways.
2002 Brymon Airways becomes British Airways Citiexpress.
2006 British Airways Citiexpress becomes BA Connect.
2006 Deutsche BA is sold to Air Berlin.
2007 BA Connect goes to Flybe.

2008 Start-up of Terminal 5 (used exclusively by BA) at Heathrow.
2008 BA announces merger with Iberia.
2008 American Airlines is added to the merger agreement.
2008 Founding of OpenSkies airline.

www.britishairways.com

BMI BRITISH MIDLAND

| | UNITED KINGDOM | **bmi** |

1949 Founding of Derby Aviation Limited.
1964 Acquisition of Mercury Airlines.
New name: British Midland Airways
(BMA).
Based at East Midlands Airport.
1970 Transatlantic flights with Boeing 707.
1994 SAS holds 40 per cent of shares in
BMA.
1999 Acquisition of stake by Lufthansa.
2001 New name: BMI.
2009 Lufthansa secures all shares in
BMI through its London-based
holding company.

www.flybmi.com

LOGANAIR

LOGANAIR
SCOTLAND'S AIRLINE

UNITED KINGDOM

Scottish regional airline, specializing in
flights to Shetland and the Orkney Islands.
Uses beach at low tide for landing and
take-off on the Isle of Barra.

www.loganair.co.uk

CIMBER STERLING

DENMARK **CIMBER AIR**

1950 Founded by aircraft captain as
an air-taxi company. Running
scheduled services since 1966.
1995 Start of collaboration with SAS.
2008 Partial acquisition of Sterling Airlines,
which had become insolvent.

www.cimber.com

NORWEGIAN AIR SHUTTLE

NORWAY **norwegian.no**

Low-cost airline founded in 1993 to take
over the Braathens Airline network.
Has portraits of famous Norwegian
personalities such as Roald Amundsen on
its tailplanes.

www.norwegian.com

WIDEROE

NORWAY **wideroe**

1934 Airline founded as Wideroes
Flyveselskap ASA.
Air-taxi, photographic, air ambulance
and advertising flights.
1935 Relocation to Kirkenes.
1958 New base in Tromsø.
1960 Construction of new airports with
800-m/2625-ft long runways.
1960 First DHC-6 Twin Otter.
1981 First DHC-7.
1992 First DHC-8.
1999 Sold to SAS.

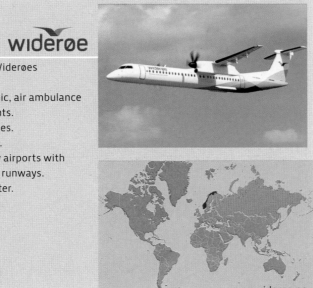

www.wideroe.no

SKYWAYS EXPRESS

SWEDEN **SKYWAYS**

Founded as Avia by Salenia Aviation in
1976. Merged with Salair in 1991. Salenia
owns 75 per cent of shares in the
company; SAS own the rest. Maintains an
extensive network of routes in Sweden.
Operates as a feeder for SAS Loganair.

www.skyways.se

SCANDINAVIAN AIRLINES

 SWEDEN

1946 Merger of the leading airlines of Norway, Sweden and Denmark to form a partnership.
1951 This gives rise to Scandinavian Airlines System (SAS)

Turi Widerøe, first female pilot for a major Western airline.

1954 First transpolar route from Copenhagen via Kangerlussuaq in Greenland to Los Angeles.
1957 First polar route to Tokyo via Anchorage, Alaska.
1986 Launch of Spanair.
1997 Founding member of Star Alliance.
2008 Sale of Spanair.

www.flysas.com

FINNAIR

 FINLAND *FINNAIR*

1923 Founded as Aero O/Y.
1946 Nationalization.
1953 Renamed Aero O/Y Finnair.
1960 Purchases Caravelles.

1962 Takes over Finnish company Kar-Air.
1975 Purchases McDonnell Douglas DC-10-30s.
1979 Regional subsidiary Finnaviation.

1983 First non-stop flight from Europe to Japan.
1988 First non-stop flight from Europe to Beijing.
1990 Launch customer for the McDonnell Douglas MD-11.
1990 Gradual conversion of medium-haul fleet to Airbus aircraft.
1999 Member of Oneworld Alliance.
2004 Purchases Embraers for short-haul flights.
2005 Orders Airbus long-haul jets.

BLUE1

 FINLAND *Blue1*

1987 Founded as Air Botnia by the Pakari family. Blue1 initially flew for Finnair until it was purchased by SAS. Has been a member of the Star Alliance since 2004.

www.blue1.fi

ESTONIAN AIR

 ESTONIA *ESTONIAN AIR*

1991 Founded by the Estonian government using aircraft previously operated by Aeroflot. SAS owns shares in 49 per cent of the company and Estonian Air is a part of the SAS loyalty programme.

www.estonian-air.com

www.finnair.com

LOT Polish Airlines

POLAND

1929 Founded by the government.
1940s Total loss of fleet in World War II.
1949 Relaunch with Ilyushins, Antonovs and Tupolevs.
1989 Converts to Boeings.
2003 Member of the Star Alliance.
2004 Launches low-cost subsidiary Centralwings.
2008 Purchases Embraer E-Jets.

www.lot.com

SkyEurope

SLOVAKIA

SkyEurope was once regarded as the best Eastern European low-cost carrier. In 2007, it shut down its Hungarian subsidiary. SkyEurope filed for bankruptcy in 2009 and it suspended all flights in September that year.

www.skyeurope.com

Czech Airlines

CZECH REPUBLIC

1923 Founded by the government.
1930 First international routes.
1938 Closure of CSA as a result of German occupation.
1945 Relaunch with Soviet aircraft.

2007 Launch of low-cost subsidiary click4sky.
2009 Possible take-over by Air France-KLM, which later falls through.

www.czechairlines.com

Wizz Air

HUNGARY

Wizz Air is based in Hungary. This low-cost carrier flies mainly to Eastern European destinations. However, since 2009 it has been seen increasingly often at German regional airports.

www.wizzair.com

Malev Hungarian Airlines

HUNGARY *MALEV* Hungarian Airlines

1918 Founded as an airmail service.
1946 Closure and relaunch by Russia.
1954 Russians withdraw from management.
1966 First Tupolev jets.
1992 Privatization.

2007 Take-over by the Russian company AIRUnion.

Member of Oneworld Alliance.

www.malev.com

Hemus Air

BULGARIA

In 2002, airlines belonging to the former Balkan Airlines were sold to private investors as bankruptcy assets. This company is showing sound growth. It has already swallowed up two other airlines: Bulgaria Air and Viaggio Air.

www.air.bg

TAROM

ROMANIA

1945 Founding of TARS with help from the Soviet Union.
1954 Withdrawal of Russians from management.
1954 Renamed TAROM.
1966 First Tupolev jets.
1968 Procurement of BAC 1-11s.
1990 Switch to Western aircraft.
2000 Withdrawal from intercontinental business.
2007 Expansion of domestic network.

www.tarom.ro

ONUR AIR

TURKEY **Onurair**

Turkish charter airline. Since 2004 has also been operating a scheduled service on Turkish domestic routes. However, its core business is carrying package tourists between Turkey and the rest of Europe.

www.onurair.com

TURKISH AIRLINES

TURKEY

TURKISH AIRLINES
TÜRK HAVA YOLLARI

1933 Founded as Türkiye Devlet Hava Yolları.
1947 First international routes.
1967 First jets.
1972 First DC-10s outside the United States.
1974 Purchases Boeing 727s.
1974 Founding of subsidiary Cyprus Turkish Airlines (KTHY).
1986 First routes to the United States.
1989 Founding of Türk Hava Taşımacılık.
1989 Launch of Sun Express jointly with Lufthansa.
1994 THT merges with THY.
2005 New corporate identity.
2008 Launch of low-cost subsidiary AnadoluJet.

2008 Acquisition of 49 per cent stake in B&H Airlines.
2008 Member of Star Alliance.

www.thy.com

SUN EXPRESS

TURKEY **SunExpress**

Joint venture between Lufthansa and Turkish Airlines, established in 1989. Now part of Condor Airlines. Very popular airline.

www.sunexpress.com

CYPRUS AIRWAYS

CYPRUS **CYPRUS AIRWAYS**

1947 Founded with the aid of BEA. From the first day onwards, operates only international routes.
Most important route: Nicosia–Athens–Rome–London.
Until 1974 Flies to all major European cities.
1974 Turkish invasion; destruction of the fleet.
Nicosia airport under UN administration.
1975 Larnaca airport opens as main base.
1980 Majority of shares in government ownership.
1984 Switches to Airbus aircraft.

www.cyprusairways.com

EUROCYPRIA

 CYPRUS

Established by Cyprus Airways in 1990 as a subsidiary charter airline. Sold to the Cypriot government in 2006. Flights to over 70 destinations in 20 countries.

www.eurocypria.com

AEGEAN AIRLINES

 GREECE

1987 Founded as Aegean Aviation. Executive service with small business jets.
1994 Purchases Learjets.
1999 Expansion into present-day Aegean Airlines. Amalgamation with Air Greece.
2001 Merger with Cronus Airlines.
2005 Partnership with Lufthansa.
2010 Joins Star Alliance.

Most successful Greek airline.

www.aegeanair.com

OLYMPIC AIR

GREECE **OLYMPIC**

Successor to failed state airlines. Renamed Olympic in 1956 by Greek magnate Aristotle Onassis and transformed into a successful airline. Operations suspended in 2009. Privatized and almost immediately relaunched as Olympic Air.

www.olympicair.com

MAT MACEDONIAN AIRLINES

MACEDONIA **MAT** *Macedonian Airlines*

Founded in 1994. As there is an airline in Greece with the same name (with no aircraft), MAT is a thorn in the side of the Greeks. In 2009, some planes are grounded by Eurocontrol due to arrears on payments of route charges.

MONTENEGRO AIRLINES

MONTENEGRO AIRLINES

MONTENEGRO

1994 Founded. Flying operations begin.
1997 Connections betweens Podgorica and cities in Central Europe as well as in the Balkans. Scheduled and charter traffic.

www.montenegroairlines.com

BH AIR

BH Airlines

BOSNIA-HERZEGOVINA

Launched in 1994 as Air Bosna at the time of the collapse of Yugoslavia. Grounded in 2003 because of its involvement in criminal practices. Re-established under new management in 2005 as BH Air.

www.bhairlines.com

CROATIA AIRLINES

CROATIA **CROATIA AIRLINES**

1989 Founded as Zagreb Airlines. Cargo operations for UPS using Cessna 402s.
1990 Name changes to Croatia Airlines.
1991 First route: Zagreb-Split.
1992 Balkan War: no flights.
1993 Fleet expansion.
1996 First airline to fly to Sarajevo.
1997 Switch to Airbus aircraft.
2004 Member of Star Alliance.
2009 Croatia Airlines celebrates its twenty-millionth passenger.

www.croatiaairlines.hr

ADRIA AIRWAYS

SLOVENIA — ADRIA / ADRIA AIRWAYS

1961	Founded as Inex Adria Airways.
1986	Renamed Adria Airways following merger with Adria Aviopromet.
1991	Aircraft stored at Klagenfurt, Austria, for the duration of the war in the Balkans.

www.adria.si

INTERSKY

AUSTRIA — InterSky / www.intersky.biz

Austrian airline with its home airport at Friedrichshafen in Germany. In private ownership. Operates low-cost flights on DHC-8s to destinations in Central Europe and the Mediterranean region.

www.intersky.biz

AUSTRIAN AIRLINES

AUSTRIA — Austrian

1957	Establishment of OELAG.
1963	First jet (Sud Aviation Caravelle).
1971	Introduction of DC-9s.
1990	Expansion into Africa and China.
1998	Take-over of Tyrolean Airways.
2000	Membership of Star Alliance.
2002	Purchase of Rheintalflug.
2002	Take-over of Lauda Air.

| 2002 | Merger of Tyrolean Airways and Rheintalflug to form Austria Arrows. |
| 2008 | Offered for sale by tender by the government due to heavy debts. |

Lufthansa wins tender process. Take-over subject to approval by the European Commission.

www.aua.com

SWISS INTERNATIONAL AIR LINES

swiss Swiss International Air Lines

SWITZERLAND

1983	Founded as Crossair.
2001	Swissair goes into insolvency.
2002	Crossair forms the legal foundation of the new airline Swiss. With assistance from the government and the banks, Crossair takes over aircraft, pilots and equipment from the former Swissair.
2005	Gradual acquisition by Lufthansa.
2005	Launch of regional subsidiary Swiss European.
2006	Member of Star Alliance.
2007	Lufthansa owns 100 per cent of Swiss.
2008	Acquisition of Edelweiss Airlines.

2008	Acquisition of Servair.
2008	Launch of Private Air by Swiss European.
2009	Swiss voted Europe's best airline.

www.swiss.com

HELVETIC AIRWAYS

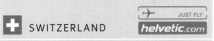

SWITZERLAND

Came into being in 2003 as the successor to Odette Airways. After discontinuing flights to many destinations in northern Europe, it now focuses on the Balkans and the Mediterranean. Leases aircraft to other airlines including Swiss. Charter flights.

www.helvetic.com

LUXAIR

LUXEMBOURG

LUXAIR

1948 Established as Luxembourg Airlines Company.
1961 Restructuring.
New name: Luxair.
Expansion of routes to all EU capitals.
1967 First jet airliner: a Caravelle.
1969 Expansion of fleet with Boeing and Embraer aircraft.
2006 Restructuring.
2006 Purchase of Bombardier Dash 8-Q400s.
2008 Orders first 737-800.

www.luxair.lu

CIRRUS AIRLINES

GERMANY

1995 Founded. In partnership with Lufthansa since 2000. Part of fleet operated for Lufthansa and Swiss. Partnership with Air Moldova.
2010 Moves to new headquarters at Saarbrücken Airport.

www.cirrusairlines.de

CONDOR

GERMANY

Condor

1955 Founding of Deutsche Flugdienst GmbH.
1965 First charter flights.
1961 Take-over of Condor-Luftreederei.
1961 Renamed Condor Flugdienst.
1962 Long-haul flights to Thailand, Sri Lanka and Kenya.
1969 Merger with Südflug.
1991 Introduction of business class.
2009 Take-over by Thomas Cook.

www.condor.com

AIR BERLIN

GERMANY

airberlin.com

1978 Founded by two American pilots. Headquarters in Miami, Florida, due to Berlin's four-power status.
1981 Palma de Majorca becomes most important destination.
Charter flights to the Mediterranean.
Licensed in Germany following reunification.
2006 Flotation.
2006 Acquisition of dba.
2007 Acquisition of LTU.
2007 Share in Swiss Belair increases to 49 per cent.
2007 New corporate identity.

2008 Joint venture with Russian S7 Airlines.
2008 Joint venture with Chinese Hainan Airlines.

www.airberlin.com

LUFTHANSA

GERMANY

1988 New corporate identity.
1997 Founding member of Star Alliance.
2003 Acquisition of Air Dolomiti.
2005 Purchase of Swiss International.
2007 Investment in 19 per cent stake in JetBlue.
2008 Acquisition of Brussels Airlines.
2009 Acquisition of BMI.
2009 Acquisition of AUA.

At Lufthansa's first class terminal in Frankfurt, a personal assistant takes care of you from the time you arrive at the airport right up to the time of departure. You are transferred to the aircraft in a Mercedes or a Porsche Cayenne.

1926 Founding of Deutsche Luft Hansa.
1945 Ceased operations.

1951 Liquidation.
1953 Launch of new company, Aktiengesellschaft für Luftverkehrsbedarf (LUFTAG).
1954 Renamed Deutsche Lufthansa AG.
1960 First Boeing 707 service to New York. Up until 1962 100 per cent state-owned.
1964 Boeing 727s.
1966 Flotation.
1968 Boeing 737-100 developed with the aid of Lufthansa.
1970 Boeing 747s.
1979 Airbus A310s.

www.lufthansa.com

GERMANWINGS

GERMANY

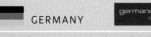

German low-cost carrier based in Cologne.
1997 Established as Eurowings.
2002 Renamed Germanwings.
2009 Wholly owned by Lufthansa. Drinks and snacks sold on board.

www.germanwings.com

BRUSSELS AIRLINES

BELGIUM

2001 Sabena goes bankrupt.
2002 Launch of SN Brussels Airlines.
2005 Majority stake sold by Virgin Express.
2007 Merges to form Brussels Airlines.
2008 Lufthansa buys 45 per cent stake in Brussels Airlines.

2009 Membership of Star Alliance.

Brussels Airlines has a well-developed network in Europe and Africa.

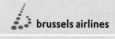

www.brusselsairlines.com

KLM

KLM Royal Dutch Airlines

1919 Founding of Koninklijke Luchtvaart Maatschappij (KLM) on the initiative of Albert Plesman, later chairman of the Dutch airline.

Oldest airline in the world still operating today.

1920 First Fokker aircraft.
1927 Establishment of flights between the Netherlands and the colony of Batavia in present-day Indonesia.
1934 Establishment of flights between Amsterdam and Paramaribo in Suriname and Curaçao in the Netherlands Antilles.
1946 Fleet renewal.
1960 Procurement of DC-8s.
1970 onwards. Establishment of Garuda Indonesian Airways, Philippine Airlines and VIASA in Venezuela.
1988 Alliance with Northwest Airlines.
1991 Eliminates first class.

2004 Merger with Air France through exchange of shares, but with retention of separate brands.
2009 Acquisition of 25 per cent stake in Alitalia by AF-KLM.
2009 Negotiations with CSA.
KLM is the only airline to have flown all aircraft types from the DC-2 to the DC-10. It is now a loyal Boeing customer.

www.klm.com

TRANSAVIA.COM

  transavia.com

Established in 1965 by a Belgian bicycle manufacturer as Transavia Limburg. Later known as Transavia Holland. Charter flights to North America. Since 2005, a low-cost carrier operating as transavia.com.

www.transavia.com

MARTINAIR

  Martinair

Founded in 1958 by a Dutch air force pilot. Begins as a charter airline with DC-3s. Buys ever larger models as it becomes increasingly successful. Operates charter, scheduled and cargo flights worldwide.

www.martinair.com

REGIONAL

  Régional

Large regional airline owned by AirFrance to supplement its domestic network. Regional flies in AirFrance livery and under the AirFrance name.

www.regional.com

AirFrance

 FRANCE

1933 Formed from the merger of four airlines.
1946 Paris–New York route.
1953 First jet: the de Havilland Comet.
1960 Jet-only operations with Caravelles and Boeing 707s.
1963 Redistribution of routes by the French government.

Long-haul routes were from that point to be serviced by UTA.
1974 First customer of the Airbus A300.
1976 First Air France Concorde flight.
1990 Merger with UTA and Air Inter.
2000 Founding member of SkyTeam Alliance.
2004 Merger with KLM through exchange of shares, but with separate brands being retained for the time being.
2009 Acquisition of 25 per cent stake in Alitalia by AF-KLM.

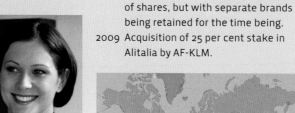

www.airfrance.fr

Corsairfly

 FRANCE

Successor to Corsair, founded in 1981 by a Corsican family. Owned since 2000 by the German tour operator TUI.

www.corsairfly.com

Air One

ITALY

Founded in 1983 as Aliadriatica. Renamed in 1995. Played an important role in the rescue of Alitalia in 2008.

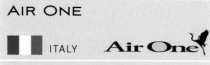

www.flyairone.it

Eurofly

 ITALY

Operates charter and scheduled flights from its base in Milan. Second hub in Sharm-el-Sheikh, Egypt. Merged with Meridiana in February 2010 to form Meridiana Fly, now Italy's second-largest airline.

www.meridiana.it

Air Dolomiti

 ITALY

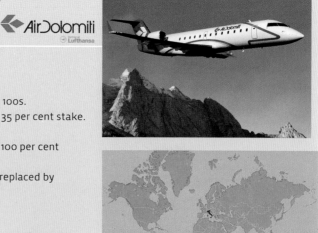

1989 Founded in Trieste.
1991 Dash 8-300s.
1995 ATR-42s.
1998 ATR-72s and Fokker 100s.
1999 Lufthansa acquires 35 per cent stake.
2001 Flotation.
2003 Lufthansa acquires 100 per cent stake.
2009 BAe-146s gradually replaced by Embraer 195s.

New hub in Munich.
Over 600 flights per week out of Munich.

www.airdolomiti.it

ALITALIA

 ITALY **Alitalia**

1946 Founded by the Italian government.
1948 First international routes.
1956 Ranked in twelfth place internationally.

1960 Introduction of DC-8s and Caravelle SE210s.
1978 First year in profit.
2009 Various investors put the airline back on its feet after it goes into liquidation. Reorganization.

www.alitalia.it

MERIDIANA

ITALY  **Meridiana** *SimplyFly.*

1963 Founded by Prince Karim Aga Khan as Alisarda, based in Olbia.
1965 First domestic routes from Sardinia.
1974 DC-9s and international routes out of Sardinia.
1990 Licensed for flights throughout Italy.

2004 Switches to Airbus aircraft.
2006 Acquires 30 per cent stake in Eurofly.
2007 Passenger volume stands at 4.6 million.
2010 Merges with Eurofly.

www.meridiana.it

AIR MALTA

 MALTA **AIR MALTA**

Malta's state airline, founded in 1973. Connections to many major European cities.

www.airmalta.com

AIR COMET

SPAIN **air**comet

Operated scheduled and charter services. Had agreements with Air Europa, Spanair, AeroSur, Aerolineas Argentinas and AeroRepublica. Numerous connections within Europe and to South America. Ceased trading in December 2009.

IBERIA

SPAIN **IBERIA**

1927 Founded.
1944 Nationalization.
1946 First route to Buenos Aires.
1997 Take-over of Air Nostrum.
1999 Member of Oneworld Alliance.
2001 Privatization.
2008 In take-over negotiations with BA.
2010 Merger with British Airways.

Iberia flies to almost all South American countries as well as to the Caribbean. The airline holds equity interests in several South American airlines.

www.iberia.es

AIR NOSTRUM

 SPAIN  IBERIA regional operado por AIR NOSTRUM

Iberia's regional airline, based in Valencia. Extensive network in Spain, but also flies to several European countries and to Morocco.

www.airnostrum.es

SPANAIR

SPAIN *Spanair*

1986 Founded by SAS.
1988 European charter flights.
1991 Intercontinental flights to the United States, the Caribbean and Argentina.
2008 Tragic crash in Madrid.
2009 Sold for 1 euro to a Catalonian investment consortium.
2009 New corporate identity.
2009 Workforce cut by a third and many routes suspended.

www.spanair.com

AIR EUROPA

SPAIN *AirEuropa*

Founded in Majorca in 1986 in order to participate in the growth in tourism to Majorca. Subsequently introduced flights to the Americas.

www.aireuropa.com

SATA AIR ACORES

PORTUGAL **SATA** *Air Açores*

Founded in 1941 as 'Serviço Açoreano de Transportes Aereos' in order to provide airline services around the Azores.

www.sata.pt

SATA INTERNATIONAL

PORTUGAL **SATA** *Internacional*

Subsidiary of SATA Air Açores. Connects the Azores with Europe and North America.

www.sata.pt

TAP PORTUGAL

PORTUGAL **TAP** TAP PORTUGAL

1945 Founded in Lisbon.
1946 First routes to Angola (Luanda), and Mozambique (Maputo).
1969 New York via Santa Maria (Azores).
1990 Switches from Boeing to Airbus.
1994 Holds 20 per cent stake in Air Macau.

1996 Service to Macau.
2005 Member of Star Alliance.
2006 Take-over of rival Portugalia.
2009 Privatization.

www.flytap.com

ERITREAN AIRLINES

ERITREA Eritrean Airlines

It was not until 2002, long after Eritrea's independence (1993), that the airline obtained its first aircraft, a Boeing 767. Due to the many regional conflicts, its development has been hesitant.

www.ertra.com/eal

ETHIOPIAN AIRLINES

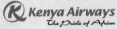

ETHIOPIA Ethiopian

1945 Founded by Emperor Haile Selassi, with support from TWA.
1946 First international route to Cairo.
1998 Transatlantic service.
2000 Upgrading of Addis Ababa into a training centre for numerous African airlines.

The American airline TWA was the force behind the founding of Ethiopian Airlines in 1945. Today, Ethiopian Airlines flies to almost all of Africa's capital cities. The airline is modern and highly reliable.

www.ethiopianairlines.com

KENYA AIRWAYS

KENYA Kenya Airways
The Pride of Africa

1977 East African Community collapses.
1977 East African Airways is wound up.
1977 Establishment of Kenya Airways in Nairobi.
1991 Beginning of privatization.
1995 KLM acquires 26 per cent stake.
2005 New corporate identity.
2005 'African Airline of the Year' award.
2007 Member of SkyTeam Alliance.

Flowers and fresh fish are important additional cargo items, providing extra revenue on passenger flights.

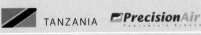

www.kenya-airways.com

AIR UGANDA

UGANDA air uganda

Private airline, founded in 2007 by the Aga Khan Fund for Economic Development. Partnership with Brussels Airlines.

www.air-uganda.com

AIR TANZANIA

TANZANIA AIR TANZANIA

Founded in 1977 after the break-up of East African Airways. Privatized in 2001. Temporarily suspended operations in 2008 due to safety deficiencies and losses. Purchased in 2009 by a Chinese investor.

www.airtanzania.com

PRECISION AIR

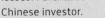

TANZANIA PrecisionAir

In operation since 1994, when it was founded as an air-taxi company for scenic flights. Due to high demand, it has also run scheduled flights since 1999. Air Kenya holds a 49 per cent stake in the airline.

www.precisionairtz.com

AIR MALAWI

 MALAWI

State-owned company. For economic reasons, most flights were suspended in 2006. Agreement with Air Zimbabwe in 2006. In 2008, South Africa-based Comair Kulula acquired a 49 per cent stake in the airline for 3,500 US dollars.

www.airmalawi.com

LAM

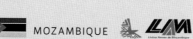 MOZAMBIQUE

1936 Founded as Direcção de Exploração de Transportes Aéreos.
1980 Renamed Linhas Aéreas de Moçambique (LAM).
1998 Partially privatized. Close links with Portugal and the Cape Verde Islands.

www.lam.co.mz

AIR SEYCHELLES

1977 Founded.
1978 Launch of domestic flights.
1983 Long-haul routes to Frankfurt and London. Other destinations include Singapore, Paris and Moscow.

www.airseychelles.com

AIR MADAGASCAR

MADAGASCAR

1962 Founded as Madair.
1963 Change of name to Air Madagascar. Air France owns a 44 per cent stake; the Malagasy Government owns 39 per cent.
1964 Boeing 707s.
1979 Boeing 747s.
2004 Major financial problems.
2005 Government holds 89 per cent stake.
2005 Restructuring.

Long-haul routes to Bangkok and Paris. Regional traffic carried in ATR-42s and ATR-72s.

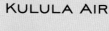
www.airmadagascar.com

AIR MAURITIUS

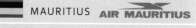 MAURITIUS

Founded in 1967 in order to be able to provide regular access to the 600-km/ 373-mile-distant neighbouring island of Rodrigues. From 1977 onwards, long-haul routes were added. Due to the high demand, it has even purchased Boeing 747s.

www.airmauritius.com

AIR AUSTRAL

 REUNION

It connects the French island paradise in the Indian Ocean to the rest of the world. Due to its strategically favourable position, flights can also be made from Paris to Australia on Boeing 777s with a stopover in Réunion.

www.air-austral.com

AIR ZIMBABWE

 ZIMBABWE

Founded in 1967 as Air Rhodesia. It was renamed after independence in 1980. Financial problems in 2003. In 2005, a maiden flight on a new route from Dubai to Harare carried just one passenger!

www.airzimbabwe.aero

KULULA AIR

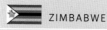 RSA

Low-cost airline established in 2001 by parent company Comair South Africa. Regional destinations in South Africa, Namibia, Zimbabwe and Mauritius.

www.kulula.com

SOUTH AFRICAN AIRWAYS

RSA

SOUTH AFRICAN AIRWAYS

1929	Founded.
1934	Emergency sale to the government.
1945	Route to London.
1953	Purchase of de Havilland Comets.
1957	Route to Perth.

1960	Boeing 707s.
1971	Boeing 747s.
1980	Beginning of decade of decline due to boycott during apartheid.
1991	Routes worldwide.
2006	Member of Star Alliance.

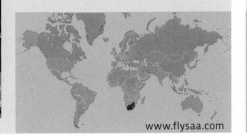

www.flysaa.com

AIR BOTSWANA

AIR BOTSWANA

BOTSWANA

State airline of Botswana. Operated at a loss initially. The first year with a positive balance sheet was 1999, when a suicidal sacked pilot crashed his ATR-42 into the parked fleet, and insurance companies had to pay for the damage.

www.airbotswana.co.bw

AIR NAMIBIA

NAMIBIA

Air Namibia
First Class World Class

South West Air Transport was founded in 1946. Air Namibia has held its current name only since 1991. It expanded its long-haul operations to the United Kingdom and Germany with several leased Boeing 747s before switching to Airbus A340s.

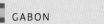

www.airnamibia.com.na

TAAG ANGOLA AIRLINES

ANGOLA

TAG · LINHAS AEREAS DE ANGOLA ANGOLA AIRLINES

Founded in 1938. Established Angola Air Charter as a subsidiary with destinations in Africa and Europe in 1987. Close links with the Soviet Union. Long-haul service to Cuba.

www.taag.com

AIR SERVICE GABON

GABON

Air Service

Founded in 1965. Connects Gabon to cities in West Africa. Features on the EU blacklist.

www.airservice.aero

GABON AIRLINES

GABON

GABON AIRLINES

Established by the government in 2006. Personnel and aircraft are managed by Ethiopian Airlines. Its network covers neighbouring countries, as well as Paris, Beirut, Dubai and Johannesburg.

www.gabonairlines.com

NIGERIAN ARIK AIR

 NIGERIA

Westernized airline with modern aircraft. Extensive domestic network in Nigeria with two long-haul routes to Johannesburg and London.

www.arikair.com

NIGERIAN EAGLE AIRLINES

NIGERIA

Formerly a Nigerian subsidiary of the Virgin Group, although the majority share was in government hands. Virgin sold their stake in 2008 and the airline changed its name from Virgin Nigeria Airways to Nigerian Eagle Airlines.

www.virginnigeria.com

AIR IVOIRE

IVORY COAST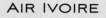

In operation since 1960. The airline belonged to the Ivory Coast government until the company went bankrupt in 1999. It has been revived with support from a French corporation.

www.airivoire.com

TACV CABO VERDE AIRLINES

CAPE VERDE

Based on its strong links with Portugal, it operates frequent flights to the former colonial power and to Brazil.

www.flytacv.cv

AIR ALGERIE

ALGERIA الخطوط الجوية الجزائرية AIR ALGERIE

1947   Founded.
1958   First jet – a Caravelle.
1963   Partially nationalized.
1970   Launch of domestic airline STA.
1974   100 per cent state-owned.
2007   Construction of new maintenance centre.

Air Algerie maintains an extensive network of flights to 26 domestic airports, a dozen destinations in Africa and over 20 cities in Europe.
Air Algérie carries three million passengers annually.

www.airalgerie.dz

TUNISAIR

 TUNISIA الخطوط التونسية TUNISAIR

1948   Founded.
1954   Charter flights from Europe to Djerba.
1956   First non-stop flights to Paris.
1961   First jet – a Caravelle.
1982   Airbus A300s.
1991   40 per cent stake in Tuninter.
1991   Launch of subsidiary Sevenair.

Founding member of the 'Arabesk Alliance' which is made up of airlines from North Africa and the Middle East.
Tunisair has been flying accident-free for 60 years.

www.tunisair.com

LIBYAN AIRLINES

LIBYA

Founded in 1964. Restricted to domestic flights for 20 years due to the boycott following the Lockerbie bombing of 1988. The passenger fleet is composed of Western aircraft types, the cargo fleet entirely of Russian aircraft.

www.ln.aero

190

AFRIQIYAH AIRWAYS

LIBYA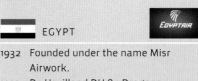

2001 Founded.
Under Libyan government ownership.
2003 Switches to Airbus.
2009 Travels to 19 destinations in Africa and major cities in Europe.

Destinations include the former colonial powers in Europe and their former colonies in Africa. All routes pass via Tripoli. Routes to the Far East are now planned. The airline's logo 9.9.99 is the date on which the declaration calling for the formation of the African Union was issued.

www.afriqiyah.aero

SAUDI ARABIAN AIRLINES

SAUDI ARABIA

1945 Establishment as the national airline. The CEO is the defence minister.
1949 onwards: Bristol DC-3s, Convair 340s.
1962 Boeing 720Bs.
1965 Member of the Arab Air Carriers Organization.
1972 New name: Saudia.
1979 First direct flights to the United States.
1994 Boeing order for 7.5 billion dollars.
1997 Name changed back to old name of Saudi Arabian Airlines.
2007 Boeing, Airbus and Embraer aircraft.

In the past, Saudi Arabian Airlines has purchased mainly widebodied aircraft. From 2010 onwards, regional jets will also be joining the fleet. Prior to each take-off, an imam recites a *surah* from the Qur'an over the on-board loudspeaker system. The text flashes up on the screen in several languages. During the flight, an arrow appears in a corner of the display indicating the direction in which Mecca is located. There is no alcohol on board. Arabian airlines were also the last to disallow smoking onboard.

www.saudiairlines.com

EGYPTAIR

EGYPT

1932 Founded under the name Misr Airwork.
1933 De Havilland DH 84 Dragons.
1935 DH 89 Dragon Rapides.

1946 Numerous types of aircraft: Airspeed Consul, Percival Proctor, Bristol 170, North American AT-6, Avro Ansons, Vickers Viking, Dragon Rapide, Beech C-45 and AT-11.

1949 Renamed MisrAir.
1956 Merger with Syrian Airlines and United Arab Airlines.
1958 Change of name to United Arab Airlines (UAA).
1961–71 Over 20 total hull losses.
1971 Renamed EgyptAir.
1981 Ex-general takes over management. Sound management leads to success.
2007 Launch of EgyptAir Express.
2008 Membership of Star Alliance.

www.egyptair.com

MIDDLE EAST AIRLINES

🌲 LEBANON

1945 Founded in Beirut as a joint regional airline by Pan Am and BOAC.
1963 Jet operations with Caravelles.
1968 Destruction of the fleet by Israeli air attack.
1975–90 Operating from abroad.
1998 Restructuring.
2007 Membership of SkyTeam Alliance.

Banque du Liban owns a 99 per cent stake in the airline.

www.mea.com.lb

ARKIA ISRAEL AIRLINES

✡ ISRAEL

Subsidiary of EL AL. Only narrowly escaped a terrorist attack involving anti-aircraft missiles in Mombasa on 28 November 2002. Just 20 minutes later, the Paradise Hotel in Mombasa was blown up.

www.arkia.com

EL AL ISRAEL AIRLINES

✡ ISRAEL

1948 Founded.
1949 First route to Paris.
1950 onwards: Acquisition of de Havilland Comets, Boeing 707s, DC-8s.
1961 First route to New York.
1968–70 Several attacks on EL AL.
1970 New security procedures.
1977 Subsidiary Sun D'Or.
2000 Boeing 777s.

All meals and drinks on board EL AL are kosher, prepared under the supervision of a rabbi. EL AL aircraft are all fitted with anti-missile systems.

www.elal.com

ROYAL JORDANIAN AIRLINES

🇯🇴 JORDAN ROYAL JORDANIAN

1963 Founded as ALIA.
1965 Caravelle jets put into service.
1971 Boeing 707s.
1977 Boeing 747s and first routes across the Atlantic.
1990 Switches to Airbus aircraft.
2001 Privatization.

www.rj.com

KUWAIT AIRWAYS

KUWAIT

1953 Founded as Kuwait National Airways
       Company with support from BOAC.
1955 New name: Kuwait Airways.
       Government-supported.
1962 Under full government control.
1964 Merger with Trans Arabia Airlines.
1964 First jets.
1968 Boeing 707s.
1978 Boeing 747s.
1980 Order for Airbus aircraft.
1990 Iraqi invasion.
       A dozen aircraft destroyed, five seized.

1991 Relaunch with Boeing and Airbus
       aircraft.
2009 Privatization.

Kuwait Airways is exposed to tough
competition in a small market that it would
like to win over with new aircraft.

www.kuwaitairways.com

GULF AIR

BAHRAIN

1950 Founded as Gulf Aviation.
1951 Investment by governments of
       Bahrain, Qatar, Abu Dhabi and Oman.
1970 First BAC 1-11 jets.
1970 Vickers VC-10s.
1974 Lockheed TriStars.
1974 New name: Gulf Air.
1980 Switches to Boeing and Airbus
       aircraft.
2006 Abu Dhabi, Qatar and Oman
       withdraw from the alliance to
       promote their own airlines.

www.gulfair.com

QATAR AIRWAYS

QATAR   QATAR AIRWAYS القطرية

1993 Founded by the government.
1997 Partial privatization.
1997 Switch to Airbus aircraft.
2006 Routes to the United States.
       Skytrax Award: World's Best First
       Class.
2008 First successful attempts at
       flying with natural gas instead of
       conventional kerosene.
2009 Qatar Airways wins the title 'World's
       Best Economy Class' from Skytrax.

www.qatarairways.com

EMIRATES

UNITED ARAB EMIRATES

1985   Founded by the government.
       Aircraft leased initially from PIA.
1987   Destinations in Europe.
1990   Destinations in Far East and Africa.
1998   Stake in Sri Lankan.
       Emirates becomes one of the

fastest growing airlines in the world, providing a first-class service in all categories.
       58 firm orders for the Airbus A380.
2000   Non-stop flights to Australia.
2001   Non-stop flights to Argentina.
2008   Flight operations with the A380.

After its founding, scarcely anyone took any notice of this airline. However, since the end of the last millennium, it has caused a stir in the airline industry. Everyone knows, especially following its order of 58 A380s, 79 A350s and 31 Boeing 777s, that this is a company to be reckoned with.

www.emirates.com

ETIHAD AIRWAYS

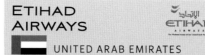

UNITED ARAB EMIRATES

2003   Founded by royal decree.
2004   Aircraft order for eight billion dollars.
2005   Flights to America.
2006   Flights to Australia.
2006   In 30 months the network expands to 30 destinations.

'We don't fly passengers. We entertain guests.' That is how Etihad describes itself and its service. As other airlines are cutting their services, Etihad view this as an opportunity to entice Europeans aboard their aircraft. Etihad has also ordered ten A380s and 25 A350s. Airports

in the Persian Gulf are all being expanded in order to accommodate the anticipated growth in the numbers of passengers changing planes in Dubai or Abu Dhabi instead of Frankfurt or London.

www.etihadairways.com

AIR ARABIA

UNITED ARAB EMIRATES

Arabian low-cost airline operating out of Sharjah. Has only been in the market for a few years but already flies to 50 destinations in the Middle East, India and North Africa. Operates a subsidiary airline called Air Arabia Maroc.

www.airarabia.com

OMAN AIR

OMAN

As every emirate needs its own airline, there has also been one in Oman since 1981. The government owns an 82 per cent stake in the airline, which focuses on long-haul routes. This is reinforced by the fact that it has six Boeing 787s on order.

www.omanair.com

YEMENIA

YEMEN   Yemenia اليمنية

Yemenia – Yemen Airways has been in existence since 1961. It has operated under its new name since 1978. In 2009, one of its aircraft had a tragic accident off the coast of the Comoros, in the Indian Ocean, as it was coming in to land in Moroni.

www.yemenia.com

MIAT MONGOLIAN AIRLINES

 MONGOLIA

National airline of Mongolia, founded in 1956. Part of the Mongolian air force, it has been under civil administration only since 1993. Operates using Airbus A310s and Boeing 737s.

www.miat.com

ROSSIYA RUSSIAN AIRLINES

RUSSIAN FEDERATION РОССИЯ

1992 Founded.
2006 Take-over of Pulkovo Airlines.

Rossiya is also due to take over other loss-making companies from Russia's AIRUnion alliance. These will then be subject, like

Aeroflot, to state control. The airline's headquarters and principal hub are at Moscow's Vnukovo airport.

www.rossiya-airlines.ru

AEROFLOT RUSSIAN AIRLINES

RUSSIAN FEDERATION AEROFLOT Russian Airlines

1976 Hundred-millionth passenger.
1990 Over 10,000 aircraft.
1992 Divided up into 300 regional airlines.
1993 Restructured.
2006 Membership of SkyTeam Alliance.

On 23 March 1994, an Aeroflot captain allowed his two children to sit in the cockpit. The 15-year-old son unwittingly switched off the autopilot. As the aircraft began to fly increasingly tight turns, the G-forces that were generated were so powerful that the pilots could not regain their seats. In the end, the Airbus A310 climbed vertically until it nearly stalled, whereupon the aircraft began to spin and went into a nosedive. The captain made it back to his seat and brought the airbus under control again, but they were so close to the ground that their altitude was insufficient to recover completely. Just three minutes after the autopilot had been switched off, the plane struck the ground, killing everyone on board.

1923 Founded by resolution of the Communist Party of the Soviet Union. An association was founded that collected donations for purchasing aircraft. Workers had to 'donate' their wages and in return received shares in 'Dobrolet'.
1923 A few months later, 15 Junkers F13s were purchased.
1937 International connections.
1939 Largest airline in the world with 4,000 aircraft and 400,000 employees.
1971 Membership of IATA.

www.aeroflot.ru

Before every take-off, the crew check the landing gear, control surfaces and engines for foreign bodies and damage.

KD AVIA

RUSSIAN FEDERATION

Private airline from Kaliningrad. Like many Russian airlines, it has had difficulties due to the credit crunch and declining passenger numbers.

www.kdavia.ru

URAL AIRLINES

RUSSIAN FEDERATION

1993 Founded in Yekaterinburg.
1997 Privatized.
2008 Carried 1.5 million passengers.

Russian successor to Aeroflot's Sverdlovsk Division in Yekaterinburg. It stuck with the old Russian aircraft types for a long time and was confronted with dwindling passenger numbers. Several auctions have been held, but they failed to come up with a buyer. Now the airline is being revamped and replacing its Tupolevs with Airbus aircraft.

www.uralairlines.ru

S7 AIRLINES

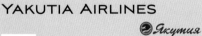

RUSSIAN FEDERATION

1992 Founded in Novosibirsk under the name Siberia.
2005 Renamed S7 Airlines.
       Russia's second-largest airline.
2007 Switch from Russian aircraft types to Airbus and Boeing aircraft for long-haul routes.
2008 Codesharing with Air Berlin.

After the accidental shooting down of a passenger aircraft by the military, all of its aircraft have been repainted in bright green colours. It is not known whether or not this is a coincidence.

www.s7.ru

YAKUTIA AIRLINES

RUSSIAN FEDERATION

Russian successor to Aeroflot's Yakutsk Division. Flies exclusively domestic routes and predominantly Russian aircraft types.

www.yakutia.aero

ARMAVIA

ARMENIA

Private airline based in Yerevan. On 3 May 2006, an A320 crashed near Sochi. During the night of 4 May, an aircraft hangar in Brussels, containing two further Armavia aircraft, burned down. The airline thus lost three aircraft in the space of two days.

www.armavia.aero

AZAL AZERBAIJAN AIRLINES

AZERBAIJAN

Founded in 1992 with Russian machines. Has since undergone a massive fleet renewal with Boeing and Airbus aircraft.

www.azal.az

AIR ASTANA

KAZAKHSTAN   air astana

2001 Founded in Astana, Kazakhstan, with three leased Boeing 737s.
2004 Boeing 757s.
2004 Fokker 50s for domestic services. 51 per cent state-owned.

2008 Partnership with Lufthansa.

CEO Peter Foster is an experienced manager who has led airlines all over the world to success. This huge country is crying out to be opened up for tourism.

www.airastana.com

KYRGYZSTAN AIRLINES

KYRGYZSTAN

State airline based in Bishkek. Domestic and international scheduled services. Made it onto the EU blacklist in 2005. The airline is 81 per cent state-owned, with 11 per cent of shares in private ownership and 8 per cent owned by employees.

www.kyrgyzair.com

PIA

PAKISTAN   PIA

1951 Founded as the state airline.
1952 Flights between West and East Pakistan.
1955 International traffic.
1960 Boeing 707s. Routes to New York.
2007 PIA on EU blacklist.
2008 Removed from blacklist.

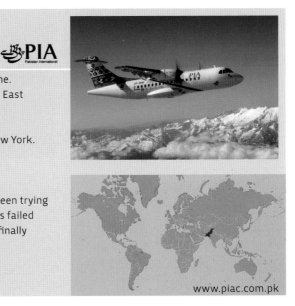

The Pakistani government has been trying to privatize PIA for years, but has failed to find any investors. In 2009 it finally abandoned these plans.

www.piac.com.pk

ARIANA AFGHAN AIRLINES

ARIANA AFGHAN AIRLINES

AFGHANISTAN

Founded in 1955; in state ownership. Built up with assistance from Pan Am and TWA. Ruined by the Taliban. With the exception of one Airbus A310, its planes are prohibited from flying into the European Union.

www.flyariana.com

JET AIRWAYS

INDIA   JET AIRWAYS

1992 Founded in Mumbai.
1993 Starts commercial operations with four leased 737-300s.
2004 Begins international flights (to Sri Lanka).
2007 Acquisition of Air Sahara.
2007 Establishes a hub in Brussels for North American flights.
2008 Alliance with Kingfisher Airlines.
2009 Jet Airways sacks two pilots; 430 of the airline's pilots call in sick. After five days, 800 cancelled flights and losses of 27 million euros, Jet Airways reinstates the sacked pilots and the other pilots return to work.

www.jetairways.com

AIR INDIA

INDIA

1932 Founded as Tata Airlines.
1971 Boeing 747s.
2007 Merger with Indian Airlines. Air India is now the country's third-largest airline, behind Jet Airways and Kingfisher. Air India has since then

been flying domestic routes again. The plan is for its subsidiary Air India Express to cover the budget sector.
2010 Membership of Star Alliance.

www.airindia.com

KINGFISHER AIRLINES

INDIA

2003 Founded in Bangalore.
Subsidiary of a brewery.
Operates almost exclusively domestic flights.
Only a few international routes.
2008 Take-over of the Indian low-cost carrier Air Deccan.

Kingfisher is currently the largest airline in India.
It has five Airbus A380s on order.
Tailplanes are adorned with kingfishers.
Places major emphasis on service and luxury.

www.flykingfisher.com

NEPAL AIRLINES

NEPAL

Successor to Royal Nepal Airlines.
Following the abolition of the monarchy in 2008, the prefix 'Royal' was dropped from the name.
Serves 40 domestic and international destinations.

www.nepalairlines.com.np

SRI LANKAN AIRLINES

SRI LANKA

SriLankan

1948 Founded as Ceylon Airways.
1949 Name changed to Air Ceylon.
1978 First Tamil attack on an HS-748.
1979 Name changed to Air Lanka.
1986 Second Tamil attack.
1998 Name changed to Sri Lankan Airlines.
2001 Third Tamil attack: half the fleet is destroyed.
2002 SARS crisis.
2004 Indian Ocean tsunami.
2007 Expansion of routes.

www.srilankan.aero

AIR CHINA

1939 Founded as CAAC.
Russian aircraft.
1970 Boeing and Ilyushin long-haul aircraft.
1987 Reorganization. New name: Air China.
1988 Boeing 747s.
2001 Merger with China Southwest Airlines and China International Airlines.

2004 Take-over of Zhejiang Airlines.
2007 Joins Star Alliance.

Majority shareholder in Air Macau, Shandong Airlines and Air China Cargo. Has 17 per cent holding in Cathay Pacific.

www.airchina.com

HAINAN AIRLINES

CHINA

1989 Established by HNA Group.
Affiliates: Shanxi Airlines, Chang'an Airlines, China Xinhua Airlines, Lucky Air, Deer Jet, Shilin Airlines, Grand China Express Air, Yangtze River Express, Hong Kong Airlines and Hong Kong Express.
1993 Start of operations.
2008 Route from Beijing to Seattle.
2009 Flights to Berlin.
2010 Beijing–Brussels and Shanghai–Brussels.

www.hnair.com

CHINA EASTERN AIRLINES

CHINA

CHINA AIRLINES

1988 Founded in Huadong.
2001 Take-over of Air Great Wall.
2003 Merger with China Yunnan and China Northwest Airlines.
2009 Merger with Shanghai Airlines.

The amalgamation of Shanghai Airlines and China Eastern has created a mega airline. Possibility of joining Skyteam Alliance, but since Air China owns 24 per cent of China Eastern shares, this could mean that a Star Alliance member was the airline's major shareholder.

www.flychinaeastern.com

CHINA SOUTHERN AIRLINES

CHINA   中国南方航空 CHINA SOUTHERN

1989   Founded in Guangzhou.
1997   Flotation in New York and Hong Kong.
2003   Take-over of China Northern Airlines,

Beiya Airlines, China Northern Swan and China Xinjiang Airlines.
2004   Take-over of China Northern and China Xinjiang.

2004   Enters the world top ten.
2007   Largest airline in Asia.
2007   Membership of SkyTeam Alliance.
2009   Opens branch in Taiwan.
2009   Airbus A380s.
2009   Skytrax votes China Southern best Chinese airline.

Has ordered around 150 aircraft, including five A380s.

www.csair.com

SHANGHAI AIRLINES

CHINA   上海航空股份有限公司 SHANGHAI AIRLINES CO.,LTD.

1985   Founded by the city of Shanghai. Limited to domestic flights.
1997   First international flights.
2002   Flotation.

2006   Launch of a cargo subsidiary, Shanghai Airlines Cargo, jointly with Eva Air of Taiwan.
2007   Membership of Star Alliance.

2009   Merger with China Eastern Airlines. This could mean the end of its membership of Star Alliance, as China Eastern is attempting to join SkyTeam Alliance.

Shanghai Airlines will amalgamate with China Eastern, with both airlines retaining their identities. They will, however, be joining the same alliance. Air China is a member of Star Alliance, China Southern of SkyTeam Alliance. There's always Oneworld...

www.shanghai-air.com

CHINA XINHUA AIRLINES

CHINA   China Xinhua Airlines 中国新华航空

Subsidiary of Hainan Airlines, with headquarters in Haikou and a base in Tianjin.
Commenced operations in 1992.

www.chinaxinhuaair.com

XIAMEN AIRLINES

CHINA   厦门航空 XIAMEN AIRLINES

1984   Established as China's first non-state-owned airline.
1985   Commences flying operations.
1990   A Xiamen Boeing 737 is hijacked. When it lands in Guangzhou, a fight breaks out in the cockpit between the pilots and the hijackers. The aircraft comes off the runway, slices another aircraft open and crashes into a third, leaving 128 dead.

1991   Feeder services for China Southern. Six hubs established. International flights to South-East Asia.

China Southern Airlines holds a 60 per cent stake in Xiamen.

www.xiamenair.com.cn

BIMAN BANGLADESH AIRLINES

BANGLADESH **Biman** BANGLADESH AIRLINES

Founded in 1972. No-one would have expected such an impoverished country to set up its own airline. In fact its first aircraft was a gift from the armed forces. In 2008, Biman ordered four Boeing 787s.

www.biman-airlines.com

VIETNAM AIRLINES

VIETNAM **Vietnam Airlines**

1956 Founded by the government.
1975 First international route.
       Soviet aircraft types.
1996 Restructuring of the company, purchase of Boeing 777s.
       Services to four continents.

Vietnam Airlines has overcome all past crises without any adverse effects. When passenger numbers worldwide declined following the 11 September attacks, Vietnam Airlines' figures actually rose.

www.vietnamairlines.com

LAO AIRLINES

LAOS *ภาพขึบลาอ* **Lao Airlines**

Founded in 1976, this state airline flies from Vientiane and Luang Prabang to major cities in Indochina. As Luang Prabang is a UNESCO World Heritage site, the airline is experiencing a rapid growth in tourism.

www.laoairlines.com

ORIENT THAI

THAILAND **ORIENT THAI AIRLINES**

Obtained its first Boeing 727 in 1995. Since then, has grown into a national airline operating domestic and international flights and even has a low-cost subsidiary, One-Two-GO, which had a tragic accident in Phuket in 2007.

www.orient-thai.com

THAI AIRWAYS INTERNATIONAL

THAILAND **THAI**

1959 Founded with support from SAS. 70 per cent of capital injected by the government.
1971 Intercontinental flights.
1975 Internal financing with no borrowed capital.
1978 Airbus A300s.
1979 Boeing 747s.
1988 Merger of TAC and Thai Airways to form Thai Airways International.
1997 Founding member of Star Alliance.
2005 New corporate design.

Thai Airways is one of the best airlines in Asia. Its service and its lounges in Bangkok are exemplary. The son of King Bhumibol, Somdech Phra Boroma Orasadhiraj Chao Fah Maha Vajiralongkorn, sometimes flies a Thai Airways passenger jet himself.

www.thaiairways.com

BANGKOK AIRWAYS

▬ THAILAND

Bangkok Airways has three airports of its own: Ko Samui, Sukhothai and Ko Chang. These airports run their own shops and resorts. Of course, the airline also flies to all of Thailand's other major airports.

www.bangkokair.com

AIRASIA

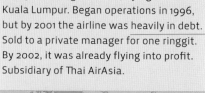

MALAYSIA

Malaysian budget carrier, flying out of Kuala Lumpur. Began operations in 1996, but by 2001 the airline was heavily in debt. Sold to a private manager for one ringgit. By 2002, it was already flying into profit. Subsidiary of Thai AirAsia.

www.airasia.com

MALAYSIA AIRLINES

MALAYSIA

1947 Founded as Malayan Airways, the airline of the Federation of Malaya from Penang to Singapore with headquarters in Kuala Lumpur.

1963 Restructuring to form Malaysian Airways.

1965 Amalgamation with Borneo Airways.

1967 Reorganization. Malaysia-Singapore Airlines with headquarters in Singapore.

1972 Separation from Singapore. Reorganization. Malaysian Airlines System. Headquarters in Kuala Lumpur.

1987 Malaysian Airlines. New corporate design.

2000 onwards: Launch of two low-cost subsidiaries: MASwings and Firefly. Launch of MASCharter. Launch of cargo company MASkargo.

Malaysia Airlines was voted a five-star airline by Skytrax and is considered to be one of the best airlines in the world.

SINGAPORE AIRLINES

SINGAPORE

A great way to fly
SINGAPORE AIRLINES

1947 Founded as Malayan Airways, the airline of the Federation of Malaya, from Penang to Singapore with headquarters in Kuala Lumpur.

1963 Restructuring to form Malaysian Airways.

1965 Amalgamation with Borneo Airways.

1967 Reorganization. Malaysia-Singapore Airlines with headquarters in Singapore.

1968 Introduction of the sarong kebaya for female flight attendants, designed by the French designer Pierre Balmain.

1972 Separation from Malaysia. Singapore Airlines becomes an airline with no domestic network.

Largest Boeing 777 fleet in the world.
First to order Airbus A380.
Several times voted best airline in the world.

www.singaporeair.com

www.malaysiaairlines.com

SILK AIR

 SINGAPORE

Regional arm of Singapore Airlines. Same technical quality, with simplified cabin service. Extremely reliable.

www.silkair.com

TIGER AIRWAYS

 SINGAPORE

With this low-cost carrier, Singapore Airlines is able to meet the full range of its customers' needs. The recipe for success: new aircraft, reliability, keeping costs down. Moreover, one of the best airlines in the world is behind it.

www.tigerairways.com

BATAVIA AIR

INDONESIA

Founded in 2002 as Metro Batavia. Regional services with an extensive domestic network. In 2007, the Indonesian transport minister threatened to close some airlines, including Batavia Air, due to concerns over safety.

www.batavia-air.co.id

GARUDA INDONESIA

INDONESIA

1949 Founded as Garuda Indonesian Airways.
       Management agreement concluded with KLM.
1954 Nationalization.
1957 Expulsion of all KLM staff.
1963 First jets.
1973 DC-10s.

As of 2010, Garuda was on the EU blacklist, along with all other Indonesian carriers.

www.garuda-indonesia.com

LION AIR

INDONESIA Lion Air

Lion Air was the first airline in the world to fly the Boeing 737-900ER.
Low-cost carrier. Also flies to Singapore, Malaysia and Vietnam, in competition with Tiger Airways.

www.lionair.co.id

MANDALA AIRLINES

INDONESIA mandala

Founded in 1969 by an air force colonel. It forms part of Indonesia's strategic transport command but flies with a civil aviation remit. Following a tragic accident in 2005, the airline was sold to a civilian investor in 2006.

www.mandalaair.com

MERPATI NUSANTARA AIRLINES

INDONESIA Merpati

Established by the government in 1962 as a domestic airline to complement Garuda. Taken over by Garuda in 1978. Continued to operate under its own brand name. In 1993, it returned to government ownership.

www.merpati.co.id

ROYAL BRUNEI AIRLINES

BRUNEI ROYAL BRUNEI

The sultanate of Brunei is a sought-after destination among luxury holidaymakers. RBA's aircraft, by contrast, are somewhat dated.

www.bruneiair.com

PHILIPPINE AIRLINES

 PHILIPPINES   Philippine Airlines

1941 Established, together with a pilot, by the San Miguel brewery in Manila.
1942 Supports the United States with logistics flights.
Interruption of services during World War II.

1945 Acquisition of 28 per cent stake by Howard Hughes.
1946 Flights to the United States.
1947 Flights to Europe.

1960 Boeing 707.
1972 Forced merger with Air Manila and Filipinas Orient Airways under Marcos. Nationalization.
Plagued by corruption for many years.
1992 Reprivatization.
2000 Lufthansa Technik takes over maintenance.
2005 New aircraft.
2009 First of six Boeing 777s is delivered.

Philippine Airlines currently features on the EU blacklist and the FAA's blacklist.

www.philippineairlines.com

CEBU PACIFIC AIR

 PHILIPPINES   CEBU PACIFIC

Following years of successful domestic operations, the private airline Cebu Pacific turned its hand to conquering the budget market. As with Southwest Airlines, the flight attendants entertain their guests with quizzes in which they can win free flights.

www.cebupacificair.com

CHINA AIRLINES

 TAIWAN

Founded in Taipei in 1959. State airline of Taiwan. For years considered the most unsafe airline in Asia. In the last 20 years, 750 people lost their lives in various accidents. However, the airline has since renewed its fleet and changed its working practices. Since 2004, China Airlines has been considered safe.

www.china-airlines.com

AIR MACAU

 CHINA   AIR MACAU 澳門航空

This airline from the former Portuguese colony specializes in connections from China via Macau to Taiwan. They have 42 flights a week departing to Taipei and 30 to Kaohsiung.

www.airmacau.com.mo

EVA AIR

TAIWAN   EVA AIR

1989   Founded as a subsidiary by a
      Taiwanese shipping company.
1991   First international flights.
1992   Boeing 747 aircraft.

China Airlines, the state airline of Taiwan,
had numerous accidents towards the end of
the last century. Demand at very safe Eva Air
rose correspondingly and it rapidly became a
global player.

www.evaair.com

CATHAY PACIFIC

CHINA/HONG KONG   CATHAY PACIFIC

1946   Founded by two Americans in Hong
      Kong.
      'Cathay' is the medieval name for
      China.

1948   Investment by Swire Group.
      First routes to South-East Asia and
      Australia.
1959   Take-over of Hong Kong Airways.
1960   Most successful airline in Asia.
1980   Expansion into Europe.
1985   Launch of subsidiary Dragonair.
1990   Recession.
1994   New corporate identity.
1998   Following a temporary suspension of
      service by Philippine Airlines, Cathay
      Pacific took over domestic flights
      between five cities in the Philippines
      within 48 hours.

1999   Change of ownership with Hong
      Kong's return to Chinese sovereignty.
      Two groups of Chinese investors are
      now the majority shareholders.

www.cathaypacific.com

DRAGONAIR

CHINA/HONG KONG

Founded in 1985. Once a bitter rival to Cathay Pacific. Was therefore forced to concentrate on the Chinese domestic market, which only later worked to its advantage. Taken over by Cathay in 2006.

www.dragonair.com

AIR KORYO

NORTH KOREA

Military airline of North Korea with a civil aviation remit. Due to North Korea's isolation, serves only six international destinations. All bar two of its aircraft are prohibited from flying into the European Union.

www.korea-dpr.com/airkoryo

AIR NIPPON

JAPAN

Japanese regional airline. Air Nippon is one of the six subsidiaries of All Nippon Airways. It services an extensive network across the whole of Japan, including Okinawa, under ANA's flight code.

ASIANA AIRLINES

SOUTH KOREA

1988 Founded as Seoul Air International. Aided state-owned Korean Air with the demand generated by the Olympics.
1988 New name of Asiana.
1990 Boeing 767s. International routes.

2003 Membership of Star Alliance.
2009 'Airline of the Year' awarded by *Air Transport World*.

Asiana was supposed to be kept small and restricted to flights to neighbouring countries. However, in the run-up to the Olympics, Korean Air was unable to meet the demand and this paved the way for Asiana's worldwide route network.

http://flyasiana.com

ANA All Nippon Airways

For political reasons, it used its own Air Nippon flight numbers on the route to Taiwan until 2008.

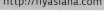

www.air-nippon.co.jp

KOREAN AIR

SOUTH KOREA

1962 Founded by the government.
1972 Boeing 707s.
1973 Boeing 747s.
1978 Following a navigational error, a Boeing 707 enters Russian airspace and comes under fire. It is able to

make an emergency landing on a frozen lake.
1983 Shooting down of a Boeing 747 which, following a navigational error north of Sakhalin in Russia, strays off course. All on board are killed.
1984 Change of name to Korean Air.
1990 MD-11s.
2000 Founding member of SkyTeam Alliance.

www.koreanair.com

JAPAN AIR LINES

JAPAN

1951 Founded as Japan Air Lines with leased aircraft.
1953 Renamed Japan Airlines.
1954 Flights to the United States.
1960 DC-8s.
1967 Tokyo–Moscow.

1970 Boeing 747s.
1973 Boeing 747 with capacity for 545 passengers used for domestic flight operations.
1985 747 carrying 520 passengers crashes on a domestic flight.
1987 Privatization and new corporate identity.
2000s onwards: Mergers with Japan Asia Airways, Japan Air System and TOA Domestic.
Division into Japan Airlines International and Japan Airlines Domestic.

www.jal.com

ALL NIPPON AIRWAYS

JAPAN

1952 Founded as Japan Helicopter and Aeroplanes Transport Company.
1960 Flights to Okinawa.
1963 Merger with Fujita Airlines.
1964 Boeing 727s.
1973 Lockheed TriStars.

1978 Boeing 747s.
1986 International flights.
1999 Membership of Star Alliance
2004 Launch of low-cost airline Air Next.
2007 'Airline of the World' awarded by *Air Transport World*.

www.ana.co.jp

QANTAS

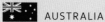 AUSTRALIA

1920 Founded as Queensland and Northern
Territory Aerial Services.
1934 Catalina flying boats.
1935 Kangaroo route: Sydney–Darwin–
Singapore–Calcutta–Karachi–Cairo–
Tripoli–London.

1952 Wallaby route: Sydney–Perth–Cocos
Island–Mauritius–Johannesburg.
1954 Southern Cross route: Sydney–
Auckland–Nadi–Honolulu–San
Francisco–Vancouver.
1958 Around-the-world service.
1959 Boeing 707s.
1966 Fiesta route: Sydney–Tahiti–Mexico
City–London.
2009 Airbus A380s.

www.qantas.com.au

SKYWEST

AUSTRALIA

A small air-taxi company in Perth was
given some coastal surveillance work
by the customs authorities. This then
grew into a scheduled service. The fleet
expanded and Skywest now serves the
whole of western Australia.

www.skywest.com.au

VIRGIN BLUE

AUSTRALIA

Australian low-cost airline from the
Virgin Group. Has an extensive network
in Australia and has risen to become
Australia's second-largest airline. A
number of island states in the Pacific are
also served by its subsidiary Pacific Blue.

www.virginblue.com.au

AIR NIUGINI

 PAPUA NEW GUINEA   **Air Niugini**

Air Niugini is Papua New Guinea's largest
airline. It now operates only regional
flights and acts as a feeder airline for
Qantas.

www.airniugini.com.pg

SOLOMON AIRLINES

Solomon Airlines
 SOLOMON ISLANDS

Solomon Airlines serves almost 30
destinations on the Solomon Islands, as
well as connecting to Brisbane, Nadi (Fiji)
and Port Vila (Vanuatu). There are scarcely
any paved runways on the islands.

www.flysolomons.com

AIR TAHITI NUI

 TAHITI   **Air Tahiti Nui**

It seems that five A340s are enough
to carry visitors from Tokyo, Paris, Los
Angeles, Sydney and Auckland to Tahiti.
The government owns 61 per cent of
shares in the airline.

www.airtahitinui.com

AIR VANUATU

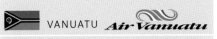 VANUATU

Founded in 1981 as New Hebrides Airways. After independence, the name was of course changed – to Air Vanuatu. International destinations: Sydney, Brisbane, Auckland and Nouméa.

www.airvanuatu.com

AIR PACIFIC

 FIJI

Founded in 1947. The government of Fiji owns 51 per cent of the shares, but the governments of Nauru, Kiribati, Samoa and Tonga also each hold a small percentage stake.

www.airpacific.com

AIR FIJI

 FIJI

You might assume that Air Fiji, with its small regional aircraft, was a subsidiary of Air Pacific. It was, however, independent and, of course, profited from the tourists who enter the country in larger aircraft. It ceased operations in 2009.

OUR AIRLINE

 NAURU

The national airline of the world's smallest island state is now called 'Our Airline' – Our meaning both 'belonging to us' and being an abbreviation for 'Oceanic United Republics' – as Kiribati, the Solomons and Fiji also hold stakes in it.

www.ourairline.com.au

AIRCALIN

NEW CALEDONIA

This New Caledonian airline has been in existence since 1983. It has connections to Japan, Korea, Australia, New Zealand and, of course, several of the island states of Oceania.

www.aircalin.com

AIR NEW ZEALAND

NEW ZEALAND

AIR NEW ZEALAND

1940   Founded by the government as TEAL (Tasman Empire Airways Limited).
1965   Renamed Air New Zealand.
1981   Boeing 747s.
1990   Privatization.
2001   Renationalization.

For short domestic routes to minor airports, Air New Zealand uses its regional subsidiaries Air Nelson, Eagle Airways and Mount Cook Airlines.

www.airnewzealand.co.nz

UK
bmib[...]
Easy[...]
Flybe[...]
Jet2[...]
Mona[...]

Iceland
Iceland Express

Ireland
Aer Lingus
Ryanair

N
tra[...]

Franc[e]
Aigle Azu[...]

Spain
Clickair
Vueling AL

Moroc[co]
Jet4you
Atlas Blu[...]
Air Arabi[...]

Canada
WestJet

USA
AirTran
Allegiant
Frontier
Horizon
JetAmerica

USA
JetBlue
Southwest
Sun Country
Virgin America
USA3000

USA (Hawaii)
Go!
Island Air
Mokulele

Mexico
Interjet
Viva Aerobus
Vollaris

Colombia
EasyFly

Brazil
Azul Brazilian
GOL
Oceanair
WebJet

LOW-COST CARRIERS

Norway
Norwegian Air Shuttle

n
usten Flyg
g
Aviation
allsflyg

Poland
AirItaly Polska

ustria **Czech Republic**
Niki Smart Wings

terSky

aly
ess
ana
Air
djet

Bulgaria/Hungary
Wizz Air

Albania
Belle Air

Turkey
Anadolujet
Pegasus
Atlasjet
Onur Air

Kuwait
Jazeera AW
Wataniya AW

Bahrain
Bahrain Air

Saudi Arabia **UAE**
Sama AL Air Arabia
Nas Air Flydubai

Yemen
Felix AW

Russia
SkyExpress

Ukraine
Wizz Air Ukraine

Pakistan
Air Blue
Shaheen Air

India
Air India Express
JetLite
Kingfisher Red
Spicejet
Goair
IndiGo

Sri Lanka
Mihin Lanka

Nepal
Cosmic Air

Bangladesh
GMG AL
Royal Bengal
Best Air

Thailand
Nok Air
1-2-Go
Thai AirAsia
Bangkok AW

Malaysia
AirAsia
AirAsia X
Firefly
Maswings

Indonesia
Indonesia AirAsia
Linus AW
Lion Air
Mandala AL
Batavia Air

China
Spring AL
United Eagle
Juneyao
Okay AL
Lucky Air

China
Shenzhen
Deer Jet
Kunpeng
Chang An

Macau
Viva Macau

Hong Kong
Hong Kong Airlines
Hong Kong Express

Vietnam
Jetstar Pacific

Singapore
Jetstar Asia
Tiger Airways
Valuair

S. Korea
Eastar Jet
Jeju Air
Air Korea
Air Busan

Japan
JAL Express
Hokkaido International
Skynet Asia
StarFlyer
Air Next

Philippines
Cebu Pacific
Spirit of Manila
Zest
Air Philippines
PAL Express

Kenya
Fly540

South Africa
Kulula.com
1Time
Mango

Australia
Virgin Blue
Jetstar AW
Tiger AW Australia

New Zealand
Pacific Blue AL

Numerous low-cost carriers have established themselves in the last 15 years. The network is now so extensive that you can fly around the world on this type of carrier.

Name	Country	◉	IATA CODE	IATA NO.	ICAO	*	Base Airport	Call-Sign	Current Fleet	Planned Fleet	✈	✈	✈
North America													
Air Canada	CANADA	NA	AC	14	ACA	1936	Montreal/ Toronto/ Vancouver	AIR CANADA	3 B.747; 8 A330/A340; 18 B.777; 47 B.767; 88 A318–321; 1 B.737 Classic; 1 DC-9/MD-80/90; 15 EMB-170/175; 45 EMB-190/195	37 B.787	226	37	263
Air North	CANADA	NA	4N	287	ANT	1977	White-horse, YT	AIR NORTH	4 B.737 Classic; 4 HS.748/Andover		8	0	8
Air Transat	CANADA	NA	TS	649	TSC	1986	Montreal	TRANSAT	6 A330/A340; 15 A300/A310		21	0	21
Canadian North	CANADA	NA		518	ANX	1990	Yellow-knife, NWT	NOR-TERRA	9 B.737 Classic; 1 F.28; 4 DHC-8		14	0	14
First Air	CANADA	NA	7F	245	FAB	1946	Ottawa/ Edmonton	FIRST AIR	1 B.767; 3 B.727; 6 B.737 Classic; 2 C-130/L.100; 1 HS.748/Andover; 9 ATR-42/72		22	0	22
Kenn Borek Air	CANADA	NA	4K		KBA	1971	Calgary	BOREK AIR	2 DC-3		2	0	2
WestJet	CANADA	NA	WS		WJA	1995	Calgary	WESTJET	1 B.737 Classic; 79 B.737 NG	33 B.737 NG	80	33	113
Virgin America	USA	NA	VX		VRD	2004	S. Francisco		29 A318–321	10 A318–321	29	10	39
JetBlue Airw.	USA, NY	NA	B6	279	JBU	1998	New Y. JFK	JETBLUE	110 A318–321; 42 EMB-190/195	58 A318–321; 61 EMB	152	119	271
Alaska Airlines	USA, ALASKA	NA	AS	27	ASA	1932	Seattle/ Anchorage	ALASKA	84 B.737 NG; 35 B.737 Classic; 14 DC-9/MD-80/90	12 B.737 NG	133	12	145
US Airways	USA, ARIZONA	NA	US	37		1937	Phoenix	CACTUS	20 A330/A340; 20 B.767; 1 B.727; 69 B.757; 215 A318–321; 110 B.737; 1 DC-9/MD-80/90; 25 EMB-190/195	22 A350; 13 A330/A340; 71 A318–321; 17 EMB-190/195	461	123	584
Frontier Airlines	USA, COLORADO	NA	F9		FFT	1994	Denver-Int.	FRONTIER FLIGHT	52 A318–321; 1 B.737 Classic	11 A318–321	53	11	64
AirTran Airways	USA, GEORGIA	NA	FL	332	TRS	1992	Atlanta	CITRUS	50 B.737 NG; 4 DC-9/MD-80/90; 86 B.717	55 B.737 NG	140	55	195
ASA	USA, GEORGIA	NA	EV	862		1979	Atlanta	ACEY	48 CRJ 700/900/1000; 113 CRJ 100/200; 12 ATR-42/72	2 CRJ 700/900/1000	173	2	175
Delta Air Lines	USA, GEORGIA	NA	DL	6	DAL	1929	Atlanta	DELTA	2 L.1011; 16 B.777; 102 B.767; 36 B.727; 132 B.757; 9 B.737 Classic; 78 B.737; 134 DC-9/MD-80/90	2 B.777; 3 B.737 NG; 2 DC-9/MD-80/90	509	7	516
Hawaiian Airl.	USA, HAWAII	NA	HA	173	HAL	1929	Honolulu	HAWAIIAN	18 B.767; 16 B.717; 3 DC-9/MD-80/90	6 A350; 10 A330/A340	37	16	53
United Airlines	USA, ILLINOIS	NA	UA	16	UAL	1934	Chicago/ San Francis-co/Denver	UNITED	33 B.747; 1 DC-10/MD-11; 52 B.777; 41 B.767; 1 B.727; 97 B.757; 152 A318–321; 82 B.737 Classic		459	0	459
Chautauqua Airlines	USA, INDIANA	NA	RP	363	CHQ	1973	Indianapolis	CHAU-TAUQUA	18 CRJ 100/200; 86 EMB-135/145		104	0	104
Northwest Airlines	USA, MINNESOTA	NA	NW	12	NWA	1926	Minneapo-lis-St.Paul	NORTH-WEST	32 B.747; 1 DC-10/MD-11; 32 A330/A340; 1 B.727; 67 B.757; 126 A318–321; 122 DC-9/MD-80/90	18 B.787; 7 A318–321	381	25	406
Comair	USA, OHIO	NA	OH	886	COM	1976	Cincinnati/ Orlando	COMAIR	28 CRJ 700/900/1000; 117 CRJ 100/200	1 CRJ 700/900/1000	145	1	146
American Airlines	USA, TEXAS	NA	AA	1	AAL	1934	Dallas	AMERI-CAN	47 B.777; 32 A300/A310; 73 B.767; 2 B.727; 125 B.757; 89 B.737 NG; 312 DC-9/MD-80/90; 4 F.28	7 B.777; 42 B.787; 83 B.737 NG	684	132	816
American Eagle Airlines	USA, TEXAS	NA	MQ		EGF	1992	Dallas-DFW	EAGLE FLIGHT	25 CRJ 700/900/1000; 222 EMB-135/145	1 EMB-135/145	247	1	248
Continental Airlines	USA, TEXAS	NA	CO	5	COA	1934	Houston	CONTI-NENTAL	3 DC-10/MD-11; 20 B.777; 26 B.767; 2 B.727; 58 B.757; 272 B.737; 2 DC-9/MD-80/90; 1 DC-3	7 B.777; 25 B.787; 4 B.757; 26 B.737 NG	384	62	446
Southwest Airlines	USA, TEXAS	NA		526	SWA	1967	Dallas-L.F. Houston-H.	SOUTH-WEST	215 B.737 Classic; 341 B.737 NG	90 B.737 NG	556	90	646
SkyWest Airlines	USA, UTAH	NA	OO	302	SKW	1972	Salt Lake City/L.A.	SKY-WEST	90 CRJ 700/900/1000, 139 CRJ 100/200	14 CRJ 700/900/1000	229	14	243
Horizon Air	USA, WASH-INGTON	NA	QX	481	QXE	1981	Seattle-Boeing Field	HORI-ZON AIR	3 F.28; 18 CRJ 700/900/1000; 45 DHC-8	11 DHC-8	66	11	77
Air Wisconsin	USA, WISCONSIN	NA	ZW	303	AWI	1965	Appleton/ Denver/ Chicago	AIR WISCON-SIN	5 BAe 146; 70 CRJ 100/200		75	0	75

◉ Region * Created ✈ Current Fleet ✈ Planned Fleet ✈ Total Fleet

Name	Country	⊙	IATA CODE	IATA NO.	ICAO	✳	Base Airport	Call-Sign	Current Fleet	Planned Fleet	✈	✈	✈
Central America & Caribbean													
LIAT	ANTIGUA	CR	LI	140	LIA	1956	Antigua	LIAT	17 DHC-8		17	0	17
Bahamasair	BAHAMAS	CR	UP	111	BHS	1973	Nassau	BAHAMAS	3 B.737 Classic; 1 HS.748; 6 DHC-8		10	0	10
Cubana	CUBA	CR	CU	136	CUB	1929	Havana	CUBANA	3 Il-96; 1 B.767; 2 Il-62; 2 Tu-154; 5 Yak-42; 4 Tu-204/214/234; 4 An-24	1 Yak-42; 3 An-72/74/148	21	4	25
TACA	EL SALVADOR	CA	TA	202	TAI	1931	San Salvador-Int.	TACA	29 A318–321; 1 B.737 Classic; 3 EMB-190/195	16 A318–321; 4 EMB-190/195	33	20	53
Air Jamaica	JAMAICA	CR	JM	201	AJM	1968	Kingston	JAMAICA	16 A318–321		16	0	16
AeroMexico	MEXICO	CA	AM	139	AMX	1934	Mexico City	AERO-MEXICO	4 B.777; 7 B.767; 45 B.737 NG; 2 DC-9/MD-80/90	5 B.787; 8 B.737 NG	58	13	71
Mexicana	MEXICO	CA	MX	132	MXA	1921	Mexico City	MEXICANA	2 A330/A340; 4 B.767; 74 A318–321	4 A318–321	80	4	84
Mexicana Click	MEXICO	CA	QA	723	CBE	1975	Mexico City	AERO-CARIBE	5 DC-9/MD-80/90; 5 B.717; 24 F.28; 4 F-27/FH-227	11 B.717	38	11	49
Aeroperlas Reg.	PANAMA	CA	WL	54	APP	1969	Panama	AEROPERLAS	1 ATR-42/72		1	0	1
Copa Airlines	PANAMA	CA	CM	230	CMP	1944	Panama-T.	COPA	28 B.737 NG, 13 EMB-190/195	21 B.737, 4 EMB-190/195	41	25	66
South America													
Aerolineas Argentinas	ARGENTINA	SA	AR	44	ARG	1950	Buenos Aires/Ezeiza	ARGEN-TINA	3 B.747; 6 A330/A340; 1 A300/A310; 5 B.737 NG; 38 B.737 Classic; 5 DC-9/MD-80/90	5 A330/A340; 7 B.737 NG; 2 DC-9/MD-80/90	58	14	72
LAN Argentina	ARGENTINA	SA	4M	469	DSM	2005	B. Aires-AEP	LAN AR	2 B.767; 10 A318–321		12	0	12
AeroSur	BOLIVIA	SA	5L	275		1992	Santa Cruz		1 B.747; 1 B.767; 5 B.727; 4 B.737		11	0	11
GOL Trans. Aer.	BRAZIL	SA			GLO	2000	Sao Paulo-C.	GOL TRANSPORTE	2 B.767, 109 B.737 NG, 13 B.737 Cl.	91 B.737 NG	124	91	215
TAM Airlines	BRAZIL	SA	JJ	957	TAM	1961	Sao Paulo-Congonhas	TAM	18 A330/A340; 4 B.777; 3 B.767; 108 A318–321	22 A350; 4 A330/A340; 4 B.777; 46 A318–321	133	76	209
VARIG Log	BRAZIL	SA		183	VLO	2000			2 DC-10/MD-11; 4 B.727; 3 B.757	3 A330/A340	9	3	12
LAN Airlines	CHILE	SA	LA	45	LAN	1929	Santiago	LAN	5 A330/A340; 23 B.767; 25 A318–321; 3 B.737 Classic; 3 DC-3	38 B.787; 7 B.767; 21 A318–321	59	66	125
Sky Airline	CHILE	SA	H2	605	SKU	2001	Santiago	AEROSKY	13 B.737 Classic		13	0	13
Avianca	COLOMBIA	SA	AV	134	AVA	1940	Bogotá	AVIANCA	4 A330/A340; 8 B.767; 7 B.757; 12 A318–321; 10 DC-9/MD-80/90; 29 F.28; 28 F.27	10 A350; 6 A330/A340; 12 B.787; 39 A318–321	98	67	165
SATENA	COLOMBIA	SA	9N		NSE	1962	Bogotá	SATENA	7 ERJ		7		7
TAME	ECUADOR	SA	EQ	269	TAE	1962	Quito	TAME	4 B.727; 3 A318–321; 2 F.28; 2 EMB-170/175; 3 EMB-190/195; 1 DC-3	1 A318–321	15	1	16
Aero Condor	PERU	SA			CDP	1973	Lima/Nazca	CONDOR-PERU	1 B.737 Classic; 3 F.27; 2 An-26; 2 An-24		8	0	8
Star Perú	PERU	SA	2I	156	SRU	1997	Lima	STAR UP	5 BAe 146; 3 B.737; 8 An-24-32		16	0	16
Surinam Airw.	SURINAME	SA	PY	192	SLM	1954	Paramaribo	SURINAM	1 B.747; 2 B.737 Classic		3	0	3
PLUNA	URUGUAY	SA	PU	286	PUA	1936	Montevideo	PLUNA	3 B.737 Classic; 6 CRJ 700/900/1000		9	0	9
Aeropostal	VENEZUELA	SA	VH	152	LAV	1997	Caracas-M.	AEROPOSTAL	1 B.727; 38 DC-9/MD-80/90		39	0	39
ConViasa	VENEZUELA	SA	Vo	308	VCV	2004	Caracas	CONVI-ASA	2 A330/A340, 7 B.737 Classic, 2 CRJ 700/900/1000, 3 DHC-7, 7 ATR-42/72	2 Il-96, 2 CRJ 700/900/1000	21	4	25
Europe													
Armavia	ARMENIA	CS	U8	669	RNV	1997	Yerevan-Zvartnots	ARMA-VIA	1 Il-86; 4 Yak-42; 5 A318–321; 1 Tu-134; 1 CRJ 100/200	2 Sukhoi RRJ	12	2	14
Austrian Airlines	AUSTRIA	WE	OS	257	AUA	1957	Wien	AUS-TRIAN	4 B.777; 6 B.767; 20 A318–321		30	0	30
InterSky	AUSTRIA	WE	3L	576	ISK	2001	Bern	INTERSKY	4 DHC-8		4	0	4
Azal Azerbaijan Airlines	AZERBAIJAN	CS	J2	771	AHY	1992	Baku-Bina/Gyandzha	AZAL	7 Yak-40; 4 B.757; 5 A318–321; 13 Tu; 1 An-140; 6 ATR-42/72	2 B.787; 2 B.767; 4 B.737 NG; 1 ATR-42/72	36	9	45
Brussels Airlines	BELGIUM	WE				2007	Brussels	B-LINE	4 A330/A340; 32 BAe 146; 4 A318–321; 11 B.737 Classic		51	0	51
VLM Airlines	BELGIUM	WE	VG	978	VLM	1992	Antwerp	RUBENS	22 F.27		22	0	22
BH Air	BOSNIA-HERZEGOVINA	EA	JA	995	BON	1994	Sarajevo	AIR BOSNA	1 B.737 Classic; 4 ATR-42/72		5	0	5
Hemus Air	BULGARIA	EA	DU	748	HMS	1986	Sofia	HEMUS AIR	4 BAe 146; 5 Yak-40; 1 B.737 Classic; 1 Tu-134; 1 ATR-42/72		12	0	12
Croatia Airl.	CROATIA	EA	OU	831		1989	Zagreb	CROATIA	8 A318–321; 4 DHC-8	4 A318–321; 2 DHC-8	12	6	18

⊙ Region ✳ Created ✈ Current Fleet ✈ Planned Fleet ✈ Total Fleet

The year in which the present-day company was created may differ from the year in which operations commenced.

Name	Country	⊙	IATA CODE	IATA NO.	ICAO	∗	Base Airport	Call-Sign	Current Fleet	Planned Fleet	✈	✈	✈
Cyprus Airw.	CYPRUS	NE	CY	48	CYP	1947	Larnaca	CYPRUS	2 A330/A340; 9 A318–321	2 A318–321	11	2	13
Czech Airlines	CZECH REPUBLIC	EA	OK	64	CSA	1923	Prague	CSA	2 A300/A310; 17 A318–321; 18 B.737 Classic; 12 ATR-42/72	9 A318–321	49	9	58
Cimber Sterling	DENMARK	WE	QI	647	CIM	1950	Sønderborg	CIMBER	5 B.737 NG; 7 CRJ 100/200; 6 ATR-42/72		18	0	18
Air Greenland	DENMARK GREENLAND	WE	GL	631	GRL	1960	Nuuk	GREEN-LANDAIR	1 A330/A340; 2 B.757; 6 DHC-7		9	0	9
Estonian Air	ESTONIA	EA	OV	960	ELL	1991	Tallinn	ESTONIAN	1 Yak-40; 6 B.737 Classic	3 CRJ 700/900/1000	7	3	10
Blue1	FINLAND	WE	KF	142	KFB	1987	Helsinki-Vantaa	BOTNIA	7 BAe 146; 7 DC-9/MD-80/90; 1 ATR-42/72; 4 SAAB 2000		19	0	19
Finnair	FINLAND	WE	AY	105	FIN	1923	Helsinki-Vantaa	FINNAIR	4 DC-10/MD-11; 9 A330/A340; 7 B.757; 29 A318–321; 20 EMB	11 A350; 5 A330/A340; 3 EMB-190/195	69	19	88
AirFrance	FRANCE	WE	AF	57	AFR	1933	Paris	AIR-FRANS	25 B.747; 34 A330/A340; 57 B.777; 11 BAe 146; 151 A318–321; 33 F.28; 29 CRJ; 9 EMB-190/195; 5 EMB-170/175; 41 EMB-135/145; 19 ATR-42/72	12 A380; 18 B.777; 12 A318–321	414	42	456
Corsairfly	FRANCE	WE	SS	923	CRL	1981	Paris-Orly	CORSAIR	11 B.747; 2 A330/A340		13	0	13
Regional	FRANCE	WE		977		1992	Nantes	REGIONAL EUROPE	1 F.28; 1 EMB-190/195	4 EMB-170/175; 2 EMB-190/195	2	6	8
Air Berlin	GERMANY	WE	AB	745	BER	1978	Berlin-Tegel	AIR BERLIN	12 A330/A340; 2 B.757; 49 A318–321; 51 B.737 NG; 1 B.737 Classic	28 B.787; 24 A318–321; 76 B.737 NG	115	128	243
Cirrus Airlines	GERMANY	WE	C9	251	RUS	1995	Saar-brücken	CIRRUS AIR	2 EMB-170/175; 3 Do 328 Jet	1 DHC-8	5	1	6
Condor	GERMANY	WE			CIB	1997	Berlin-Schönef.	CONDOR BERLIN	12 A318–321		12	0	12
Condor Flugd.	GERMANY	WE		881		1955	Frankfurt	CONDOR	9 B.767; 13 B.757		22	0	22
Germanwings	GERMANY	WE	4U		GWI	1997	Cologne	GERMAN-WINGS	26 A318–321; 1 B.737 NG	4 A318–321	27	4	31
GOAL	GERMANY	WE				1998	n/a	n/a	5 A300/A310; 1 B.757; 5 B.737 Classic; 12 CRJ; 6 DHC-8		29	0	29
Lufthansa	GERMANY	WE	LH	220	DLH	1926	Frankfurt/München	LUFT-HANSA	30 B.747; 66 A330/A340; 8 A300/A310; 91 A318–321; 67 B.737; 3 B.737	15 A380; 20 B.747; 50 A318–321; 30 C; 1 Starl.	265	116	381
Aegean Airl.	GREECE	WE	A3	390	AEE	1987	Athens	AEGEAN	6 BAe 146; 21 A318–321; 7 B.737	6 A318–321	34	6	40
Olympic Air	GREECE	WE	OA	50	OAL	1956	Athens	OLYMPIC	4 A330/A340; 19 B.737 Classic; 14 ATR-42/72; 4 DHC-8		41	0	41
Malev Hunga-rian Airways	HUNGARY	EA		182	MAH	1946	Budapest	MALEV	1 B.767; 2 Tu-154; 18 B.737 NG; 5 F.28; 1 CRJ 100/200; 4 DHC-8	4 DHC-8	31	4	35
Wizz Air	HUNGARY	EA			WZZ	2003	Budapest	WIZZAIR	22 A318–321	65 A318–321	22	65	87
Air Iceland	ICELAND	WE		882		1997		FAXI	5 F.27; 2 DHC-8		7	0	7
Icelandair	ICELAND	WE	FI	108	ICE	1937	Keflavík	ICEAIR	16 B.757; 2 DC-3	4 A330/A340; 4 B.787	18	8	26
Aer Arann	IRELAND	WE	RE	809	REA	1970		AER ARANN	10 ATR-42/72	4 ATR-42/72	10	4	14
Aer Lingus	IRELAND	WE	EI	53	EIN	1936	Dublin	SHAM-ROCK	10 A330/A340; 36 A318–321	6 A350; 4 A330/A340; 3 A318–321	46	13	59
Ryanair	IRELAND	WE		224	RYR	1985	Dublin/Stansted	RYANAIR	202 B.737 NG	112 B.737 NG	202	112	314
Air Dolomiti	ITALY	WE		101	DLA	1989	München	DOLO-MITI	3 BAe 146; 5 EMB-190/195; 16 ATR-42/72	5 EMB-190/195	24	5	29
Air One	ITALY	WE	AP	867	ADH	1995	Rome-Fiuminico	HERON	2 A330/A340; 1 BAe 146; 18 A318–321; 21 B.737 Classic	12 A350; 12 A330/A340	42	24	66
Alitalia	ITALY	WE	AZ	55		1946	Rome-Fiuminico	ALITALIA	6 DC-10/MD-11; 10 B.777; 12 B.767; 60 A318–321; 47 DC-9/MD-80/90	48 A318–321	135	48	183
Eurofly	ITALY	WE				1989	Milan-Orio	SIRIOFLY	4 A330/A340; 9 A318–321		13	0	13
Meridiana	ITALY	WE	IG	191	ISS	1963	Firenze	MERAIR	4 A318–321; 22 DC-9/MD-80/90		26	0	26
Air Astana	KAZAKH-STAN	CS		465		2001	Astana	ASTANA-LINE	2 B.767; 4 B.757; 10 A318–321; 5 F.27	3 B.787; 6 A318–321	21	9	30
Kyrgyzstan Airlines	KYRGYZ-STAN	CS		758		1992	Bishkek	KYRGYZ	9 Tu-154; 12 Yak-40; 1 B.737 Classic; 5 Tu-134		27	0	27
Luxair	LUXEM-BOURG	WE	LG	149	LGL	1948	Luxem-bourg	LUXAIR	1 B.737 Classic; 3 B.737 NG; 8 EMB-135/145; 3 DHC-8	2 DHC-8	15	2	17
MAT Macedo-nian Airlines	MACE-DONIA	EA	IN	367	MAK	1994	Skopje	MAKAVIO	1 B.737 Classic		1	0	1

⊙ Region ∗ Created ✈ Current Fleet ✈ Planned Fleet ✈ Total Fleet

Name	Country	⊙	IATA CODE	IATA NO.	ICAO	✷	Base Airport	Call-Sign	Current Fleet	Planned Fleet	✈	✈	✈
Air Malta	MALTA	WE	KM	643	AMC	1973	Luqa	AIR MALTA	12 A318–321		12	0	12
Montenegro Airlines	MONTE-NEGRO	EA		409	MGX	1994	Podgorica/Tivat	MONTE-NEGRO	11 F.28; 2 EMB-190/195	1 EMB-170/175	13	1	14
Martinair	NETHER-LANDS	WE	MP	129	MPH	1958	Amsterdam	MARTIN-AIR	4 B.747; 7 DC-10/MD-11; 6 B.767		17	0	17
Transavia.com	NETHERL.	WE	HV		TRA	1965	Amsterdam	TRANSAVIA	32 B.737 NG	7 B.737 NG	32	7	39
KLM	NETHER-LANDS	WE	KL	74	KLM	1919	Amsterdam	KLM	21 B.747; 10 DC-10/MD-11; 10 A330/A340; 19 B.777; 1 BAe 146; 31 B.737 NG; 23 B.737 Classic	3 A330/A340; 4 B.777; 9 B.737 NG	115	16	131
Cyprus Turkish Airlines	NORTHERN CYPRUS	NE	YK	56	KYV	1974	Ercan	AIR-KIBRIS	3 A318–321; 4 B.737 NG		7	0	7
Norwegian Air Shuttle	NORWAY	WE			NAX	1993	Oslo-Fornebu	NOR SHUTTLE	15 B.737 NG; 28 B.737 Classic	46 B.737 NG	43	46	89
Wideroe	NORWAY	WE	WF	701	WIF	1934	Oslo	WIDEROE	29 DHC-8	6 DHC-8	29	6	35
LOT Polish Airlines	POLAND	EA	LO	80	LOT	1929	Warsaw-Okęcie	LOT	6 B.767; 12 B.737 Classic; 16 EMB-170/175; 6 EMB-135/145; 1 Il-18	8 B.787; 12 EMB-170/175	41	20	61
SATA Air Acores	PORTUGAL	WE	SP	737	SAT	1941	Ponta Delgada	SATA	5 BAe ATP; 2 DHC-8	4 DHC-8	7	4	11
SATA International	PORTUGAL	WE	S4	331	RZO	1998	Lisbon/P. Delgada	AIR AZORES	4 A300/A310; 4 A318–321		8	0	8
TAP Portugal	PORTUGAL	WE	TP	47	TAP	1945	Lisbon	AIR POR-TUGAL	16 A330/A340; 40 A318–321	1 A330/A340; 12 A350; 4 A318–321	56	17	73
Tarom	ROMANIA	EA	RO	281	ROT	1945	Bucharest-Baneasa	TAROM	2 A300/A310; 4 A318–321; 4 B.737; 7 B.737 NG; 9 ATR-42/72; 2 An-24		28	0	28
Ural Airlines	RUSSIA	CS	U6	262	SVR	1993	Ekaterinb. Koltsovo	SVERD-LOVSK AIR	4 Il-86; 13 Tu-154; 11 A318–321; 3 An-24	7 A318–321	31	7	38
Yakutia Airlines	RUSSIA	CS		840	SYL	1925	Yakutsk	AIR YAKUTIA	10 Tu-154; 4 Yak-40; 4 B.757; 1 B.737; 3 An-12; 3 An-140; 4 An-26; 16 An-24	2 An-140	45	2	47
KD Avia	RUSSIA	CS	KD		KNI	1976	Kaliningrad	KALININ-GRAD AIR	16 B.737 Classic; 3 Tu-134		19	0	19
Aeroflot Russian Airlines	RUSSIAN FEDERATION	CS	SU	555	AFL	1923	Moscow-Shereme-tyevo	AERO-FLOT	6 Il-96; 4 Il-86; 1 Il-76; 3 A330/A340; 11 B.767; 7 Il-62; 26 Tu-154; 55 A318–321; 3 Tu-134	22 A350; 7 A330/A340; 22 B.787; 1 B.767; 33 wA318–321; 30 Sukhoi RRJ	116	115	231
Rossiya Russian Airlines	RUSSIAN FEDERATION	CS	R4	948	SDM	1992	Moscow-Vnukovo	RUSSIA	4 Il-96; 2 Il-86; 3 B.767; 9 Il-62; 26 Tu-154; 6 Yak-40; 5 Tu-204/214/234; 14 A318–321; 5 B.737; 12 Tu-134; 2 Il-18	1 Il-96; 4 Il-76; 2 B.767; 4 Tu-204/214/234; 12 An-72/74/148	88	23	111
S7 Airlines	RUSSIAN FEDERATION	CS	S7	421	SBI	1992	Novosibirsk	SIBERIA AIRLINES	9 Il-86; 2 B.767; 8 A300/A310; 23 Tu-154; 26 A318–321; 2 B.737 Classic; 4 B.737 NG	27 A318–321; 10 B.737 NG	74	37	111
SkyEurope	SLOVAKIA	EA	NE		ESK	2001	Bratislava	RELAX	12 B.737 Classic; 7 B.737 NG	7 B.737 NG	19	7	26
Adria Airways	SLOVENIA	EA	JP	165	ADR	1961	Ljubljana	ADRIA	6 A318–321; 2 B.737 Classic; 4 CRJ 700/900/1000; 7 CRJ 100/200	1 CRJ 700/900/1000	19	1	20
Air Comet	SPAIN	WE	A7	352	MPD	1996	Madrid	RED COMET	6 A330/A340; 3 A318–321	2 A380; 3 A330/A340	9	5	14
Air Europa	SPAIN	WE		996	AEA	1986	Palma/Madrid	EUROPA	6 A330/A340; 2 B.767; 29 B.737 NG; 4 EMB-190/195	8 B.787; 30 B.737 NG; 7 EMB-190/195	41	45	86
Air Nostrum	SPAIN	WE	YW	694		1994	Valencia	NOS-TRUM AIR	11 CRJ 700/900/1000; 35 CRJ 100/200; 5 ATR-42/72; 16 DHC-8	35 CRJ 700/900/1000; 10 ATR-42/72; 9 DHC-8	67	54	121
Iberia	SPAIN	WE	IB	75	IBE	1927	Madrid	IBERIA	37 A330/A340; 5 A300/A310; 3 B.727; 116 A318–321; 23 DC-9/MD-80/90	3 A330/A340; 13 A318–321	184	16	200
Spanair	SPAIN	WE		680		1986	Palma Gran Can.	SPANAIR	24 A318–321; 37 DC-9/MD-80/90; 4 B.717		65	0	65
Scandinavian Airlines	SWEDEN	WE	SK	117	SAS	1946	Copenha-gen/Stock-holm/Oslo	SCANDI-NAVIAN	13 A330/A340; 5 BAe 146; 13 A318–321; 48 B.737 NG; 59 DC-9/MD-80/90; 9 CRJ 700/900/1000; 6 CRJ 100/200; 1 ATR-42/72; 9 DHC-8	1 B.737 NG; 6 CRJ 700/900/1000	163	7	170

⊙ Region ✷ Created ✈ Current Fleet ✈ Planned Fleet ✈ Total Fleet

Name	Country	◉	IATA CODE	IATA NO.	ICAO	✱	Base Airport	Call-Sign	Current Fleet	Planned Fleet	✈	✈	✈
Skyways Express	SWEDEN	WE	JZ	752	SKX	1976	Linköping	SKY EXPRESS	11 F.27		11	0	11
Helvetic	SWITZERL.	WE	2L		OAW	2003	Zürich		4 F.28		4	0	4
Swiss Int'l Air Lines	SWITZERL.	WE	LX	724		1975	Zürich/ Basel	SWISS	26 A330/A340; 33 A318–321; 1 B.737	8 A330/A340; 2 A318–321	60	10	70
Onur Air	TURKEY	NE	8Q		OHY	1992	Istanbul	ONUR AIR	2 A300/A310; 9 A318–321; 9 DC-9/MD-80/90		20	0	20
Sun Express	TURKEY	NE	XQ	564	SXS	1989	Antalya		3 B.757; 18 B.737 NG	6 B.737 NG	21	6	27
Turkish Airlines	TURKEY	NE	TK	235	THY	1933	Istanbul/ Ankara	TURKAIR	16 A330/A340; 3 B.777; 5 A300/A310; 46 A318–321; 48 B.737 NG; 3 B.737	12 B.777; 4 B.737 NG	121	16	137
British Airways	UK	WE	BA	125	BAW	1974	Heathrow/ Gatwick	SPEED-BIRD + SHUTTLE	57 B.747; 46 B.777; 21 B.767; 11 B.757; 83 A318–321; 47 B.737 Classic	12 A380; 6 B.777; 24 B.787; 16 A318–321	265	58	323
Loganair	UK	WE			LOG	1962	Glasgow	LOGAN			0	0	0
Thomson Airways	UK	WE			TOM	2003	Coventry	THOM-SON	7 B.737 Classic		7	0	7
EasyJet	UK	WE	U2		EZY	1995	Luton	EASY	153 A318–321; 20 B.737 NG	79 A318–321	173	79	252
bmi	UK	WE	BD	236	BMA	1949	East Midlands	MID-LAND	3 A330/A340; 1 B.757; 30 A318–321; 1 B.737 Classic	3 A318–321	35	3	38
Flybe	UK	WE	BE	267	BEE	1969	Exeter	JERSEY	8 BAe 146; 14 EMB-190/195; 9 EMB-135/145; 57 DHC-8	22 DHC-8	88	22	110
Monarch Airlines	UK	WE		974	MON	1967	Luton	MO-NARCH	2 A330/A340; 4 A300/A310; 1 B.767; 3 B.757; 33 A318–321	6 B.787; 1 A318–321	43	7	50
Thomas Cook Airlines	UK	WE	MT		TCX	1999	Manchester	KESTREL	9 A330/A340; 2 B.767; 23 B.757; 22 A318–321		56	0	56
Virgin Atlantic Airways	UK	WE		932	VIR	1982	Gatwick/ Heathrow	VIRGIN	13 B.747; 26 A330/A340	6 A380; 10 A330/A340; 15 B.787	39	31	70
Africa													
Air Algerie	ALGERIA	AR	AH	124	DAH	1947	Algier	AIR ALGERIE	5 A330/A340; 5 B.767; 6 A300/A310; 8 B.727; 15 B.737 Classic; 18 B.737 NG; 1 C-130/L.100; 8 F.27; 8 ATR-42/72		74	0	74
TAAG Angola Airlines	ANGOLA	ZA	DT	118	DTA	1938	Luanda	DTA	5 B.747; 3 B.777; 4 B.737 NG, 4 B.737 Classic, 4 F.27		20	0	20
Air Botswana	BOTSWANA	ZA	BP	636	BOT	1965	Gaborone	BOTS-WANA	3 BAe 146; 5 ATR-42/72		8	0	8
TACV Cabo Verde Airlines	CAPE VERDE ISLANDS	EQ	VR	696	TCV	1958	Praia	CABO VERDE	2 B.757; 4 ATR-42/72		6	0	6
EgyptAir	EGYPT	AR	MS	77	MSR	1932	Cairo	EGYPT-AIR	10 A330/A340; 5 B.777; 1 B.767; 16 A318–321; 4 B.737 Classic; 7 B.737 NG	5 A330/A340; 6 B.777; 13 B.737 NG	43	24	67
Eritrean Airl.	ERITREA	EQ	B8	637	ERT	2002	Asmara	ERI-TREAN	1 B.767		1	0	1
Ethiopian Airlines	ETHIOPIA	EQ	ET	71	ETH	1945	Addis Ababa	ETHIO-PIAN	3 B.747; 1 DC-10/MD-11; 10 B.767; 10 B.757; 5 B.737 NG; 1 C-130/L.100; 5 F.27	1 DC-10/MD-11; 12 A350; 5 B.777; 10 B.787; 3 B.737 NG; 8 DHC-8	35	39	74
Air Service Gabon	GABON	EQ			AGB	1965	Libreville	AIR SERVICE GABON	2 CRJ 100/200; 5 DHC-8		7	0	7
Gabon Airlines	GABON	EQ	GY	13	GBK	2006	Libreville	GABON-AIRLINES	2 B.767		2	0	2
Air Ivoire	IVORY COAST	EQ		943	VUN	1960	Abidjan	AIR IVOIRE	3 A318–321; 1 B.737 Classic; 2 DC-9/MD-80/90; 3 F.28	3 B.737 Classic	9	3	12
Kenya Airways	KENYA	EQ	KQ	706	KQA	1977	Nairobi	KENYA	4 B.777; 6 B.767; 9 B.737 NG; 6 B.737 Classic; 3 EMB-170/175	9 B.787	28	9	37
Afriqiyah Airways	LIBYA	AR	8U	546	AAW	2001	Tripoli	AFRIQI-YAH	1 A330/A340; 1 A300/A310; 9 A318–321	3 A330/A340; 6 A350; 10 A318–321	11	19	30
Libyan Airlines	LIBYA	AR	LN	148	LAA	1964	Tripoli	LIBAIR	8 A300/A310; 1 B.707/720; 7 B.727; 2 A318–321; 2 BAC-111; 5 F.28; 5 CRJ 700/900/1000; 10 F.27	4 A350; 4 A330/A340	40	8	48

◉ Region ✱ Created ✈ Current Fleet ✈ Planned Fleet ✈ Total Fleet

Name	Country	⊙	IATA CODE	IATA NO.	ICAO	*	Base Airport	Call-Sign	Current Fleet	Planned Fleet	✈	✈	✈
Air Madagascar	MADAGASCAR	ZA	MD	258	MDG	1962	Antananarivo	AIR MADAGASCAR	2 B.767; 2 B.737 Classic; 5 ATR-42/72	1 B.737 Classic	9	1	10
Air Malawi	MALAWI	ZA		167	AML	1964	Blantyre	MALAWI	3 B.737 Classic; 1 ATR-42/72		4	0	4
Air Mauritius	MAURITIUS	ZA	MK	239	MAU	1967	Mauritius	AIRMAURITIUS	9 A330/A340; 2 A318-321; 2 ATR-42/72	1 A330/A340	13	1	14
LAM	MOZAMBIQUE	ZA	TM	68	LAM	1936	Maputo	MOZAMBIQUE	4 B.737 Classic; 1 EMB-190/195; 2 DHC-8	1 EMB-190/195	7	1	8
Air Namibia	NAMIBIA	ZA	SW	186	NMB	1946	Windhoek	NAMIBIA	2 A330/A340; 2 B.737 Classic		4	0	4
Arik Air	NIGERIA	EQ	W3		ARA	2006	Lagos	ARIK	2 A330/A340; 2 B.737 Classic; 11 B.737 NG; 4 CRJ 700/900/1000; 7 F.27; 4 DHC-8	1 A330/A340; 5 B.777; 7 B.787; 22 B.737 NG; 4 DHC-8	30	39	69
Nigerian Eagle Airlines	NIGERIA	EQ	VK		VGN	2004	Lagos	VIRGIN NIGERIA	5 B.737 Classic; 2 EMB-190/195	7 EMB-170/175; 1 EMB-190/195	7	8	15
Air Austral	REUNION	ZA	UU	760	REU	1975	St. Denis	REUNION	5 B.777; 2 B.737 Classic; 3 ATR-42/72		10	0	10
Air Seychelles	SEYCHELLES	EQ	HM	61	SEY	1977	Mahé	SEYCHELLES	5 B.767	2 B.787	5	2	7
South African Airlines	SOUTH AFRICA	ZA	SA	83	SAA	1934	Johannesburg-Int.	SPRINGBOK	2 B.747; 21 A330/A340; 11 A318-321; 17 B.737 NG; 4 B.737 Classic	4 A318-321	55	4	59
Precision Air	TANZANIA	EQ	PW	31	PRF	1991	Arusha	PRECISIONAIR	1 B.737 Classic; 11 ATR-42/72	3 ATR-42/72	12	3	15
Tunisair	TUNISIA	AR	TU	199	TAR	1948	Tunis-Carthage	TUNAIR	4 A300/A310; 15 A318-321; 4 B.737 Classic; 7 B.737 NG	3 A350; 3 A330/A340; 10 A318-321	30	16	46
Air Uganda	UGANDA	EQ	U7	926	UGB	2007	Entebbe		3 DC-9/MD-80/90		3	0	3
Air Zimbabwe	ZIMBABWE	ZA		168	AZW	1967	Harare-Int.	AIR ZIMBABWE	2 B.767; 1 BAe 146; 3 B.737 Classic; 3 Viscount; 3 Yun Y-7		12	0	12

Middle East

Name	Country	⊙	IATA CODE	IATA NO.	ICAO	*	Base Airport	Call-Sign	Current Fleet	Planned Fleet	✈	✈	✈
Gulf Air	BAHRAIN	ME	GF	72	GFA	1950	Bahrain	GULF AIR	34 A330/A340; 4 B.777; 4 B.767; 21 A318-321	20 A330/A340; 24 B.787; 15 A318-321	63	59	122
Eurocypria Airlines	CYPRUS	NE	UI		ECA	1990	Larnaca	EUROCYPRIA	8 B.737 NG		8	0	8
Arkia Israeli Airlines	ISRAEL	NE	IZ	238	AIZ	1950	Tel Aviv-Ben Gurion	ARKIA	2 B.757; 1 EMB-190/195; 5 DHC-7; 4 ATR-42/72	4 B.787	12	4	16
EL AL Israel Airlines	ISRAEL	NE	LY	114	ELY	1948	Tel Aviv-Ben Gurion	ELAL	8 B.747; 6 B.777; 9 B.767; 1 B.757; 13 B.737 NG	4 B.777	37	4	41
Royal Jordanian Airlines	JORDAN	NE	RJ	512	RJA	1963	Amman	JORDANIAN	6 A330/A340; 9 A300/A310; 12 A318-321; 7 EMB	8 B.787	34	8	42
Kuwait Airways	KUWAIT	ME	KU	229	KAC	1953	Kuwait	KUWAIT	1 B.747; 5 A330/A340; 2 B.777; 9 A300/A310; 4 A318-321		21	0	21
Middle East Airlines	LEBANON	NE	ME	76	MEA	1945	Beirut	CEDAR JET	4 A330/A340; 10 A318-321	3 A318-321	14	3	17
Oman Air	OMAN	ME	WY	910	OMA	1981	Muscat-Seeb	KHANJAR	2 A330/A340; 13 B.737 NG; 2 ATR-42/72	13 A330/A340; 6 B.787; 9 B.737 NG	17	28	45
Qatar Airways	QATAR	ME		157	QTR	1993	Doha	QATARI	34 A330/A340; 8 B.777; 3 A300/A310; 21 A318-321	5 A380; 80 A350; 1 A330/A340; 19 B.777; 30 B.787; 27 A318-321	66	162	228
Saudi Arabian Airlines	SAUDI ARABIA	ME	SV	65	SVA	1945	Jeddah	SAUDIA	27 B.747; 4 DC-10/MD-11; 2 A330/A340; 23 B.777; 38 A300/A310; 5 B.757; 2 A318-321; 1 B.737 Classic; 29 DC-9/MD-80/90; 15 EMB-170/175	8 A330/A340; 12 B.787; 45 A318-321	146	65	211
Air Arabia	UAE	ME	G9		ABY	2003	Sharjah		17 A318/A319/A320/A321	46 A318/A319/A320/A321	17	46	63
Emirates	UAE	ME	EK	176	UAE	1985	Dubai	EMIRATES	5 A380; 7 B.747; 47 A330/A340; 78 B.777	51 A380; 10 B.747; 70 A350; 32 B.777	137	163	300
Etihad Airways	UAE	ME	EY		ETD	2003	Abu Dhabi	ETIHAD	26 A330/A340; 5 B.777; 2 A300/A310; 12 A318-321	10 A380; 10 A330/A340; 25 A350; 10 B.777; 2 A300/A310; 35 B.787; 24 A318-321	45	116	161
Yemenia	YEMEN	ME	IY	635	IYE	1961	Sana'a	YEMENI	3 Il-76; 2 A330/A340; 4 A300/A310; 6 B.727; 4 B.737 NG; 3 B.737; 2 C-130/L.100; 2 DHC-7; 3 DHC-8; 2 DC-3	10 A350; 6 DHC-8	31	16	47

⊙ Region * Created ✈ Current Fleet ✈ Planned Fleet ✈ Total Fleet

Name	Country	⊙	IATA CODE	IATA NO.	ICAO	*	Base Airport	Call-Sign	Current Fleet	Planned Fleet	✈	✈	✈
Asia													
Ariana Afghan Airlines	AFGHAN-ISTAN	ME	FG	255	AFG	1955	Kabul	ARIANA	4 A300/A310; 5 B.727; 2 An-24		11	0	11
Bangladesh Biman Airlines	BANGLA-DESH	ME	BG	997	BBC	1972	Dhaka	BANGLA-DESH	1 B.747; 5 DC-10/MD-11; 2 A300/A310; 4 F.28	4 B.777; 4 B.787; 1 A300/A310; 2 B.737 NG	12	11	23
Royal Brunei	BRUNEI	FE	BI	672	RBA	1974	Bandar Seri	BRUNEI	6 B.767; 4 A318-321	4 B.787	10	4	14
Air China	CHINA	FE	CA	999	CCA	1988	Beijing-Capital	AIR CHINA	10 B.747; 26 A330/A340; 10 B.777; 8 B.767; 13 B.757; 53 A318-321; 77 B.737 NG; 32 B.737; 1 An-12; 4 Yun Y-7	20 A330/A340; 15 B.777; 15 B.787; 15 A318-321; 42 B.737 NG	234	107	341
Air Macau	CHINA	FE	NX	675	AMU	1994	Macau	AIR MACAU	3 A300/A310; 19 A318-321		22	0	22
China Eastern Airlines	CHINA	FE	MU	781	CES	1988	Shanghai/Nanchang/Hefei	CHINA EASTERN	30 A330/A340; 7 A300/A310; 3 B.767; 5 BAe 146; 107 A318-321; 19 B.737; 44 B.737; 9 DC-9/MD-80/90; 5 CRJ; 10 EMB; 9 Yun Y-7	15 B.787; 44 A318-321; 14 B.737 NG	248	73	321
China Southern Airlines	CHINA	FE	CZ	784	CSN	1989	Guangzhou	CHINA SOUTH-ERN	2 B.747; 14 A330/A340; 12 B.777; 6 A300/A310; 19 B.757; 127 A318-321; 24 B.737; 75 B.737; 25 DC-9/MD-80/90; 6 EMB-135/145; 5 ATR-42/72	5 A380; 10 A330/A340; 6 B.777; 10 B.787; 48 A318-321; 61 B.737 NG	315	140	455
China Xinhua Airlines	CHINA	FE		779	CXH	1992	Beijing-Tian	XINHUA	7 B.737 NG; 9 B.737 Classic		16	0	16
Hainan Airlines	CHINA	FE		880	CHH	1989	Haikou	HAINAN	9 A330/A340; 3 B.767; 46 B.737 NG; 8 B.737 Classic	4 A330/A340; 8 B.787; 25 A318-321; 13 B.737 NG	66	50	116
Shanghai Airlines	CHINA	FE		774		1985	Shanghai-Hongqiao	SHANG-HAI AIR	7 B.767; 10 B.757; 1 A318-321; 30 B.737 NG; 5 CRJ 100/200	9 B.787; 9 A318-321; 7 B.737 NG; 5 ARJ21	53	30	83
Xiamen Airlines	CHINA	FE		731	CXA	1984	Xiamen	XIAMEN AIR	8 B.757; 43 B.737 NG; 2 B.737 Classic	41 B.737 NG	53	41	94
Dragon Air	CHINA HK	FE		43	HDA	1985	Hong Kong	DRAGON-AIR	5 B.747; 17 A330/A340; 16 A318-321	2 A318-321	38	2	40
Cathay Pacific Airways	CHINA HK	FE	CX	160	CPA	1946	Hong Kong	CATHAY	76 B.747; 64 A330/A340; 32 B.777	11 B.747; 8 A330/A340; 19 B.777	172	38	210
Air India	INDIA	ME	AI+ IC		AIC	2007	Delhi	INDAIR	10 B.747; 2 A330/A340; 17 B.777; 10 A300/A310; 76 A318-321	10 B.777; 27 B.787; 18 A318-321	115	55	170
Jet Airways	INDIA	ME	9W	589	JAI	1992	Mumbai	JET AIRWAYS	10 A330/A340; 3 B.777; 48 B.737 NG; 14 ATR-42/72	5 A330/A340; 3 B.777; 10 B.787; 28 B.737 NG; 6 ATR-42/72	75	52	127
Kingfisher Airlines	INDIA	ME	IT		KFR+ BEZ	2003	Mumbai	KING-FISHER	5 A330/A340; 1 B.727; 25 A318-321; 18 ATR-42/72	5 A380; 17 A330/A340; 23 A318-321; 14 ATR	49	59	108
Batavia Air	INDONESIA	FE	7P	671	BTV	2002	Jakarta	BATAVIA	6 A318-321; 34 B.737 Classic	2 A330/A340; 1 B.737 Classic; 10 ATR-42/72	40	13	53
Garuda Indonesian	INDONESIA	FE	GA	126	GIA	1949	Jakarta-Hatta	INDO-NESIA	3 B.747; 9 A330/A340; 38 B.737 Classic; 14 B.737 NG; 4 DC-9/MD-80/90	1 A330/A340; 10 B.777; 25 B.737 NG	68	36	104
Lion Air	INDONESIA	FE	JT	990	LNI	2000	Jakarta-Hatta	LION INTER	2 B.747; 11 B.737 Classic; 25 B.737 NG; 10 DC-9/MD-80/90	157 B.737 NG	48	157	205
Mandala Airlines	INDONESIA	FE			MDL	1969	Jakarta	MAN-DALA	9 A318-321; 3 B.737 Classic; 1 DC-3	25 A318-321	13	25	38
Merpati Nusantara Airlines	INDONESIA	FE	MZ	621	MNA	1962	Jakarta	MERPATI	18 B.737 Classic; 22 F.28; 4 F.27; 2 Yun Y-7	1 B.737 Classic; 13 Yun Y-7	46	14	60
All Nippon Airways	JAPAN	FE	NH	205	ANA	1952	Tokyo-Haneda	ALL NIPPON	15 B.747; 43 B.777; 57 B.767; 29 A318-321; 4 B.737 NG	4 B.777; 55 B.787; 4 B.767; 21 B.737 NG	148	84	232
JAL Domestic	JAPAN	FE	JL	234	JLJ	1964	Tokyo-Haneda	AIR SYSTEM	7 B.777; 22 A300/A310; 25 DC-9/MD-80/90		54	0	54
JAL International	JAPAN	FE	JL	131	JAL	1951	Tokyo-Han./Narita	JAPAN-AIR	52 B.747; 36 B.777; 50 B.767; 12 B.737 NG	10 B.777; 35 B.787; 9 B.767; 31 B.737 NG	150	85	235
Air Nippon	JAPAN	FE	EL	768	ANK	1974	Tokyo	ANK AIR	21 B.737 NG; 5 B.737 Classic		26	0	26
Air Koryo	KOREA (NORTH)	FE	JS	120	KOR	1950	Pyongyang	AIR KORYO	3 Il-76; 5 Il-62; 6 Tu-154; 1 Tu-204/214/234; 2 Tu-134; 4 Il-18; 6 An-24	2 Tu-204/214/234	27	2	29

⊙ Region   * Created   ✈ Current Fleet   ✈ Planned Fleet   ✈ Total Fleet

Name	Country	⊙	IATA CODE	IATA NO.	ICAO	✱	Base Airport	Call-Sign	Current Fleet	Planned Fleet	✈	✈	✈
Asiana Airlines	KOREA (SOUTH)	FE	OZ	988	AAR	1988	Seoul-Incheon	ASIANA	12 B.747; 7 A330/A340; 10 B.777; 8 B.767; 24 A318–321; 7 B.737 Classic	30 A350; 1 A330/A340; 4 B.777; 3 A318–321	68	38	106
Korean Air	KOREA (SOUTH)	FE	KE	180	KAL	1962	Seoul-Incheon/ Gimpo	KOREAN-AIR	50 B.747; 20 A330/A340; 23 B.777; 8 A300/A310; 31 B.737 NG	10 A380; 5 B.747; 6 A330/A340; 16 B.777; 10 B.787; 5 B.737 NG	132	52	184
Lao Airlines	LAOS	FE	QV	627	LAO	1976	Vientiane	LAO	4 ATR-42/72; 3 An-24; 7 Yun Y-7	1 ATR-42/72	14	1	15
AirAsia	MALAYSIA	FE		807	AXM	1993	Kuala Lumpur	ASIAN EXPRESS	44 A318–321; 1 B.737 Classic	114 A318–321	45	114	159
Malaysia Airlines	MALAYSIA	FE	MH	232	MAS	1947	Kuala Lumpur	MALAY-SIAN	23 B.747; 15 A330/A340; 17 B.777; 1 A300/A310; 3 B.737 NG; 38 B.737	6 A380; 35 B.737 NG	97	41	138
MIAT Mongolian Airlines	MONGOLIA	FE	OM	269	MGL	1956	Ulaan-baatar	MONGOL AIR	2 A300/A310; 2 B.737 NG; 1 An-30; 17 An-24		22	0	22
Nepal Airlines	NEPAL	ME	RA	285	RNA	1958	Kathmandu	ROYAL NEPAL	2 B.757; 1 HS.748/Andover	2 Yun Y-7	3	2	5
PIA	PAKISTAN	ME	PK	214	PIA	1951	Karachi	PAKIS-TAN	8 B.747; 9 B.777; 12 A300/A310; 7 B.737 Classic; 7 ATR-42/72		43	0	43
Cebu Pacific Air	PHILIP-PINES	FE	5J	203	CEB	1995	Manila	CEBU AIR	21 A318–321; 8 ATR-42/72	15 A318–321; 2 TR-42/72	29	17	46
Philippine Airlines	PHILIP-PINES	FE	PR	79	PAL	1941	Manila	PHILIP-PINE	11 B.747; 28 A330/A340; 23 A318–321; 1 B.737 Classic; 5 DHC-8	6 B.777; 3 A318–321; 2 DHC-8	68	11	79
SilkAir	SINGAPORE	FE	MI	629	SLK	1975	Changi	SILKAIR	16 A318–321	13 A318–321	16	13	29
Singapore Airlines	SINGAPORE	FE	SQ	618	SIA	1972	Singapore-Changi	SINGA-PORE	9 A380; 12 B.747; 13 A330/A340; 77 B.777	10 A380; 11 A330/A340; 20 A350; 20 B.787	111	61	172
Tiger Airways	SINGAPORE	FE	TR		TGW	2003	Singapore	GO CAT	10 A318–321	55 A318–321	10	55	65
Sri Lankan Airlines	SRI LANKA	ME	UL	603		1979	Colombo	SRI LANKAN	9 A330/A340; 3 A318–321; 4 An-12		16	0	16
China Airlines	TAIWAN	FE	CI	297	CAL	1959	Taipei	DYNASTY	34 B.747; 23 A330/A340; 11 B.737 NG	14 A350	68	14	82
EVA Air	TAIWAN	FE	BR	695	EVA	1989	Taipei-Chiang Kai Shek	EVA	22 B.747; 8 DC-10/MD-11; 11 A330/A340; 12 B.777; 1 A318–321; 9 DC-9/MD-80/90	3 B.777	63	3	66
Bangkok Airways	THAILAND	FE		829	BKP	1968	Bangkok	BANG-KOK AIR	10 A318–321; 2 B.717; 8 ATR-42/72	4 A350; 1 A318–321; 1 ATR-42/72	20	6	26
Orient Thai Airlines	THAILAND	FE	OX	578	OEA	1995	Bangkok	ORIENT EXPRESS	7 B.747; 1 DC-9/MD-80/90		8	0	8
Thai Airways International	THAILAND	FE	TG	217	THA	1959	Bangkok	THAI	18 B.747; 25 A330/A340; 20 B.777; 17 A300/A310; 6 B.737; 2 ATR-42/72	6 A380; 2 B.747; 5 A330/A340	88	13	101
Vietnam Airlines	VIETNAM	FE	VN	738	HVN	1956	Hanoi/ Ho Chi Minh City	VIET-NAM AIRLINES	5 A330/A340; 10 B.777; 2 Yak-40; 25 A318–321; 1 Tu-134; 2 F.28; 3 Il-18; 10 ATR-42/72; 2 An-26; 8 An-24	10 A350; 16 B.787; 28 A318–321; 12 ATR-42/72	68	66	134

Australia and Pacific

Name	Country	⊙	IATA CODE	IATA NO.	ICAO	✱	Base Airport	Call-Sign	Current Fleet	Planned Fleet	✈	✈	✈
Qantas	AUSTRALIA	OC	QF	81	QFA	1920	Sydney	QANTAS	3 A380; 34 B.747; 16 A330/A340; 29 B.767; 17 B.737; 38 B.737 NG; 1 Const.	17 A380; 4 A330/A340; 50 B.787; 31 B.737 NG	138	102	240
Skywest	AUSTRALIA	OC		608		1963	Perth, WA	SKYWEST	8 F.28; 7 F.27		15	0	15
Virgin Blue	AUSTRALIA	OC	DJ		VOZ	1999	Brisbane	VIRGIN	46 B.737 NG; 12 EMB-190/195; 6 EMB-170/175	27 B.737 NG; 5 EMB-190/195	64	32	96
Air Pacific	FIJI	OC	FJ	260	FJI	1947	Nadi	PACIFIC	3 B.747; 1 B.767; 3 B.737 NG	8 B.787	7	8	15
Air Tahiti Nui	FRANCE POLYNESIA	OC	TN	244	THT	1996	Papéeté	TAHITI AIRLINES	5 A330/A340		5	0	5
Our Airline	NAURU	OC	ON	123	RON	1970	Nauru	AIR NAURU	1 B.737 Classic		1	0	1
Aircalin	NEW CALEDONIA	OC	SB	63	ACI	1983	Noumea-La Tontouta	AIRCA-LIN	2 A330/A340; 1 A318–321		3	0	3
Air New Zealand	NEW ZEALAND	OC		86	ANZ	1940	Auckland	NEW ZEA-LAND	7 B.747; 8 B.777; 5 B.767; 21 A318–321; 19 B.737 Classic; 1 F.27	5 B.777; 8 B.787	61	13	74
Air Niugini	PAPUA NEW GUINEA	OC	PX	656	ANG	1973	Port Moresby	NIUGINI	1 B.767; 1 B.757; 10 F.28; 8 DHC-8; 2 DC-3	1 B.787	22	1	23
Solomon Airlines	SOLOMON ISLANDS	OC	IE	193	SOL	1968	Honiara	SOLO-MON			0	0	0
Air Vanuatu	VANUATU	OC	NF	218	AVN	1981	Port Vila	AIR VAN	1 B.737 NG; 1 ATR-42/72	1 ATR-42/72	2	1	3

⊙ Region ✱ Created ✈ Current Fleet ✈ Planned Fleet ✈ Total Fleet

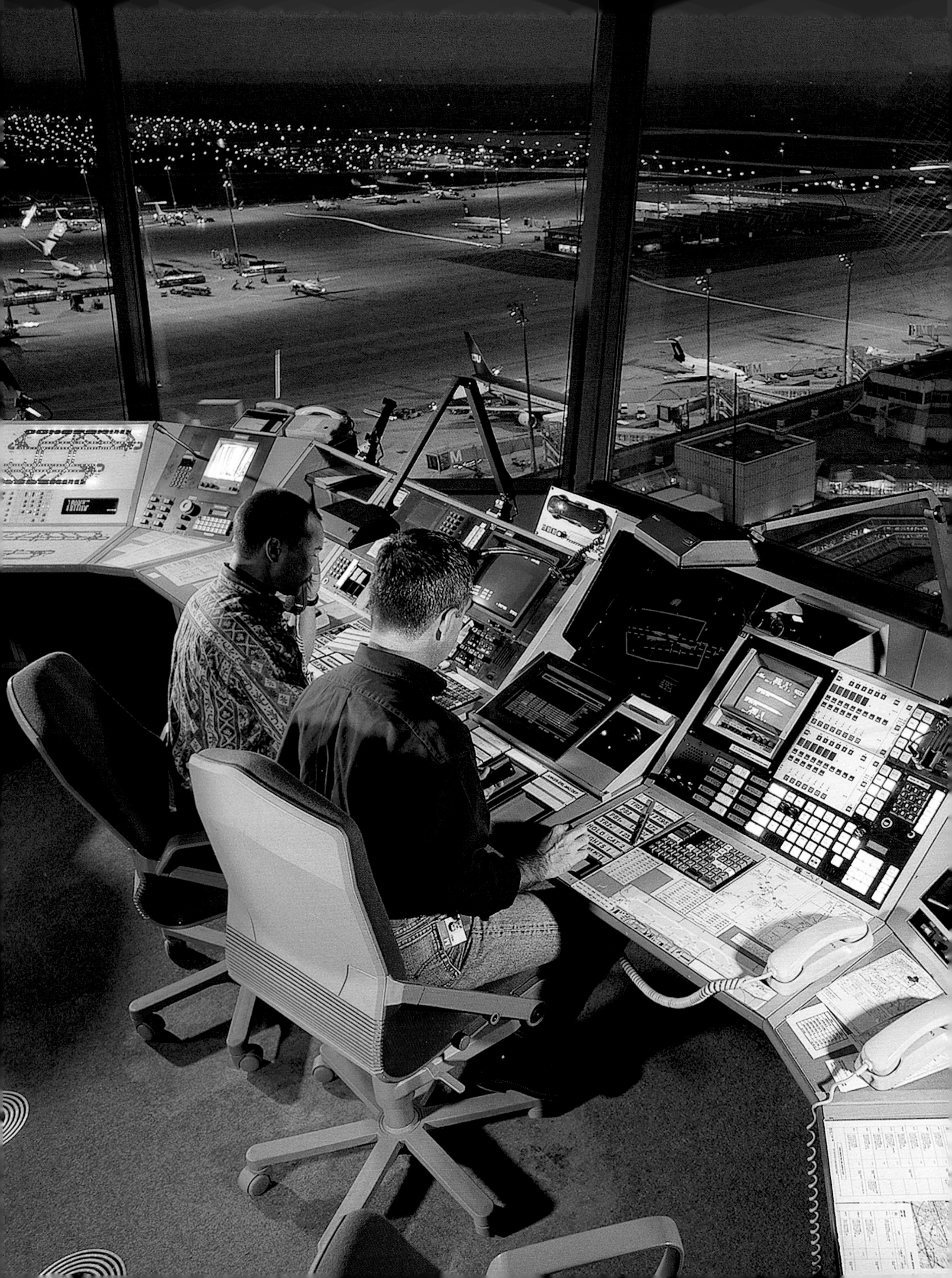

ABOUT
FLYING

The Ticket

History of the Airline Ticket

1920 First airline ticket.
1930 First standardized IATA ticket with multiple flight coupons.
1972 First universal ticket in BSP (billing and settlement plan) format. IATA agencies use blank documents. The computer calculates the fare and prints out the paper ticket. All the data is forwarded to BSP, which in turn settles payment with the airlines. Today, BSP operates in over 150 countries worldwide and handles nearly 80 per cent of airline ticket sales.
1983 First ticket with a magnetic strip.
1994 First e-ticket.
2008 Start of the age of ticketless travel.

From Travel Agency to E-ticket

The traditional, complicated-to-issue ticket is making way for the electronic ticket. Travel agencies will generally no longer receive any commission, but will charge a service fee to customers who continue to buy their tickets from them, rather than booking directly via the internet.

Travel agencies will be needed to handle more complex bookings: for example, booking flights from Rome to Moscow, from there on to Singapore, with a side trip to Laos, Bangkok and Hong Kong, and then back again to Rome would cause any booking engine to crash. Moreover, booking the cheapest fare on every leg of the journey carries a huge risk: in the event of a delay, you would not be able to change the booking on the subsequent legs of the journey.

The E-ticket

The issuing of a conventional ticket manually could take a good 20 minutes. Since 1 June 2008, however, the customer's passport or credit card suffices for most of the world's airlines. This personal data is used to call up the flight details. Travellers with hand luggage only can even order their electronic boarding card via SMS or using an internet-capable mobile phone, then proceed directly to the security check and place their mobile phone on the scanner – and that's it. You can also check in via the internet the day before you travel and print out your boarding pass on your own printer.

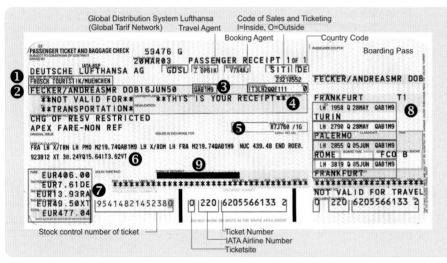

1 = Issuer
2 = Passenger, including DOB
3 = Fare basis
First letter is the booking class
4 = Authorization code for inclusive tour
5 = Booking code/computer reservation system
6 = Fare calculation
Frankfurt–Turin–Palermo 219.74
(+Palermo)–Rome–Frankfurt 219.74 = 439.48 NUC
(NUC = Neutral Unit of Construction; ROE = Rate of exchange
1 NUC = 1 dollar)

XT = Refers to combined charges in the tax box
YQ = Airline's own charge (30.24)
IT = Airport charge for Italy (15.64)
VT = Security surcharge Italy (3.62)
7 = Taxes and charges
DE = German sales tax (7.61)
International passenger service charge (13.93)
XT = combined charges and taxes from fare calculation
8 = Boarding pass copy
9 = Credit card number

Booking a Flight

There are hundreds of booking engines on the internet. These compare specific routes, sorting them by fare, journey duration or number of stopovers. However, the airlines are involved in many of these. The basic rule is that the cheaper the ticket, the fewer the privileges. Also, the earlier you book, the more likely you are to obtain a cheaper fare.
Expedia.com
Travelocity.com
fly.com
cheapflights.com
orbitz.com
priceline.com
hotwire.com
farecompare.com
kayak.com
tripadvisor.com
SideStep.com
skyscanner.net
Alternatively, simply google the names of two cities, and all of the relevant booking engines, including those of the airlines themselves, will come up.

HOW ARE TICKET PRICES ARRIVED AT?

Previously, the (mainly government-owned) airlines were monopolies. Only airlines from country A and country B could fly from country A to country B. A flight within Europe might very well cost four times as much as an intercontinental flight. Tickets became amazingly cheap (85 per cent discount) if a Saturday night fell between the dates of the outward and return flights. The reason for this was that such tickets were not purchased by business travellers who wanted to be with their family at the weekend.

Tickets were also cheaper if the journey started in a third country. Paris–London–New York was significantly less expensive than London–New York.

CROSS-TICKETING AND CROSS-BORDER-SELLING

Savvy air passengers soon got the hang of this vexing pricing system and simply purchased two cheap return tickets, which they used to get around the minimum stay requirements. They then flew just the outward segment of the first ticket and the return segment of the other. Alternatively, instead of purchasing a Frankfurt–Tokyo ticket, they bought the less expensive Madrid–Frankfurt–Tokyo flight and simply discarded the Madrid–Frankfurt coupon. Lufthansa brought a legal action to prevent this at the Cologne Higher Regional Court and won (Cologne HRC judgement of 31 July 2009, 6 U 224/08). Accordingly, anyone who does not fly a segment of a ticket can be charged subsequently. Lufthansa does not have to accept tickets which are not flown in the sequence booked. Low-cost airlines and airlines with open pricing, on the other hand, allow the unused portion of the ticket to lapse without any further consequences.

CODESHARING

While the airline alliance system definitely has its benefits for customers (for example, you can collect miles worldwide and use partner airlines' lounges), one feature of them is downright annoying: codesharing flights. They may have benefits for the airlines, from the transportation of luggage to their use as a marketing tool, but for passengers they are more likely to be seen as confusing, if not as an outright fraud.

An alliance airline's flight no longer has one flight number, but two, three or even four. You might book a flight with American Airlines and end up flying with British Airways; or you want to fly with Lufthansa from Stuttgart to Tenerife, but have to change in Madrid to a Spanair plane flying under a Lufthansa flight number. Even if most airlines indicate at the booking stage which partner will actually be operating a flight, this is not necessarily obvious to the customer.

The rotating logos on the information board, where for 20 seconds the flight number of one airline, then that of another, and possibly even that of a third is displayed, are an irritation for customers. Otherwise, the same flight is displayed three times. Customers in a hurry might have to wait for several minutes until the relevant screen page appears on the monitor. Then, at the destination airport, the person meeting them may end up at the wrong terminal.

BOOKING CLASSES

Tariff		Class	Remarks
A	●	First	Discounted fares, round-the-world
B	●	Economy	Fully flexible
C	●	Business	Fully flexible
D	●	Business	Discounted fares, round-the-world
E	●	Economy	Discounted fare
F	●	First	Fully flexible
G	●	Economy	Discounted fare, also for group travel
H	●	Economy	Discounted fares, student fare
I	●	Business	Premium ticket
J			
K	●	Economy	Discounted fare, one-way domestic
L	●	Economy	Discounted fare
M	●	Economy	Fully flexible, round-the-world
N	●	Economy	Non-revenue *
O	●	First	Award ticket
P	●	Economy	Premium ticket
Q	●	Economy	
R	●	Business	Non-revenue *
S	●	Economy	Heavily discounted fare, international
T	●	Economy	Heavily discounted fare
U	●	Economy	Discounted fare
V	●	Economy	Discounted fare, cheapest class with 100 per cent miles, cheapest upgradeable class
W	●	Economy	Discounted fare, intercontinental, internet specials
X	●	Economy	Premium ticket
Y	●	Economy	Fully flexible
Z	●	Business	Discounted business class fare, round-the-world, 60-day advance bookings

* Staff, guests, competition winners

WHAT SOME AIRLINES ADD SURCHARGES FOR

Fee for online check-in	5 euros
Processing fee – per passenger per flight	5 euros
First item of luggage	10 euros
Second and third items of luggage – per passenger per flight	20 euros
Items for children (infant carriers/travel cots) fee per item per flight (one pushchair is carried free of charge)	10 euros
Sports equipment – per item per flight	30 euros
Musical instruments – per item per flight	30 euros
Flight rebooking fee – per passenger per flight	35 euros
Name change fee – per passenger	100 euros
Alcoholic drink on board	5 euros
Meal	10 euros
Blanket and pillow	10 euros
Seat at emergency exit with more legroom	25 euros

Lo

Ma

Vancouver

Air Canada

Atlanta

⊗ New York

American Airlines

Air Canada

San Francisco

USAirways

Lufthansa

Los Angeles

United Airlines

★ Dallas

American Airlines

Miami

American Airlines

Honolulu

Mexico City

Caracas

Air New Zealand

American Airlines

Iberia

South African

Lima

Star Alliance

Day	City	Miles	Day	City	Miles
	FRANKFURT			**AUCKLAND**	
1.10.	Bangkok	5584	1.10.	Honolulu	4406
6.10.	Shanghai	1787	5.10.	Los Angeles	2736
11.10.	Honolulu	4942	8.10.	New York	2461
15.10.	Vancouver	2706	12.10.	Johannesburg	7975
18.10.	Caracas	4481	16.10.	Hong Kong	6641
22.10.	**Frankfurt**	5019	21.10.	Sydney	5506
		24519	27.10.	**Auckland**	1342
					31067
	Economy	2976 EUR		Economy	3614 USD
	Business	6435 EUR		Business	10239 USD
	First	11354 EUR		First	14360 USD

Oneworld Alliance

Day	City	Miles	Day	City	Miles
	LONDON			**DALLAS**	
1.10.	Dubai	3450	1.10.	Rio de Janeiro	5261
4.10.	Hong Kong	3671	7.10.	Madrid	5068
9.10.	Taipei	528	13.10.	Bangkok	6369
13.10.	Tokyo	1275	18.10.	Perth	3328
19.10.	San Francisco	5153	21.10.	Sydney	2039
23.10.	Miami	2590	24.10.	Honolulu	5083
24.10.	**London**	4510	25.10.	**Dallas**	3783
		21177			**30931**
	Economy	1425 GBP		Economy	3960 USD
	Business	3875 GBP		Business	9711 USD
	First	6395 GBP		First	13340 USD

Caracas

Rio de Janeiro

Santiago de Chile

Star Alliance

Oneworld

SkyTeam

AIR MILES

Airlines have been running loyalty programmes since the 1980s. Air miles can be gained for economy class (single), business class (double) and first class (triple). For example, a person booking a round-the-world trip of 39,000 miles in first class will receive 117,000 air miles. These are best exchanged for upgrades,

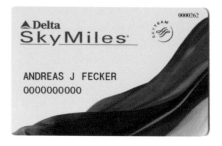

SkyTeam Alliance					
1			**2**		
Day	City	Miles	Day	City	Miles
	SEOUL			NEW YORK	
1.10.	Honolulu	4535	1.10.	Paris	3839
4.10.	Los Angeles	2510	4.10.	Rome	688
7.10.	Mexico City	1601	7.10.	Madrid	833
11.10.	Lima	2630	11.10.	Prague	1108
15.10.	Atlanta	3183	15.10.	Moscow	1035
19.10.	New York	747	19.10.	Amsterdam	1337
23.10.	Prague	4084	23.10.	Bangkok	5697
26.10.	Paris	545	26.10.	Seoul	2311
30.10.	Rome	688	30.10.	Beijing	593
3.11.	**Seoul**	5577	3.11.	Tokyo	1320
		26100	6.11.	San Francisco	5153
			10.11.	Mexico City	1874
			15.11.	Santiago de Chile	4093
			20.11.	Buenos Aires	709
			25.11.	Atlanta	4985
			27.11.	**New York**	747
					36322
	Economy	2984 USD		Economy	6011 USD
	Business	5395 USD		Business	11558 USD
	First	10568 USD		First	18185 USD

but they can also allow you to enjoy the magnificent airport lounges or to be chauffeur-driven to the plane. Some tax authorities view air miles as a pecuniary benefit. A frequent flyer who uses his miles for a free first-class holiday flight might subsequently be asked to pay tax on it. So a person receiving a free flight from Europe to Sydney in first class (worth approximately 10,000 euros) as a bonus might have to pay tax on this free flight as if it were income.

First Business Economy

An intercontinental flight can cost anywhere between 800 and 10,000 dollars. Anyone who gets the chance to fly **first class** tends to be bowled over by the creature comforts available at 12,000 m/39,000 ft: a glass of champagne before take-off, caviar with vodka, lobster with Meursalt (white wine), Chateaubriand with Margaux (red wine) and finally a dessert with a small glass of Chateau Yquem (dessert wine). Of course, the value of the meal, at perhaps 250 dollars, does not justify the exorbitant fare. The difference lies in the legroom and the size of the seat. A first class seat takes up around four or five times as much space as a seat in economy class. You could buy food on the ground and bring it on board with you: an airline cannot refuse to allow you to eat food you have brought with you on board. However, you are not allowed to open a good Bordeaux for yourself!

In **business class** you are also seated quite comfortably, although it is less expansive than first class. The price for this is around 4,000–6,000 dollars. Business class is a little more down-to-earth, yet still roomier than economy seating. The wine is decent and the films are the same throughout the plane (and censored for everyone too).

Economy can be rather uncomfortable, it is true, but costs just a fraction of the price. If you take games with you or use the games provided in the entertainment system, the few – considerably cheaper – hours will fly by. When you arrive at passport control, you'll end up standing in the same queue as the equally jetlagged first class passengers.

A Curtain Separates the Classes

Where the classes cannot be physically divided, this function has to be performed by a curtain. During take-off, the curtain has to be left open for safety reasons, but once cruising altitude is reached, the curtain is drawn, in a manner ranging from the discreet to the ostentatious. The seating in business and economy is thus the same. In front of the curtain you get scrambled egg and bacon with a glass of champagne, behind it a thin sandwich and sparkling mineral water. If anyone pays around 600 euros more for this difference, it's probably not coming out of their own pockets. Frequent flyers will notice that although the curtain has steadily been moved forward, the few remaining seats are still empty. The trend is universal: first class passengers are shifting to business, and business passengers to economy (or even straight to the low-cost carriers).

On board Gulf Air's long-haul aircraft, the food for the first class passengers is prepared by a chef.

	First Class	Business Class	Economy Plus	Economy
Booking:				
Changes free of charge	●	●	●	●
Changes for a surcharge	-	-	o	o
Switch to another IATA airline	●	o	●	●
Switch to another airline within the same alliance	●	●	o	o
Free cancellation	●	●	●	●
Bonus miles	●	●	●	●
Arrival:				
Limousine service	●	●	●	●
Valet parking or hire car return	●	●	●	●
At the airport:				
Personal assistant from arrival to departure	●	●	●	●
First Class Terminal	●	●	●	●
Lounges:				
First Class Lounge	●	●	●	●
Business Lounge	●	●	●	●
Check-in:				
Priority Check-in	●	●	●	●
Security Fast Lane	●	●	●	●
Boarding:				
Priority Boarding	●	●	●	●
Private chauffeur service to the plane	●	●	●	●
On board (international):				
Free drink(s)	●	●	●	●
Free alcoholic drink(s)	●	●	o	o
Alcoholic drinks sold on board	-	-	o	o

	First Class	Business Class	Economy Plus	Economy
Free meals	●	●	●	o
Meals sold on board	-	-	-	o
Flexible meal times	●	o	●	●
Travel kit	●	●	●	●
On board (domestic):				
Free drink(s)	●	●	●	●
Free alcoholic drink(s)	●	●	o	o
Alcoholic drinks sold on board	-	-	o	o
Free meals	●	●	o	o
Meals sold on board	-	-	o	o
Further amenities on board:				
In-flight entertainment	●	●	●	●
Video library	●	●	●	●
Seat width in cm	50+	50+	40–45	40–45
Seat pitch in cm	200+	150	90	81
Sleeper seat	●	o	●	●
Extra legroom (surcharge)	-	-	●	o
Newspapers and magazines	●	●	o	o
Baggage:				
Baggage allowance on international routes in kg	40	30	20	20
(Additional) hand luggage	2	2	1	1
Priority baggage handling/ reclaim	●	●	●	●
Departure:				
Limousine service	●	●	●	●

● yes ● no   o sometimes o usually

THE SEAT

It should look smart, not too hard, not too soft. The cover should absorb sweat, but the foam core should not. If it is made of leather, it should be resistant to sweat and butyric acid. Aircraft seats are, of course, flame-resistant and must not generate any toxic gases in a fire. They must be light, crease-resistant, washable and hard-wearing.

Otherwise it comes down to size and technology, depending on the class: ten seats per row in economy, seven or eight seats per row in business class and a maximum of six seating units (often reclinable right down to a horizontal position and complete with a massage function) in each first class row. Frequent flyers often choose an airline by its seating. If you are spending 12 hours in a confined space, you want to be comfortable, and if you are flying business class on a long-haul route, you do not want to miss out on a seat that is adjustable through 180 degrees.

Organizations and Treaties

IATA

The International Air Transport Association was founded in Cuba in 1945 as an umbrella organization for the airlines. Its headquarters are in Montreal and its goal is the safe, orderly and efficient transportation of passengers, mail and freight. It unites almost 250 airlines, which make up approximately 95 per cent of global air traffic.

ICAO

The International Civil Aviation Organization was founded in Chicago in 1944. It is a specialized agency of the United Nations. The full assembly of the ICAO and its specialist committees issue binding standards and recommendations that have to be implemented by the 190 member states. These cover areas including international traffic laws, flight corridors, infrastructure and airports.

ICAO headquarters, Montreal.

FAA

Every sovereign state maintains an aviation authority, which is generally subordinate to its transport ministry. One of the most powerful of these is the Federal Aviation Administration in the United States. It issues and monitors guidelines and regulations for safe air traffic in the United States, working within the ICAO framework. Since many aircraft manufacturers based in the United States produce goods that are used throughout the world, its scope is global. It monitors the supervision and implementation of air traffic in many regions of the world and issues recommendations to its own staff. The FAA also operates air traffic control in the United States and United States territories.

The Warsaw Convention of 1929

This international treaty regulated, among other things, liability for personal injury and damage to baggage during air transportation. It was revised in 1955 in The Hague and in 1975 in Montreal. The upper limit was set at 250,000 Swiss francs per passenger and 250 Swiss francs per kilo of baggage, unless the airline could be shown to have caused the accident through intent or gross negligence.

The Montreal Convention of 1999

The members of the International Civil Aviation Organization (ICAO) signed a convention in 1999 revising the regulations on compensating passengers and their relatives. It limited liability again, this time to just 135,000 dollars per person. The airline is now liable only for physical injuries and not psychological trauma.

Some people see these sums as insulting and scandalous because a jumbo jet is insured for a value of around 300 million dollars, while the 250 passengers on board would, according to these regulations, be worth just 30 million dollars – barely a tenth of the sum for material damage. However, the upper limit does not apply in cases of gross negligence.

Another new feature is that the families of victims can sue the airline in their own country of residence rather than in the airline's place of jurisdiction. If the country of residence then happened to be the United States, this could spell ruin for some airlines.

Airline Philosophies:

Hub-and-Spoke System (with stops)...

The **hub-and-spoke** system is characterized by central 'hubs', like that of a wheel, from which flights to secondary destinations radiate like spokes.
- Very efficient on long-haul routes.
- Traffic between the hubs is on large aircraft, while the spokes are served by smaller planes. Instead of flying Phoenix–Alice Springs direct, you fly Phoenix–Los Angeles on a 737, Los Angeles–Sydney on a 747 or A380, and Sydney–Alice Springs on a 737.
- Better utilization of aircraft capacity.
- Passengers have to put up with periods of waiting when changing planes.
- Sometimes weather-related bottlenecks occur at a hub, which then affect the entire network.
- Short feeder flights to hubs place a disproportionate burden on the environment and should ideally be replaced by train connections.

...Point-to-Point System (non-stop)

Point-to-point connections are offered depending on market demand.
- No need to change planes.
- Often seasonally determined.
- If demand falls below a certain level, the connection will be axed.
- The cost of maintenance is higher due to aircraft being based regionally.
- Possible increased pressure on airspace, which could lead to delays in the entire system.

If an airline has several hubs, the obvious solution is a combination of these two systems: frequent point-to-point connections can be flown direct as well as being linked via the hubs.

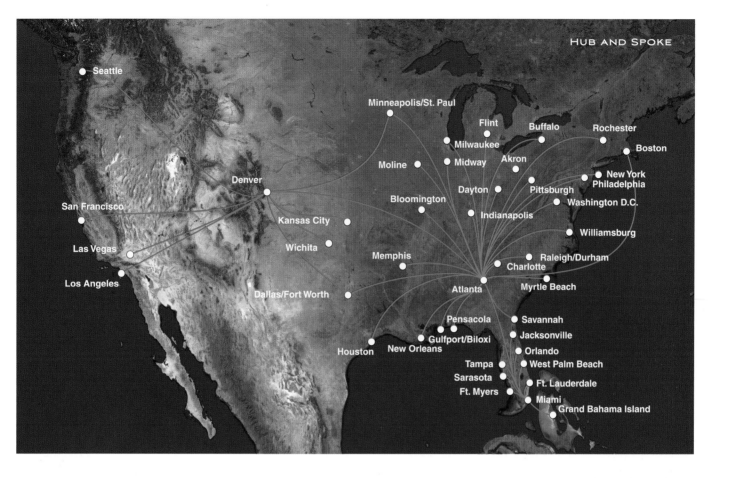

Seattle
Minneapolis/St. Paul
Flint
Buffalo
Rochester
Milwaukee
Boston
Moline
Midway
Akron
Denver
Dayton
Pittsburgh
New York
Philadelphia
San Francisco
Bloomington
Washington D.C.
Kansas City
Indianapolis
Las Vegas
Wichita
Williamsburg
Los Angeles
Memphis
Raleigh/Durham
Charlotte
Dallas/Fort Worth
Atlanta
Myrtle Beach
Pensacola
Savannah
Gulfport/Biloxi
Jacksonville
Houston
New Orleans
Orlando
Tampa
West Palm Beach
Sarasota
Ft. Lauderdale
Ft. Myers
Miami
Grand Bahama Island

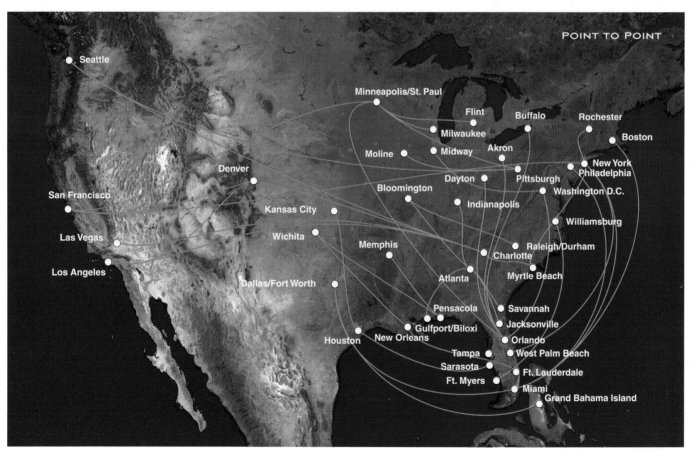

Seattle
Minneapolis/St. Paul
Flint
Buffalo
Rochester
Milwaukee
Boston
Moline
Midway
Akron
Denver
Dayton
Pittsburgh
New York
Philadelphia
San Francisco
Bloomington
Washington D.C.
Kansas City
Indianapolis
Las Vegas
Wichita
Williamsburg
Los Angeles
Memphis
Raleigh/Durham
Dallas/Fort Worth
Charlotte
Atlanta
Myrtle Beach
Pensacola
Savannah
Gulfport/Biloxi
Jacksonville
Houston
New Orleans
Orlando
Tampa
West Palm Beach
Sarasota
Ft. Lauderdale
Ft. Myers
Miami
Grand Bahama Island

CHECK-IN

Check-in is the name given to the process between arriving at the airport and the purser announcing 'boarding completed'. Check-in marks the beginning of the journey. Airports can be very hectic places, so the airlines vie with each other to provide a process that is easy and convenient, especially for first and business class passengers, often using separate check-in terminals.

At the Counter
The counter is where people are parted from their luggage, and it is here that they receive their boarding cards, if they have not already done so. In the past, passengers had to show their ticket and passport. Nowadays, a computer print-out or credit card is usually all that is required.

Seats are allocated when the boarding card is issued, if not before. The system ensures that men travelling alone are not seated next to children travelling alone and that families can sit together. Incidentally, seats next to the emergency exits always have more legroom.

The luggage is weighed and the weight added to the cumulative total

only, you will receive a text message from the airline on your mobile phone approximately 12 hours before departure containing up-to-date flight information. Once you have texted to confirm receipt, you will receive an electronic boarding card in the form of a barcode which you can take directly to the gate. Luggage can be handed in at a dedicated counter.

With internet check-in, the passenger uses a link and a password to access a check-in site, chooses a seat and can then print out a boarding card.

A slightly more personal alternative is to speak to a friendly voice in a call centre. In this case, boarding cards are printed out at the baggage check-in.

Automated Check-in Machines
These self-service terminals are becoming increasingly popular. Your credit card, passport or identity card is passed through a slot and machine-read; using the touch screen you can then receive your boarding card in a matter of seconds.

weight of the plane. This is also where excess baggage is calculated – often an expensive surprise. Each extra kilo costs up to 1 per cent of the first-class fare, so heavy luggage can rapidly amount to several hundreds or even thousands of euros. Some airlines permit you to check in the evening before you fly. You take your luggage to the counter in the evening, and the following morning you go straight to the gate.

Check-in via SMS, Internet or Telephone
Once you have registered for SMS check-in, which needs to be done once

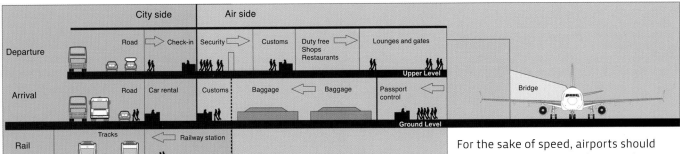

ANATOMY OF AN AIRPORT

For the sake of speed, airports should really be designed in such a way that travellers can get to the boarding gate in the shortest possible time. However, in recent times the philosophy has changed: nowadays passengers have to pass large numbers of shops, an important source of additional revenue for airport operators, on their way to the gate.

TYPES OF TERMINAL

Simple

Pier

Elliptic

Concourse

Multiconcourse

Satellites

Multiconcourse with underground rail

Multiconcourse with carrier lounges

SECURITY

These days there is no room for presumption of innocence in passenger aviation. In the age of organized terrorism, an error in security checks could be a death sentence for hundreds of people. It would make the job of security staff much easier if all passengers were to arrive without any luggage. However, as this is obviously not the norm, rigorous checks are carried out, including screening and scanning, with baggage items sometimes removed, confiscated and destroyed.

WE CHECK YOUR LUGGAGE...
Hand luggage, laptops and cameras are screened and examined for explosives using spectral analysis. All metal objects and shoes must also be placed in the luggage scanner (when the U-shaped

x-ray machines cannot detect metal objects in shoes the passenger has to take them off and run them through the luggage scanner). Many items are not permitted on board at all, such as any substantial quantity of liquid. At times of high security alert, even books and newspapers brought from outside are not allowed on board, in case they contain paper-based explosives.

...AND WE CHECK YOU
Until recently, metal detectors were sufficient for most airports. Body scanners are, however, more effective. They scan through all clothes,

revealing any solid object, such as a perspex knife. Initial reservations about violations of passenger privacy are now being outweighed by the terrorist threat.

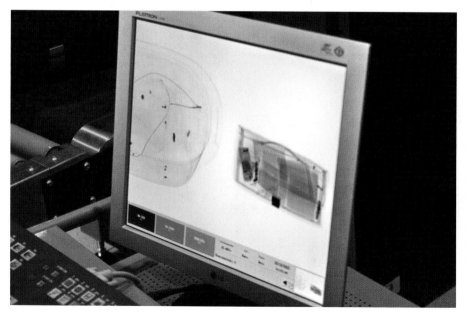

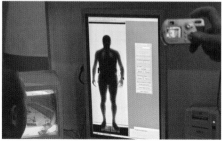

What is and Isn't Allowed on Board

What is not Allowed Through Security Screening

- liquids in containers larger than 100 ml
- sharp objects such as nail files, scissors or knives
- razor blades
- weapons of any kind
- ammunition
- sports equipment such as baseball bats, golf clubs, snooker cues or hockey sticks
- harpoons
- tools such as hammers, drills, saws, screwdrivers or pliers
- more than one ordinary cigarette lighter
- gel insoles in shoes
- snow globes

What is not Allowed in the Aircraft at all

- easily flammable material
- strike-anywhere matches
- spray cans
- batteries containing fluid
- tear gas
- flares

On flights beginning in the European Union, there are restrictions on what liquids, creams, pastes, gels, sprays and lotions can be taken with you.

Medicines, baby food and food for special diets which are needed on board during the flight can be transported outside the plastic bag.

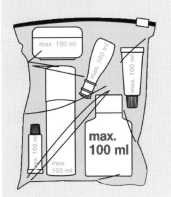

- maximum volume 1 litre
- resealable
- transparent

Stamps and Visas

Colourful visa and immigration stamps are seen by some as trophies and by others as sentimental reminders of wonderful journeys. However, they are far more than just that: they document entries and exits to different countries and can be used as evidence by the authorities. One unforgettable tragedy was the death of a German prince who missed his plane from Bangkok to Hawaii and thereby overstayed his transit visa. He foolishly altered his visa stamp from 1 August 2005 to 1 August 2006. This was noticed on his departure, whereupon he was arrested for passport forgery and placed in a cell with 40 other people. He died ten days later.

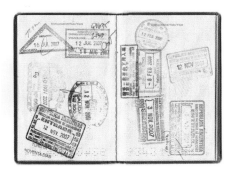

Airport Tax

Handling fees, departure tax, passenger facility charges, airport authority tax, airport passenger tax, airport development tax – there are lots of names for it, but the aim is the same: to make money. Most airports are satisfied with between 10 and 15 dollars per passenger, payable on departure. However, it can be as much as 100 dollars per person (as in Barbados). In most cases these taxes, fees and charges are only payable in the domestic currency and credit cards are not always accepted. This is most often the case in those countries where no local currency can be exported. First you have to go with your boarding card and your passport to check-in, then to a special counter for the tax, possibly already having had to go to the bank counter. Having paid, you receive a slip and go back to the first barrier, where the payment is checked. Only from there can passengers proceed to passport control. Hastily you fill out your customs declaration and departure card. Meanwhile you have a jumbled heap of papers in your hand, which you give to the customs official, who then stamps everything.

In places such as these, it would be so much easier if the price of the airport tax were just added to the price of the ticket, as happens at most of the world's major airports.

Duty Free

To make travelling between countries easier, the global community has agreed to allow small quantities of goods that would otherwise be taxable to be brought into countries as tax-free gifts. In order to avoid abuse of the system, you need your boarding card and passport to purchase these.

The first duty-free shop was opened in 1947 by Aer Rianta in Shannon, Ireland. Shannon was once the westernmost airport in Europe, where many aircraft made a last refuelling stop before flying across the Atlantic. Since then, duty free has developed into an important sales market for the perfume, spirits and tobacco industries.

As journeys within the European Union are now treated as domestic trips in terms of tax, this practice has become less important. In Europe, duty free has become known as 'travel value'. Prices, however, are sometimes higher than in city centres.

Problems Changing Planes

Duty-free goods bought at an EU airport or in Norway, Switzerland, Iceland, Croatia, Changi Airport in Singapore or on board an aircraft belonging to an EU airline can be taken through security by passengers if they are in a sealed transparent bag. These goods have been previously checked. Liquids from duty-free shops outside the European Union are not checked to EU standards. These may not, therefore, be carried in your hand luggage when transferring in an EU airport.

Since the restrictions on liquids were introduced, the ICAO has decreed that passengers should also be able to buy duty-free goods on arrival at their destination, before leaving the airport. This is a decision that goes some way towards solving the problem. It would be better if there were no duty-free sales at all at departure airports. On a 10,000-km/6,200-mile flight, 1 kg/ 2.2 lb of duty free consumes around 4 litres/0.9 gallons of fuel.

From top to bottom: Dubai, Bangkok, Stuttgart.

LOUNGES

Above: Frankfurt/Lufthansa; Below: Bangkok/Thai Airways.

Lounges are stress-free oases for frequent flyers or business and first class passengers. Comfortable armchairs, an extensive range of drinks and snacks, newspapers and magazines, TV and internet, along with manicures, massages, luxury spas and jacuzzis all help to shorten the waiting time. Alternatively, there is the ultimate in lounge terminals: the passenger is conducted to a luxury terminal away from the main airport building. Check-in, passport control and security take just a few seconds and then you find yourself – as for example at Lufthansa's terminal in Frankfurt – in stylish surroundings with a cigar lounge, showers, quiet rooms and a restaurant. You can sit comfortably and look out through the huge glass front at the hectic comings and goings on the apron. Then, 20 minutes before departure, a car of your choice will take you directly to the plane.

In the hope of attracting new customers, magazine publishers pay the airlines for the privilege of displaying their products. Wine merchants, too, are happy to use the airport lounges to show off their wares.

The arrival lounges are also a very sensible idea. Following a 12-hour flight, you arrive at Heathrow, for example, at around 6.30 am. In the arrival lounge, you can have breakfast, take a shower or a bath, read the paper and turn up refreshed at a business meeting at 9 am.

LOUNGES AROUND THE WORLD

Airline	Lounge Name
Air Canada	Maple Leaf Lounge
Air India	Maharaja Lounge
Air New Zealand	Koru Lounge
Alitalia	Sala Freccia Alata
American Airlines	Admirals Club
	Flagship Lounge
Asiana	OZ Club Lounge
British Airways	Concorde Room
	Galleries Club
China Airlines	Dynasty Lounge
Continental Airlines	Presidents Club
Delta Air Lines	Delta Sky Club
Emirates	Emirates Lounge
Korean Air	Korean Air Lounge
Lufthansa	Senator Lounge
Malaysia Airlines	Golden Lounge

Airline	Lounge Name
Qantas	Qantas Club
Royal Jordanian	Crown Lounge
Scandinavian Airlines System	Scandinavian Lounge
Singapore Airlines	Silver Kris Lounge
South African Airways	Baobab Lounge
	Cycad Premium Lounge
Thai Airways International	Royal Orchid Lounge
United Airlines	Red Carpet Club
US Airways	US Airways Club
Virgin Atlantic Airways	Virgin Atlantic Clubhouse
Virgin Blue	The Lounge

In some places there are access restrictions. For example, the Senator Lounge is only available for first class passengers. In such cases, business class passengers are offered a slightly less sumptuous business lounge.

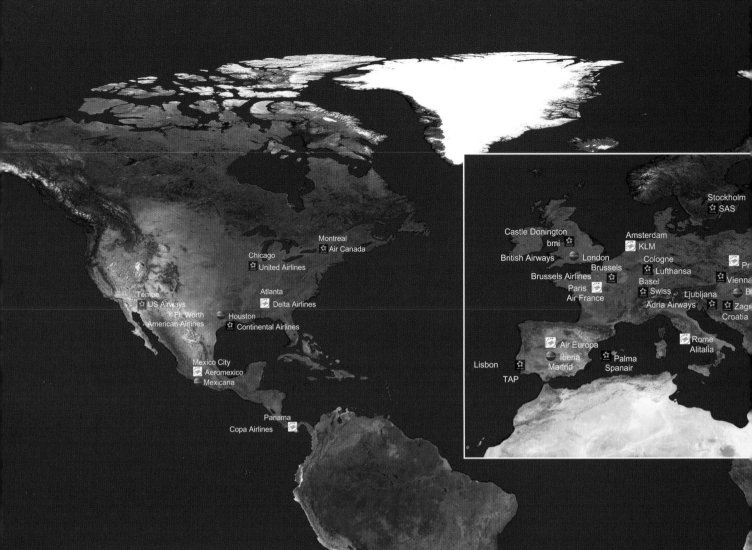

STAR ALLIANCE

Member airline	Country	Joined
Air Canada	Canada	1997 Founding member
Lufthansa	Germany	1997 Founding member
Scandinavian Airlines	Sweden Denmark Norway	1997 Founding member
Thai Airways International	Thailand	1997 Founding member
United Airlines	USA	1997 Founding member
Air New Zealand	New Zealand	1999
All Nippon Airways	Japan	1999
Austrian Airlines	Austria	2000
bmi	UK	2000
Singapore Airlines	Singapore	2000
Asiana Airlines	South Korea	2003
LOT	Poland	2003
Spanair	Spain	2003
US Airways	USA	2004
TAP Portugal	Portugal	2005
South African Airways	South Africa	2006
Swiss International	Switzerland	2006
Air China	China	2007
Shanghai Airlines	China	2007
Egypt Air	Egypt	2008
Turkish Airlines	Turkey	2008
Continental Airlines	USA	2009
Brussels Airlines	Belgium	2009

Regional member airline	Country	Joined
Adria Airways	Slovenia	2004
Blue1	Finland	2004
Croatia Airlines	Croatia	2004

Future member airline	Country	Joining
TAM Airlines	Brazil	May 2010
Air India	India	late 2010
Aegean Airlines	Greece	June 2010

Moscow
  S7 Airlines (2010)
  Aeroflot

...s
...ish Airlines
...s (2010)

Amman
  Royal Jordanian

Nairobi
  Kenya Airways

...nnesburg
...South African Airways

Beijing
Air China

Seoul
Asiana
Korean Air

Tokyo
  ANA
  JAL

Shanghai
Shanghai Airlines

Guangzhou
China Southern

Hong Kong
Cathay Pacific

Mumbai
  Air India (2010)

Bangkok
  Thai Airways

Singapore
  Singapore Airlines

Sydney
Qantas

Auckland
Air New Zealand

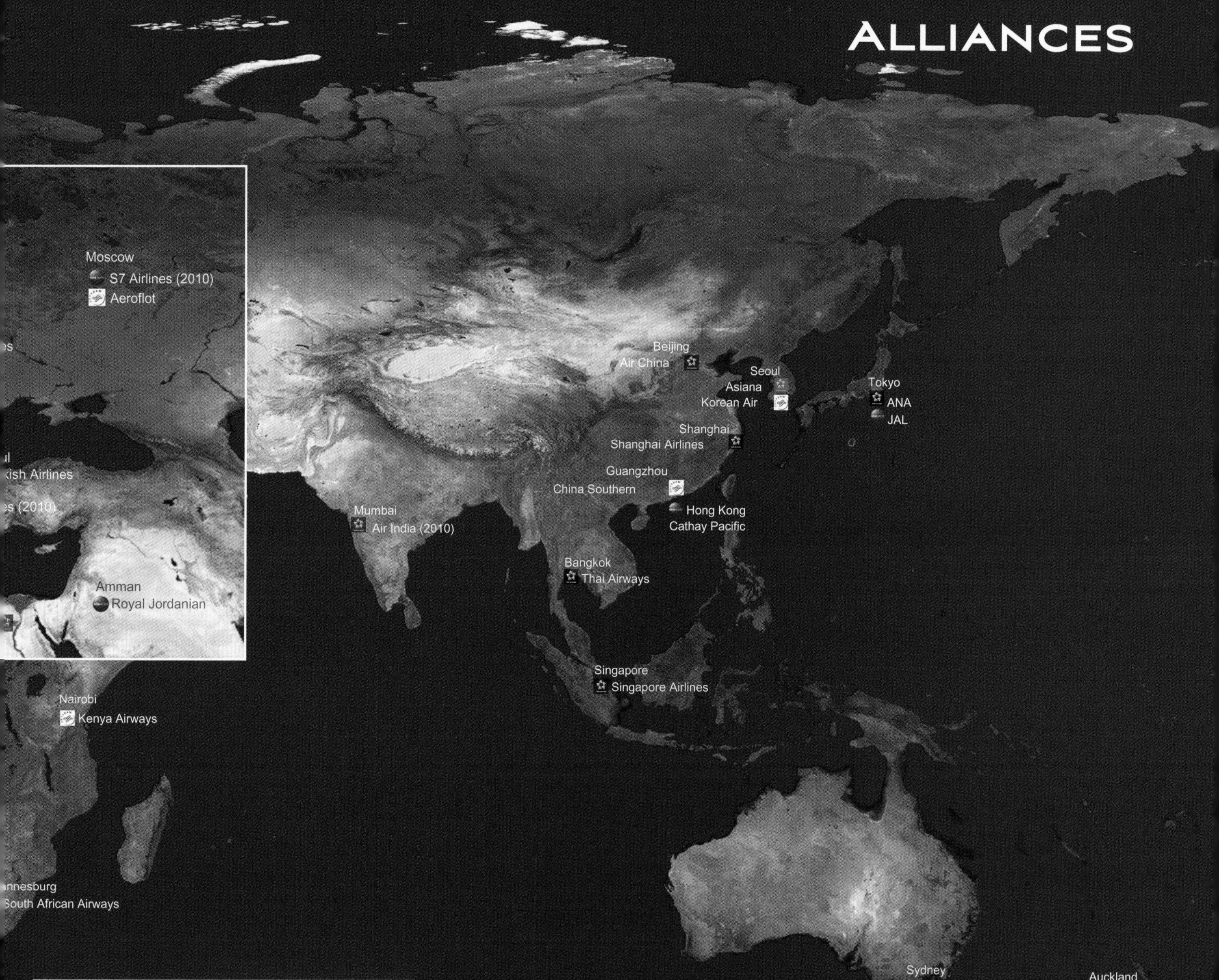

ONEWORLD ALLIANCE

Member airline	Country	Joined
American Airlines	USA	1999 Founding member
British Airways	United Kingdom	1999 Founding member
Cathay Pacific	Hong Kong	1999 Founding member
Qantas	Australia	1999 Founding member
Finnair	Finland	1999 Founding member
Iberia	Spain	1999 Founding member
LAN	Chile	2000
Japan Airlines	Japan	2007
Malév	Hungary	2007
Royal Jordanian	Jordan	2007
Mexicana	Mexico	2009

Future member airline	Country	Joining
S7 Airlines	Russia	2010

SKYTEAM ALLIANCE

Member airline	Country	Joined
Aeroflot	Russia	2000
Aeroméxico	Mexico	2000
Air France	France	2000
Alitalia	Italy	2000
China Southern Airlines	China	2000
Continental Airlines	USA	2000
Czech Airlines	Czechia	2000
Delta Air Lines	USA	2000
KLM	Netherlands	2000
Korean Air	South Korea	2000

Future member airline	Country	Joining
Air Algerie	Algeria	n/a
Garuda Indonesia	Indonesia	n/a
Malaysia Airlines	Malaysia	n/a
Uzbekistan Airways	Uzbekistan	n/a
Vietnam Airlines	Vietnam	June 2010

SEAT MAPS

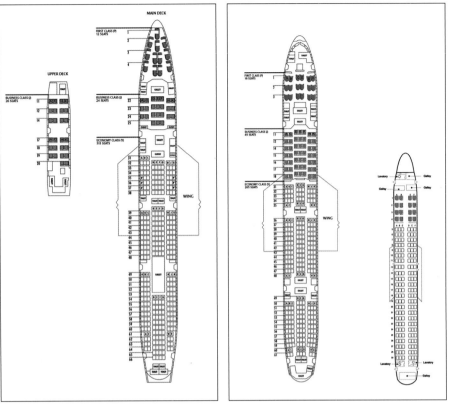

B.747-400

777, 737

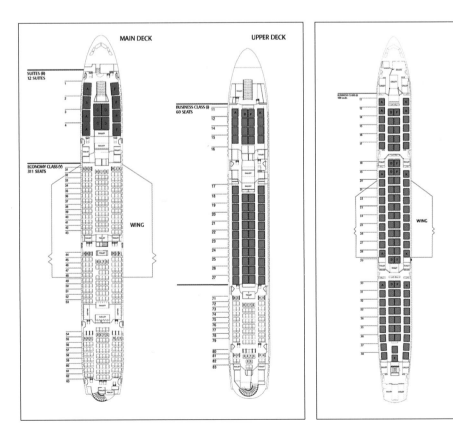

A380

A340-500J

BOARDING

The layout of passenger aircraft varies from airline to airline. In almost all of them, the economy class section is at the rear. In the Boeing 747, most carriers reserve the upper deck for business class, with first class at the front of the lower deck. Air France, Air Pacific, Eva Air and JAL have their economy seats on top. Lufthansa has its first class section upstairs. Aircraft are most profitable while they are in the air. For this reason, airlines have awarded research contracts to universities in order to work out the fastest model for boarding.

The usual practice is:

1. first class
2. business class
3. disabled people and parents with children
4. economy class, from the rear to the front and from the window seats to the aisle.

Some low-cost carriers have dispensed with the allocation of seats altogether.

TIPS AND ETIQUETTE

- Cut down on your luggage. On a long-haul flight, each kilo of luggage requires 6-8 times its own weight in fuel. One Japanese airline even made the headlines for asking its passengers to go to the toilet before the flight.
- Limit your carry-on baggage to what you need in the cabin. Unused luggage takes up space.
- Large or particularly heavy passengers should not sit in a middle seat. In their own interest, they should raise this issue with the ground staff and ask for a suitable seat.
- Do not push and shove at the gate. The crew will normally organize the boarding procedure.
- When you board the plane, do not block the aisle, but move quickly to your seat.
- When standing up, do not pull yourself up on the backrest of the seat in front. This disturbs the passenger seated there. When you return, do not drop suddenly into your seat. The passenger behind you with coffee on the fold-out table will be grateful.

Provisioning: Cross-Servicing

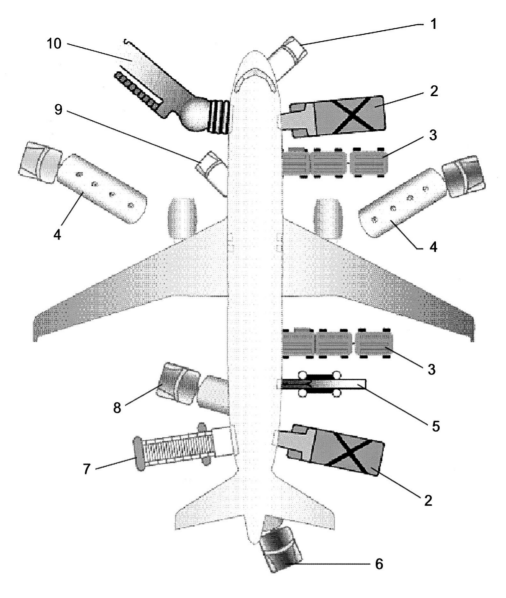

Almost as soon as an aircraft docks at the gate, the provisioning of the plane begins. This procedure is also known as the 'turnaround'.

Clockwise from front right:

1. The aircraft is connected to a **power supply** – a mobile battery, a generator or a hook-up set into the ground.
2. **Catering vehicles** remove the trolleys containing used crockery and supply the on-board kitchen with everything necessary for the next flight.
3. Baggage and cargo are unloaded using the **high-lift loader**.
4. At the same time, the aircraft is refuelled. Either large **tankers** or, at airports with underground tanks, **pump trucks** are used for this.
5. A **conveyor belt** is used to unload mailbags, for example, which have been transported in the aircraft.
6. There is also a special vehicle for emptying the **toilets**.
7. Technicians and cleaning staff can enter and leave the aircraft using the **mobile stairs**.
8. The **water tanks** are rinsed out and filled ready for the next flight.
9. Some aircraft have no APU (auxiliary power unit) of their own and rely on an **external air supply** when they are on the ground. There is a special vehicle for this, which pumps fresh air into the plane and provides the compressed air for starting the first engine.
10. Finally, the **gangway** is also a vehicle, albeit one which is firmly connected to the terminal at one end.

Remote parking positions
Many airports, especially in Europe, do not have enough gates on the buildings to keep pace with the growth in air traffic. Aircraft are then assigned to remote parking positions. This is also the case for small regional aircraft which cannot dock at the gates because the angle to the gangway would be too steep.

The Airport
Site

1   2

5   6   7   8

1-4. **Runways** The most significant
characteristic of a runway is its load-
bearing capacity. For a runway on
which heavy aircraft are to land, a
1-m/3-ft thick foundation must first
be laid. At the bottom comes gravelly
sand, covered by a layer of concrete,
followed by several layers of asphalt of
varying consistencies. Finally, a layer
of bitumen is applied, which increases
the braking effect and largely prevents
aquaplaning.

5-7. **Technical area** with engine
testbeds and laboratories. Heatable
hangars for minor maintenance work.

8, 10, 11. **Airport buildings** These include
the departure hall (with a covered

concourse, airline counters, baggage
check-in, waiting areas, customs, security
barriers, gates, cafés, sanitary facilities
and shops), arrival hall (with baggage
reclaim, car-hire counters and sanitary
facilities), and airport administration
building (with air traffic control, flight
security, weather centre, briefing rooms
and passenger loading bridges).

9. **Tower** Visually, the control tower
is at the heart of every airport. High
above the ground, the 360-degree
glazing provides a generally unimpeded
view over the entire airport and the
airspace surrounding it. The air traffic
controllers have a large amount of radio
and communications equipment at
their disposal, as well as short-range or

surface movement radar. Together
with their colleagues in approach
control, they ensure the safe and
orderly landing and take-off of
aircraft, as well as swift taxi clearance.
Large airports with a lot of taxiways
and departure gates operate their own
apron control system.

Aircraft rescue and firefighting is
also housed within the flight operations
area. Its vehicles must be able to reach
all flight operation areas within 180
seconds of the alarm sounding. If that
is not possible, additional emergency
vehicles, which are manned at all times
during flight operations, must
be stationed at strategic locations.
The size, equipment and extinguisher
tanks of these vehicles will depend on

the size of the largest plane that can
use the airport.

12. **Cargo centre** Cargo has become an
important mainstay of air transport.
Sophisticated logistics are required in
order to transport perishable goods
halfway around the world in the shortest
possible time and at acceptable prices.

13. **Multistorey car park, parking
areas** Different areas are provided
for pick-up and drop-off, short-term
parking and long-term parking. As
a rule of thumb, the closer to the
terminal, the higher the cost. Airport
employees also need somewhere to
park. Large airports have parking
spaces for up to 50,000 cars.

ICING

The aerodynamic profile of an aircraft wing forces the air which passes over it to flow faster, thereby generating lift. If this airflow is disrupted by ice, the wing loses lift. Wings which are iced over also lose elasticity and become heavy, promoting the formation of even more ice. Wings have to be elastic in order to adjust to changes in pressure and turbulence.

Extreme Conditions

Before being officially approved for operation, a new aeroplane has to pass cold-weather tests. These tests must last for a minimum of ten hours at a maximum temperature of -35°C/-31°F. During these tests, the following are checked:

- Viscosity of hydraulic fluid
- Hydraulic sealing of landing gear and pumps
- Elasticity of landing gear springs
- Pneumatic systems in flaps and control surfaces
- Behaviour of bonded metals of various alloys
- Behaviour of flaps and doors
- Behaviour of trim, sensors and movable parts.

As well as all of these checks and tests, a refuelling procedure has to be carried out, and all systems and reserve systems must be shown to function properly.

Preferred Airports for Cold-Weather Tests

YFB Iqaluit, Nunavut, Canada
YKS Yakutsk, Siberia, Russia
LLA Luleå, Norrbotten, Sweden

Similar tests are carried out in hot-weather conditions at temperatures exceeding a minimum of 40°C/104°F.

Preferred Airports for Hot-Weather Tests

AAN Al Ain, Abu Dhabi, United Arab Emirates
DXB Dubai, Dubai, United Arab Emirates
ASP Alice Springs, Northern Territory, Australia

Consequences of Icing

- The aerodynamic profile of the wings changes, reducing lift.
- Layers of ice increase air resistance and reduce wing elasticity.
- The ice increases the weight, meaning that a longer distance would be required for take-off.

Countermeasuires

On the ground:
- Spraying of de-icing agents before take-off (propylene glycol, ethylene glycol).

In flight:
- Rubber profiles on leading edges of wings, through which air is pumped periodically (de-icing boots).
- Electrostatic voltage in the wings.
- Heat pipes below the wings transport hot air from the engines to below the wing surface.
- De-icing fluid is applied in flight through tiny apertures in the wing.

The de-icing of a widebodied aircraft on the ground costs up to 25,000 euros.

How Does it Work?

The Wing

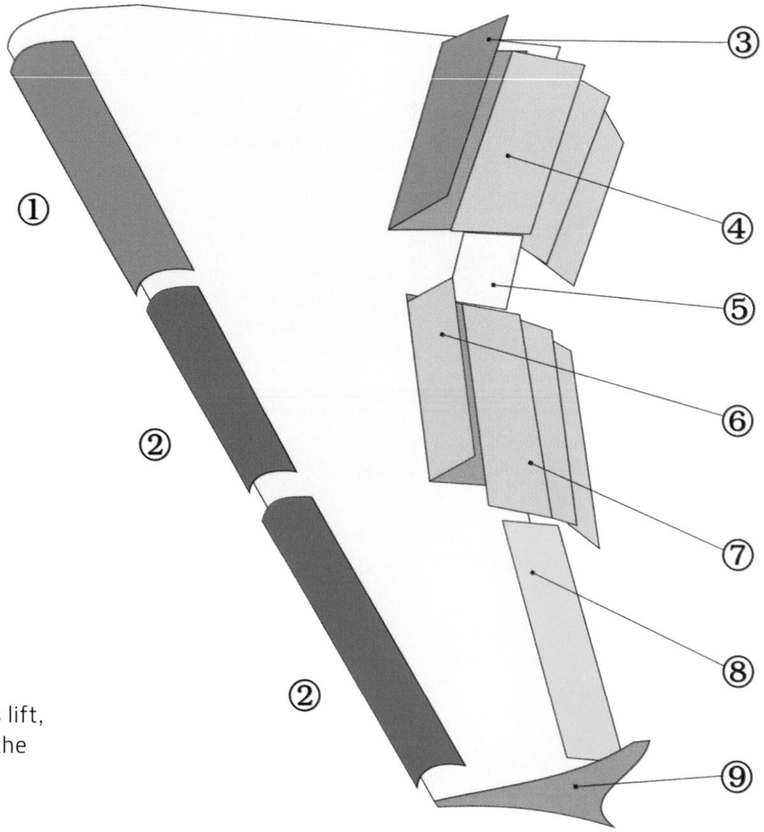

The shape of the **wing** provides lift because the air above the camber of the wing flows faster and the pressure is lower.

1. Krueger Flaps
2. Slats
3. Air Brakes
4. Inner Flaps
5. High Speed Aileron
6. Speedbrakes/Spoiler
7. Outer Flaps
8. Low Speed Aileron
9. Wingtip

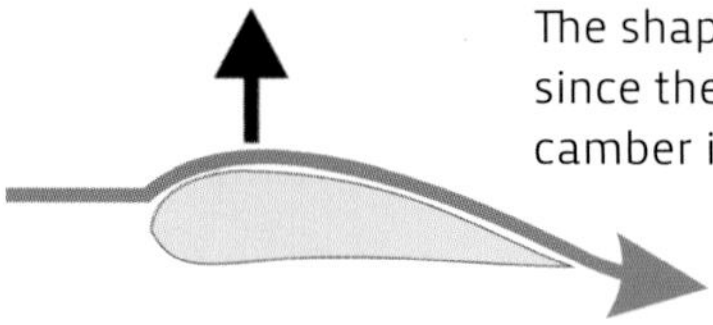

The shape of the wing provides lift, since the air which flows **over** the camber is faster.

During take-off...

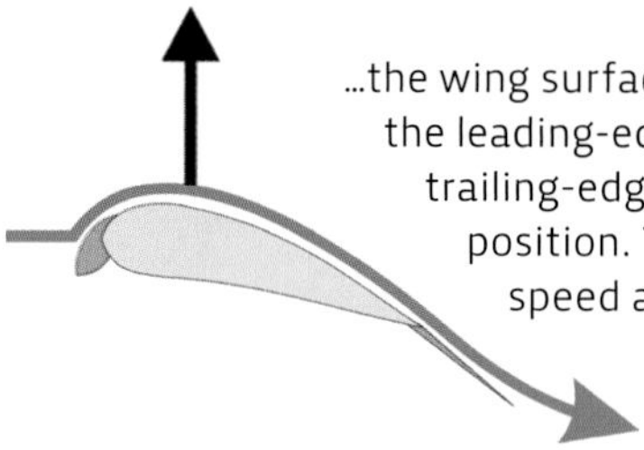

...the wing surface is enlarged by extending the leading-edge slats and moving the trailing-edge flaps to the take-off position. This permits a lower take-off speed and shorter take-off distance.

During landing...

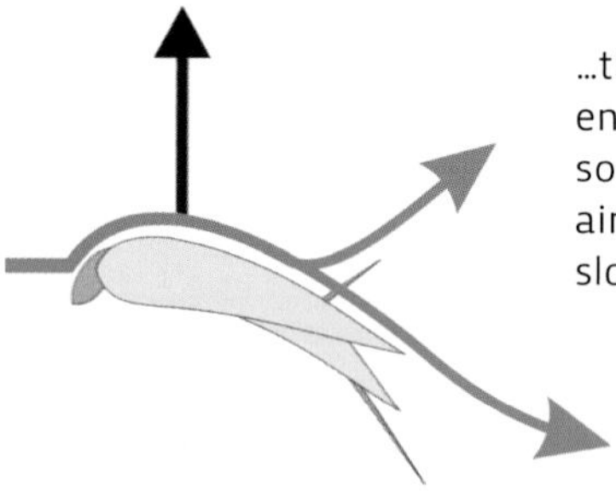

...the wing surface is enlarged even further so as to improve the aircraft's ability to fly slowly.

WING SHAPES

1. Generates a lot of lift and low drag at low speeds

2. Reduces drag at high speeds, but reduces lift. High take-off and landing speeds required.

3. Supersonic aircraft with delta wings. Less efficient on take-off and landing, which is why a lot of power is needed. It is only in the supersonic speed range that this wing shape comes into its own.

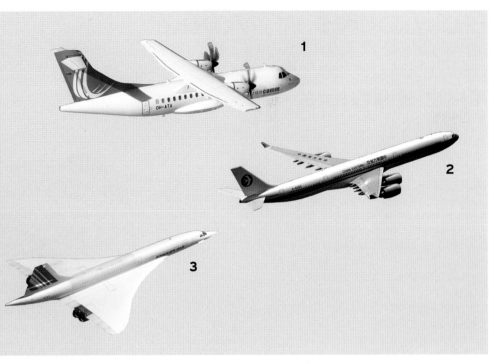

CONTROL SURFACES

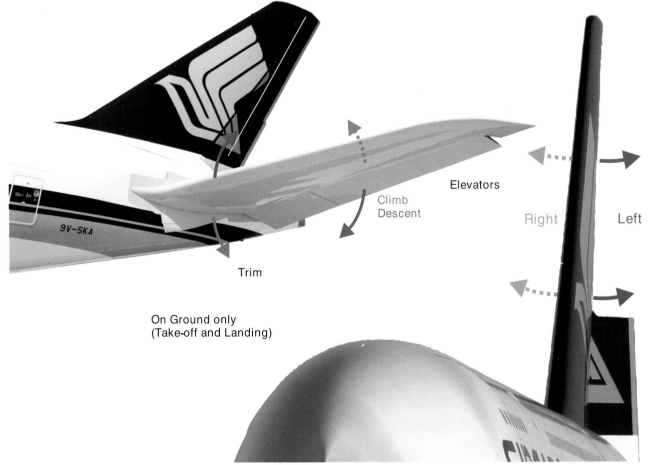

Climb
Descent

Elevators

Right   Left

Trim

On Ground only
(Take-off and Landing)

How Does it Work?

The Engine

The engines commonly used today all operate according to a similar principle: air is sucked in at the front and compressed in the engine by blade wheels. Fuel is added and ignited in a combustion chamber. The explosive mixture drives the turbine. In the jet engine, the hot air is ejected at the rear, producing the thrust. In engineering slang, this is called 'suck, squeeze, bang and blow'. The bang, however, is a powerful one: the temperature in the combustion chamber, at 1700°C/3100°F, is hotter than in the magma chamber of a volcano.

The hot air itself produces only 20 per cent of the thrust, but it drives the turbine shaft on which turbine blades of varying sizes are located. This is where the bypass, or cold air, emerges: 80 per cent of this flows past the combustion chamber and in so doing cools the oil and the blades, which would otherwise melt. The bypass air flow acts like a propeller, but is much more effective. It has a further advantage: it dampens the noise produced in the turbine. Turbofan engines are much quieter than the old jet turbines. The individual turbine blades are hollow inside, helping to cool air and save on weight. They have tolerances in the micrometer range and are made of titanium or of nickel-/tungsten-molybdenum alloys.

Fan blades are some of the most expensive parts of an aeroplane to replace. Their weight has to be absolutely identical, because otherwise the engine will be out of balance. Scrupulous airlines number each individual blade and register it on an individual lifespan card which also records every engineer and every inspector who has ever worked on it.

'Creeping', whereby over time the blades increase in length as a result of high temperatures and radial stresses, poses a risk because the lengthened blades may come into contact with the turbine edging.

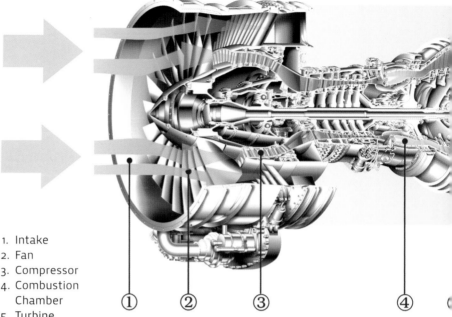

1. Intake
2. Fan
3. Compressor
4. Combustion Chamber
5. Turbine
6. Nozzle
7. Bypass

① ② ③ ④

⑦

THE PROPELLER

This is a device composed of rigid or adjustable wing-shaped blades that are seated on a hub and rotate on a shaft. The shape of the propeller blades generates a thrust by screwing into the air and pushing it behind them.

In order to construct a high-performance drive system, powerful engines and large propellers are needed. However, the traditional propeller blade tips rotate at speeds in the ultrasonic range, resulting in noise and vibrations in the aircraft. Every effort is therefore made to keep these speeds in the subsonic range by using scimitar-shaped blades, with further blades added in order to increase efficiency. The old four-blade propellers are gradually being replaced by quieter six-blade propellers. The Airbus A400 is even fitted with eight-blade propellers.

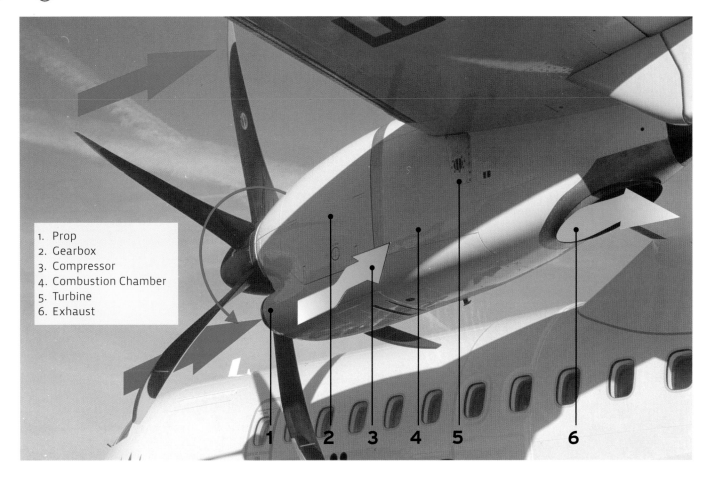

1. Prop
2. Gearbox
3. Compressor
4. Combustion Chamber
5. Turbine
6. Exhaust

1   2   3   4   5   6

English only

Aircraft and cockpit crews from countries around the world share the same airports, the same runways and the same airspace, often travelling at speeds approaching that of sound. Therefore it is essential that all those involved communicate using just one language. Giving instructions to your compatriots in German, French or Italian, for example, is grossly negligent, and has in the past contributed to accidents simply because a third party did not understand what had been said.

Furthermore, the shared language must also be standardized. In the past, the fact that the English number 'two' and the English word 'to' sound the same has proven fatal on several occasions. For example, a jumbo jet belonging to Flying Tiger Airways was handed over to Kuala Lumpur approach control on 19 February 1989 and the pilots were cleared for a direct approach to runway 33. As they made the approach, they received the instruction 'descend 2400 ft' ('descend two four zero zero feet'). This was misunderstood as 'descend to 400 ft' ('descend to four zero zero feet'). The aircraft, flying at an altitude of 122 m/400 ft, consequently crashed into a 300-m/1,000-ft-high mountain. The minimum acceptable altitude for flying over it would have been the intended 732 m/2,400 ft. The accident investigation report concluded by stating that the cause of the accident was that 'non-standard phraseology was used by Kuala Lumpur ATC, causing the crew to misinterpret the instructions.'

Approach control at an American airport guided a DC-10 to 3,050 m/10,000 ft for the approach to runway 27 L, saying 'Maintain 10,000; cleared 27.' The co-pilot confirmed 'Cleared two-seven.' The captain had heard what the co-pilot said and understood 'Cleared (descent) to seven (thousand)' and initiated his descent to 2,150 m/7,000 ft. At 2,750 m/9,000 ft he narrowly missed an aircraft travelling in the opposite direction.

In order to prevent similar misunderstandings, the word 'altitude' is now placed in front of the number, as in 'descend altitude two four zero zero feet'. This rules out the possibility of the number 'two' being interpreted as the preposition 'to'.

Sloppy use of language has also caused a number of near misses: on one occasion, a Boeing 747 landed on a runway numbered 22 L and, after taxiing to the terminal, had to cross runway 22 R. The captain asked the tower: 'May we cross?' and received the response 'Hold short'. Having misheard, the pilot then opened the throttle and crossed the runway; a Boeing 737 that was taking off was just able to get past in time. The pilot explained later, 'In response to my request "May we cross?" the tower replied "Oh, sure".' The correct response should have been 'Negative. Hold position. Departing traffic.'

However, despite standardized phraseology, there are still grey areas. Everyone knows the stereotypical response 'ROGER'. ROGER means 'I have received and understood your last transmission.' There is also the term 'WILCO', which goes a step further and means 'Your message is received, understood and will be complied with.' The important bit is 'will be complied with'. An instruction to do something should therefore never be answered with 'ROGER'.

Flight Preparation

ALL DESCRIPTIONS BASED ON THE EXAMPLE OF A FLIGHT FROM FRANKFURT TO BOSTON

Briefing

– 2 hours before pushback

Flight preparation comprises studying NOTAM and flight plans, including possible alternative airports, airport briefing folders, security advisories, printed-out documents, crew briefing, weather briefing, passengers/VIPs and any special aspects of the flight.

Signing in

– 1 hour before pushback

A crew bus carries the cockpit crew and cabin staff to the aircraft. The head of maintenance hands over the aircraft to the captain.

and by the choice of alternative airports. It only takes about 15 minutes to pump as much as 210,000 litres/46,190 gallons of kerosene into the tanks, at a rate of over 200 litres/44 gallons each second!

CATERING

– about 1 hour before pushback

For an intercontinental flight, a 747-400 needs about 114 containers and 102 trolleys, with a combined weight of 5 tonnes. A total of 800 different items are carried, from apples to newspapers, from beer to customs forms and pens – 30,000 individual items in all.

LOADING

– about 45 minutes before pushback

The outbound baggage is prepared. A high-lift loader lifts as many as 14 containers, each holding 35 to 45 suitcases, up to the loading hatch. Transfer baggage is loaded next, followed by any additional freight.

WALK AROUND

– about 30 minutes before pushback

The pilot or first officer checks whether any externally visible changes or damage can be seen on the aircraft. Here, particular attention is paid to the engines, wings, flap systems, fuselage, sensors, landing gear and brakes.

REFUELLING

– 1 hour before pushback

At this stage it is possible to see how much is being loaded onto the plane in terms of passengers, baggage, catering and additional freight. The amount of fuel required can be calculated from the total weight and the route plan. This amount is also affected by the latest weather and high-altitude wind forecasts on the assigned flight route,

COCKPIT TO CABIN CREW COMMUNICATION

'CABIN CREW, PLEASE PREPARE FOR GATE DEPARTURE'
• Overhead lockers closed
• Toilets vacant
• Seats upright
• Tables stowed away
• Electronic devices off
• Passengers' seatbelts fastened

'DOORS ON AUTOMATIC' OR 'ALL DOORS IN FLIGHT'
This means that the automatic unfolding mechanism for the emergency chutes is activated. If the doors are now opened following an emergency, then the emergency chutes will be inflated automatically. This is not desirable for a normal exit, so before docking at the gate, the crew is requested to 'select doors on manual'.

'FLIGHT ATTENDANTS, PREPARE FOR TAKE-OFF PLEASE'
The safety briefing must now be completed, all loose objects stowed away and all hatches closed. All window blinds must be open on take-off and landing so that in the event of an accident people outside can see in and people inside can see out.

'CABIN CREW, PLEASE BE SEATED'
The flight attendants must now also take their seats and fasten their seatbelts in preparation for take-off.

Their seats are arranged so that they are seated at strategic points in the cabin so that they can observe the passengers. This request may also be made during a flight if the aircraft encounters turbulence.

'CABIN CREW, FIVE MINUTES TO GROUND'
This announcement is made in order to let the flight attendants know how much time they have left to clear the cabins.

'CABIN CREW, PLEASE BE SEATED FOR LANDING'
The flight attendants must now take their seats again and fasten their seatbelts.

Preflight Check

– about 10 minutes before pushback

Battery, navigation lights and external power supply are switched on, and the cabin is supplied with power, fresh air and heat. The pilots go through the various checklists and test the technical systems. Some things can only be checked when the engines are running, but that is not possible while the aircraft is standing next to the terminal building. The navigation system is calibrated, with the exact co-ordinates of the parking position being provided at the gate for this purpose.

The flight management system (FMS) loads the pre-prepared electronic flight plan containing all the waypoints from take-off to landing. Another option is to input the two four-digit ICAO codes of the departure and destination points in order to enable the system to calculate the shortest flight path. Until recently, the pilots used to bring cases full of navigational material and airport information on board with them.

The total weight of the aircraft and the external temperature are used to calculate V1, VR and V2, speeds which are used for the take-off procedure. Trimming (alignment of the aircraft to maintain a defined aerodynamic flight attitude) is also carried out now.

In the tail, the APU (auxiliary power unit – the aircraft's own small on-board power plant) is already running. It is from here that the bleed air for starting the engines later will come.

Boarding

– about 20–40 minutes before pushback

When everything in the cabin and cockpit is ready and refuelling has been completed, the passengers are requested to board. Once all the passengers have entered the aircraft, the 'BOARDING COMPLETED' announcement is made.

The co-pilot obtains the latest information about weather and restrictions at the airport via the ATIS (automated terminal information system). This information carries a serial code letter between Alpha and Zulu from the aviation alphabet, which the pilots quote when they first contact air traffic control.

The first contact is for clearance delivery, when they are given route clearance.

Pilot: 'FRANKFURT DELIVERY, CACTUS 632 TO BOSTON, INFORMATION GOLF, REQUEST START-UP.'

Delivery: 'CACTUS 632, GOLF IS CORRECT, CLEARED TO DESTINATION BOSTON VIA BIBOS, SQUAWK 2163, WHEN AIRBORNE CONTACT LANGEN RADAR ON 120.850. START-UP APPROVED.'

Pilot: 'CLEARED TO BOSTON VIA BIBOS, SQUAWK 2163, WHEN AIRBORNE LANGEN RADAR ON 120.850. START-UP APPROVED, CACTUS 632.'

Delivery: 'READBACK CORRECT. CONTACT APRON AT 121.850.'

Pilot: '121.850, CACTUS 632.'

PUSHBACK

– about 10 minutes before take-off

The doors are closed and the connection to the external power supply is cut. All systems are now connected to the battery and APU. The jet bridges are retracted. The pilots go through the 'BEFORE START' checklist and request 'pushback' from apron control. The cabin crew receive the instruction:

'CABIN CREW, ALL DOORS IN FLIGHT' from the cockpit.

A lever is now turned on all the doors, which releases the safety lock on the emergency chutes. If the doors were now opened, their emergency chutes would immediately unfurl and inflate.

Pilot: 'FRANKFURT APRON, CACTUS 632, AT GATE A 21, REQUEST PUSHBACK.'

Apron: 'CACTUS 632 PUSHBACK

ICAO-ALPHABET

A	Alpha	N	November
B	Bravo	O	Oscar
C	Charlie	P	Papa
D	Delta	Q	Quebec
E	Echo	R	Romeo
F	Foxtrot	S	Sierra
G	Golf	T	Tango
H	Hotel	U	Uniform
I	India	V	Victor
J	Juliet	W	Whisky
K	Kilo	X	X-ray
L	Lima	Y	Yankee
M	Mike	Z	Zulu

COCKPIT-CHECKLIST

Checklist	B.747-400F	A320	ATR-42	DHC-8
Preflight	4	–	10	6
Before start (engines)	6	11	–	15
Before taxi	5	4	8	16
Taxi	–	–	7	13
Before take-off	1	10	14	6
After take-off	2	4	7	12
Cruise	–	–	4	4
Descent	4	–	6	4
Approach	4	6	6	10
Landing	3	3	7	5
After landing	–	4	9	12
Shutdown	7	6	3	15
Secure (leaving aircraft)	4	6	10	5

APPROVED, FOR TAXI CONTACT APRON ON 121.700.'

Pilot: '121.700, CACTUS 632.'

By now, the 1400 hp aircraft tug has docked with the nose wheel. It is just 1.65 m/5 ft 5 inches high and drives like a lowered truck.

TAXI

– about 7 minutes before take-off

While the tug pushes the aircraft onto the apron so that it will be free to move off later, the pilots read out the 'BEFORE START (ENGINES)' checklist. Provided all the engines are clear of obstructions, when the tug has disconnected, the pilots start up and rev the engines. In the case of a 747, engine number four is

usually started first, because this engine also generates the hydraulic pressure for the brakes. This is then followed by number one, then numbers two and three (the engines are numbered from left to right facing in the direction of flight). The APU is switched off.

Pilot: 'APRON, CACTUS 632 READY TO TAXI.'

Apron: 'CACTUS 632, TAXI TO HOLDING POINT 18 VIA GOLF AND NOVEMBER. ADVISE WHEN READY.'

Pilot: 'HOLDING POINT 18 VIA GOLF AND NOVEMBER. WILCO. CACTUS 632.'

The aircraft then taxis over the apron on the taxiways as far as the assigned holding point on the runway.

In the cabin, the flight attendants are familiarizing the passengers with the aircraft's emergency procedures.

CAN AIRCRAFT DOORS BE OPENED IN FLIGHT?

No. This is not physically possible. When in the locked position, the door is larger than the door opening. After turning the opening lever, it is first necessary to pull the door inward in order to release this lock. Since there is excess pressure in the aircraft interior while airborne, however, even the world's strongest man could not do this.

THE FLIGHT

TAKE-OFF

Apron: 'CACTUS 632 CONTACT TOWER ON FREQUENCY 124.850.'

Pilot: '124.850, CACTUS 632.'

Now comes the instruction to the cabin crew: 'CABIN CREW, PLEASE BE SEATED.'

The cockpit crew switch frequency and report to the control tower.

Pilot: 'TOWER, CACTUS 632 HEAVY, INTERSECTION NOVEMBER, READY FOR DEPARTURE.'

Tower: 'CACTUS 632 HEAVY, WIND CALM, CLEARED FOR TAKE-OFF RUNWAY 18.'

Pilot: 'CLEARED TAKE-OFF RUNWAY 18.'

Some time earlier, it will have been decided in the cockpit who the PF (pilot flying) is. It does not necessarily have to be the captain. The other pilot assists the PF and is ready to intervene at any time. Once the aircraft has straightened up on the runway, the PF pushes the throttle forwards. The co-pilot watches the instruments and calls out the speeds. V1 is the point up to which a take-off can still be safely terminated. At VR (rotation speed), the nose wheel is lifted. V2 is initial climb speed, at which the landing gear is retracted.

CLIMB OUT

As soon as the landing gear hatches are closed, terminal control takes charge of the flight and ensures that it adheres to its departure route. These routes are clearly defined in order to reduce noise pollution and keep the airspace organized. The crew is now under departure sector radar control.

Pilot: 'LANGEN RADAR, CACTUS 632 HEAVY, AIRBORNE IN FRANKFURT.'

LANGEN RADAR: 'CACTUS 632 HEAVY, RADAR IDENTIFIED, CLIMB TO FLIGHT LEVEL 100, TURN RIGHT INBOUND BIBOS INTERSECTION.'

BAGGAGE AND PASSENGERS MUST ALWAYS FLY TOGETHER

Baggage and passengers must be transported in the same aircraft. This at least helps to pre-empt attacks where the owner of a suitcase bomb stays on the ground. It also sometimes happens that people simply miss their flight and want to have their luggage back.

In any case, the electronic monitoring system reports when a passenger has not boarded the plane. Now the suitcase must be pinpointed and unloaded again. Large airlines use software that tells them exactly in which container a particular suitcase is located. The item of luggage is identified and removed within a few minutes.

EN ROUTE

When the aircraft leaves the surroundings of the airport it is handed over to national area control. While it climbs to upper airspace, the flight attendants begin the on-board service. They usually come through with drinks before serving a meal.

NORTH ATLANTIC TRACK SYSTEM

Traffic over the North Atlantic has increased to such an extent that numerous parallel routes, which are also vertically staggered, have been established there. These routes, between flight levels 310 (9,450 m/ 31,000 ft) and 400 (12,190 m/40,000 ft), are optimized and redetermined by computer several times a day, based on the prevailing wind conditions. There is no radar coverage of this airspace. The navigation computer is switched to the track that was fed into it before take-off. The aircraft will not be picked up on radar again until it approaches the coast of North America.

APPROACH

Following the rather monotonous transatlantic flight on autopilot, the demands on the cockpit crew and their workload now increase as they descend to the area surrounding the destination airport. Here, traffic density increases rapidly. The flight is assigned a published approach route and is threaded on to one of the runways for landing. It overflies an initial approach fix and executes its descent until it overflies the final approach fix.

The ground-based ILS (instrument landing system) sends out a glide path and directional information, which enables the on-board control system to make an automatic landing. Nowadays, it is even possible for a plane to land itself in thick fog and zero visibility. However, for this to be possible, it is necessary to invest in costly infrastructure on the ground. Furthermore, only the latest aircraft have the capability to do this.

For the majority of planes there are approach minima, which are expressed in terms of visibility and cloud ceiling. If these are not met, the aircraft must be diverted to an alternative airport.

TELEPHONE AND INTERNET

Why is use of mobile phones generally prohibited on board?

- Even though interference with the avionics has not yet been proven beyond doubt, there have been a few cases in which the electromagnetic waves from mobile phone systems are thought to have led to malfunctions.
- All mobile phone receivers within a radius of up to 25 km/15½ miles around a fast-flying aircraft would pick up the signals and the receivers' software would crash.
- There is a danger that with 300 passengers in the plane, the noise created would be like that of the New York Stock Exchange. Peace and quiet would be a thing of the past, with everyone automatically speaking louder and louder on the phone in an attempt to drown out their neighbours.
- People of a more temperamental disposition could become

aggressive towards persistent phone users, something that has already led to dangerous situations on planes and even to emergency landings.

Sometimes the remote control of the in-flight entertainment system has an integrated telephone. Using a credit card, you can make a call at a cost of around five dollars a minute via satellite telephone. Using the internet on board is also expensive: with a ten-dollar dial-up fee plus usage charges, the cost of this luxury could rapidly run to 50 dollars or more.

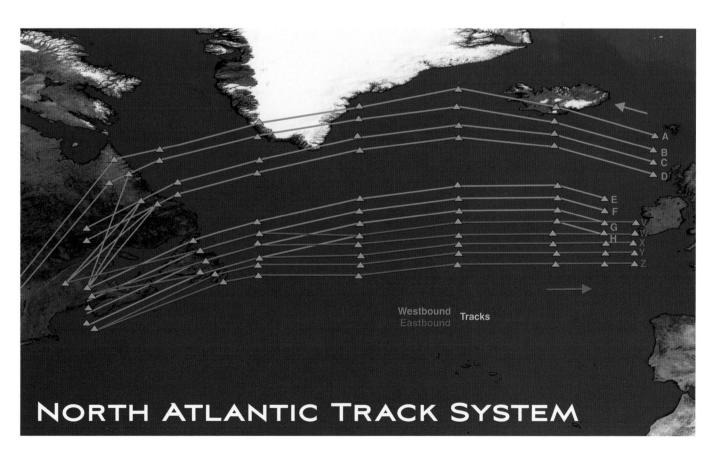

NORTH ATLANTIC TRACK SYSTEM

Westbound
Eastbound   Tracks

System Redundancy

Two are better than one, three are better than two. Based on this principle, critical systems are designed so that any one can safely fail at any given time.

Engine
A two-engined aircraft is capable of flying with just one engine. However, the regulations state that the aircraft must then fly to the closest suitable airport to land.

Hydraulic systems
Most aircraft have two separate hydraulic systems. Each of these is capable of taking over the key functions of the other.

Flaps
The wings have several pairs of flaps. They are moved symmetrically by various electric motors or hydraulic cylinders. If one pair of flaps fails, it is still possible to steer the aircraft.

other, and if one fails, another will take over. If all the computers should fail, it is always possible to fall back on the same key instruments that Charles Lindbergh would have used.

Speed measurement
This is the basis of aircraft control. The use of multiple pitot tubes (dynamic pressure sensors) should prevent failures here.

Control surfaces
Elevators and rudders are moved by means of both electric and hydraulic actuators. Large control surfaces are divided, enabling redundancy here, too.

Ram air turbines
In the event of the aircraft's entire power supply failing, it is possible to deploy an emergency power turbine, which pivots into the airstream and functions like a wind turbine, generating power for the most critical units.

Navigation
Modern aircraft have hundreds of computers on board, which help the pilots to control the aircraft. These monitor each

Tanks
The fuel tanks are contained in cavities in the fuselage and the wings. They can be selected individually, but must not be emptied asymmetrically. On the A380 it is even possible to fill the tail with 18 tonnes of fuel.

Landing gear
Should the landing gear fail to deploy automatically, it can also be lowered manually.

Brakes
Apart from reverse thrust, there are backup systems here, too. If all else fails, there is always the parking brake.

The Air We Fly Through

Clouds can lie in several layers, one above the other. They impede the view of the ground, so navigation by instruments and surveillance by air traffic control are fundamental requirements for passenger air transportation. When flying through most types of cloud, nothing happens at all. However, strong turbulence sometimes occurs in various forms of cumulonimbus. These air masses carry a lot of moisture, and sometimes also ice and an electrical charge.

Flying altitudes

Concorde . . . . 17,370 m/57,000 ft
Jet . . . . .12,190 m/40,000 ft
Turboprop . . . . 9,145 m/30,000 ft

CIRRUS

Cirrus . . . . 6,000–12,000 m

STRATUS

Stratus . . . . 0–1,000 m

CUMULONIMBUS

Cumulonimbus . . . . . 500–2,000 m

ALTOCUMULUS

Altocumulus . . . . . . 2,000–5,000 m

CUMULUS

Cumulus . . . . 500–2,000 m

STRATOCUMULOS

Stratocumulus . . . . . 500–2,000 m

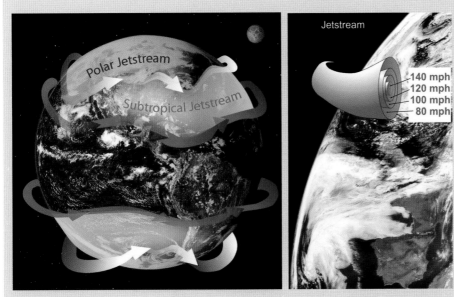

Polar Jetstream

Subtropical Jetstream

Jetstream

140 mph
120 mph
100 mph
80 mph

JETSTREAM

The jetstream is a narrow band of strong winds between the troposphere and the stratosphere. It always runs from west to east along the boundaries of major weather zones with high pressure gradients. Due to the increased density of air masses at the polar ice caps, the northern polar-front jetstream is lower and faster than the subtropical jetstream. Aviation takes advantage of these jetstreams. Aircraft flying eastward follow these fast-flowing air masses, wherever possible, to save time and fuel, while aircraft flying westward seek out flight paths where they are exposed to the currents as little as possible.

Although there is a worldwide trend of making savings in on-board services, the world's airlines still serve up more than 19.5 million litres/4.3 million gallons of wine every year. This is the equivalent of 21.7 million bottles, which would weigh a total of 28,000 tonnes. Qantas and Air New Zealand serve the best wines – they have some that would cost between 50 and 200 US dollars from a specialist supplier! Japan Airlines offers its first class passengers a Champagne Salon 1997, only 60,000 bottles of which were ever produced.

The amount of wine consumed on board also depends on where the flight departs from. For example, passengers on flights out of San Francisco tend to drink more wine than passengers on flights departing from Dallas Fort Worth.

Of course, for most passengers, in-flight catering primarily concerns the provision of food and beverages. There can be as many as 24 special meals to choose from, in addition to the standard meals. These might include Asian food, vegetarian food, baby food, diabetic food and wholefoods, as well as Hindu and kosher meals. In addition to beverages, wide-ranging in-flight services also include newspapers, refreshment towels, cushions, blankets, headphones, toys and many other items. Customs declaration forms are provided for incoming passengers. These differ depending on the destination country and the passengers' nationalities.

Biman Bangladesh Airlines operates a 300,000 sq m/ 358,797 sq yd chicken farm in Dhaka for its catering needs. This farm not only provides meat for its own requirements, but also supplies at least five of the largest airlines that fly into Dhaka. It produces 25,000 chicken meals a month.

Cathay Pacific runs the largest laundry service in Asia through its company Vogue Laundry. Here the tablecloths used for premium class passengers are washed, along with the chair covers, blankets and clothing. They also provide laundry services for 20 other airlines as well as 30 hotels.

Also invisible to passengers are the legions of kitchen workers who fill bread rolls, prepare trays to strict specifications, bake in bulk and provide washing facilities for the catering trolleys.

FOOD ON BOARD

CATERING

LSG Sky Chefs, a subsidiary of Lufthansa, is the world's biggest caterer. It provides about 400 million meals a year to more than 300 aviation companies. LSG cooks for a million people every day. LSG Sky Chefs is prominently represented in its home regions – Europe and North America – where it has 62 and 50 customer service centres respectively.

The preparation of airline meals is subject to specific regulations. Human taste buds behave differently up in the air (a flying height of 2,000 m/6,652 ft is simulated in the cabins) and this has to be taken into account. So, for example, more salt is needed to prevent the food tasting too bland. Cooks test their creations in a pressurized room.

On-board Entertainment Systems

Long flights are boring. Bored passengers stand up, move around and drink more. This means more weight and higher costs. Films and games relax people, thus bringing costs down. These range from feature films that have not been out long in cinemas, to individual multi-entertainment systems that have games, the internet, TV, 250+ films, fast-forward, rewind and slow-motion replay, as well as thousands of CDs to cater for all tastes.

Strict censorship applies on board: there is no controversial political content, no sex, no religious content and there are especially no films about aviation disasters.

Chicken or Beef?

When preparing the on-board catering, nothing is left to chance: where to put the napkins, the cutlery and individual components is all strictly specified. Pork is hardly ever served on planes, as too many people would decline it on religious grounds. The standard food served is mostly chicken or beef and pasta or rice. If there is no choice left, it becomes the flight attendant's task to tempt customers with those meals still available.

DAILY LIFE

HEART ATTACKS

'May we have your attention please? Is there a doctor on board?' In practice, this does not always happen. MedAire, a medical centre in Phoenix, Arizona, is on call to help. About 17,000 times a year its emergency doctors assist with a real emergency in the air. MedAire advises on first aid, helps make decisions about possible emergency landings and, if required, recommends the most suitable hospital. Crews have medical instruments on board, for example syringes and defibrillators, for use in the case of a cardiac arrest.

LEGAL ASPECTS

The terms and conditions of carriage for all airlines require pregnant, sick or disabled people to advise the airlines, before they book, that they may require special care. Once the traveller is accepted on board, the contract of carriage comes into effect. The customer may not be excluded from carriage on the basis of this requirement of care. Expectant mothers require a medical certificate to fly after the thirty-sixth week of pregnancy.

Should an acute medical emergency arise during a flight, as a last resort the captain must decide whether or not to land at the nearest suitable airport. Apart from the delays, the missed connections and possible complications that some passengers could face due to an unplanned trip to a third airport, such unplanned emergency landings cost a minimum of 40,000 euros, and sometimes much more. The pressure on the captain is correspondingly high. Not too long ago a pilot made the wrong decision. The signs of a heart attack were misinterpreted and the passenger died shortly afterwards on the plane. His widow successfully sued the airline for 6 million dollars in compensation.

LIABILITY

It is also important to realize that doctors' medical insurance does not cover their actions on aeroplanes. On the other hand, doctors may be found to be at fault if they fail to assist. Should a doctor make a mistake in such a situation, he himself is personally liable. Lufthansa, the German airline, has arranged insurance that protects doctors from such financial risk if they give assistance voluntarily.

AIR RAGE

Sometimes passengers with aggressive personalities become enraged because they are not allowed smoke, for example, or because they have had too much alcohol. Stewardesses have received black eyes because a passenger has not been allowed to make a phone call, does not want to do up his or her seatbelt, or has been refused a fifth vodka. In 2008, the captain of a charter flight from Munich to Bangkok decided to turn the plane round over the Ukraine and fly back to Germany. A passenger had become so violent that he had to be tied to his seat. As Munich airport had closed, the crew had to fly into Düsseldorf, where the troublemaker was handed over to the police. The 212 passengers were put up in a hotel and flew to Bangkok the next day with a different crew. The cost of this overnight stay, the fuel, the landing fees and compensation for passengers is payable by the guilty party. This quickly mounts up to over 100,000 euros.

SEVEN TIPS FOR STAYING HEALTHY ON BOARD

1.

Flying through multiple time zones plays havoc with our daytime and nighttime rhythms, causing what is known as 'jetlag'. However, there are some things you can do to alleviate the symptoms:

- before flying, get your body used to the new time zone
- at the start of your flight, change your watch immediately to the local time of the place you are flying to
- on arrival, slot into local time immediately and get plenty of fresh air.

2.

When flying west, you should eat protein-rich foods such as meat, fish, eggs and dairy products. Protein-rich food helps the body fight tiredness. On the other hand, when flying east you should eat plenty of carbohydrates such as noodles, rice, fruit and vegetables, which aid digestion and help you sleep.

3.

In a house, relative air humidity varies between 40 and 70 per cent. On a plane this fluctuates between 5 and 15 per cent, and consequently the body's need for liquids increases. At cruising height, the body needs 250 ml/8.8 fl oz of liquid per hour. A good remedy is tomato juice, ideally with salt and pepper. Tomatoes are a healthy fruit. They are rich in lycopene, which reduces the risk of cardiac and circulation illnesses, among others.

4.

Take your shoes off at the start of the flight because feet swell as altitude increases. Flight socks with non-slip rubber soles that can be worn over ordinary socks are available on the market. Loose, comfortable clothing, especially around the waist, prevents uncomfortable tightness and over-heating.

5.

Regular isometric exercises on the spot keep the circulation active. Occasionally standing up and stretching your legs, especially in narrow seats, helps counter thrombosis, also known as 'economy class syndrome'.

6.

Contact lens wearers should consider bringing spectacles for the journey, as the dry air on a plane can irritate eyes.

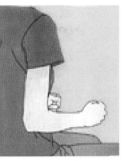

Breathe deeply   *Activate muscles*

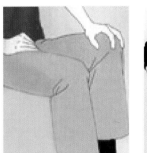

Stay alert   *Release tension*

7.

A moisturising skin cream will help prevent the skin from drying out.

SILJE

In 1986, there was no hospital in the Norwegian town of Honningsvåg. Babies were either delivered by a midwife or were born in the city of Hammerfest, 180 km/112 miles away. Silje's Jørgensen mother went into labour early and it was too late for her to reach the hospital by car. The midwife decided to take her to hospital on a short take-off Twin Otter operated by the airline Widerøe. All of the passengers had to remain behind and only the expectant mother, the midwife and the two pilots were on board.

The midwife, however, could not bear flying and started to panic, yet the baby could not wait. Just 13 km/8 miles

before the final descent into Hammerfest, a little girl first saw the light of day. After landing in Hammerfest, the happy mother was able to hold little Silje in her arms. The doctors and medical staff on stand-by then attended to the mother, the baby and the ashen-faced midwife.

Widerøe airline has a sense of humour: the Twin Otter plane was given the name 'Silje' and Silje herself received free flights on all of Widerøe's routes for the rest of her life, as well as a lifelong job offer from the airline.

Silje is currently studying biology and mathematics in Tromsø. She may well take up the job offer at a future date. The young woman loves travelling!

HOLDING

If you come in to land at an airport at rush hour, the plane may be put into a holding pattern or stack. This happens for many reasons: bad weather, snow clearance, storms over the destination airport, an incident on the runway, an emergency in the air involving another plane, an overstretched airport, a staff shortage at air traffic control, failure or damage to radar or communications equipment. Closure of a nearby airport can also lead to an overload, as another 20 or 30 planes join the queue, having been diverted from, say, Philadelphia to Boston.

The instruction for the pattern shown opposite is as follows:

'CACTUS 632, RIGHT HAND HOLDING RADIAL 360 ABC VOR BETWEEN 5 AND 10 DME. MAINTAIN FLIGHT LEVEL 100.'

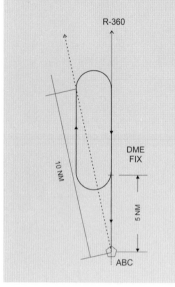

LANDING

Control of the landing is handled by the control tower.

'BOSTON TOWER CACTUS 632 HEAVY 6 MILES FINAL RWY 22 LEFT. RUNWAY IN SIGHT.'

'632 HEAVY, BOSTON TOWER, CLEARED TO LAND RUNWAY 22 LEFT. WIND 180 DEGREES 8 KNOTS.'

'CLEARED TO LAND 22 LEFT, CACTUS 632.'

In fact, every plane can be landed manually, but it is easier and more economical if it is done electronically.

The ground-based ILS (instrument landing system) sends out horizontal and vertical control beams that are received and analysed by the instruments on board. The plane is then guided very precisely, either manually or electronically, onto the centre line and the glide-path to the landing point on the runway. This is how planes are able to land even in thick fog.

The radar altimeter with a speech module also gives the altitude reading.

The crew must, of course, look after the landing configuration themselves.

Electronics land the plane gently on the runway. The Airbus A380 also has an automatic 'brake-to-vacate' system (BTV) that determines the best braking pressure to ensure that the heavy plane taxis off the runway at the desired exit.

There is a 'take-off/go-around' (TO/GA) switch for use in emergencies. The plane is put into overshoot mode using a button. The TO/GA switch not only gives the pilot maximum power in the shortest possible time, but it also switches off automatic landing and reconfigures the plane for the new flight position, so that the pilots can concentrate on the essentials.

After taxiing, the pilots receive further taxi instructions from GROUND CONTROL.

When they reach the gate, the crew will sign out on the radio as follows: 'BOSTON GROUND, CACTUS 632 AT THE GATE, SHUTTING DOWN.'

INGENIOUS: THE SARAJEVO APPROACH

Flight over ROBBY, STEFY or VINCE.

INGENIOUS BUT DIFFICULT: THE APPROACH INTO SARAJEVO AIRPORT

Since Sarajevo is situated in a hollow, it can only be approached from the northwest. Planes have to take off in the opposite direction. To stagger incoming and outgoing flights, a triangular procedure has been developed. Air crews require a special qualification for this.

When the radio compass is at 136 degrees, commence descent to 1,768 m/5,800 ft. At 124 degrees, commence curve into final descent.

Stacking over HANDY OR STEFY, as required.

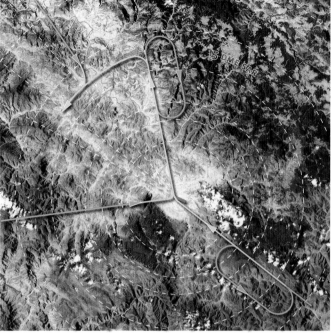

On permission to approach, arc 15 DME SAR at 2,133 m/7,000 ft.

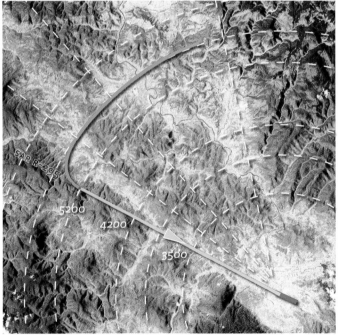

Descend to 1,585 m/5,200 ft. Continue flying on the radial SAR R-295 maintaining minimum altitude of 1,585 m/5,200ft, 1,280 m/4,200 ft and 1,067 m/3,500 ft until the decision point (visual contact with the runway) and complete landing visually.

Missed the runway? Then go back to the start...

Night Flights

THE RED-EYE FLIGHTS
Flights that take off in an easterly direction in the middle of the night and that arrive no more than five hours later are known as the 'red-eye' flights. You save a day travelling and an overnight stay in a hotel, but you generally arrive having had no sleep, hence the red eyes.

Airlines are happy to offer these flights if there is a nighttime flying ban at their home airport. Thus their medium-haul aircraft can continue to earn money at night, plus on their return journey the airport is open again. These night flights can be offered at low cost and make good money for the airlines.

TYPICAL RED-EYE FLIGHTS in the Far East would be Hong Kong–Tokyo and Singapore–Manila. Other red-eye routes are Singapore–Sydney, Perth–Sydney, Delhi–Bangkok, Frankfurt–Larnaca, Calgary–Toronto and Honolulu– San Francisco.

Beijing

Tokyo

Shanghai

Hong Kong

Islamabad

Delhi

Dhaka
Kolkata

Dubai

Muscat

Mumbai

Bangkok

Bangalore   Chennai

Beirut
Tel Aviv

Cairo

Kuwait
Dammam
Bahrain
Doha
Abu Dhabi

oli

Singapore

Entebbe

Nairobi

Dar-es-Salaam

Lusaka

Mauritius

Johannesburg

wr

Sydney

A BAG'S JOURNEY

SORTING THE BAGS

Types of luggage With the fine-tuning of barcode scanners and increasing automation, a suitcase rarely fails to reach its plane, thanks to a system of conveyor routes that in Frankfurt, for example, is 67 km/42 miles long. This is one of the most demanding tasks required of an airport – to take in the passengers' countless suitcases and bags, along with surfboards, children's pushchairs and skis, and to ensure that these arrive promptly and in good condition at the correct plane, which could be in any one of hundreds of possible parking spots.

Bags arriving, bags being transferred and bags departing all have to be sorted. It is only in single-aisled aircraft that suitcases and rucksacks are put loose into the cargo hold and restrained in luggage racks. In larger aircraft, light metal holders are used. Each of these holds 35–45 suitcases. This ensures careful transport and also enables quicker loading and unloading.

Arrivals baggage In a Boeing 747, the loading/unloading area of the storage hold is 5.2 m/17 ft above the ground. Inside the aircraft there are devices along which the containers roll to the docked hydraulic ramp which, however, can only manage two containers at a time. The ramp is then lowered, so that the container can be unloaded onto the baggage tenders. Each time about 90 suitcases are unloaded, until all the trailers of the tender are full. A large airport has about 200 luggage tenders and 1,800 trailers. Even before a plane lands, the arrivals gate and baggage carousel are organized so that the collectors know at which exit to wait. Bags are fundamentally sorted into two groups: bags going abroad and domestic bags (in Europe 'domestic' also means the Schengen countries).

Airlines try to give those paying full fares – that is, business and first class passengers – a time advantage by pre-sorting their baggage on departure so that it can be unloaded on arrival and brought to the carousel first as 'priority' baggage.

Singapore Airlines sorts its luggage into 12 different categories. Luggage that is not collected or assigned goes into 24-hour storage. If this remains uncollected a day later, it is sent to a customs warehouse and entered into a worldwide database for abandoned luggage that is accessible for enquiries.

Transfer baggage Sorted luggage that needs to be transferred to a different flight continues on a conveyor belt to a departure bag loading facility, where baggage from the departure halls is sorted and stored. This process is akin to finding 'the eye of the needle' in an airport. Some airports require a minimum window of 120 minutes between connecting flights. Modern airports require a maximum of 45 minutes: 15 minutes for unloading, 15 for transport, sorting and further transport, and 15 minutes for loading onto the connecting flight. Some incoming planes may have baggage for about 30 different connecting flights on board. So there is barely 15 minutes available to get a bag from one end of the airport to the other.

Before a plane even lands, the established airlines already have information on the number of bags that need to be transferred. Thus, in the event

United Breaks Guitars

A Canadian country music band flew with United Airlines from Halifax, Virginia, to Nebraska. They arrived in Omaha to find the top broken off a guitar worth 3,500 dollars. For nine months, the customer tried to claim 1,200 dollars needed for its repair. His complaint was continually passed on to someone else in the airline, finally ending up at a call centre in New Delhi. In a final letter from the airline, he received a curt rebuff. He replied, promising that he would write three songs about his case and broadcast them by video on YouTube. When the first video, 'United Breaks Guitars',

came out, CNN reported the story and it was viewed by five million people within a space of four weeks. Soon all the TV and radio channels in North America were reporting the story and the video was seen all around the world. United Airlines received a flood of cancellations on its flights, including its long-haul service. A newspaper calculated that this PR disaster cost the airline an estimated 150 million dollars!

Legally, under the terms of the Warsaw Convention, airlines are only liable up to a maximum limit of 20 dollars per kilo. The Montreal Convention set a limit of 1,000 dollars per person.

of late arrivals, issues can be identified and planned for.

Original departures baggage What seems simple is, in fact, a complex process. In Frankfurt, for example, passengers can check in luggage at any of 408 desks in two terminals and two railway stations. Bags go through different security procedures and are weighed and issued with a machine-readable baggage tag on which the flight number, connecting flight number, destination and individual number of the bag are printed. Depending on where the aircraft is parked, the latest 'closing time' for bags at the check-in desk is 20 minutes before take-off.

Frankfurt airport has a baggage handling system that is still unique in the world. Baggage disappears in a lift, which passengers do not see. Suitcases and flight numbers are then 'married' with 18,000 tub-like packing trays that are ready and waiting to receive them.

The trays carry a machine-readable code that can be read from any angle. Suitcases are moved on, as if by magic, at a speed of 5 m/16 ft per second (18 km/h /11 mph) through a labyrinth of 6,000 conveyor belts and 7,000 roller conveyors, around 4,000 bends,

over 1,600 switching points and via 300 lifts through halls and tunnels. They are controlled by 2,000 electronic barriers and moved by 16,000 driving mechanisms until they arrive promptly at any one of around 87 removal stations, where they can be loaded on to the baggage trolleys. The facility in Frankfurt has a sorting throughput of

Another option: on booking a premium ticket, customers may arrange for their luggage to get priority delivery on landing.

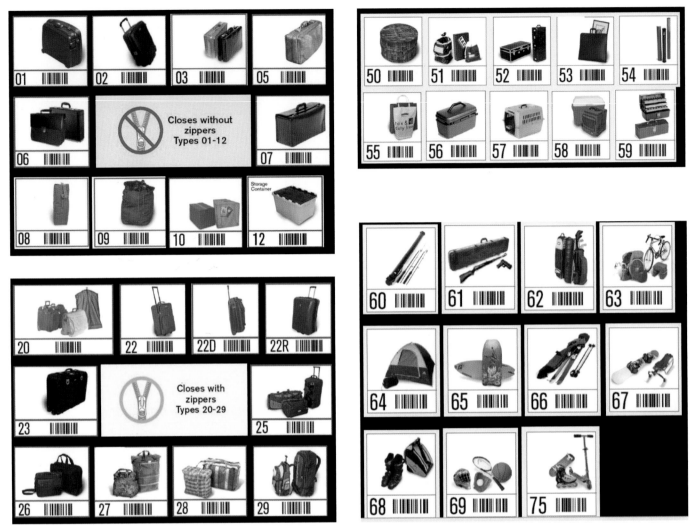

When bags go missing, passengers report them to the airline's baggage claims department. A search commences using the bag's luggage label and a baggage control table. The passenger is given an emergency kit with washing items and funds to buy other essentials. In most cases, the missing bag is delivered to the passenger's hotel the following day.

18,000 items per hour, is 67 km/42 miles long, and is operated and maintained by 270 staff. It has a value of 350 million euros.

Advance baggage Bags that are checked in several hours before a flight are sent off to an early luggage storage facility that has a capacity of 8,200 units. The bags then go round and round in circles until it is time for them to be retrieved and forwarded to the correct removal station.

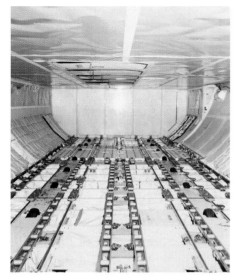

SECURITY

Stationary and mobile x-ray machines are used everywhere: each piece of luggage is x-rayed, and no bag is transported unless its owner has boarded the plane. This is called 'passenger baggage reconciliation'.

The price for this element of security is occasional delays when baggage that has already been loaded on board has to be taken off again because its owner fails to board the plane on time. Only efficient electronic records can tell which container the baggage is in. This saves valuable time.

The day London Heathrow came to a standstill

It was to be the largest terminal in Europe and the most modern. Since baggage handling is the critical factor in passenger dispatch, Heathrow's new terminal was designed around its baggage handling system. The size of 50 football pitches, it is as big as a whole urban district. Queen Elizabeth II opened the new terminal – and then chaos erupted.

A parking attendant was taking his job very seriously. He failed to open the barrier to an overflow car park promptly, because he wanted to ensure that the main car park was filled first. In the meantime, the small army of workers at Terminal 5 were unable to park their cars and drove round and round the airport's one-way system in despair. Soon, all cars at the airport got stuck in a long tailback.

Employees failed to rectify the situation as soon as the difficulties started. Passengers then started arriving late at the security gates. Passengers who failed to arrive at the gate 35 minutes before their departure time found that their luggage had been unloaded. So bags started arriving back and blocked up the system. Transit bags from arriving planes then started to pile up on top of the bags of the departing passengers. Bags for departure landed in baggage reclaim. In the terminal, computers froze and the electricity supply crashed. Heathrow was the laughing stock of the world's airline industry.

This continued for days, with more and more bags stacking up. It was weeks before a solution was found to sort out the chaos. Finally, 28,000 bags were loaded onto lorries and driven to Milan where a specialist company identified the owners of the bags and delivered them back.

Aircraft Technical Inspections

	When	What	Duration
Ramp check	Daily	External check	Between landing and take-off
A-check	250–650 hours/every 2 months	Cabins, minor superficial work	Overnight
B-check	1,000 hours/ 3–5 months	Airframe and systems (only on Boeing 737-200 and 747-200)	12 hours
C-check	15–18 months	Detailed inspection of structure and systems Exposure of panelling Inspection of airframe	1–2 weeks
IL-check	48 months	Complete overhaul of cabins, checks on the fuselage, structure, wings, electrics and hydraulics	Variable
D-check	6–10 years	Complete overhaul and dismantling	4–6 weeks

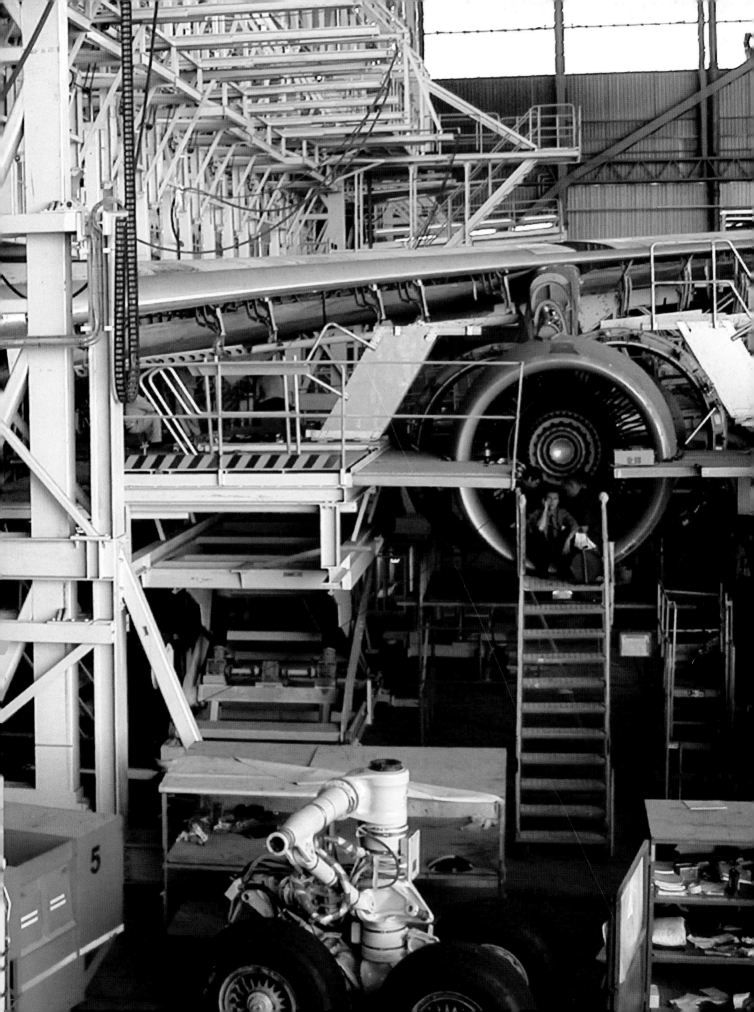

Careers in the Aviation Industry

PILOTS

Salaries for pilots depend on the airline, length of service, the type of aircraft and the distances and hours that a pilot flies in a month. Young pilots often have to repay the airline for some of their training, so their monthly income can be less than 2,000 euros a month for a number of years.

Asian airlines traditionally pay well. At Cathay Pacific a first officer earns between 60,000 and 95,000 euros and a captain earns between 110,000 and 160,000 euros. At Singapore Airlines, a captain earns between 60,000 and 120,000 euros.

European flag carriers are in the upper levels, paying from 60,000–120,000 euros (gross) for a first officer and 120,000–200,000 for a captain flying about 75 hours a month.

American Airlines has the broadest range of salaries, with incomes ranging from 17,000–189,000 euros.

Qantas pays 40,000–100,000 euros for a first officer and between 120,000 and 200,000 euros for a captain.

A first officer at Emirates earns between 40,000 and 60,000 euros, with a captain earning between 50,000 and 90,000 euros.

Throughout the world, low-cost carriers are being set up and airlines in the Middle East are experiencing growth at double digit rates. Moreover, it is not unusual for leading aircraft manufacturers to get orders from individual airlines for 50, 100 or 150 aircraft. If a long-haul plane such as an Airbus A340 is to be flown cost-effectively, it must be flown for about 18 hours a day. Thus, seven to ten crew are needed per aircraft per year. European budget airlines also pay well above average, as there seems to be a shortage of pilots.

This was not always the case. At the end of the 1990s, there was an oversupply of pilots. This did not just cause salaries to stagnate: human resources directors were receiving applications from unemployed pilots practically on their knees begging to be allowed fly so that their valuable type ratings would not lapse. Some were even prepared to work for nothing! This phenomenon reoccurs periodically.

Boeing predicted a shortage of 10,000 pilots in the next five years for the Asian region. However, this was before the current financial crisis that has forced many carriers in the Far East to reduce their fleets by 10–20 per cent.

AIR TRAFFIC CONTROLLERS

In most countries, air traffic controllers enjoy the same high standing as pilots. Good salaries, short working hours and a relatively early retirement age reflect the job's inherent level of responsibility. Since public budgets in most countries in the world are undergoing rigorous cutbacks, air traffic controllers often have to struggle with ageing equipment and staff shortages. A typical average salary in Europe is between 60,000 and 100,000 euros.

In the United States, salaries are between 45,000 and 110,000 euros, and in Australia salaries also go up to 110,000 euros.

FLIGHT ATTENDANTS

In the United States, flight attendants earn between 12,000 and 55,000 euros a year. Salaries at Asian airlines are much lower.

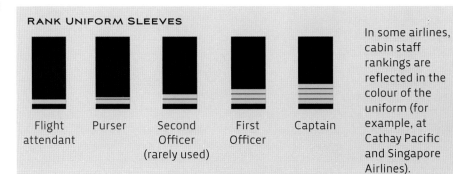

RANK UNIFORM SLEEVES

| Flight attendant | Purser | Second Officer (rarely used) | First Officer | Captain |

In some airlines, cabin staff rankings are reflected in the colour of the uniform (for example, at Cathay Pacific and Singapore Airlines).

Career	Minimum age	Description	Length of training	Income per annum
Pilot	18	Pilots commercial passenger and cargo planes.	2–3 years' or 4 years' training with an airline or aviation school.	40,000–130,000 euros
Dispatcher	18–21	Is responsible for all essential flight information such as wind and weather data. Also responsible, with the pilot, for the flight plan.	13 months with an airline.	50,000 euros
Air Traffic Controller	19	Works in the control tower or radar control rooms to ensure the safe, orderly, fluid and most efficient management of air traffic.	3–4 years' training at a flight safety school, plus on-the-job training.	60,000 – 100,000 euros
'Follow me' or marshaller	–	Guides aircraft to the correct parking positions after landing and secures them. Organizes the luggage and freight.	3–4 years' training with an airline.	20,000 euros
Flight attendant, purser	18	Looks after passengers on board the aircraft. Is responsible for safety and well-being of passengers. Serves meals and beverages. In an emergency, oversees evacuation of the plane.	6 weeks to 4 months with an airline.	30,000 euros
Technical careers in aviation:				
Aeroplane mechanic	–	Repairs and maintains aircraft and aeroplane parts.	3½ years	30,000 euros
Aviation electronics technician	–	Installs electrical and electronic systems and equipment on aeroplanes and looks after the smooth operation, repair and maintenance of these parts.	3½ years training in the industry.	30,000 euros
Aeronautic/ astronautic engineer	–	Works in the industry to develop, construct and complete aircraft or individual components. In an airline, plans and oversees the fleet and implements the maintenance programme.	3–4 years' study in aeronautic/ astronautic engineering at university level.	60,000–100,000 euros
Transport and communications engineer		Specializes in transport concepts.	3–4 years' study at university level in economic engineering.	60,000 euros
Business careers in aviation				
Customer service staff	–	Advises and looks after passengers at the airport. Provides information, sells tickets, checks in passengers and bags, performs other commercial tasks.	3 years' training with an airline or airport operator.	30,000 euros
Air transport agent	–	Plans, organizes and manages passenger and freight transport. Employed in the areas of purchasing, sales, marketing, personnel, accounts and customer service.	3 years' training with an airline or airport operator.	30,000 euros
Freight agent (forwarding and logistics services)	–	Plans and organizes national and international freight traffic. Looks after customs requirements and foreign trade regulations. Calculates prices and processes tenders	3 years' training with a forwarding agent.	30,000 euros
Catering manager	–	Implements a standardized, centrally managed food concept in all areas of a restaurant.	3 years' training in the hospitality business.	20,000 euros
Transport administrator		Performs specialist and managerial tasks in various lines of business.	3–4 years' study at a university or equivalent institute.	30,000–40,000 euros
International aviation assistant	–	Advises and looks after passengers, ticket sales and freight dispatch. Also gives managerial assistance.	2 years' training at a tourism institute.	–

* Gross salary depending on allowances, income bracket, employer and country.

INCIDENTS

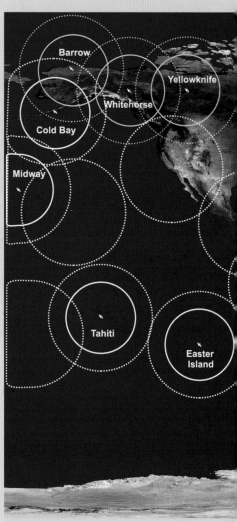

TURBULENCE

In the area around cumulonimbus clouds there is always strong turbulence. However, invisible turbulence, known as 'clear air turbulence' (CAT) is much worse. What are known colloquially as 'air pockets' are vertical currents of air going upwards or downwards. The fulminant forces are powerful enough to result in people or drinks trolleys being smashed up against the ceiling, which would cause havoc in the cabin. This is why airlines insist that passengers keep their seatbelts on even when the seatbelt signs are switched off. Turbulence does not harm aircraft.

FLIGHT ENGINE FAILURE

Possible causes include bird strikes, fire and volcanic ash. In 1982, a British Airways jumbo flew into a cloud of volcanic ash causing all four of its engines to fail. The plane dropped from 11,280 m/ 37,000 ft to 3,960 m/13,000 ft, at which point the pilot managed to restart engine number four, followed by engines number three and one. In the years which followed, nine Volcanic Ash Advisory Centres (VAACs) were established. These track the paths of ash clouds and issue warnings to aircraft. The centres are based in London, Toulouse, Anchorage, Washington, Montreal, Darwin, Wellington, Tokyo and Buenos Aires.

ETOPS

Are twin-engined planes permitted to fly over the Atlantic? Or over the Pacific? The International Civil Aviation Organization (ICAO) issues what are called 'ETOPS' rules. ETOPS stands for 'Extended-Range Twin-Engine Operation Performance Standards'. Originally, they ruled that in the event of engine failure a plane must be able to make an emergency landing within 60 minutes. Thus, a flight had to be planned in such a way that this

One small bird rarely harms an engine. The worst are birds of prey, geese and storks. They can come through cockpit windows and radomes, and can also destroy engines.

SUDDEN PRESSURE LOSS

During a flight at an altitude of 9,750 m/ 32,000 ft, the air pressure inside the aeroplane is the same as if it were flying at 2,000 m/6,560 ft. Outside, however, there are life-threatening conditions:

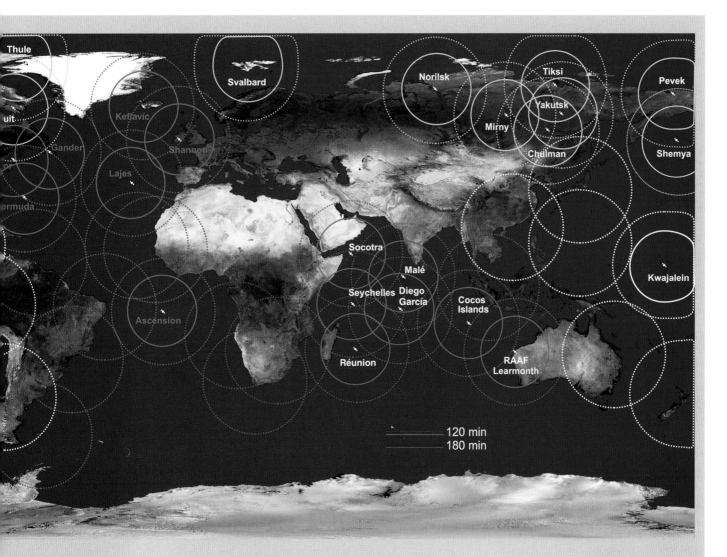

Thule

Svalbard

Norilsk

Tiksi

Pevek

Keflavic

Yakutsk

Shemya

Gander

Shannon

Mirny

Chulman

Lajes

Socotra

Ascension

Malé

Seychelles Diego
García

Cocos
Islands

Kwajalein

Réunion

RAAF
Learmonth

———— 120 min
———— 180 min

requirement was feasible at all times. However, in recent years engine reliability has improved, meaning that the target time has been increased to 75 minutes. More generous rules also apply to airlines that carry out exemplary engine maintenance schedules and to specific types of aircraft and engines. Currently, the longest ETOPS target time is 207 minutes. ETOPS, of course, relates to the distances between two points and to fuel economy. It also specifies that it must be possible for the particular plane to land at these airports. If this is not the case, longer alternative routes must be flown.

The following islands and airports are open 24 hours a day as emergency landing sites.

Atlantic routes
- Bangor airport
- Gander airport
- Keflavík airport
- Shannon airport
- Bermuda airport
- Lajes airport
- Ascension Island

Pacific routes
- Midway Atoll
- Easter Island
- Faa'a airport, Tahiti
- Wake Island
- Kwajalein Atoll
- Shemya Island
- Cold Bay airport

North polar routes
- Svalbard airport
- Thule airbase
- Iqaluit airport
- Whitehorse airport
- Yellowknife airport
- Barrow airport
- Norilsk airport
- Tiksi airport
- Yakutsk airport
- Mirny airport
- Chulman airport
- Pevek airport

Indian Ocean routes
- Socotra airport
- Seychelles airport
- Réunion
- Maldives, Male
- Diego García
- Cocos Islands airport
- Learmonth, Australia

air temperatures of -50°C/-58°F and air that is too thin to breathe. If for any reason there is a leak, the air inside the cabin escapes, the cabin pressure drops, it gets colder and oxygen masks drop down over the seats. The masks begin

to work as soon as they are pulled down and put on.

Cabin crew also carry portable oxygen equipment. The crew in the cockpit rapidly descend the plane to 3,050 m/10,000 ft, where the masks can be

removed. The remainder of the flight to the next suitable airport should pass without further impairment.

ENGINE FIRES

Thankfully, engine fires are extremely rare. The most famous occurrence is the Concorde crash in Paris in 2000: on take-off, one of its wheels rolled over a small metal part on the runway, which burst a tyre in the main undercarriage unit. Pieces of tyre then hit the overhead tank, triggering a shockwave that caused fuel to leak out. More pieces of tyre then damaged the landing gear's electrics, with the result that the landing gear could no longer be operated. Sparks ignited the leaking fuel. Both engines on the left-hand side lost thrust. At this point, the plane was already going too fast to abort take-off. The fire melted parts of the wings and the flaps. The plane banked onto its side and crashed into a nearby hotel.

If an engine fire breaks out during a flight, it can be extinguished using internal equipment.

OVERSHOOTS

The most ordinary thing in the world is an overshoot. For example, a plane that has landed earlier has not left the runway quickly enough, a vehicle is driving on the runway and is not answering its radio, or a deer is crossing the runway. In most cases, the tower gives the order to overshoot. Pilots may also make the decision if they catch a gust of wind just before landing, or because the cross-winds have increased and they would prefer to land on a different runway.

STORMS

Unstable stratification in the atmosphere, damp air close to the ground and vertical air currents lead to a build up of cumulonimbus clouds. The rising warm air cools down quickly. In the area of the storm, strong upwinds carry the raindrops to great heights where they freeze. Down currents force these down again where they accumulate more moisture. This process repeats itself until the centre of the cloud is so large and heavy that it has to fall.

Hailstones are a danger for aircraft because heavy ice crystals can bounce off the aeroplane like bullets (see picture).

BLACKLISTS

EU

The European Union oversees safety standards for airlines that wish to fly in its territory. The EU Member States work together with authorities from other countries to raise safety standards worldwide. However, there are still some airlines that operate at conditions below the required safety levels. These are put on a blacklist that is constantly updated. See http://ec.europa.eu/transport/air-ban.

FAA

The US Federal Aviation Administration (FAA), in its role as the supervisory body for airline companies, monitors state air travel authorities using its IASA program. If countries fail to maintain or implement ICAO standards, then they appear on a blacklist throughout the country. See http://www.faa.gov/about/initiatives/iasa/.

IATA

The International Air Transport Association (IATA) awards a quality mark to airlines that pass its Operational Safety Audit (IOSA). See http://www.iata.org/ps/certification/iosa/registry.htm

At high vertical speeds, different sized ice crystals may generate different electrical charges. The discharge is expressed as lightning.

The large frames of modern passenger planes, with destaticizers attached to the landing flaps, offer good protection against lightning strikes.

When they occur individually, thunder storms, hail and lightning do not pose any real danger. Most aircraft are struck by lightning several times in their lifespan. Despite this, storms are always given a wide berth and flown around. If a storm occurs over an airport, patience is needed because, unless it is an emergency, pilots prefer to stay a little longer on the ground or to circle in a holding pattern rather than to take off into the storm.

LANDING GEAR PROBLEMS

It sometimes happens that a tyre bursts. If this happens on take-off it may not be a problem, as the load is lifted increasingly off the nose of the plane. However, precautions must be taken to ensure as little damage to the aeroplane as possible when it lands. When the naked wheel rim sets down on the ground, sparks are emitted, the heat caused by the friction brings the rim to burning point, the second tyre bursts and even more damage is caused. In addition, the aeroplane becomes difficult to steer and could well veer off the runway.

In such cases, the fire brigade lays down a foam carpet starting at the spot where the damaged wheel is most likely to come into contact with the ground. Here, time is of the essence. If the carpet is laid too early, the foam – depending on the temperature – collapses in on itself and becomes ineffective. If it is laid too late, the aeroplane might have

to abort its landing because the foam carpet is not yet ready. All going well, the foam prevents the excessive build up of sparks. Once the aircraft is stationary, the fire brigade can cool the landing gear and the emergency is over.

The destaticizers are clearly visible on the landing flaps. These conduct lightning. Additional discharge points are the interim spaces between different plane components and the edges of the bolts and rivets.

SIMULATORS

Flying lessons are expensive and time-consuming. Pilots must regularly train for all possible incidents and emergency situations until they are totally in control. For this purpose, at the comparatively modest price of about 500 dollars an hour, simulators are used on which 300 different flight emergencies can be practised, including engine failure, on-board fire and emergency ditching.

Pilots must have proven mastery of certain 'by heart items'. These are actions that have to be taken in an emergency, which they must know by heart and not have to check on an emergency checklist. Although the simulator is first and foremost a training tool, it is also extremely stressful for the trainees. Everything is recorded: dates, sound and video. Does the candidate react in a calm, collected and correct manner? Depending on the airline, the results go on file.

Simulators are also used to train flight attendants for emergencies, such as evacuations or dealing with difficult passengers.

Large airlines maintain a series of simulators for every type of aeroplane. The cost of purchasing each machine runs into double-digit millions.

LIFEJACKETS

Since 1954, when a Convair flight ditched into the English Channel and some passengers drowned because they had no lifejackets, this piece of life-saving equipment has been a statutory requirement on all flights over water. In 1956, a Pan Am flight made a successful emergency landing on water and all 31 of its passengers survived. In 1963, the pilot of a Tupolev 124 managed to ditch his plane in a river. Again, all 52 passengers survived. In 1968, a Japan Airlines DC-8 missed the runway at San Francisco and came down out in the bay. All of its passengers were saved. Another 63 occupants of a DC-9 found themselves in the waters of the Caribbean when their flight ran out of fuel; 40 of them were later rescued by helicopter, although the other 23 perished. In 1996, a Boeing 767 belonging to Ethiopian Airlines had to ditch in water when it ran out of fuel. Several passengers ignored the staff's instructions not to inflate their lifejackets before exiting the plane, so most of them drowned when they were unable to leave the plane. Only 52 of the 175 people on board managed to survive. In 2002, 60 people survived an emergency water landing in Indonesia. In 2005, 23 of 39 occupants survived when an ATR-72 ditched off Sicily. Finally, US Airways flight 1549 landed on the Hudson River after a bird strike. All 155 on board survived unharmed. Some passengers even had the chutzpah to look for their hand baggage so they could take it with them in the rescue boats!

WHY ARE THERE NO PARACHUTES?

The French Foreign Legion are trained in parachute jumping.

1. Dropping 80 paratroopers from a transport aircraft requires the highest levels of courage, discipline and a lengthy period of basic training. Attaching the drop rope alone takes a few minutes and requires a lot of practice and care. It simply would not be possible to organize 300 or 400 untrained passengers to jump out of an aeroplane travelling at 400 km/h /249 mph at an altitude of 10,000 m/30,000 ft.

2. Even if the doors could be opened, the passengers jumping out would smash into the wings or the tail fins.

3. Parachutes can only be opened at 1,500 m/4,920 ft at the earliest. Given the inexperience of passengers, each parachute would have to have an automatic opening device, and for a jump at great altitude also an oxygen tank and an altimeter, all of which would have to be set up and put on.

4. Each passenger would also have to have a helmet, to avoid injuries inflicted by uncoordinated jumps made by other passengers.

5. The evacuation would also have to be operable at night.

6. Should a passenger land in water, most of the parachute would land on their heads, suffocating them. The passenger would have to remove the harness and climb out from underneath it without getting caught up in the lines. The lifejacket, which would have to be put on underneath the parachute – not easy when in a panic – could then be inflated.

7. During a storm or in high winds, the untrained parachutist would be dragged along the ground upon landing.

8. In built-up areas there is the danger that the canopy could collapse so that the person would fall the last 20 m/65 ft to the ground at full speed.

9. Evacuating 300 or more passengers from a passenger plane would take much longer than evacuating trained paratroopers from a slow-flying transport plane. A passenger plane flies at just under the speed of sound, meaning that its 'drop zone' for could be as large as 300 km/186 miles.

10. Over 90 per cent of all accidents happen either on take-off or landing and with no or very little warning. Only in the case of a bomb or rocket fire could a parachute possibly save any of the passengers. In both the Lockerbie and Sakhalin crashes, passengers lost consciousness in seconds because of the drop in cabin pressure.

11. In August 2001, an Air Transat A310 suffered a fuel leak at high altitude over the Atlantic and had to glide for 20 minutes with no power at an altitude of 6000 m/19,700 ft on to the Azores. This was one of the rare times when an orderly air evacuation could have taken place. Even so, it seems highly unlikely that 306 people would have been able to exit the plane promptly and get to the ground unhurt. The plane made an emergency landing at Lajes airbase on the island of Terceira and came to a halt undamaged.

12. As there would not be enough room in the plane to don the extra 25 kg/ 55 lb of special equipment, the passengers who had just negotiated check-in, passport control and security checks would then have to put on thermal suits, lifejackets, parachutes and oxygen tanks in the terminal berfore trudging out to the plane.

FEAR OF FLYING

All the statistics make fear of flying (or 'aerophobia') seem foolish. Yet the autonomic nervous system in humans does not respond to statistics.

At an altitude of 10,000 m/32,800 ft, travelling at just under the speed of sound, some people feel completely helpless, experiencing increased perspiration, a racing heart, shortness of breath, weak knees and a faint feeling. Any unexpected noises, such as retraction or extension of the engines or mechanical trimming can frighten the inexperienced traveller.

To help counter this, many airlines run special courses. At these, a pilot explains how the aeroplane works and how thorough the maintenance is. A short tour is made of the aeroplane and the seminar often ends with a short flight.

The real truth: the most dangerous part of flying is the drive to the airport!

Time Zones

Add time zone number to local time to obtain UTC.
Subtract time zone number from UTC to obtain local time.

WEST

Flying over the International Date Line

Every child knows that the sun rises in the east and sets in the west. So, for example, if you were to fly on Monday 18 May from Los Angeles to Honolulu, you would have to put your watch back two hours because when it is 10 am in LA, it is only 8 am in Honolulu. The flight takes about five hours, so you will arrive in Hawaii at 1 pm local time.

If you were to continue your journey to Micronesia on the same day, then you would cross the International Date Line (IDL). Starting in Honolulu at 4 pm on Monday, it is 2 pm in Majuro on the Marshall Islands. However, in Majuro it

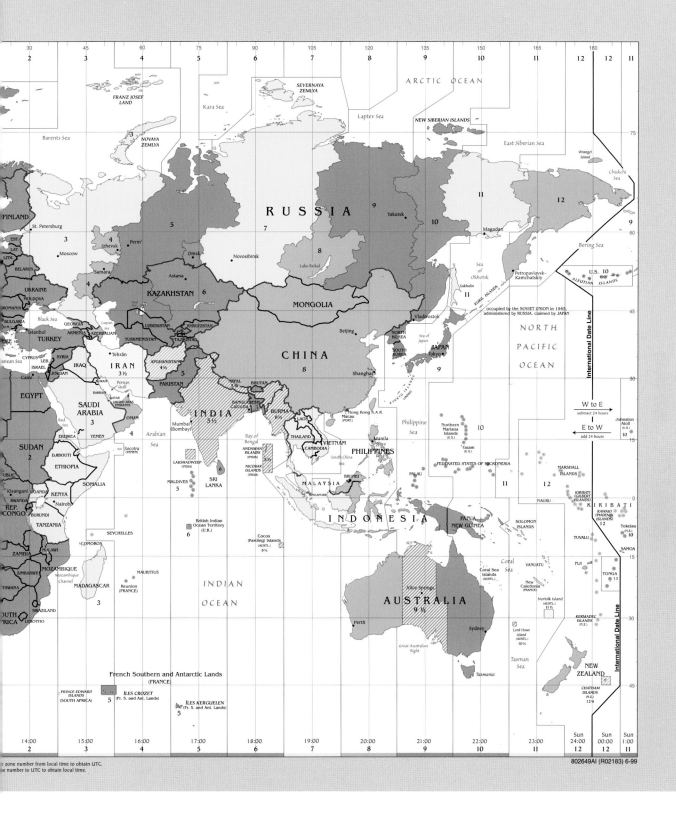

is already Tuesday 19 May. After the five-hour flight towards the west, your watch has to be put back two hours, but the date has to be put forward by a day.

It is more exciting on the way back. You leave Majuro on Wednesday 27 May at 8 pm. In Honolulu it is already 10 pm, but it is only Tuesday 26 May. Five hours later you land in Honolulu at 3 am local time, where it is also 27 May. Thus, you land in Hawaii 17 hours before your departure time. So if you want a particularly long birthday celebration...

Be careful when you are booking hotels. It is better to recheck it five times rather than paying for one night too many on the flight out or finding yourself without a room after the flight back!

CABIN ANNOUNCEMENTS

	UNITED KINGDOM	GERMANY	FRANCE	SPAIN	JAPAN
1	Good morning/afternoon/evening, ladies and gentlemen! On behalf of XXX we would like to welcome you on this flight to ... on board our Airbus.../Boeing.../Fokker ...	Guten Morgen/Tag/Abend, sehr geehrte Damen und Herren! Im Namen von XXX heißen wir Sie sehr herzlich willkommen an Bord dieses Airbus .../dieser Boeing .../dieser Fokker ... auf diesem XXX-Flug nach ...	Bonjour/bonsoir mesdames et messieurs! Au nom de XXX, nous aimerions vous souhaiter la bienvenue sur ce vol à destination de XXX à bord de notre Airbus .../Boeing .../Fokker ...	Buenos/as (días, tardes, noches), y bienvenidos. Sobrecargo responsable del servicio a bordo. Muchas gracias por volar con XXX en este vuelo con destino a ... servicio con el deseo de que tengan un vuelo agradable. Es necesario que tengan la mesa plegada, el respaldo de su butaca vertical y el cinturón de seguridad abrochado.	Joyoukyaku no minasama Ohayou gozaimasu/Konnichiha/Konbanwa. xxx ni kawari, minasama ni touki Airbus .../Fokker ... heno gotoujou wo kokoro yori kangei moushiagemasu.
2	We kindly ask you to stow your carry-on baggage either under the seat in front of you or in the overhead compartment. Please note that the emergency exit rows and the first seat row(s) must be cleared of any carry-on baggage. Thank you.	Bitte verstauen Sie Ihr Handgepäck entweder unter Ihrem Vordersitz oder in einem Gepäckfach. Beachten Sie bitte, dass Reihen beim Notausstieg, sowie die erste(n) Sitzreihe(n) frei von Handgepäck sein müssen. Vielen Dank.	Nous vous prions de bien vouloir ranger vos bagages à main, soit sous le siège devant vous ou dans le compartiment à bagages. S'il vous plaît noter, que la première rangée de sièges doit être maintenue libre de tout bagage à main. Merci.	Para agilizar el embarque, agradecemos que ocupen su asiento lo antes posible, y coloquen su equipaje en los compartimentos superiores o debajo del asiento delantero. Muchas gracias.	Tenimotsu ha mae no zaseki no shita ka mata ha zujou no nimotsu ire ni goshunou kudasai. Tsuuro ya hijou guchi, soshite ichiban mae no ozaseki no mae ha nani mo okanaiyou onegai moushiagemasu.
3	We'll be leaving very shortly, so please switch off your mobile phone and any other electronic devices and respect the smoking ban on board. Thank you!	Wir starten in wenigen Minuten: Schalten Sie bitte Ihr Mobiltelefon und Ihre elektronischen Geräte aus, und beachten Sie das Rauchverbot an Bord. Herzlichen Dank!	Nous partons très bientôt, donc s'il vous plaît, veuillez éteindre votre téléphone portable et autres appareils électroniques et respecter l'interdiction de fumer à bord. Merci!	Por favor, ahora deben apagar sus teléfonos, manteniéndolos desconectados durante todo el vuelo. Otros dispositivos electrónicos solo deberán estar apagados durante el despegue y el aterrizaje. Muchas gracias	Touki ha mamonaku ririku itashimasu. Okyakusama no keitai denwa ya denki kiki no dengen ga kireteiruka imaichido gokakunin kudasai. Nao toukinai ha kinenn desu
4	Ladies and gentlemen, we want to inform you about the international safety regulations:	Meine Damen und Herren, wir informieren Sie über die internationalen Sicherheitsbestimmungen:	Mesdames et Messieurs, Nous tenons à vous informer sur les règles de sécurité internationales:	Por favor presten atención. A continuación vamos a realizar una demostración sobre los aspectos de seguridad de este vuelo.	Gotoujou no minasama, korekara kokusaianzenkitei ni tuite gosetumei moushiagemasu:
5	Our aircraft has 6 emergency exits: 2 exits in the rear of the cabin, 2 overwing exits and 2 exits in the front of the cabin. They are marked with AUSGANG and EXIT. Floor-mounted escape path lights will guide you to the exits.	Unser Flugzeug hat 6 Notausgänge: 2 Notausgänge befinden sich im hinteren Bereich, 2 über den Tragflächen und 2 befinden sich im vorderen Bereich der Kabine. Sie sind als AUSGANG und EXIT gekennzeichnet. Lichter an den Sitzreihen führen zu diesen Ausgängen.	Notre avion a 6 issues de secours: 2 sorties dans la cabine arrière, 2 sorties sur les ailes et 2 sorties à l'avant de la cabine. Ils sont marqués avec AUSGANG et EXIT. Un sentier de lumières au sol vous guidera vers les sorties.	Observen que hay ... puertas de salida, ... a cada lado del avión. Cada una de ellas está señalizada con la palabra SALIDA. En el lateral inferior de las butacas o en el suelo a lo largo del pasillo, hay unas luces que se iluminan en caso de emergencia, marcando las vías de evacuación. Todas las salidas de emergencia, incluidas las ventanillas sobre las alas disponen de una rampa inflable de evacuación.	Kono hikouki ha 6kasho no hijouguchi ga gozaimasu. Sonouchi 2 tsu ha kouhou ni, 2 tsu ha kitai tsubasa bubun, 2 tsu ha zenpou ni gozaimasu. AUSGANG mataha EXIT no moji ga mejirushi desu. Tsuuro no raito ga michishirube desu.
6	There are oxygen masks located in panels above your seats. These will open automatically with a decrease in cabin pressure. Pull the mask towards you, place it firmly over your mouth and nose and secure the elastic band. Important: first help yourself before assisting children.	Unser Flugzeug ist mit Sauerstoffmasken ausgerüstet, die sich über Ihren Sitzen befinden, und bei einem Druckverlust automatisch herausfallen. Ziehen Sie die Maske zu sich heran, drücken Sie die Öffnung auf Mund und Nase und befestigen Sie das Band um Ihren Kopf. Wichtig: Legen Sie zuerst Ihre eigene Maske an, und helfen anschließend Sie Ihren Kindern.	Il existe des masques à oxygène dans les panneaux situés au dessus de votre siège. Ils s'ouvriront automatiquement en cas de dépressurisation de la cabine. Tirez le masque vers vous, placez-le fermement sur la bouche et le nez en garantissant l'étanchéité avec la bande élastique. Important: faîtes-le d'abord à vous-même avant d'aider les enfants.	En caso de despresurización de la cabina se abrirá automáticamente un compartimento situado encima de sus asientos que contiene las máscaras de oxígeno. Si esto ocurriera, tiren fuertemente de la máscara, colóquenla sobre la nariz y la boca, y respiren con normalidad.	Minasama no ozaseki no joubu niha sanso masuku ga zozaimasu. Kore ha kyuugeki na kiatu no henka ni yori jidouteki ni orite kimasu. Masuku wo hikiyose kuchi to hana ga kabusaru youni souchaku shi, bando ha atama ni kakete kudasai. Juuyou: mazu hajime ni gojibun ga masuku wo souchaku saretekara, okosama ni souchaku shitekudasai.

The captain on a flight out of JFK: 'Welcome on our flight non-stop to LA. The weather ahead is fine and therefore we should have a smooth and uneventful flight. Now sit back and relax – oh my God!'

Silence in the cabin. A short time later the captain comes back on: 'Sorry if I scared you earlier, but while I was talking, the flight attendant brought me a cup of coffee and spilled the hot coffee in my lap. You should see the front of my trousers.' A passenger called the stewardess and asked her to tell the captain 'Never mind the front of his trousers. He should really see the back of mine!'

English engineers developed a 'chicken gun' that they used to fire chicken carcasses into aeroplane windscreens, in order to test their resistance. In one test the bird shattered the windscreen, broke the pilot's headrest and flew like a bullet to the end of the cabin. NASA's response was to tell them to 'first defrost the chicken'.

Tower: 'Have you reached Flight Level 200 or not?'
Pilot: 'Yes.'
Tower: 'Yes, what?'
Pilot: 'Yes, SIR.'

A stressful check-in. An exasperated passenger pushes his way to the front of the queue but is sent back. Furiously he shouts: 'Do you know who I am?' The agent at the desk makes the following announcement: 'There is a man at the Delta ticket counter who does not know who he is. Anyone who may be able to help this man is asked to please step forward and identify him.'

Quite a few years ago, a Frankfurt ground controller had to intervene several times when a British Airways pilot who had just landed took some wrong turns on the way to his gate. Finally he asked impatiently: 'Have you never been to Frankfurt before?' The answer came back: 'Yes. 1944, but I didn't land that time."

Pilot: 'Good morning, Frankfurt ground, KLM 242 request start up and push back, please.'
Tower: 'KLM 242 expect start up in two hours.'
Pilot: 'Please confirm: two hours' delay?'
Tower: 'Affirm.'
Pilot: 'In that case forget about the good morning.'

The flight was 20 per cent full at the most. The stewardess announced to the passengers boarding: 'Please take the window seats so that the competition will think our flight is full.'

Announcement after a very rough landing in Amarillo, Texas: 'Please remain in your seats with your seatbelts fastened while the captain taxis what is left of our aeroplane to the gate.' When disembarking, an elderly woman asked: 'Sorry, mind if I ask you a question?'

'Why not,' said the pilot. 'What is it?'

She answered: 'Did we land or were we shot down?'

After another hard landing, the purser announced 'Remain seated as Captain Kangaroo bounces us to the terminal.'

AND DESPITE THIS...
FLYING IS GETTING SAFER ALL THE TIME

HOW SAFE IS FLYING?
In Europe, if you were to board a plane every day, 365 days a year, statistically it would take 5,708 years before your chances of being in an accident came to 50:50.

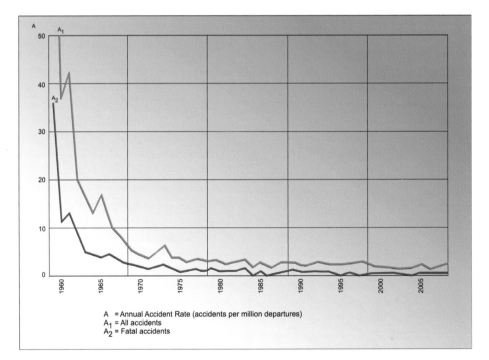

A = Annual Accident Rate (accidents per million departures)
A₁ = All accidents
A₂ = Fatal accidents

WHY ACCIDENTS HAPPEN

In the aviation world, air crashes are a source of regret all round. In 1926 and 1927 there were 24 airline accidents. In 1928, there were 26 and in 1929 another 51. To date, this is the worst record in the accident statistics: with one accident for every 1.6 million km/994,190 miles flown. Were we to use the same ratio with today's air traffic volume, the figure would be 7,000 casualties per year. In the meantime, however, statistically the accident rate for air travel has come down to one accident for every 3.2 billion km/2 billion miles flown. An accident is rarely caused by one incident alone, but almost always occurs at the end of a sequence of adverse events.

The most common causes of accidents are:

ENVIRONMENTAL
Wind, storms, cloud, fog, rain, hail, lightning, heat, cold, ice and snow all make flying demanding. However, birds in the sky or animals on the ground can also pose a latent risk to aeroplanes. People try to minimize all of these possible dangers, but it is impossible to avoid them completely.

TECHNICAL
The old DC-3 is an example of the skill in metalwork of its time. Back then, rivets were still driven with a hammer into the sheet metal. Today, malleable composite materials are used and honeycombed synthetic materials are laid down, which surpass the strength of the heavy floor plates of the past. The technology has become much more costly, but it has made flying demonstrably safer. All systems are reworked many times. Today, a large aircraft can accommodate up to 900 passengers. The engines are bigger, stronger and more reliable and their range is longer. Aeroplanes fly higher in calmer air layers. Even such complex technology can sometimes fail, but more commonly accidents are caused by human error.

EQUIPMENT
When an aeroplane descends from a great height to land in the heat of the desert, only a few minutes previously it will have been flying in temperatures that may have been as low as -60°C/-76°F. All of the equipment must be able to deal with such rapid temperature fluctuations, from the windows to the landing gear, whose tyres have to accelerate immediately from 0–250 km/h /0–155 mph on runways hotter than 60°C/140°F, at the same time bearing the multi-ton weight of the aeroplane. For this reason, all of the equipment is inspected and replaced at regular intervals. And yet, a hairline crack might go undetected, a bolt might break or a motor could fail. Here again, human error plays a significant part.

ELECTRONICS
In the old days, aeroplanes were flown with physical strength. The steering column was tied with cables and wires that controlled the rudder and the flaps. Today, hundreds of computers on board have replaced the Bowden cables of old. They give electronic steering commands to actuators and motors, while pilots fly with a joystick so they ultimately have overall charge of navigation. The autopilot monitors the altitude and the course, the computer calculates the most efficient engine output, the Flight Management System (FMS) informs the pilot about fuel consumption, distance to travel, the heading to the next alternative airport and the soundness of the systems – all in a multitasking interface, which of course has a backup. Monitors replace the 'clockshops' of old; the multifaceted computers can oversee and also prevent or limit false reactions from the pilot. Computers cease to function if they are fed illogical data, as, for example, may have been the case in the Air France crash in Brazil in 2009.

COMMUNICATIONS
It is only when all parties involved communicate with each other – that is, exchange and comprehend all essential information – that courses of action can be agreed upon. Therefore it is of the utmost importance that information given is correctly received, processed and confirmed. For this purpose, general standards are essential, most importantly requiring that a common language (English) be used exclusively by all persons involved.

THE HUMAN FACTOR
It is the human being that always poses the greatest accident risk. Opinions, feelings, abilities, intellect and knowledge all determine human behaviour. At the same time, external circumstances affect or influence our judgement or scruples. This concerns technical staff as much as the pilots, planners and air traffic controllers. Every effort is made to exclude undesirable behaviour in the organization of work, staff, training, quality control and remuneration.

That the aviation industry has all of these possible accident causes largely under control is evident in the outstanding, and ever improving, accident statistics. That there is still much to be done, however, can be seen when looking at the individual accidents that have resulted in a tragic number of victims. These accidents usually occur at the end of a chain of events, a chain that in most cases could have been avoided by just one factor – the human factor.

Region	IATA accident factor 2008	Accident per x flights	Number of years
World	0.90	1 111 111	3044
Europe	0.48	2 083 333	5708
North America	0.58	1 724 138	4724
Asia	0.58	1 724 138	4724
North Africa & Middle East	1.89	529 101	1450
Africa	2.12	471 698	1292
Central & South America	2.55	392 157	1074
CIS	6.43	155 521	426

Emergency Training

Theory...

Evacuation

Large airlines have cabin simulators at their training centres and staff undergo emergency training several times a year. Dealing with panic, lifejacket procedures and escapes using emergency slides must be practiced regularly in case the real thing happens. How vital this training is was demonstrated when a French A340 overshot the runway when landing at Toronto airport in 2005. All 309 of the passengers and crew on board managed to escape the plane, even though it was already on fire and two of the emergency exits were blocked.

Regulators give manufacturers stringent rules on the maximum time in which a plane has to be evacuated, and under what circumstances. It must be possible for all passengers on a plane to be evacuated within 90 seconds.

Tests are carried out under the following conditions:
• Darkness
• A representative group of passengers in normal health
• 40 per cent female

• 35 per cent over 50
• 15 per cent of the over 50s must be female
• Three life-size baby dolls
• Windows closed from the outside
• Gangways are obstructed with cushions, blankets and hand luggage
• Passengers do not know what the test conditions are
• Only half of the doors may be used
• Sides are temporarily fixed
• Passengers must be wearing seatbelts
• Only emergency lighting may be switched on in the cabin
• Flight attendants must carry out a standard emergency demonstration
• Cabin crew must be working at an active airline
• Crew may not have taken part in a similar exercise in the previous six months
• They must include members of an average crew, with regards to gender, age, size and experience.

The evacuation test for the A380 resulted in 873 people exiting from both storeys in 78 seconds!

...AND PRACTICE

CRASH FIRE RESCUE

The emergency services at every airport in the world follow strictly controlled training programmes. Every two years these are checked by the International Civil Aviation Organization (ICAO). The following are looked at in particular:

- Readiness for action
- Equipment
- Fire extinguishers
- Rescue of injured persons
- First aid
- Co-operation between services (airport firefighters, local fire brigades, doctors, hospitals, police, military)
- Management of services.

Huge crash tenders, such as the Simba, are the most visible. These are all-terrain vehicles, usually over 1,000 hp strong, carrying 12,000 litres/2,639 gallons of water in which 2 x 600 litres/2 x 132 gallons of foam and/or 2 tons of extinguishing powder can be mixed, as required. Powerful 280 hp pumps on a roof-mounted extinguishing arm are controlled remotely by a joystick in the fire station or by onboard equipment. Crash tenders have special protection fittings for the tyres. If, for example, the vehicle has to drive through burning kerosene, it can spray 60 litres/13 gallons of water per minute onto its tyres from seven water-foam nozzles.

Depending on the size and capabilities of the airport, their Rescue and Firefighting Services are required to have up to two large-tank tenders, auxiliary tenders, equipment vehicles,

hose carts, armoured vehicles and rescue trucks.

If an emergency is declared, rapid response tenders can reach the plane within seconds from a stationary position, and they can set up extinguishers to deal with any possible fire. Additional vehicles arrive, including special tenders with ladders. Firefighters, wearing fireproof suits and equipped with breathing apparatus, are ready to extinguish any fire on the aircraft and to board and rescue passengers.

BOATS

Airports located on the waterfront must also be prepared for emergencies occurring offshore. These have permanently manned and ready-to-operate boats with fire-fighting capabilities.

TRIAGE

In a real crash situation, the longer the rescue operation continues, the more

rescue vehicles arrive. Deployment plans provide for rescue convoys arriving from surrounding towns and cities, and ensure that the police and army are notified. Rescue helicopters fly in. Here discipline is essential: all authorities must report to the on-scene commander.

Within minutes, tents are erected and a triage station is set up. In the case of a major incident, emergency medics follow what is known as the '30 second rule': for every person involved in an accident, a maximum of 30 seconds is initially spent on sorting them into different categories marked up as red, yellow or green. After 30 seconds, they move on to examine the next patient. The word 'triage' comes from the French verb 'trier' meaning 'to sort'.

'Red' means that a patient is so badly injured that he or she needs urgent medical assistance if they are to survive the accident. Patients marked 'yellow' also require medical assistance, but are not in acute danger and will survive the accident even without immediate help. 'Green' casualties are those who have only minor injuries, who can move by themselves and who may not require any medical assistance.

Signs, bands or stickers may be attached to the victims. As more doctors arrive, they can quickly identify and treat the injured according to the priority they have been given.

Aeroplane Crashes

Date Airline Place	Flight number Type of aircraft Registration	No. of victims	Type of accident
3.6.1962 Air France France	AF 117 Boeing 707-300 F-BHSM	130	The Boeing 737 overshot the end of the runway and collided with a building.
4.2.1966 All Nippon Japan	NH 60 Boeing 727-81 JA8302	133	The Boeing 727 crashed into Tokyo Bay on its approach into the airport.
30.7.1971 All Nippon Japan	NH 58 Boeing 727-281 JA8329	162	The Boeing 727 collided with a fighter jet.
3.12.1972 Spantax Spain	--- Convair CV-990-30A-5 EC-BZR	155	Accident occurred on take-off.
3.3.1974 THY France	TK 981 DC-10-10 TC-JAV	346	It is thought that a cargo door that was not closed properly caused the crash when it opened during the flight. The sudden drop in cabin pressure tore six passengers out of the plane. Parts of the plane's structure were also damaged, which caused failure of engine number two and parts of the controls. The DC-10 could no longer be controlled, and so crashed.
20.11.1974 Lufthansa Kenya	LH 540 Boeing 747-130 D-ABYB	59	The Lufthansa jumbo jet crashed on take-off from Nairobi.
10.9.1976 British Airways Croatia	BA 475 Hawker Siddeley HS-121 Trident G-AWZT	176	A Douglas DC-9 owned by the Yugoslavian Inex Adria Aviopromet collided with the Hawker Siddeley HS-121 in the sky.
27.3.1977 KLM Spain	KL 4805 Boeing 747-206B PH-BUF	583	A Pan Am jumbo collided with a KLM jumbo in thick fog. This is the deadliest accident in civilian aviation history. The KLM jet had not been given clearance to take off.
19.11.1977 TAP Portugal	TP 425 Boeing 727-282 CS-TBR	131	The aircraft failed to land on what at the time was a very short runway and rolled off a steep bank.
1.1.1978 Air-India India	AI 855 Boeing 747-237B VT-EBD	213	The Boeing 747 crashed into the sea a couple of minutes after take-off when the pilot became spatially disoriented due to instrument failure.
25.9.1978 PSA USA	PS 182 Boeing 727-214 N533PS	144	The Boeing 727 collided with a Cessna 172 sports plane over San Diego.
25.5.1979 American Airlines USA	AA 191 DC-10-10 N110AA	271	The McDonnell Douglas DC-10 (American Airlines flight 191) crashed after an engine failed during take-off.
28.11.1979 Air New Zealand Antarctica	TE 901 DC-10-30 ZK-NZP	257	On a flight over the Antarctic, the New Zealand McDonnell Douglas DC-10 crashed into Mount Erebus.
19.8.1980 Saudi Arabian Saudi Arabia	SV 163 Lockheed L-1011-200 TriStar HZ-AHK	301	Despite an emergency landing of the Lockheed L-1011 Tristar after a fire on board, the 301 passengers could not be saved. They perished after the crew and ground staff failed to evacuate swiftly enough after landing.

Date Airline Place	Flight number Type of aircraft Registration	No. of victims	Type of accident
9.7.1982 Pan Am USA	PA 759 Boeing 727-235 N4737	145	The Boeing 727 crashed shortly after take-off.
1.9.1983 KAL Pacific	KE 007 Boeing 747-230B HL7442	269	The Soviet air force shot down a Boeing 747 that had strayed off course and was flying over Sakhalin Island.
27.11.1983 Avianca Spain	AV 011 Boeing 747-283B HK-2910	181	Avianca's Boeing 747 crashed on approach to Madrid Airport.
19.2.1985 Iberia Spain	IB 610 Boeing 727-256 EC-DDU	148	The Boeing 727 hit an aerial on its approach into Bilbao airport. The wing on the left came off and the plane crashed.
23.6.1985 Air-India Atl. Ocean	AI 182 Boeing 747-237B VT-EFO	329	The Boeing 747 crashed into the Atlantic ocean after a bomb exploded on board.
2.8.1985 Delta Air Lines USA	DL 191 Lockheed L-1011-385-1 TriStar 1 N726DA	134	The Lockheed L-1011 Tristar crashed during a storm near Dallas airport.
12.8.1985 JAL Japan	JA 123 Boeing 747SR-46 JA8119	520	The Boeing 747 crashed after its vertical stabilizer was torn off. The probable cause was faulty maintenance carried out seven years previously.
16.8.1987 Northwest Airlines USA	NW 255 DC-9-82 N312RC	154	The McDonnell Douglas MD-80 crashed onto a busy street shortly after take-off.
28.11.1987 SAA Indian Ocean	SA 295 Boeing 747-244B ZS-SAS	159	The Boeing 747, on a scheduled flight from Taiwan to South Africa, was attempting an emergency landing in Mauritius after a fire broke out in the cargo hold. The plane crashed into the sea.
17.3.1988 Avianca Colombia	AV 410 Boeing 727-21 HK-1716	143	The Boeing 747 crashed close to the Colombian city of Cúcuta.
3.7.1988 Iran Air Indian Ocean	IR 655 Airbus A300B2-203 EP-IBU	290	The Airbus A300 was mistakenly shot down by the US Navy missile cruiser, the USS Vincennes.
21.12.1988 Pan Am UK	PA 103 Boeing 747-121A N739PA	259	After a bomb exploded on board, the Boeing 747 crashed over the town of Lockerbie in Scotland. It was 16 August 2003 before Libya admitted responsibility for this terrorist attack and paid 2.7 billion dollars in compensation to relatives of the victims.
2.10.1990 Xiamen Airlines China	UM 8301 Boeing 737-247 B-2510	128	During an emergency landing of the Boeing 737, the pilot and the hijacker started to fight and the plane went out of control. It crashed into a Boeing 707 from China Southwest Airlines and then crashed into another Boeing 757.
26.5.1991 Lauda Air Thailand	NG 004 Boeing 767-3Z9ER OE-LAV	223	After taking off from Bangkok, a system failure caused the thrust reverser on the Boeing 767 to deploy during the flight. This caused the aeroplane to crash near Bangkok.
27.12.1991 SAS Sweden	SK 751 McDonnell Douglas MD-81 OY-KHO	0	The plane was not properly de-iced and so, after take-off, the engines ingested ice that had broken loose from the wings. The engines were damaged and the plane crashed and broke up into three parts. Everyone on board survived.

Date Airline Place	Flight number Type of aircraft Registration	No. of victims	Type of accident
24.11.1992 China Southern China	CS 3943 Boeing 737-3Yo B-2523	141	The Boeing 747 crashed on its approach, 20 km/12 miles from Guilin.
8.9.1994 USAir USA	US 427 Boeing 737-3B7 N513AU	132	The Boeing 737 crashed on its approach after losing control of the rudder.
20.12.1995 American Airlines Colombia	AA 965 Boeing 757-223 N651AA	160	The Boeing 757 crashed on its approach. The pilot gave an incorrect navigation target during the flight. When trying to correct the course, the plane crashed into a mountain.
6.2.1996 Birgenair Atl. Ocean	KT 301 Boeing 757-225 TC-GEN	189	The Boeing 757 crashed into the sea shortly after take-off from the coastal airport of Puerto Plata in the Dominican Republic. The probable cause of the crash was an air speed indicator reading that was too high, causing the pilots to take incorrect action.
17.7.1996 TWA USA	TW 800 Boeing 747-131 N93119	230	Shortly after take-off from New York City, the Boeing 747 exploded at an altitude of 4,000 m/13, 120 ft. The most likely cause was a fuel-air explosion in the wing fuel tank.
12.11.1996 Saudi Arabian India	SV 763 Boeing 747-168B HZ-AIH	349	Mid-air collision between the Boeing 747 that had left New Delhi and an Air Kazakhstan Iljuschin Il-76 that had descended below its assigned altitude.
6.8.1997 Korean Air Guam	KE 801 Boeing 747-3B5 HL7468	228	On its approach, the Boeing 747 crashed into a hill about 5 km/3 miles from the airport. The ILS had been switched off. The pilot flew the plane in too low, which went unnoticed by air traffic control.
26.9.1997 Garuda Indonesia	GA 152 Airbus A300B4-220 PK-GAI	235	The Airbus A300 crashed on its approach to Medan. Probable cause was bad communication between the pilots and air traffic control, and poor visibility.
16.2.1998 China Airlines Taiwan	CI 676 Airbus A300-600R B-1814	196	The Airbus A300 was too high when trying to land at Taipei airport in overcast and wet conditions, so it attempted a go-around. The plane then went out of control and crashed.
2.9.1998 Swissair Canada	SR 111 MD-11 HB-IWF	229	A fire broke out in the cockpit on a flight from New York City to Geneva, about an hour after take-off, causing smoke and instrument failure. En route to an emergency landing in Halifax, the plane crashed into the Atlantic off the coast of Nova Scotia.
31.10.1999 EgyptAir Atl. Ocean	MS 990 Boeing 767-366ER SU-GAP	217	The Boeing 767 crashed into the Atlantic during its flight from New York City to Cairo in Egypt. Shortly before crashing, the plane was apparently put into a nosedive by one of the pilots.
19.4.2000 Air Philippines Philippines	3G 541 Boeing 737-2H4 RP-C3010	131	The Boeing 737-200 crashed 6 km/3½ miles before landing in Davao.
23.8.2000 Gulf Air Bahrain	GF 072 Airbus A320-212 A4O-EK	143	After an aborted landing, the Airbus A320 crashed into the sea.
31.10.2000 Singapore Airlines Taipei	SQ 006 Boeing 747-412 9V-SPK	83	During a typhoon, the Boeing 747 attempted to take off on a runway that had been closed. It crashed into construction equipment, broke into pieces and burst into flames.
8.10.2001 SAS Italy	SK 686 McDonnell Douglas MD-87 SE-DMA	114	The McDonnell Douglas MD-87 collided on take-off with a Cessna Citation II that was on the wrong runway in dense fog.

Date Airline Place	Flight number Type of aircraft Registration	No. of victims	Type of accident
12.11.2001 American Airlines USA	AA 587 Airbus A300B4-605R N14053	260	The Airbus A300 crashed less than three minutes after take-off from John F. Kennedy International Airport in a residential area. The plane's vertical stabilizer had fallen off during the ascent.
15.4.2002 Air China South Korea	CA-129 Boeing 767-200ER B-2552	129	The Boeing 767 crashed into a hill on its approach to Gimhae airport.
25.5.2002 China Airlines Pacific	CI 611 Boeing 747-209B B-18255	225	The China Airlines Boeing 747 disintegrated shortly after take-off due to metal fatigue.
3.1.2004 Flash Airlines Egypt	FSH 604 Boeing 737-3Q8 SU-ZCF	148	The Boeing 737 crashed into the Red Sea. The probable cause of the crash was spatial disorientation and failure of communication on the part of the pilots.
29.9.2006 Gol Brazil	G9 1907 Boeing 737-8EH PR-GTD	154	The Boeing 737 crashed into rainforest in the northern state of Mato Grosso, after it collided at 11,000 m/36,000 ft with an Embraer Legacy jet.
17.7.2007 TAM Brasil Brazil	JJ 3054 Airbus A320-233 PR-MBK	187	The Airbus A320 failed to come to a halt after landing on a rain-drenched runway at Congonhas-São Paulo airport. The plane then crashed into a fuel station at 175 km/h /109 mph and a building outside the airport.
20.8.2008 Spanair Spain	NR 5022 MD-82 EC-HFP	154	The MD-82 crashed immediately after take-off from Madrid airport. It disintegrated and was completely burnt out.
1.6.2009 Air France Atl. Ocean	AF 447 Airbus A330-200 F-GZCP	228	The Airbus A330-200 crashed into the Atlantic during flight 447 from Rio de Janeiro to Paris for reasons that remain unknown.
30.6.2009 Yemenia Airways Comoros	IY 626 Airbus A310-324 7O-ADJ	152	The Airbus A310-300 crashed 5–10 km/4–6 miles from the main island of Grande Comore. Only a 12-year-old girl survived.

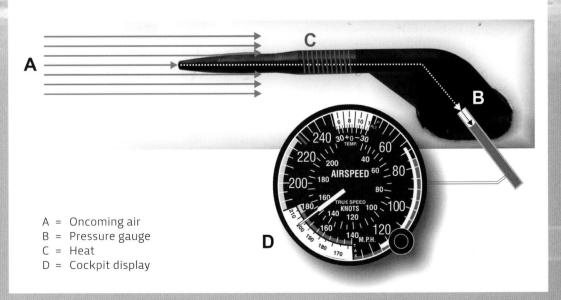

The pitot tube: blocked, obstructed or iced-up tubes have in the past been the cause of avionics computers malfunctioning, which can cause serious difficulties for the crew.

A = Oncoming air
B = Pressure gauge
C = Heat
D = Cockpit display

HIJACKINGS

The first hijacking took place on 16 July 1948 when a Cathay Pacific Catalina seaplane was hijacked and crashed into the Pacific Ocean off the coast of Macao.

During the 1960s and 1970s, several planes were hijacked or overrun by Palestinian terrorists.

In 1971, a man called Dan Cooper seized control of a Northwest Orient Airlines Boeing 727. He was extremely polite and circumspect during the hijack. He informed a flight attendant that he had a bomb in his briefcase, and on landing in Seattle he demanded 200,000 dollars in exchange for the passengers. With the intention of continuing the flight, he also demanded four parachutes. To avoid his own parachute being tampered with, he claimed the other three were for the pilot, the co-pilot and the stewardess. Having freed the passengers, Cooper ordered the captain to fly the plane towards Mexico at an altitude of 3,000 m/10,000 ft and to raise the flaps by 15 degrees. Supposing that fighter planes would follow them, he jumped out of the plane from the rear steps when it was flying through dense cloud.

For 18 days, the FBI combed the probable jump zone, without ever finding a trace of the man, the money or his parachute.

FBI identikit picture of Dan Cooper.

Inevitably, there were copycat hijackings. None of these were so successful, partly because the authorities had become better prepared and partly because the hijackers chose the wrong type of plane and were killed on exit by the rear elevator.

There was an excellent outcome in the case of a GSG 9 hijacked in Mogadishu, Somalia, in 1997. After five days, the plane was stormed, three of the four terrorists were shot and all 86 passengers on board were freed.

Not all rescue operations pass off so smoothly. In 1982, the storming of a plane in Malta by Egyptian soldiers resulted in the deaths of 59 people. In 1986, 22 people died when Pakistani commandos stormed a hijacked Pan Am 747 in Karachi, Pakistan.

A hijack in China ended particularly tragically on 2 October 1990. A hijacker with a 15 kg/33 lb bomb demanded to be flown to Taiwan. The captain was advised by the state authorities to pretend to accede to the request, but to secretly fly back to Guangzhou. The hijacker noticed the change of plan on landing and a fight broke out in the cockpit. The Boeing 737 crashed on the runway, sideswiped a parked 707 and then collided with a taxiing 757, which burst into flames. The 737 then flipped onto its back before skidding to a halt. From the two planes, 127 people were killed.

On 23 November 1996, an educational piece of criminal incompetence was demonstrated by three men of Ethiopian origin. They stormed the cockpit of an Ethiopian Airlines Boeing 767 and demanded to be flown to Australia. The crew tried to explain to the men that they did not have the amount of fuel necessary to do this. Unfortunately, the hijackers only spoke their own tribal dialect, so could not be convinced of the futility of their request. When the fuel ran out between Madagascar and the Comoros islands, Captain Leul Abate tried to ditch the 767 in shallow water. However, fighting broke out in the cockpit, the tip of a wing dipped into the water and the plane broke up into three pieces. Of the 175 people on board, 125 died. Many could not be saved because, contrary to the urgent instructions of the crew, they inflated their lifejackets on board and were then unable to escape in the ensuing chaos. All three hijackers died.

However, the biggest and most deadly hijacking of all occurred on 11 September 2001.

WHY NOT FLY PLANES REMOTELY?

Technology and electronics are now so advanced that planes can be flown completely automatically, taking off from one place and landing in another. Military drones such as the *Predator* and *Global Hawk* drones, with a range of 25,000 km/15,500 miles, are the flying proof of this. However, these are flown without passengers – to do otherwise would be a paradigm shift that many people are still not ready for.

It has also been considered whether in hijacking cases the cockpit should simply be shut down and the plane controlled remotely from the ground. Pilots and hijackers are not always prepared, as has been shown, to land at the next suitable airport. However, this would probably lead to an escalation of violence that could not be judged properly from the ground.

Computer hackers always seem to be a step ahead of technological developments, so terrorists could perhaps seize control of an aeroplane and carry out a hijacking from the ground, at no risk to their own lives.

11 September 2001

Time	Event
6.20	Hijackers arrive in Boston and board Flight AA 11.
6.20	Hijackers board Boeing 767, Flight UA 175, from Boston to Los Angeles.
7.03	Hijackers check in for Flight UA 93 in Newark.
7.25	Three hijackers board Flight AA 77 in Washington.
7.40	Pushback of Boeing 767 Flight AA 11 Boston–Los Angeles.
7.59	Hijackers telephone each other.
8.01	Flight UA 93 is delayed.
8.13	AA 11 final communication with air traffic control.
8.13	AA 11 transponder switched off
8.14	AA 11 is hijacked
8.14	UA 175 takes off 16 minutes late.
8.19	AA 11 flight attendant Betty Ong reports the hijacking by telephone. The call is not taken seriously at first.
8.20	AA 11 veers off course.
8.20	AA 77, Boeing 757 Washington–Los Angeles takes off 10 minutes late.
8.22	AA 11 flight attendant Madeline Sweeney gives further details over the phone to American Airlines.
8.33	Betty Ong reports the death of a passenger.
8.37	UA 175 pilots are asked to look out for Flight AA 11.
8.38	Air force personnel still think they are involved in an exercise.
8.39	AA 11 flies over a nuclear power station.
8.40	UA 175 flies into the airspace of the New York Center; radio contact.
8.42	Hijackers take over Flight UA 175.
8.42	UA 93, Boeing 757 takes off 41 minutes late from Newark heading to San Francisco.
8.44	AA 11 flight attendants describe the unravelling catastrophe in hushed voices.
8.46	AA 11 crashes into the North Tower of the World Trade Center.
8.46	Air traffic control at New York Center identifies difficulties with Flight UA 175.
8.48	The early warning centre of the National Security authority learns on TV that the United States has been attacked.
8.50	UA 175 goes off course.
8.51	Final radio contact with AA 77.

Time	Event
8.52	UA 175 flight attendant reports the hijacking by telephone.
8.54	AA 77 veers off course.
9.03	UA 175 crashes into the South Tower of the World Trade Center.
9.04	Airspace over New York and Washington is closed down.
9.09	Fighter squadrons at Langley Air Force Base take up command posts.
9.09	Numerous false announcements about hijackings cause confusion.
9.12	AA flight attendants describe six hijackers on board AA 77.
9.15	American Airlines requests all of its pilots to land immediately.
9.17	All New York airports are closed.
9.19	UA Flight 23 aborts take-off, perhaps preventing another hijacking.
9.21	All bridges and tunnels into New York City are closed.
9.26	FAA bans all planes taking off throughout the United States.
9.27	UA 93 passenger Tom Burnett makes several telephone calls to his wife.
9.28	Hijackers take over UA 93.
9.31	UA 93 flight attendant is suffocated.
9.34	UA 93 passenger Tom Burnett receives an update from his wife.
9.34	Washington DC hospital is informed of an incoming plane and activates its catastrophe plan.
9.37	AA 77 crashes into the Pentagon.
9.45	New FAA manager, on his first day in the job, orders airspace in all 50 states to be cleared.
9.54	UA 93 passenger Tom Burnett makes the decision to recapture control of the plane.
9.57	Passengers fight with the hijackers in the cockpit.
9.59	South Tower of the World Trade Center collapses.
10.06	UA 93 crashes in Pennsylvania.
10.15	Part of the Pentagon collapses.
10.28	North Tower of the World Trade Center collapses.
12.16	Airspace over the United States is empty.
13.27	In Washington, the government declares a national emergency.

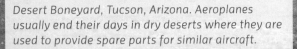

Desert Boneyard, Tucson, Arizona. Aeroplanes usually end their days in dry deserts where they are used to provide spare parts for similar aircraft.

INDEX

PICTURE CREDITS

This edition published by Parragon in 2010
Copyright © Parragon Books Ltd 2010

Parragon Books Ltd
Queen Street House
4 Queen Street
Bath BA1 1HE, UK

ISBN: 978-1-4454-0442-4

Printed in Indonesia

Created and produced by: Frechmann Kolón GmbH
Layout: Rheinische Umbrechereien, Werk Düsseldorf-Süd and Verlagsservice Peter Schneider

English-language edition produced by Cambridge Publishing Management Ltd

Translated by Richard Elliott, David Darrah-Morgan and Eithne McCarthy

H007 SAA AZ971 SAB DG SAC CDG SAD
AF HUD SAG MD-11 SAH ILS SAI DME
AM FMS SAN OY SAO LQ SAP NM WX
AT KU 204 FA MXP SAU VN SAV OU631
AZ A4 AN AY A340 BG BI DA 747-400
B ED DH3 EE CPH BT302 EF A310 EG A
MD-90-30 EP ES ET HRE EV EY FB ANC
Y FM FM A319 FN FO HHI TU FP FQ
Q006 DC-2 A380 GB GC GE SKP GF UIO
GA NJJ PVR GM ORD GO RJK GQ GS
FCO SK1588 KF664 JK023 TXL KF682 743
311 MSP D9S D8F AB3 JRO HH HK BBF
YD NEL LB TU154 BBZ LC MVD EZE LD
FXY LK LL KUL LM LN A320-200 LO LP A
WK BNE POM MEM LZ MB MD SAAB20
AN GVA MP MR FLY MS JFK MT BAH
AZ PRG NC NF CLK NG NI AB6 ET0421
NS NT DXB KTM NV NW FLA NZ OA AM
TL OK DO328 OL OM SIN OO SEL YVR
K FZO MHD PM IST WAW PT SPU PW
SC ACA SE LGW ISB TUS SF SG SK YIK
K021 CPH ONU SY EE (AY) MUC TA LHR
L SJJ VIE MD-90 JNB TN OBX KHI TQ SE
NRT TX UA UB DUS UE TXL UG UH PEW
US UT UU MCT PHX MIA AUS DFW UW
ERJ145 CRJ LUX VO DXB VQ VR VT VY
VR WS ZM FRA OAM AF1567 FAA LBA
RN FCO RUH GIG F50 Y FJY JY GF162
GF024 4U330 IB8260 UTC CVG MAD B757
V322 AT7 PX090 POM QF384 MDU GUG
CZ 5J 9 W AI BR EK S2 TG VN OZ MH13
BJ BCN BSL VCE VNO SXB LGW TU964
UH MAA LHE MNL TRV A320 S7 LY337